THE
EASTERN
EUROPE
COLLECTION

HUNGARY

IN THE

EIGHTEENTH CENTURY

Henry Marczali

Henrik Marczali

ARNO PRESS & THE NEW YORK TIMES

New York · 1971

Reprint Edition 1971 by Arno Press Inc.

LC# 75-135818

ISBN 0-405-02760-5

The Eastern Europe Collection
ISBN for complete set: 0-405-02730-3

Manufactured in the United States of America

HUNGARY

IN THE EIGHTEENTH CENTURY

CAMBRIDGE UNIVERSITY PRESS

London: FETTER LANE, E.C.

C. F. CLAY, Manager

Edinburgh: 100, PRINCES STREET

Berlin: A. ASHER AND CO.

Leipzig: F. A. BROCKHAUS

New York: G. P. PUTNAM'S SONS

Bombay and Calcutta: MACMILLAN AND CO., Ltd.

HUNGARY
IN THE EIGHTEENTH CENTURY

BY

HENRY MARCZALI

WITH AN

INTRODUCTORY ESSAY ON THE EARLIER HISTORY OF HUNGARY

BY

HAROLD W. V. TEMPERLEY M.A.
FELLOW OF PETERHOUSE, CAMBRIDGE

Cambridge:
at the University Press
1910

𝕮𝖆𝖒𝖇𝖗𝖎𝖉𝖌𝖊:

PRINTED BY JOHN CLAY, M.A.

AT THE UNIVERSITY PRESS

PREFACE.

IN 1878 the Hungarian Academy of Science invited me to write a History of Hungary in the time of Joseph II and Leopold II (1780–92).

I went to work with the purpose of not being content with superficial motives and results, but of getting to the bottom of the problems. The greatest problem, the adaptation of Western civilization to Hungary, in such a way as not to jeopardise the originality and independence of our nation, interested me most. I sought the solution of this problem—which dominates the epoch I desired to study—not in previously accepted conclusions, but in indubitable historic facts. In a word, my ambition was to write a genetic history, though at that time this term was as yet unknown to me.

A knowledge of the country and of its inner forces, of its economic, intellectual and moral qualities, was of more importance to me than the struggle of political parties. Therefore, before writing the history of the reign of the Emperor Joseph II, I wrote a volume on the state of Hungary at the time of his accession.

The principal aim was to exhibit a clear view of the home administration and of all the conditions of life connected with it. The Archives of the Royal Chancellery, which contain the documents of this period, to the number of 8000—17,000 a year, were my principal sources. Then came the investigation of the more important facts in the Archives of the Royal Council and of the Treasury. To obtain further material, I also studied the Archives of the Archbishops, of several counties, and of the most prominent families of Hungarian magnates. For intellectual developments, the library and the large collection of manuscripts in the National Museum and in the Academy of Science at Budapest were my chief sources. State documents and folklore were of equal value for me.

I had no conscious bias at all, and no design except the furtherance of truth. If my book is patriotic, it is so because I think that what my country most needs is that the truth should be told to her.

If I worked hard, my best reward is the decision of the Cambridge University Press to publish my book in English.

The first Hungarian edition of this volume appeared in 1882, and was succeeded after some weeks by a second. For the present English edition I have not only revised the text, but I have also utilised the results of my recent studies in bringing it up to date.

For the translation I am much obliged to my colleague and friend, Dr Arthur B. Yolland, Extraordinary Professor in the University of Budapest.

The Essay of Mr H. W. V. Temperley on earlier Hungarian History will make it possible for the English reader to plunge at once *in medias res*.

HENRY MARCZALI.

BUDAPEST.
31 *January*, 1910.

ANALYSIS AND TABLE OF CONTENTS.

	PAGE
Map (for explanation v. xv—xvi)	*end of book*
Author's Preface	v—vi
Analysis and Table of Contents	vii—xii
List of Kings of Hungary and of Princes of Transylvania . .	xiii—xiv
Explanation of Map	xv—xvi
Introductory Essay on the earlier History of Hungary . . .	xvii—lxiv

INTRODUCTION.

HUNGARY FROM 1711—1740. (pp. 1—16.)

I. Consequences of the expulsion of the Turks and of the peace of Szatmár. pp. 1—3

II. The Ruling Class of Hungary. The prelates and magnates. The gentry. The counties. Comparison with Poland. The *Tripartitum* (1514). Protestantism. The towns. The influence of native and foreign dynasties. Comparison with France and England . . . . pp. 3—12

III. Why the peace of Szatmár had more effect than the preceding pacifications. End of the Rákóczi movement. Hungary remains an independent nation. pp. 12—16

HUNGARY IN 1780.

CHAPTER I.

ECONOMIC CONDITIONS. (pp. 17—99.)

Error of considering as a national trait what is merely the characteristic of a certain grade of evolution.

I. *System of Taxation*, pp. 18—37. Direct taxes. *Ne onus inhaereat fundo.* Amount of taxes. The *portae*. The *dica*. Croatia's privilege. Scarcity of coined money. Difference between the North-West counties and the Lowlands (Alföld). The mountain districts are industrial, but their wealth is on the decline. The population of the Alföld ; its wealth and the amount of its taxes are fast increasing. The various counties in arrears with their payment of taxes. *Regulamentum militare* and the supply of food and fodder. Decadence of North-West districts. Preference given by the Government to Austrian manufactures. Hungarian industry and mining on the decline. The counties with a Magyar population on the increase, the German and Slovak populations relatively on the decline. This change is natural and not the consequence of a design. The meaning of nationality in the eighteenth century. Distribution of the estates of the Crown, of the Church, of the magnates and the gentry in the different districts. The districts of the Magyar gentry rising in importance.

II. *Customs Duties*, pp. 37—46. Commerce disturbed by the period of the wars. Saltpetre. Cattle-driving. The *commissio in oeconomicis*. Commercial policy since 1723. Austrian commercial oppression. Its geographical and historical causes. Austrian tariffs. Opposition in the Parliament and elsewhere. Obstacles to the exportation of Hungarian wines. Commercial treaties damaging to Hungary.

III. *Agriculture and Cattle-breeding*, pp. 46—61. Colonial features in Hungary. Exportation of cattle is the chief staple. Importance of the *latifundia*. Struggle between pasture and agriculture. System of cultivation, three fields and two fields. Primitive character of the farming. Exportation of dairy and garden produce and of fowls. Sericulture. Obstacles in the way of its advance.

IV. *Industry and Commerce*, pp. 61—94. Comparison with England and its colonies. Factories and domestic industry. Scarcity of workmen. Chief articles of industry. The Austrian Government hostile to Hungarian industries. Guilds and their influence. Greek merchants. Fairs; Debreczen, Pest. Acquisition of Fiume and opening for Hungarian maritime trade. School of navigation. Count Benyovszky's projects. Tobacco, preserved meat. Attempts to improve the navigation on the rivers. Resistance of the counties. Poems of Baron Orczi on commerce and luxury. Weirs and sluices. Bad roads. Mail-coaches. Hawkers. Joseph II's judgment on Austrian commerce. " Active " balance. The figures of the returns are not trustworthy.

V. *Conclusion*, pp. 94—99. Hungarian industry in decay, Austrian fast developing. Hungary is treated as a colony, though only one part of it was new territory; the other part was a rival to Austrian manufacture and agriculture, and therefore subjected to this treatment by the Emperor Joseph II.

CHAPTER II.

THE SOCIAL SYSTEM. (pp. 100—195.)

The medieval State and Joseph II, pp. 100—102.

I. *The Nobility*, pp. 102—111. Based on conquest. Foreign elements. Croatian nobles. *Indigenae*. Chief privileges of nobles. Different from the French and English nobility. *Armalistae. Banderia*. Hereditary magnates. Their services against the Turk. Lack of a national dynasty and of a national *bourgeoisie*. The Holy Crown. Exemption of the nobles from taxation.

II. pp. 112—127. Increase of the estates and of the wealth of the magnates. Their dignities and offices. Count Palatine. Lord Chief Justice. Ban of Croatia. Chancellor. All are members of Parliament. *Föispán's* (high sheriffs). Signs of decadence. Revolts punished by law. Beginnings of an aristocracy of office. The magnates at the Court. Their luxury, debts. The Court at Pozsony. New manners. Foreign culture. Tendency of magnates to become estranged from the national feeling.

III. *The Gentry*, pp. 127—148. The gentry economically independent both of magnates and Court. Influence of Protestantism. Cessation of military service, Acts of 1715 and 1723. Administration of the counties. The *táblabiró*. Importance of the county courts. Hungary becomes the nation of lawyers. The gentry the ideal of patriotic writers. Francis Kazinczy on them. Money and time have no value for the *táblabiró*. Their influence, their culture, their home life. Women and children. Patriotism. The *congregatio* or county assembly. County elections, their abuses. Other abuses. Cruelty in inflicting punishments, example in the county of Hont. Relation of the high sheriff (*föispán*) to the county. Joseph II's struggle against the counties.

IV. *The Bourgeoisie and the Royal Free Boroughs*, pp. 148—170. Abuses and corruptions of the town councils. Embezzlement and malversation. The citizens are, for the most part, Germans or strangers. Their privileges. The burgess franchise or privilege of citizenship. The town councils (*magistratus*). The *tribunus plebis*. Dependence upon the Royal Chamber. Oppression of journeymen. Fees of citizenship. Counties declare for free industry and against the guild system in the towns. The *patricii* in the towns. Poverty of the towns. Nobles in the towns (pp. 156—159). Oppression of Greek merchants. The Lutheran intellectual class in the towns. Representation of the towns in Parliament. Sympathies of the towns with Austria. " Town and gown." The medieval towns an exotic plant on Hungarian soil. Small number of their population. The Towns actually pay no more taxes than the peasants. Transitory classes. *Armalistae*; nobles with one session. Jász-Kún districts, i.e. Iazygia and Cumania. The " Hajdú " towns. Their decline in importance during the eighteenth century.

V. *The Peasants and Serfs*, pp. 170—195. The pillars of society. Peasant revolt in 1514. The right of migration restored (1547) and abolished (1715-23). Burdens of the serf. Socage. The serfs must seek justice in the courts, over which their feudal superiors presided. *Jus gladii*. The position of the serfs better than that of those in France and Germany. Protection of serfs. The poetic and sentimental view of the peasant as expressed by Baron Orczi and Bessenyei. Complaints and wishes of the peasants. The peasants still incapable of maintaining religious convictions and nationality without assistance. Their political creed before 1711. Their resignation. Particular grievances—the burdens of socage. They seek protection from the Court of Vienna. The *Urbarium* (1767). Maria Teresa's views. Joseph II's reforms. Redemption of service in socage.

CHAPTER III.

NATIONALITY. (pp. 196—246.)

Disastrous consequences of the Turkish occupation. The Magyar element in the Alföld. The seats of ancient civilization suffered most. Lady Montague's remarks on the depopulation of Hungary. Its speedy recovery. Kollonics's project of colonisation.

I. *The Rascians (Serbs) in the Alföld*, pp. 201—204. Their colonisation. Their relations to Russia and the Czar. Want of civilization. Their character.

II. *The German Settlers in the Alföld*, pp. 204—211. Districts from which they came. Their distribution in both town and country. Character of German peasants and artisans. The causes of Hungarian hatred of Germans.

III. *The Magyar Settlers in the Alföld*, **pp. 211—246**. Their distribution. The Harrucker family send the immigrants into the county of Békés. Croatian colonies. Changes in nationality since that time. The Slovak colonists a bar to German and Rascian expansion, an aid to Magyardom. Magyar colonies. Advance of civilization. Cessation of the Oriental plague. Danger of religious persecution. Influence of Prussia for toleration. The Catholic Church and the Serbs. The nobles are Magyars. Their influence on the settlers. Magyar language and dress largely adopted in Croatia and elsewhere. Examples to prove that the Slovak and Croatian counties were actually foremost in the struggle of the Magyar against the German language. The process of Magyarisation imperceptible and not forcible. Magyar names. Opinions of the writers George Bessenyei, Lawrence Orczi, Paul Ányos. Magyar Literature (**pp. 235—243**). Endeavour to polish the language. 1772 not the starting-point of a new era in Hungarian literature. Religious dissensions prove the principal obstacle to progress. The influence of the Hungarian noble guard at Vienna. Foreign influences and Hungarian patriotism illustrated from Orczi. The Magyar peasant (**pp. 243—246**), Emperor Joseph's opinion of. Chief qualities of the Magyar serf. The development consisted in the victory of the farmer over the herdsman, and the transformation of the Alföld from pasture into arable land. The struggle between nobles and peasants constituted no danger to Hungarian nationality.

CHAPTER IV.

THE CHURCH. (pp. 247—300.)

Connection between Church and State. Advance of Protestantism (Lutheran and Calvinist). The prelates and the Counter-Reformation. Catholicism and the Habsburg. The two faiths and national tradition. Causes of the victory of Catholicism illustrated. The epic of the *Zrinyiász* (1646). The Catholic magnates and Peter Pázmány. Francis Rákóczi II and the policy of religious toleration and political union against Germans. The *Regnum Marianum* and Leopold I's intolerance towards Protestantism. Articles of 1681-87. Restriction of the exercise of Protestant worship to specified places (*articularis*). Comparison with Spain and France.

I. **pp. 254—261.** Legal situation since 1715. The *Carolina Resolutio*. Foreign powers and Protestantism. Maria Teresa more intolerant than her father Charles III (VI). Exclusion of Protestants from office. The oath. Bishop Biró of Veszprém's attack. Cases of persecution. Bajtay's advice. Frederick II and the Pope Benedict XIV condemn Bishop Biró's book, the *Enchiridion de fide*, published 1750.

II. **pp. 261—269.** Grievances of the Protestants. *Reversalis*. Mixed marriages. Apostasy. Case of Agnes Bánffy. Intolerance in Transylvania. Protestants and their guilds forced to take part in Catholic ceremonial processions, etc. Their churches and schools taken away. Burial and Christening fees demanded of Protestants by the Catholic Priests. Superintendents forced to undergo the visitation of Catholic Bishops. Renegades. *Juramentum decretale*. Exclusion of Protestants from office in the chief cities and also to some extent in the counties. Union of Catholics and Protestants against arbitrary government.

III. pp. 269—277. Strength of the Catholic party. Policy of converting and teaching. Influence of the Franciscan friars. Restoration of the Church in the districts formerly occupied by the Turks. Kalocsa. Veszprém. The Jesuits. Their merits in regard to historiography. Their interpretation of national history. Marian congregations. Wonder-working images. Prayers and preaching. Religious life.

IV. pp. 277—288. Power of the Catholic Hierarchy. Incomes of the prelates. Political influence. The Primate (Archbishop of Esztergom). Privileges of the prelates. Count Batthyány. Count Ch. Eszterházy. Visitation. *Föispán*-prelates. Prelates in the King's Bench. The official language. The canons. The lower clergy—half gentlemen, half peasants. *Congrua*. The Piarists. Difference between them and the Jesuits. Methods of education. Catholic and Greek Church union. Results more pretentious than important.

V. pp. 288—297. Organisation and strength of Protestantism. Lutherans and Calvinists. Political characteristics of Calvinism. Religion of the gentry and of the Magyar towns. Struggle for the constitution. In what the wealth of Hungarian history consists. Lutheranism is the religion of the German and Slav *bourgeoisie*. Education of Calvinists. Foreign universities. School organisation. Colleges of Debreczen and Sáros-Patak. Morals. Learning. Accounts given by Kazinczy and Bessenyei. Lutheran schools. Relations between the teachers and the nobles. Low position of the Protestant pastors and teachers. Struggle for the schools. Prayers. The Court and the Protestants.

VI. pp. 297—300. Beginnings of a better understanding between Catholics and Protestants. Literature, social intercourse. Humanity. Influence of Freemasonry. Indifferentism. Government against it. Religious schism no longer a national danger nor a source of fundamental division in 1780.

CHAPTER V.

THE ROYAL POWER AND THE GOVERNMENT OF THE STATE.
(PP. 301—357.)

Principles of the Hungarian monarchy. Relation of the King to the Estates in Parliament.

I. pp. 303—307. The Holy Crown as representative of the State. The King is the State personified. The decadence of kingdom. The Estates become unable to fulfil their mission. They invest the King with a dictatorship before Mohács (1526). Merits of the Habsburg Kings. The two alternatives: absolutism and strength; opposition and discord. The modern conception of the State appears as a foreign innovation to Hungarians. The compromise arrived at between the modern sovereign and the medieval society.

II. pp. 308—320. Position of the King. Hereditary in both lines. The apostolic title. Theory of his power. Personal prerogative: *jus patronatus*; education; power over the Protestant churches. *Jus nobilitandi*. Granting of privileges. He is judge in cases of *lèse-majesté*. His Jurisdictional power. Devolution of noble estates. Power of interpreting the laws. Law and custom. Appointment of magistrates. Granting of pardons. Rights over the coinage. Limits of

King's power. War and peace. His power in Parliament. Hungarian Kingship does not correspond with Montesquieu's description [of it or with his theories. The King as head of foreign organisations. The Army. The Serbs. The Jews. The King's control over the revenues of the Mines. Only part of his income is voted by Parliament. The *quota* of the Court. Postal Service. Great difference between the legal right and the actual power of Parliament in Hungary.

III.   pp. 321—327.   The King of Hungary as sovereign of Bohemia and Austria. Confederation of the Estates (1606). Conquest of Bohemia (1620-21). "Empire" of the Habsburgs. Catholicism; aristocracy. Results in Hungary. Protestantism vanquished; *jus resistendi* abolished (1687). Obstacles. National feeling. Hungary is content.

IV.   pp. 327—347.   Instruments of the King. *Dicasteria.* Chancellery. Its activity. Dependence upon the King. Its members. *Consilium locumtenentiale.* Its legál independence and actual nullity. Its instructions. Weak side of its system. The *Curia* and the King's Bench. Abuses. National spirit. The Royal Chamber. Foreign spirit; unpopularity. The counties and the *föispán.*

V.   pp. 347—357.   The *diploma inaugurale.* History. Power of law. Coronation. Its singular importance. Maria Teresa's *diploma.* Influence of Parliament. The Palatine. The taxes. The nobles have exemption from taxation. Insurrection. Decadence of Parliament. National organs really to be found in the assemblies of the counties and in the Courts of Law.

	PAGE
Appendix I. Money, Weights and Measures	358—9
Appendix II. Dicas of the County of Pest	360—1
Appendix III. Number of the Portae of the Counties and Royal Free Boroughs, 1723–1847	362—4
Appendix IV. Speculum Moderni Temporis	365—7
Glossary and Subject-Index	369—77

I. LIST OF THE KINGS OF HUNGARY.

I. *House of Árpád.*

Prince Árpád, about 900.
  „   Géza, 972–997.
  „   Stephen (Vajk), 997–1000, then afterwards
King Stephen (Saint), 1000–38.
  „   Peter, 1038–41.
  „   Sámuel Aba, 1041–44.
  „   Peter (re-established), 1044–46.
Andreas I, 1046–60.
Béla I, 1060–63.
Salomon, 1063–74.
Géza I, 1074–77.
Ladislas I (Saint), 1077–95.
Koloman, the Scholar, 1095–1116.
Stephen II, 1116–31.
Béla II, the Blind, 1131–41.
Géza II, 1141–62.
Ladislas II, 1162.
Stephen III, 1162–72.
Stephen IV (Anti-King), 1163.
Béla III, 1172–96.
Emeric, 1196–1204.
Ladislas III, 1204–5.
Andreas II, 1205–35.
Béla IV, 1235–70.
Stephen V, 1270–72.
Ladislas IV (Kún), 1272–90.
Andreas III, 1290–1301.

II. *Kings of different Houses.*

Charles Robert of Anjou, 1301–1342[1].
Anti-Kings[2]. Wenceslas of Bohemia, 1301–4; Otto of Bavaria, 1305–8.
Louis I the Great, 1342–82.
  [After 1370 also King of Poland.]

Mary, 1382–85.
Charles I of Anjou, 1385–86.
Mary and her husband Sigismund of Luxemburg, 1387–95.
Sigismund (alone), 1395–1437.
  [From 1410 also Emperor.]
Albert (Habsburg), 1438–39.
  [Also Emperor as Albert II.]
Wladislav I Jagello, 1440–44.
  [Also King of Poland.]
Ladislas V, Habsburg, 1445–57.
(John Hunyadi, Regent, 1446–53.)
Matthias I Hunyadi (Corvinus), 1458–90.
  [After 1469 also King of Bohemia.]
Wladislav II Jagello, 1490–1516.
  [Also King of Bohemia.]
Louis II, 1516–26.
  [Also King of Bohemia.]

III. *House of Habsburg.*

Ferdinand I[3], 1527–64.
  [Emperor from 1556.]
(Anti-King John Zapolya, 1526–40.)
Maximilian I, 1564–76.
  [As Emperor Maximilian II.]
Rudolph, 1576–1608.
  [As Emperor Rudolph II.]
Matthias II, 1608–19.
Ferdinand II, 1619–37.
Ferdinand III[4], 1637–57.
Leopold I, 1657–1705.
Joseph I, 1705–11.
Charles III, 1711–40.
  [As Emperor Charles VI.]
Maria Teresa, 1740–80.
Joseph II, 1780–90.

---

[1] Stephen V's great grandson in the female line.
[2] Both descending in the female line from Béla.
[3] Wladislav II's son-in-law. N.B. Ferdinand and all the subsequent rulers of Hungary were also Kings of Bohemia and Holy Roman Emperors except, of course, Maria Teresa, who could not succeed to the last dignity.
[4] His son Ferdinand IV was crowned King of Hungary, but died (1654) before his formal accession.

II. LIST OF PRINCES OF TRANSYLVANIA.

1526-40.	[John I Zapolya, also claimant to Hungarian Crown.]
1540-71.	John II Sigismund Zapolya.
1571-75.	Stephen I Báthory [after 1575 King of Poland.]
1576-81.	Christopher Báthory, regent.
1581-1600.	Sigismund II Báthory.
1600-4.	Emperor Rudolph II.
1604-6.	Stephen II Bocskay.
1607.	Sigismund III Rákóczi.
1608-13.	Gabriel Báthory.
1613-29.	Gabriel Bethlen (Bethlen Gabor).
1630-48.	George I Rákóczi.
1648-60.	George II Rákóczi.
	[Claimants, Francis Redei, Achatius Barcsai, 1658-61.]
1661-63.	John Kemeny.
1663-90.	Michael I Apafi.
1690-91.	Michael II Apafi, d. 1702.
1691.	Emperor Leopold I, recognised by the Estates of Transylvania, 1694.
	[Claimant, Francis II Rákóczi, 1703-11.]
1764.	Transylvania becomes a Grand-Duchy.

EXPLANATION OF THE MAP (1).

LIST OF THE COUNTIES IN HUNGARY

Cis-Danubian District.

Bács.
Pest.
Nógrád.
Zólyom.
Hont.
Esztergom.
Bars.
Nyitra.
Pozsony.
Trencsén.
Turócz.
Árva.
Liptó.

Trans-Danubian District.

Moson.
Sopron.
Györ.
Komárom.
Fejér.
Veszprém.
Vas.
Zala.
Somogy.
Tolna.
Baranya.

Cis-Tiszan District.

Szepes (Zips district, part of which was recovered by Hungary from Poland, 1772).
Gömör.
Heves.
Borsod.
Torna.
Abauj.
Sáros.
Zemplén.
Ung.
Bereg.

Trans-Tiszan District.

Máramaros.
Ugocsa.
Szatmár.

Szabolcs.
Bihar.
Békés.
Csongrád.
Csanád.
Arad.
Krassó.) The BANAT (outside Hun-
Temes. } garian administration till
Torontál.) 1780, v. p. 318).

PARTIUM (PARTES REGNI HUN-GARIAE ADNEXAE), i.e. Cis-Tiszan Counties attached to Transylvania, v. pp. 332 note and 350.

Zaránd.
Kraszna.
Közép-Szolnok.
Kövár vidéke.

District of the Drave (SLAVONIA-TÓTORSZÁG annexed to Hungary, 1750–51).

Szerém.
Veröcze.
Posega.

CROATIA (HORVÁTORSZÁG).

Körös.
Varasd.
Zágráb.

PRIVILEGED DISTRICTS.

Jaszság (Iazygia).
Kis-Kunság (Little Cumania, v. pp. 104, 197).
Nagy-Kunság (Great Cumania, v. pp. 104, 197).
Hajdu-városok. ("Hajdu" towns, v. pp. 104, 167—70).
Tenger-Part (Coast or Littoral, i.e. Fiume, Buccari, etc., annexed to Hungary, 1776, v. pp. 76—80).

The Military Frontiers remained outside the jurisdiction of Hungary even after 1780 (v. pp. 318—9).

EXPLANATION OF THE MAP (2).

LIST OF COUNTIES AND DISTRICTS IN TRANSYLVANIA (ERDÉLY).

Hungarian (Magyar) Counties (Megyék).

Hunyad.
Belsö-Szolnok.
Doboka.
Kolozs.
Torda.
Küküllö.
Alsó-Fehér
Felsö-Fehér.
Fogaras vidéke.

Szekler Seats or Districts (Székek).

Aranyos.
Maros.
Udvarhely.
Csik.
Háromszék.

Saxon Seats or Districts (Székek).

Köhalom.
Segesvár.
Nagy Sink.
Medgyes.
Ujegyház.
Nagy Szeben.
Szerdahely.
Szászszebes.
Szászváros.
Besztercze vidéke.
Brassó vidéke.

CORRIGENDA.

Page 14, l. 4 from bottom, *for* George Rákoczy *read* Rákóczi and *for* Tököly *read* Tököli (*ib.* p. 162, l. 3).

,, 105, last line but 3, *for* Geyza II *read* Géza II.

,, 105, n. 2, *for* Frising *read* Freising.

,, 117, n. 1, *for* Orczic *read* Orczi.

,, 273, l. 5 from bottom, *for* Ladislas IV (1272–92) *read* (1272–9c).

INTRODUCTORY ESSAY.

A GENERATION ago a Regius Professor of History at one of our ancient Universities could allude to the constitution of Hungary, and express regret that he was unable to discover the terms of its coronation-oath. To-day our knowledge is greater and a number of essays, pamphlets, romances or solid works, dealing with various aspects of Hungary, have been presented to English readers. But as yet there has appeared in English no work on Hungarian history—as distinguished from its politics—which bases its conclusions on study of unpublished authorities at first-hand, and which presents the results of original research.

The work of my friend, Professor Marczali of the University of Budapest, needs, therefore, no apology for its publication in English, since it is based on the labour of ten years among the official records at Vienna and Budapest, and in many private archives. Yet something may perhaps be said as to its contents and as to the subjects there treated in a manner which has been recognised as classical by historians of the Continent. The work deals primarily with the history of Hungary under Joseph II—the one Habsburg never crowned King of Hungary, that gifted and hapless ruler, whose wonderful energy and enthusiasm could not save him from becoming one of the most tragic failures of history. His relations with Hungary are at once the key to his whole life and policy. As Professor Marczali writes (p. 101), "The importance of Joseph II in the history of the world consists in the fact that he represented the conception of the unified State, which perceived a disavowal of its own existence in the privileges, restraints and classes of medieval society. As its representative he fought strenuously against the organisation that had previously predominated in his dominions, and sought the overthrow of the older Hungarian society as one of the principal objects in his life. His defeat was the greatest misfortune which he experienced, and the fact that his principles were carried out by other men and by other means, renders his failure all the more tragical."

The point is that Joseph II viewed and treated Hungary— the home of all that was medieval, customary and traditional— according to the hard reason and doctrinaire theories of an eighteenth-century philosophy. Any work, therefore, which seeks to explain the stubborn and successful resistance which Hungary offered to him, must start by presenting a complete picture of Hungary in the eighteenth century and by carefully explaining the historic features of that strange medieval society. It is this portion of the work of Professor Marczali that is here presented to English readers. The peculiar circumstances enable us to behold a portrait of a medieval society, complete and finished in all its outlines, and drawn with a wealth of detail and accuracy of information that can hardly be paralleled elsewhere in Europe.

Even to-day in Hungary there are still many relics of an immemorial past. Traces of the most primitive savagery still abound in the folk-lore, the songs and the customs of the peasants. In the Eastern Carpathians bears, lynxes and wolves are still to be found, buffaloes may be seen in the marshes of Hungary, and in Transylvania men are still living who have seen horses tread out the corn in true Biblical style. Even to-day a hussar stands with drawn sword before the county assembly hall, ready if necessary to resist the King and his soldiers in the true spirit of medieval autonomy. Seventy years ago the peasants were still serfs, the nobles still wore the hussar dress (no uniform but their native costume) and the forms of Parliament were still medieval. Fifty years before that in the reign of Joseph (1780–90) the whole medieval society was, as it were, still crystallised in Hungary, and by a unique stroke of good fortune it was at this moment that bureaucrats set to work to analyse, to criticise, to describe and to report upon it. The result is an enormous mass of material which forms the groundwork of the present book. Instead of having to piece out our knowledge of this country in the Middle Ages from study of coins and portraits and inscriptions, from doubtful interpretations of parliamentary statutes or of monastic chronicles, we merely have to look in the pigeon-holes of a bureau. There we find complete tables of statistics of economic growth, memoranda on social and political subjects of all kinds, and the comments of Joseph and his bureaucrats upon every conceivable aspect and phase of the political and social institutions in Hungary. In the nineteenth century we have had ethnological and statistical surveys of many tribes in primitive conditions, and the resultant gain to anthropology has been enormous. A similar process applied to Hungary in the eighteenth century can hardly fail to be of great advantage to the fuller understanding of medieval conditions, even if Joseph's investigators had not always the patience or the accuracy of the compilers of an Indian Census Report. The picture of the medieval and the primitive system of economics, of the county assembly and its primitive autonomy, as drawn in their concrete reality by eighteenth century officials, is an advantage that it is difficult to overrate.

Professor Marczali's work opens with a sketch of the general conditions of Hungary at the beginning of the eighteenth century which is carried down to the reign of Joseph. Then the various separate forces and elements of society are analysed and fully described, with frequent references to their past history or origin. The whole treatment opens up numerous vistas into the older history of Hungary, and often takes us far back into the middle ages. As with every country of true historic traditions, the earliest origins and the remote past of Hungary's story are inextricably intertwined with her later evolution. Hence I believe that the best introduction to his work will be an attempt to give a broad general survey of some of the more striking facts in Hungarian history, hardly known to English readers and too little appreciated by English scholars, and to insist upon those aspects which are subsequently treated in the text.

The influence of physical conditions and of geography on historical and racial development cannot be more strikingly exhibited in any country than in Hungary. Few races have indeed more individuality than the Magyar, yet none have been more profoundly affected by natural environment[1]. The map of Hungary shows an irregular square bounded by the Save and the Danube on the south, and by the gigantic and continuous wall of the Carpathians on east and north. The mountains contained within its borders comprise three large groups forming natural fortresses, which, in each case, secure the inhabitants against invasion. The smallest of these lies in the extreme south where the inland spurs of the Dalmatian Alps wall off Croatia from Hungary proper. The next in extent lies in the Tatra district of the north, where the high peaks of the Western Carpathians form a refuge and a barrier, behind which the Slovaks entrenched themselves. Thirdly, the Eastern Carpathians form a compact mass separating Transylvania sharply from the wide plains of the centre, and giving to it a character and population wholly different from the other parts of Hungary. For the rest the western part of Hungary is broken by hills, but fully one half of Hungary—the central part of the whole land— is flat, fertile, and well watered. Here are the characteristic Hungarian Lowlands (or Alföld), the little Alföld lying between Pozsony (Pressburg) and Budapest, the great Alföld comprising the vales of the Danube and the Tisza (Theiss), and the great watershed between them. The character of these great plains is singular, the eye beholds an endless flat, now covered by reeds and marshes, at times completely inundated with water, or now stretching away—bare and sandy—to a seemingly infinite distance. Nothing more monotonous or dismal can be conceived, though—as in the fens of England—there is a certain grandeur in its melancholy and a certain majesty in the endless

---

Hungary still encloses within its borders the most extraordinary diversity of races and languages, and from A.D. 300—900 fragments of almost every people in Europe found refuge there. Since the ninth century the following have been the chief groups: first and foremost the Magyars and their kinsmen in Transylvania the Szeklers; then a number of different Slavonic races, the Slovaks, Rascians and Serbs, and the Croats; then the Roumans or Wallachs, who claim to be descended from Trajan's soldiers, but whom other authorities declare to have migrated into Transylvania in the thirteenth century from the Balkans; and last of all the Germans—divided into the Saxons who inhabit the towns of the North-West and Transylvania, and the Swabians of the South.

sweep of its horizon. To the historian as well as to the artist this part of the country is of the greatest interest and importance. Such a land invited invasion, for its fertility suggests wealth and its situation weakness; mounted invaders could pour up the valleys of the Danube and the Tisza, and sweep over its wide plains with ease. Like Sparta such a land has no walls, and its strength could only lie in stout hearts and strong hands. On the other hand, in the natural fortresses of the Tatra, of the Eastern Carpathians, and of the Dalmatian Alps, the original inhabitants could resist all invasions with ease. Therefore the race, which dominates the two Alfölds in Hungary, will either be at once overcome or else will become fierce and strong, steeled and disciplined by hard necessity. Such are the probabilities of the natural situation, and the historic evolution has tended to conform to them. The Magyars, in the ninth, the Tartars in the thirteenth, and the Turks in the sixteenth centuries, overcame little and great Alföld with ease, but either could not easily conquer or were repelled with great loss from the three natural fortresses[1].

It was traditionally at the end of the ninth century (about 900) that the Magyars, led by Prince Arpád, descended upon Hungary from the north. His host of wild riders swarmed over the fertile plains from Debreczen as far as the Danube. In the Alföld was a great confusion of races, the loam deposited there by the streams of countless previous invasions, but the predominant element was Slav. These races now sank for the most part into the position of serfs, a lot eventually shared by a large number of the poorer and weaker Magyars. In the outlying parts and in the natural fortresses the other races preserved more

[1] The racial origin of the Magyars is an unsolved puzzle to which it would be impossible here to attempt any definite answer. The evidence of biology shows that their physical formations are Asiatic, but have been, to a certain extent, Europeanised, a process which has been carried much further in the case of their political and social systems. The best opinion appears to regard them as a mixed nationality, compounded partly of some race akin to the Turks, and partly of an Ugrian tribe possibly akin to the Finns. The Turkish tribe appears to have conquered the Ugrian, and—as is frequent with conquering races—to have adopted much of the language and customs of the conquered. This explanation disposes of some difficulties, particularly the undoubted fact that Magyars were described by the Greeks as Turks till late in the middle ages. But the whole problem is still in a very unsettled state.

individuality, such as the Croats in the lands near the Dalmatian Alps, the Szeklers and perhaps the Roumans (Wallachs) in Transylvania, and the Slovaks in Slovakia (the Tatra district)[1]. In military respects the Magyars proved much the strongest and most effective of the races then in Hungary, and were strong enough to hold both Alfölds in force. It should, however, be realised that the centre of the power and rule of the Magyar was not the great Alföld, now their recognised home. The main seat of the Hungarian princes and kings lay in the western portion of their kingdom, and centred round Buda, Esztergom, and Fehérvár.

The wild Magyar riders were not satisfied with their victories in Hungary, and for half a century longer no part of Germany, or indeed of almost any country, was safe from their incursions. They were to inland states what the Danes were to maritime ones, and the celerity of their movements and the savagery of their raids make the parallel more close. Before the end of the ninth century they beat to pieces an Empire of Moravian Slavs, established beyond the Tatra mountains, and carried their victorious arms far into the heart of Germany. Eventually in 955 they were decisively beaten by Otto I of Germany, truly called the Great, in that victory on the Lechfeld, which is probably as memorable for Europe as the defeat of the Saracens by Leo the Isaurian. For Hungary at any rate, if not for Europe, this battle was a decisive and significant land-mark. Henceforward the Magyars gave up wandering beyond their own borders, ceased to have an effective foreign policy, and concentrated every energy on internal organisation and develop-ment. In the tenth century Germany was only able to defend herself, though retaliation was to come in a short space. Hungary

[1] In the Danubian flats the Serb populations (though subsequently strengthened by later immigrations) preserved independent characteristics. Other tribes, such as Cumanians and gipsies, did the same thing. The German immigrations into Hungary took place chiefly after the reign of St Stephen (1000–38). Migrations after the fifteenth century are fully described on pp. 204—211 sqq. of the text. Transylvania was eventually occupied by Szeklers (akin to the Magyars) and also by German (Saxon) colonists and by Magyars. The Roumans (Wallachs), as has been said, may have migrated there in the thirteenth century. In any case they became the subjects of the three other nations, Magyars, Szeklers and Saxons (v. *infra*, p. xlviii, note).

had a breathing-space, and meanwhile the energy and strength of the Magyars were well spent in organising and constructing their own institutions.

With the reign of St Stephen in Hungary (1000–38) we reach an epoch in her history that is from every point of view— both national and international—of unspeakable importance. After their disastrous overthrow at the Lechfeld the Magyars had withdrawn within their borders, and shut themselves off from Western influences, thus abandoning external warfare, and with it one of the best medieval means for obtaining new ideas. King Stephen, who realised their necessity for Hungary, devised another way—that of peace—by which he could intro-duce them. The influence of the Papacy was international, and it represented the highest traditions of culture in the West, though as a repository of learning and civilization it had a serious rival in the Byzantine Empire and the Greek Church. Stephen decided to make Hungary Christian by means of the Papacy, and by this decision he turned its development and civilization away from the East, freed it from the Oriental influences to which it was naturally prone, and brought it into contact with the new and vigorous West. The change was the more signifi-cant because the inhabitants of the Balkans, in so far as they were Christians, were usually Greek and Orthodox. Hence at one stroke the position of Hungary was changed, instead of being the bridge between the East and the West she became the outwork or advanced post of Rome. The surrounding nations of the Orient, and the Slavonic immigrants from them into Hungary, became hostile, and Hungary was drawn into the vortex of Occidental politics. That Stephen really received the famous Holy Crown of Hungary from the Pope is not very likely, but the legend that he did is as significant in its way as the famous " Donation of Constantine." Like that celebrated fable it embodies a truth, and shows how subsequent ages read back the realities of their own age into the past. The Popes certainly showed special favour to Hungary, bestowed on two of her kings the title of Saint, and gave to all of them a position of independence quite unusual in the Middle Ages, feeling instinc-tively that Hungary was a proselyte worth having, and a valuable guardian of the true faith against the hated Eastern rival in the Balkans.

That St Stephen was fully conscious of the advantages of civilization might be deduced from his connection with the Papacy, it is also proved by other actions of his. His energies were all devoted to introducing his subjects to the new civilizing agencies of all kinds, he expressly encouraged foreign (chiefly German) immigrants to settle, and explicitly promised them security and encouragement. A royal edict of his expresses the great advantages that Hungary will derive from foreign manners, customs, and ideas. Indeed, whatever may be said of Hungarians at a subsequent stage, it cannot be contended that they showed any aversion to foreign customs at this age. Slavonic influences played a large part at this early stage in the development of the government of the counties, German influences were important at this time and later both in the government of the towns and in other institutions. Moreover, the Magyar nobles were no exclusive caste, for both at this and at a much later time foreigners—Germans, Slovaks, Croats, Czechs, and Roumans— were freely ennobled and admitted into their ranks. The result was in the highest degree beneficial, the Hungarian nation gained a wholly unexpected strength and wealth of vitality from this absorption of new ideas and elements, and from the composite character of their institutions. That they borrowed feudal notions from the Germans and the system of the counties from the Slavs is no reproach to them, for they certainly improved them in the borrowing, a striking tribute to their singular political ability.

St Stephen appears to have been no less distinguished as an organiser than as a farseeing statesman. At any rate it is in his time that we first see definite traces of these Hungarian institutions, which can alike be so strangely compared, and so strangely contrasted, with our own. At this period the Hungarian King found means of asserting his power, which gave him a strength and authority almost unique in the early Middle Ages, and which is often and rightly held to resemble that of our own Norman kings. In centralising his power the King possessed two very great advantages—one spiritual, the other material. First the support of the Church and Papacy was given him with a readiness that was quite unusual and which had important effects. Nor was it only her spiritual thunders that made the Church formidable, the bishops would lend the King the Church *banderia* or feudal levies at need, and money could often be raised from vacant benefices or by loans from the clergy. Hence the King was soon able to consolidate his power and to extend his rule to the foot of the Eastern and Western Carpathians and to the Dalmatian Alps. Transylvania and Croatia were both subjected to the authority of the Hungarian King. Both retained provincial Estates but were governed in each case by a royal official appointed by the King, the Governor of Transylvania being termed the *voivode*, that of Croatia the *Banus* or *Ban*.

One obvious source of the King's power is the fact that the dominant Magyar nobility remained so numerous[1]. Gradually there arose a distinction between the great lords or magnates and the lesser ones or gentry, and gradually also a large number of Magyars were degraded to the position of serfs. But none the less the gentry—as opposed to the magnates—were extremely numerous, powerful, and filled with a sense of equality. Their excessive number, and the important part they played in shaping the constitution, are the most singular features of Hungarian political development. They continued to be the dominant class, to which the King could always appeal in his struggle with the magnates. The King also possessed the advantage that the Magyars remained a nation of warriors, and were ever ready at the slightest provocation to rush to arms. Hence the old fyrd or national militia, the *posse comitatus* of each county headed by the *föispán*, in a word the *generalis insurrectio*, remained a living reality. It was not infrequently summoned by the King. The magnates or gentry did not

---

[1] It appears best to speak of Hungarian nobles and of nobility from the beginning, though the terms involve a measure of anachronism. The Hungarian *nemes* implies tribesman, *serviens*, for which freeman seems the nearest equivalent. The title and distinctions of the nobility do not really appear till the thirteenth and fourteenth centuries. With this qualification I believe the description of the Hungarian *nemes* as noble is the most intelligible and convenient term that can be applied to him in English.

for some time begin to surround themselves with feudal levies of their own (*banderia*), and, even when they did, the fyrd was likely to prove the stronger. Of the fyrd the King was the natural leader and recognised chief, and he often used it with effect against the rebellious nobles with their *banderia*, in very much the same way as William Rufus once used the English national fyrd to crush Norman rebel barons (1088). Hence, so long as the fyrd remained in active existence, the King retained his advantage as against rebellious or turbulent nobles.

The administrative organisation of the whole land followed the models pursued in other countries, after the conquering race had thoroughly settled on the soil. The King sought to consolidate his power and to counteract feudalism by turning the chief local representatives into royal officials. The land was divided like England into counties, over each of which the King sought to set a high sheriff (*föispán*) who should be appointed by and solely responsible to the royal power[1]. The attempt was not altogether successful, and, just as in England, some sheriffs managed to make their office hereditary. Moreover, the *föispán* who was the chief official in the county, was almost always a local noble. As commander of the county forces, he naturally exercised greater influence than he would have done among races whose instincts were less military. The King's only resource with the *föispán* was to select them from among the gentry rather than from among the magnates. In this way he pleased the gentry and played off their influence against the magnates. The result of all these causes was that, until the thirteenth century, the Hungarian King remained one of the strongest in Europe. This fact appears even more remarkable when we contemplate the great size of his kingdom, and remember that the monarchy remained elective, though confined to the Arpád family. As it was, royal control was so great that—in spite of much local independence in some districts—the rights of private coinage were never exercised by the noble, and those of building private fortresses and of engaging in private war were but seldom

---

[1] There was a further subdivision of the county into *járás* or hundreds.

claimed. It was the strength of the royal power that prevented disintegration and, during. the confusion that came after the twelfth century, the unity that had already been obtained was too strong to be dissolved. None the less, in the thirteenth century a number of causes contributed to break down the power of the King in Hungary as in England. Some of these causes were more or less accidental; for example there was a series of weak kings, of minorities, and of disputed successions, which culminated in military and financial disasters. But there were other and deeper causes of the decline of monarchy, for the intense military spirit, which had once animated everyone in Hungary, had decayed. The fyrd had become antiquated and the King had thus lost his chance of making his most impressive appearance before his people as head of the nation. Henceforward he had to depend on his personal guards (who were limited in number) or upon the *banderia* lent to him by the nobles and the Church. In any case he had not the same power of asserting his authority, while dangerous privileges were constantly being extended to the nobles. The magnates naturally sought to evade his authority, to make offices hereditary, and to establish petty sovereignties; among the local gentry the spirit of liberty —often of turbulence—had always been strong, and, as the central authority weakened and war became more of a specialised trade, they developed both the strength and the theory of independence. This fact is of very great importance, much more so than if the lesser tenants in England had developed the same ideas, for the Hungarian gentry interfered in the national government in addition to controlling local affairs[1]. In England the lesser tenants either did not attend the national Parliament at all or merely sent representatives, in Hungary every one of the gentry had a right to attend it in his own person, which many of them actually exercised. Hence the growth of ideas of independence among the Hungarian gentry had direct and immediate effects upon the national assembly.

---

[1] It is in the thirteenth century that the local autonomy of the counties first becomes apparent. Then the authority of the *föispán*, high sheriff, and the *alispán*, his sheriff—*vice-comes*—or representative, the two nominated officials, begins to be limited by the powers of the county assembly (*congregatio*).

They viewed with indignation the weakness of their kings and their disastrous foreign policy, and determined on their own remedy. In 1222—seven years after *Magna Carta*—the weak, extravagant, and militarily incompetent Andreas II was forced by the combined action of magnates and gentry to subscribe to a document entitled *Bulla Aurea*. This is, just as truly as *Magna Carta*, the first in a long line of statutes and customs which form an unwritten constitution. In the same way it, in a sense,. expresses an aristocratic reaction and the *Bulla*, like the *Carta*, is the sign and seal of royal submission. Apart from this the two documents are very different. In theory, at any rate, *Magna Carta* was more for the whole people, but *Bulla Aurea* was a victory for the nobles only, though the latter were so numerous that they might for the moment almost think themselves the nation. *Bulla Aurea* is evidently not a victory for the magnates as against the gentry, in fact the very reverse is true. The gentry saw that it was to their interest that the King should not be too weak, and aimed alike at strengthening his power and their own against the magnates. The King's jurisdiction is admitted to be legal and supreme throughout the counties. Neither entire counties nor dignities of state are in future to be conferred as hereditary estates nor held in perpetuity—an evident blow at the magnates. At the same time the power of the *főispán* in each county was defined and restrained. Hence the county system still remains controlled by the King, though the gentry take care that they shall not have too little power or the magnates too much.

Other provisions aim at interposing the Palatine (the chief official of the realm corresponding roughly to the Norman or Arragonese "justiciar") as intermediary between the King and the "nation." Thus all law-suits concerned with the nobles are to be judged by the Palatine without knowledge of the King. Therefore the Palatine is really entrusted with the execution of the law, and here a distinct concession is made to the magnates, for the Palatine was usually a magnate. But the privilege of trial by the Palatine is the first of the great provisions erecting the nobles as a whole (i.e. both magnates and gentry) into a privileged class. A second of these provisions—also expressed in *Bulla Aurea*—is that of immunity from extraordinary taxation, no noble or ecclesiastic is to be taxed. These and all other privileges are guarded by the famous article which contains the *jus resistendi*[1]. In case of the King or his successors acting contrary to the provisions of the *Bulla*, bishops or nobles have each the right of resisting and opposing him by arms *sine nota alicujus infidelitatis*. It is characteristic of the military character of the gentry as a class that they close a compact otherwise remarkable for legality and tranquillity, by extorting an admission from the King that armed rebellion is, under certain circumstances, lawful.

The situation thus outlined in *Bulla Aurea* leads at once to the typical medieval system of restraint upon the King by an Assembly of Estates, to that system of government by contract between King and people (usually embodied in an assembly) which has become the root of every modern constitution through the agency of Locke. It is singular that Hungary and England are the only countries whose institutions still bear upon them the proof that Locke's theory was essentially a medieval idea. In Hungary the contract was enforced in a very definite form by the *jus resistendi*. A similar provision to it exists indeed in *Magna Carta*, but its operation was only temporary; in Hungary it was a permanent principle of public law and was a recognised basis of the constitution until its repeal in 1687[1]. A breach of contract by the King was immediately followed by armed rebellion and, since the nobles attended Parliament on horseback and in armour, they could proceed to execute their threats of resistance directly they uttered them.

The relations of the King with the nobles find their best expression in the period when Hungary was ruled by the foreign Angevin kings (1308–85). Charles Robert (1308–42), the first of the line, had French ideas of dealing with rebellious barons and was arbitrary enough, but under his son Louis the Great (1342–82) a complete harmony was established between King and nobles. The splendours of his reign are surpassed in Hungarian history only by those of Corvinus, and we see in him the best type of

---

[1] The *jus resistendi* also existed in Arragon—and Professor Marczali has traced its adoption in Hungary to imitation of that country, but the point has been disputed.

medieval monarch, who knew how to take the lead, and yet could work in thorough harmony with the system of government by Estates.   The Palatine or premier stood at the head of the King's Council (*consilium regis*) and exercised great powers both as commander-in-chief and civil administrator, resembling the Anglo-Norman justiciar in power, and the Arragonese *justiza*, as being the intermediary between King and "nation." Both he and other ministers were admittedly responsible to the Parliament or National Assembly of Estates.   Already in 1290 and 1298 it had been agreed that the King should be always accompanied by ministers, and that his Acts should be invalid without their counter-signature, and even before this in 1231 the Palatine was a responsible official.   Thus we get even in the thirteenth century in Hungary a very fair realisation of the principle of ministerial responsibility, which was carried much further by Louis the Great.

It is characteristic of the constitution of this country, so abounding in contrasts, enshrining so much that is old with so much that is new, that while the principle of ministerial responsibility was more highly developed than in any medieval constitution, the system of government by Estates was the least advanced.   Even under Louis the Great it was most imperfectly developed.   Originally the National Assembly under Arpád had merely been the whole people in arms, the wild riders gathered on the *puszta* or prairie, whom Arpád harangued before leading into battle.   Leaving the uncertainties of the early period we find definite evidence of the existence of the National Assembly under St Stephen in 1001.   It bears a character very similar to that described above, for in theory at any rate every free man—that is every noble—could attend.   In literal fact the Rákos—the plain near Pest where this Assembly met—was often covered with thousands of wild horsemen, who came mounted and armed to take part in the deliberations of the National Assembly.   The special peculiarity of this Assembly was that it was not split into two or three Chambers, as in the case of other medieval legislatures.   The magnates and the prelates and the numerous gentry all appeared in person and voted together and by heads not by orders.   Hence the magnates, being much the fewer, could always be outvoted, though their moral influence and importance often allowed them to prevail. The fact of the numbers and power of the gentry, not only in the local but in the national life, is the most unique and fundamental influence of Hungarian history. It is also of extraordinary interest because it shows how a conservative people could maintain far down into the Middle Ages a species of government by assembly, which was rudimentary in the highest degree. For there is not much difference—either in theory or practice— between the free men of Tacitus and the free nobles of Hungary, between the armed gathering of warriors in Homer who assemble in the ἀγορά and the wild Hungarian riders who thronged in the Rákos in the Middle Ages[1]. The fundamental idea of equality, which permeated the whole class of nobles, is one that was essentially primitive, and which disappeared much more quickly in every other European land. It was the moral force of this idea, just as much as the numerical superiority of the gentry, which preserved their peculiar privileges against the magnates and imparted its special form to the Hungarian constitution.

It is once more in keeping with this singular constitution that, while its Parliament is most remarkable for its disregard of the representative principle in the middle ages, yet in the eleventh century (1061) we find almost the earliest instance of it in Hungary. The representative principle never indeed took deep root in her national government, save in one instance. In the later Middle Ages the wealth and importance of the towns in Hungary procured them a voice in the National Assembly, and a number of them were permitted to send borough or burgess representatives to it. But unfortunately prejudice was too strong, against the upstart burgesses the noble class—whether magnates or gentry—was united. It was a serious misfortune for Hungary that the towns were relatively unimportant and were not regarded with favour by the nobles, since their inhabitants were chiefly German. The result of this disfavour shown to the towns was

---

[1] Even so late as the sixteenth century general assemblies *en masse* of the nobility were held, and it was not till 1608 that a permanent system of electing representatives of the nobles from each county was devised (v. *infra*, pp. xlvii—xlviii, note).

that the burgess-members never attained adequate weight or importance, and, though they were allowed to speak, were very seldom permitted the privilege of voting in any way by which their numbers could exercise an important influence on the assembly as a whole. The result was that the nobility was unable to mix with the *bourgeois* element or to link it to the national life. The evil was less than among most nobilities— for the Hungarian was perhaps the most numerous and the least exclusive of aristocracies—but, none the less, its inability to make common cause with the *bourgeoisie* stereotyped it into a privileged caste. The vast class of nobles became the *populus* or "nation" in the technical sense, endowed with every privilege and liberty ; beneath them was the people properly so-called, a vast body of the unprivileged—*bourgeoisie* and serfs of all kinds and nationalities—including many Magyars. To all of these the appropriate description of *misera plebs contribuens* was applied in the sixteenth century.

Under Louis the Great we see very evident signs that the influence of German and Western ideas was transforming the free Magyar noble into the feudal baron or knight of the West. Louis the Great is as much the creator of the magnate as a political force, as Matthias Corvinus was of the gentry. Titles for the first time became common and tended to become hereditary, the rights and privileges of the nobles were carefully worked out and defined, the magnates began to draw apart from the gentry, and the whole noble class became organised in a sort of close hereditary corporation. The whole body formed the Corporation of the Sacred Crown (*Corpus Sacrae Coronae*) of which every individual noble, whether a magnate or one of the gentry, was admitted a member. This is one of the reasons why the Hungarian Crown has been invested with a reverence which attaches not even to that of Charlemagne. Another is that the King and the Crown appear to have been considered as separable from one another. Hungarians revered the Crown not only as the symbol of majesty but as the visible embodiment of their rights ; it was not only the ornament and property of the King, but, as it were, the palpable title-deed of the whole nobility.

The national Parliament was so exclusively an aristocratic assembly, that its importance naturally implied the predominance of the nobles. None the less the continual strife between the magnates and the gentry served both King and constitution in good stead. Louis the Great, though he favoured the magnates, looked also to the gentry for their support. It was freely given and produced a result extremely rare in the Middle Ages, for the National Assembly, though powerful, refused to use its power to attack and to reduce the authority of the King. The characteristic feudal tendencies were never given full rein, and the traditional authority of the King was able to check the baser kinds of feudal abuses. For instance, subinfeudation was never practised, the gentry held directly of the King, and the meanest of them was as much an individual member of the Sacred Crown as the loftiest magnate. The rights of private war and private coinage were rarely recognised, those of private justice were strictly defined ; and, even where the county offices tended to become hereditary, the gentry continued to operate as a check on the magnates. For instance, these great lords occasionally obtained rights to separate jurisdictions independent of the counties, but these cases were, on the whole, rare and hardly affected the general principle. Under the firm hand of Louis the Great the magnates were kept in submission, the gentry were encouraged to take part in political life, and the whole system of government by Estates was worked with a simplicity and harmony, which is a better testimony to his memory and his greatness than the numerous conquests and victories that he achieved. There is no more instructive contrast than between this truly great monarch and Edward III of England, his contemporary. Each had a great personality and won great victories and renown, each had to deal with a powerful and growing Parliament, but the skill with which Louis managed his Assembly contrasts markedly with the continual bitterness between Edward and his Parliament.

From the death of Louis the Great (1382) to the accession of Matthias Corvinus (1458) stretches a dreary period of anarchy, bloodshed and disunion. Hungary is misgoverned by minors and weaklings at home, harassed by foreign invasions from

M. H.

without. The inevitable result of weakness at the centre was an increase in the power of the magnates, whose interest it was at the moment to promote disunion or to ally themselves with enemies. In fact this is probably the most critical period of all Hungarian history; at other times she has been saved either by a great king, by the magnates, or by the gentry. During this period there were no great kings; the magnates refused to play a patriotic part; the gentry were weak and the county system, always the seat of their strength and power, was in danger of actual dissolution. Some gleam of hope indeed there was, the heroic John Hunyadi, the *voivode* of Transylvania, was the light and hope of Hungary in the war against the Turks, and the "White Knight" was acknowledged as the hero of Christendom. Several times victorious in border-warfare, he was at length defeated at the disastrous battle of Varna (1444), where Wladislav I (Ulaszló) King both of Hungary and of Poland was killed. Nothing, however, could shake the nation's belief in Hunyadi's military talents. He became Regent or Governor for the infant King during the last decade of his life (1446–56), and his military triumphs and adventures resemble those rather of a paladin than of a ruler. His last achievement, the heroic defence of Belgrade against the Turks in 1456, was also the most glorious of his life. The Turkish retreat was marked by heavy losses, and his defence impressed their leaders so deeply that they made no serious effort to conquer Hungary for a generation. But great warrior and heroic man as Hunyadi showed himself in repelling the Turks, he was far less successful in circumventing the magnates at home. He was supported in the main by the gentry, but his position as Regent was weak, for he needed the magic title of King to win the authority and respect sufficient to unite around him all the elements of national life. Under happier auspices his son Matthias Corvinus Hunyadi was raised to the throne (1458). In him the gentry had named their representative, in him the magnates had discovered one determined to be their master, in him the people as a whole had found one who could conform to every ideal and promote every object of national greatness.

Much as St Stephen and Louis the Great may have accomplished for Hungary, neither of them can compare with Matthias Corvinus, who is undoubtedly one of the great rulers of history. His acts bear the evident stamp of greatness, and his policy and achievements exhibit a farseeing statesman, a wise ruler, and a triumphant warrior. The greatness and versatility of his character need no demonstration. It is sufficient to say that the man, who has always been the ideal of the Magyars, was Rouman by extraction, polyglot by speech, and a worshipper of the Classical Renaissance. Few rulers have combined such judicious patronage of literature and art with the gifts of a soldier and a statesman, none have possessed a more magical personality or more power to awaken enthusiasm among his followers. Like Alfred in England, Henry IV in France, and Barbarossa in Germany, he is one of those rulers of whom legend is never weary, and of whom a thousand traits are preserved in ballad and anecdote. As with so many great soldiers his military gifts have obscured his other services, in his case perhaps almost more than with anyone. His victories over Czechs and Austrians are regarded as wasted efforts, since it is held that he should have concentrated all his attention on defeating the Turks, whose power was increasing with every year. In reality it appears more probable that he realised that Hungary could not resist the Turks alone, and was anxious by arms and alliances to bring other countries and nations into the scale against them. At any rate it seems clear that he did not love war for its own sake, for the decrees of his later years indicate an ardent desire for peace and a systematic attempt to organise the administration of the country. The difficulties confronting him were enormous, for the whole fabric of government had been gradually disintegrating since the end of the fourteenth century. Even under Louis the Great the *insurrectio* was already antiquated, and it had become a practice for the King to employ the *banderia* lent to him by nobles or ecclesiastics for the purpose of suppressing disturbance or revolt. Such a procedure—dangerous enough even under a great king—became simply anarchical in the reign of a weakling or a minor, for it delivered the King wholly to the mercy of one set of nobles or another. Matthias was not the man to depend on the goodwill of his vassals for military support, and rightly

saw that it was essential to strong government that the King
should maintain an efficient professional army quite separate and
distinct from the feudal levies. He had his way and maintained
his famous " Black Army " in defiance of all the protests that it
was against the law and the constitution. Matthias was probably
influenced by autocratic ideas derived from the classics, and by
the avowed absolutism of contemporary sovereigns like Ferdinand
of Spain and Louis XI of France. But he was far too wise to
offend the prejudices of the Hungarian nobles too deeply, and,
though he wished that the King should be strong, perhaps too
strong, it would be harsh to say that he aimed definitely at
absolutism. After all he was sprung from the gentry, he was an
elective not a hereditary King, and he perfectly understood the
need of conciliating a proud and passionate nobility, and of giving
to the National Assembly full opportunities of consultation and
deliberation. He took care to repress the magnates, and relied
chiefly for support on the gentry whom he sought in every way
to strengthen and conciliate. A series of decrees endeavoured
to vitalise and recreate the spirit of the county system. Nobles
were forced to undertake official duties in the counties, such as
to accept the post of *szolgabiró* (under-sheriff) if elected to it, while
a committee of eight or twelve nobles was elected annually to
hear lawsuits in each county (v. *infra*, p. 131). Matthias kept the
chief control by insisting on retaining the royal nomination of
the high sheriff of the county (*föispán*). At the same time
there was always a danger that a magnate might become *föispán*
and overawe the gentry in the county assembly. To provide
against this Matthias abolished, so far as he could, the special
privileges and jurisdictions of the magnates, and endeavoured to
base the whole working of the county system on the cooperation
of the more numerous gentry against them. It is to Matthias
that we may trace a deliberate and definite attempt to give a
firm autonomy to the county government. When his strong
hand no longer controlled from above disintegration became
apparent. Each county developed into an autonomous unit, a
sort of *imperium in imperio*, each county assembly became a
miniature parliament, and the state was dissolved into some fifty
independent communities. This result came from the weakening

of control at the centre, and, though it may have produced immediate weakness, was a source of ultimate strength. The struggle between the local freedom of the gentry in the county assembly, and the authority of the King or the magnate ended in the complete victory of the former. During the Turkish wars (1526–1718), while the King was weak and the magnates were fighting along the borders, the gentry won victory at home. The powers of the *föispán* (high sheriff), who was nearly always a magnate, were definitely restricted. The *alispán* (*vice-comes* or sheriff) had hitherto been his mere mouthpiece and representative, but in 1548 he became subject to election in the same way as the other county magistrates. Henceforth the self-government of the county was admitted as supreme, and this recognised autonomy of the gentry was at least better than the arbitrary rule of magnates. Such a system was not indeed suited for military purposes, but its political vitality was such that it could maintain itself against every effort to crush it. The county system and the county assembly are far the most peculiar and characteristic institutions of Hungary. In the evil days which followed, had it not been for the vigour which Matthias breathed into the county system, the whole fabric of government must have collapsed under the stress of the Turkish invasions. As it was, the local government attained its most striking development just at the moment when the central government reached the lowest depth of weakness and degradation.

On the death of Matthias without legitimate heir (1490) Hungary fell into a state of great confusion. The magnates, repressed by his iron hand, endeavoured to bring about a feudal reaction, but they were stubbornly resisted by the gentry both in the county *congregatio* and in the National Assembly. The moderating influence of a King was gone, for the new ruler Wladislav II was utterly weak, and the fact that he was a Jagello and a King of Bohemia, as well as of Hungary, destroyed any claim which he might have upon the loyalty of Hungarians as a real national King. Hence the magnates and the gentry continued their furious faction-fight without disturbance and without cessation. As if this chaos was not sufficient it was

increased by a terrible peasant revolt (1514). Goaded by the
heavy taxes and by their exclusion from all political power, a
large number of peasants (of whom most appear to have been
Magyars) rose in a fierce revolt headed by George Dózsa—the
Hungarian Jack Cade[1]. It was savagely repressed, and the
triumphant nobility (for once united) passed a series of vindic-
tive laws against them, which are described more fully in the
text of this work (pp. 171 sqq.). At the same moment Verböczy
produced and laid before Parliament his famous legal text-book
—the *Tripartitum*—which may be described as an unofficial
code of the laws, and which subsequent generations have
worshipped as a masterpiece of legal wisdom. Nothing could
reconcile the magnates and the gentry, but, after a most
chequered struggle, at the last moment the latter seemed to be
gaining the day. In 1525 Verböczy was chosen Palatine by the
young King Louis II in deference to the wishes of the gentry.
Verböczy was a great lawyer, bearing a remarkable resemblance
to our English Coke, in that he was at once the author of the
classic legal text-book of his land, and also the stout parliamentary defender of her liberties. But, while he might have been a
great leader in quiet times, he was wholly unequal to a crisis in
which only a warrior or an iron-willed diplomatist could have
succeeded. While the constitutional pedants were wrangling in
the Parliament a grim army of professional soldiers was advancing to settle their disputes for them in a manner that should
be decisive enough. The Turks were then the finest soldiers in
the world, and already

"The Orient moon of Islam rode in triumph
From Tmolus to th' Acro-Ceraunian shore."

They had long been encroaching on the Hungarian frontier,
Belgrade was already in their hands, and no great fortress barred
their way up to the Alföld. Finally in 1526 they moved up
the Danube from Belgrade. Mindful of the coming danger the
pedants at length ceased to wrangle, and Parliament at last
recovered its senses and invested the King with a dictatorship.
But it was too late, and the concession was fruitless. King Louis

[1] The insurgents were known as Kuruczes (Crusaders), a term afterwards applied
to all Hungarian insurgents, as the followers of Bocskay, Tököli, and Rákóczi.

went to meet the Turks only to be vanquished and slain with many of his troops on the fatal field of Mohács, the most disastrous battle of Hungarian history (1526).

The disaster of Mohács was the most important event in the later history of Hungary whether regarded from the constitutional or political point of view. Two-thirds of Hungary were conquered by the Turk and were not recovered for a century and a half. But this was the least evil: in order to resist the Turk Hungary had to accept a German ruler in the Habsburgs—who have ever since ruled as Kings in Hungary and as Archdukes or Emperors in Austria and its adjacent lands. Now Hungary had had foreign dynasties before, Kings from Naples, from Bohemia or Poland, who had also ruled Hungary. But in the fourteenth century such things did not matter; in all countries the nobles were then too strong to be permanently crushed, and, though a foreign ruler might—and frequently did—stimulate useful tendencies to reform, he would have been quite unable to overthrow the balance of the constitution. In the sixteenth century it mattered a good deal, for everywhere absolutism was abroad, medieval Parliaments were dying, and Kings were stimulated to new life under the influence of economic conditions, military power, classical ideas, and Lutheran and Machiavellian advocacies of Divine Right.

In the sixteenth century almost all rulers sought to be absolute, and it will be found that this aim was more easily realised by a sovereign who ruled over more kingdoms than one. Ferdinand and Charles of Castile found it easy to subdue Arragon; the Ferdinands of Austria found it easy to subdue Bohemia, and had the resources of both to turn against Hungary. However, absolutism was more easily attained where the dynasty was native; in France, Sweden, and in many German States the native patriotic dynasty was gradually made despotic by universal consent. But where the dynasty was foreign, resistance was inevitable and in two cases successful—in England under the Stuarts, in Hungary under the Habsburgs. In neither case could the absolutising alien King subdue a stubborn prejudiced and alien people.

The fact of a foreign or Scotch dynasty, though important in

England, is far less momentous than the fact of a foreign or
German dynasty in Hungary. The Magyars hated the Germans
worse than the English hated the Scots, and the ruler of Austria-
Hungary, who controlled so many different lands and nations,
necessarily thought that his only salvation lay in absolutism.
There was also a serious religious difficulty, the Habsburgs have
always been good Catholics, but in the seventeenth century they
definitely adopted the ideals of Catholicism and of religious
intolerance as a principle of state-policy. Hence they desired
uniformity throughout their realm for conscience sake as well as
for military needs.

In a similar way conscience inspired Hungary to resist the
Habsburgs, for many Magyars had become Calvinists, and, as
everyone knows, Calvinism and absolutism agreed as well with
one another, as God with the Devil. Hence the effect of a
foreign dynasty, imposed on Hungary in the sixteenth century,
was to provoke a bitter struggle between medieval Hungarian
constitutionalism and modern Austrian absolutism ; the result
was the survival of the former crystallised, perfected, almost
unimpaired down to within the memory of living man. By
medieval, I mean that which is of the fourteenth, not of the
ninth, century. The statement is not intended to mean that the
Hungarian constitution did not develop at all under Habsburg
rule—it did, none the less it remained medieval and fourteenth
century in character. At the time of Mohács (1526) it was
actually primitive or of the ninth century in many of its features.
Under a native dynasty, and with favouring conditions, it might
gradually, but in no very short time, have become an absolutist
state of the normal continental type. Under Corvinus these
tendencies were certainly present, in 1526 Parliament had
actually granted the King a dictatorship. But under the foreign
Habsburg dynasty the conflict between King and people became
so sharp that, though the Hungarians could not prevent the
constitution from ceasing to be primitive, they managed to prevent it from ceasing to be medieval.

Great as was the defeat of Mohács it is unquestionable that
its effect would not have been so profound but for the internal
chaos which it so dramatically displayed. The cause of defeat

was not a decline in Hungarian valour, for the long history of the war on the frontiers abounds in episodes of romantic bravery. It was rather the hopeless nature of internal dissensions—there was now no longer a King, there was to be a disputed succession, the magnates still hated the gentry, and the peasants still hated both. Moreover the system of county-autonomy, though admirable for maintaining the existence of each county by itself, was almost fatal to national defence or to united effort. The self-government, which Matthias had given to the counties, could not fail to bring military disaster unless the King controlled a "Black or professional Army" which could fight immediately at his bidding. Now that the King and his army were gone, the magnates, with their dependants and *banderia*, were the only men who could readily undertake the national defence. But some of them were dead and others disheartened, and from their very nature they were the last men to unite with one another in great military movements, though admirably suited to warfare of the marches. For the moment they were useless, and there was only one chance to save Hungary. She must accept a foreign ruler, and he must be a German and a Habsburg. Already in 1526 the crown had been offered to and accepted by John Zapolya, a Hungarian noble, but he was powerless and became dependent on the Turk. Therefore in 1527 the gift was revoked and the crown offered to Ferdinand, a Habsburg and brother of the Emperor Charles V, then the mightiest potentate in the world. It was hoped that the Emperor would assist Hungary, as he had already sent troops to her aid, and in fact the advance of the Turks gave him no option. In 1528 Buda was captured, and in 1529 the Turks knocked rudely enough on the gates of Vienna itself, but here their limit of conquest was reached. They were repulsed with loss, and the Emperor himself headed an army against them in 1532, backed by Luther, who denounced the Turks for not drinking wine. However, even this alcoholic crusade did not succeed in shaking the Turkish hold on Hungary, which soon developed into a formal annexation. Ferdinand's rival in the kingship—John Zapolya—had made an alliance with the Turks, and the Sultan professed to regard him as an independent King. When Zapolya died in 1540, the

Sultan took the opportunity to destroy the idea of Hungarian independence and to establish a Hungarian pashalik in the Alföld, leaving only the Principality of Transylvania to John Zapolya's son. From 1540 onwards for almost a century and a half a pasha dwelt on the rock of Buda, kept a slave market in the town below, and a harem on the famous Margaret island in mid-Danube. The cathedral of Pest became a mosque, and minarets and crescents adorned both towns, while the whole Alföld between Transylvania and the West became a Turkish province divided into sanjaks. Only the strips running along the boundary, which joined together the impregnable natural citadels of the Tatra and of Croatia, remained in Habsburg hands. In the strong rock-fortress of Transylvania a Hungarian prince or duke maintained his ground, and kept the land relatively free from Turkish troops and influences. Hence there were now three Hungaries, the western part which was Habsburg, the centre—the Alföld—Turkish, the south-eastern part Transylvanian. Though Transylvania remained autonomous it was yet a state tributary to the Turks, and its prince was constantly subject to deposition by the Sultan. None the less, after the Habsburg had been enthroned at Pozsony and the Turk at Buda, Hungarian sentiment gravitated towards Transylvania where free Magyar nobles, Szeklers and Saxons still preserved something more than the form of old liberties and kept their prince in a state of submission that was highly gratifying to their neighbours under the rule of the Habsburg. A patriotic Hungarian considered that there was as much reliance and safety to be placed upon the Turk as upon the German. Each was acceptable only so long as he could be used to prevent the other crushing the last remnants of Hungarian liberty, and the greatest patriots and statesmen of the time—men like Martinuzzi (Frater György) and Bocskay in Transylvania—are found using the Turk as often as the Habsburg for this purpose.

Their attitude may seem strange to us but, paradoxically enough, the powerful influence of religion recommended it. One cause of disunion in 1526 had been that Hungary was threatened not only by political but by religious division. Matthias Corvinus, in true Renaissance style, had shown himself thoroughly alive to the abuses of the Church, and hatred of the corruption and moral laxity of the Church had spread far before 1526. After that time a doctrinal reformation speedily set in, or rather two reformations together, the Lutheran and the Calvinist, and progressed with great rapidity because political disunion rendered the suppression of heresy impossible[1]. The importance of this religious reformation was very great because Calvinism affected the majority of the gentry. The Habsburgs were Catholic, the gentry—the strength and core of Hungarian patriotism—became largely Calvinistic, and their religious differences strengthened them in the resolve to maintain their parliamentary liberties against the Habsburg. The autonomy of the religious assembly and the stubborn spirit of Calvinism strengthened the autonomy of the county *congregatio* and the proud obstinacy of ancestral liberty.

Calvinism, as in France, showed itself aristocratic and was partly taken up by the nobles, because it suited their ideal of resistance to the sovereign. In no land has Calvinism exercised a more important effect than in Hungary, and without it there can be little doubt that its constitution would have perished. Here as elsewhere Calvinism lent strength and fibre and a fierce spirit of defiance to its adherents. The iron entered into their souls with such a doctrine, and steeled its worshippers to defy their sovereign and to die for their religion. Calvinism appealed much to the Magyar and spread far over the Alföld, especially in the wide plains around Debreczen, which city earned and has retained the name of the "Calvinist Rome." It also spread into Transylvania where, in the latter half of the sixteenth century, it became more popular than Catholicism, and where toleration for both religions—almost the earliest instance in Europe—was admitted in 1557. Calvinism, here as elsewhere, was not primarily the incentive to strife and "the creed of rebels," but it speedily became so. As the Habsburgs eventually fell under the influence of Jesuits and became bigoted, and as the Turks—though politically oppressive—showed some religious tolerance, the choice between an Austrian and a Turkish master became a

[1] Lutheranism was recognised in Hungary in 1550, in Transylvania in 1545, Calvinism in Hungary in 1564, and in Transylvania in 1562.

hard one. At all events during the sixteenth and seventeenth centuries the patriotic Hungarian was evenly balanced in his inclinations and had no more love for the one than for the other. The plumed helmets of the Kaiser's soldiers were seen with as little pleasure as the turbans of the Sultan's, for in the shadow of the one came a black army of Jesuits to dispossess the Calvinist of his conscience; in the train of the other a rabble of Serbish settlers to rob him of his land. It was a balance between opposite oppressions, and entailed a hard choice between the claims of the soul and the body.

The rule of the Habsburgs in Hungary marks a most decisive stage in her history. Ferdinand and his successors were Kings of Bohemia, as well as of Hungary, and usually Archdukes of Austria and Emperors as well. It was inevitable that sovereigns, who ruled over other lands, should offend Hungarian susceptibilities by slighting their keen national feelings. In Hungary, where passion and sentiment run high, such indifference was likely to be more serious than elsewhere. But there was an even greater danger for, while Hungary was exceptionally jealous of her constitutional liberties, her sovereign was willing to sacrifice them to military efficiency. A sovereign, who ruled over other states, might be able to draw his revenues from them, dispense with the Parliament of Hungary, and gradually destroy its constitution by disuse. In this wise the Spanish Habsburgs had treated the kingdom of Arragon, whose liberties had been defended by a nobility quite as proud and independent as the Hungarian. But the Austrian Habsburg needed money more than the Spanish one, and—happily for Hungary—he found the frequent summoning of her Parliament a necessity, if he wished to obtain his taxes. But like Matthias Corvinus the Habsburgs saw that a professional standing army was also a necessity, though it was directly opposed to the traditions of Hungary and calculated to engender strong suspicions of royal good faith. Hence they came into constant conflict with their Parliaments and subjects in Hungary. The county system was for military purposes almost useless, yet it was most formidable as a means of political resistance, whether to Habsburg or Sultan. Therefore even if the Habsburg ruler could sometimes coerce the

Parliament he had only gone one step, he had then to coerce each of the autonomous counties in turn. Even after he had got his money voted for an efficient professional army of mercenaries, he could never be sure of his rule, for the Hungarian counties were quite capable of summoning the Turk to their assistance if the Habsburg interfered too much with their privileges. Some blunders and some breaches of the constitution were inevitable under these conditions and at this time of crisis and necessity ; and, considering their extreme difficulties and their temptation to sacrifice everything to military efficiency, the first two Habsburg rulers got along fairly well in Hungary. In addition at times both showed political moderation and some appreciation of the value of religious tolerance. Unhappily the third Habsburg, the gifted but bigoted and intolerant Emperor Rudolph II (1576–1607), proved a very different ruler. With him we trace a definite design to destroy religious tolerance and, as a natural consequence, to attack constitutional autonomy. This hardly disguised attempt was opposed primarily by passive resistance and at last by open rebellion ; and it is significant of the time that in the end the constitutional freedom of Hungary could only be maintained by the aid of a Hungarian rebel, of a Transylvanian Prince, and of a Turkish Sultan. Rudolph's first attempt had been to concentrate the control of Hungarian affairs in Vienna, and to subordinate Hungarian local independence to his military council there. His particular desire was to appoint the commanders of the frontier garrisons, and he chose German mercenaries for the chief posts, as he not unreasonably thought that Hungarian nobles, suspicious of his good faith towards their constitution, were not always likely to be the best officers. A vote of the Parliament in 1583 was the first significant mark of Hungarian resistance. It declared that no further supplies would be voted until Hungarians were appointed to the military posts, and were consulted in matters relating to financial and military concerns common to both Hungary and Austria (perhaps the earliest momentary anticipation of the modern Aus-gleich of 1867). Rudolph, who alternated between weakness and ungovernable passion, gave way for the moment but ultimately revived his old demands. Just at this time the religious strife greatly increased in intensity, the Calvinists were in the majority in Hungary, while Rudolph, under the influence of Jesuits, had begun to display the fiercest intolerance. The renewal of war with the Turks (1593) afforded a diversion, but in the end Rudolph's military disasters only served to increase his unpopularity. Finally in 1600 he acquired Transylvania, partly by negotiation, partly by arms, and proceeded to rule that land and its high-spirited nobles in a spirit of brutal savagery and intolerance. General Basta, who was appointed Governor, ruled by means of German soldiers, treating the land like a conquered territory and sending out his soldiers, as missionaries in jackboots and apostles with pikes, to shepherd converts into the Catholic fold. No more impolitic or brutal policy could be imagined, and the best justification of Rudolph is that his reason was unhinged. Rudolph's *coup d'état* in Transylvania in 1600 had the same reflex effect on Hungary as Charles I's attack on Scotland had on England in 1638. A concrete example taught England, in the one case, and Hungary in the other, that their King was meditating treason against them. But Transylvania was far more important to Hungary than Scotland was to England. Transylvania had been the home of Hungarian exiles, where Calvinist and Catholic had lived side by side undisturbed, the land of free men and free opinions, of liberty and toleration ; it was the Holland of East Europe to which Basta had now become the Alva. For it was as dangerous and as useless for Rudolph to force the nobles of Transylvania into rebellion as it had been for Philip II to stir up the burghers of Holland. In 1604 Rudolph seized a pretext to apply his Transylvanian policy to a district in Hungary, one of his generals seized the town of Kássa and hunted out its Protestant preachers. This outrage drove the Hungarians to desperation for it brought the danger to their very doors. It was clear that Rudolph intended to be absolute both in Church and State, and that rebellion had become the only refuge of conservatives, and at this critical stage a really great man arose to save the situation. Stephen Bocskay, a Transylvanian noble, took up arms on behalf of the imperilled liberties of both Hungary and Transylvania, prepared to resist in

Transylvania, and called in the Turk to his aid (1604). So moderate were his demands, so swift his preparations for war, and so skilful his diplomacy, that he carried everything before him. He speedily overran the whole of Upper Hungary—the chief centre of Calvinism—and made constant raids into Austrian territory, where his followers gave short shrift to Catholic priests and nóbles. Bocskay himself was thus formidable enough, but behind Bocskay was the still more formidable Turk, and the knowledge of this fact forced Rudolph to make terms. The result was the Treaty of Vienna (June 23, 1606) between the Emperor and Bocskay, and on November 11 of the same year, that of Zsitva-Torok between him and the Turks. By the latter arrangement, Rudolph was compelled to acknowledge the independence of Transylvania and to recognise Bocskay as its Prince.

The real negotiator of these treaties was Rudolph's brother, Matthias, who practically deposed the mad Emperor in 1607, and who in the next year arrived at a working agreement with the Hungarian Parliament on the basis of the Vienna Treaty. This arrangement has been described as the first Aus-gleich or Compromise between Austria and Hungary, but the term is somewhat misleading. It was really a recognition of the power of the medieval Parliament or Assembly of Estates as against the King, and, as a consequence, of the full privileges of the Hungarian nobility. The monarchy, which the Habsburg had evidently been striving to make hereditary, was once more declared to be elective and in the gift of the Parliament. The Office of the Palatine—which visibly symbolized the independence of the nobles of the crown—was solemnly revived after half a century of suppression. The legal power of the Palatine to judge nobles without any intervention from the King, except in cases *de capite et bonis*, was expressly restored. Hungarians and not Germans were to be chosen for all the chief offices and posts, and finally toleration for both Lutherans and Calvinists, and full admission of both to political office, was to be established[1].

[1] The legislative machinery also received its final shape and an organisation which it retained until 1847. The single chamber and the personal representation of the gentry were both done away with. Henceforth two representatives were elected by

As a final seal of the treaty—the famous Holy Crown of St Stephen was to be brought back to Hungary.

In reality Bocskay's victory had been too complete. This great patriot and statesman died before the end of 1606, but even he could not perhaps have secured the complete execution of all the terms of the Vienna Treaty. They were too humiliating for the ruler to observe them, but they were none the less of immense moral significance. The Emperor Matthias (1608–18) made some attempt to recover Transylvania but his efforts ended in complete failure, and from 1613–29 it was ruled by Prince Gabriel Bethlen (Bethlen Gábor), the most renowned of Transylvanian Princes and by no means the least powerful of European rulers. He secured the complete independence of Transylvania from Habsburg influence, and, though an ally of the Turk, was not a subservient one. He insisted on complete toleration of Lutheranism and Catholicism in his dominions, and made Transylvania once more the Holland of the Balkans—the home of toleration and freedom. In proportion as breaches were made in the Vienna Treaty, Hungarians turned eyes of longing towards Transylvania, where a powerful State arose, ruled by strong Princes, many of whose nobles were Hungarian in blood and sympathy, and who welcomed exiles from Hungary itself[1]. The fact that an autonomous independent State, which possessed the institutions and ideas of liberty, existed in the immediate neighbourhood of Hungary was perhaps the most powerful of all incentives to its nobles to retain their freedom. By this example they were constantly urged to resist all attempts to destroy their old rights or to infringe the new obligations of

each county assembly to represent the gentry and these, together with the burgess representatives, formed the Lower House or Table. The Upper House or Table consisted of the magnates and the bishops, each represented in person. Hence the line between magnates and gentry, which had long existed in fact, was now definitely and legally drawn, and the personal representation of the gentry as a whole, the witness to a most primitive political condition, was finally abolished.

[1] Transylvania was inhabited by four races—Magyars, Szeklers, Saxons, and Roumans or Wallachs. The first three were called the three nations and possessed full political rights. Eventually (1691) four religions were recognised and tolerated, Catholicism, Calvinism, Lutheranism, and Unitarianism. In respect to territory, the boundaries of Transylvania were often extended to include several counties of Hungary or *partes regni Hungariae*.

the Vienna Treaty. If the Habsburg ruler made any serious attempt to overthrow the latter, there was the ever-present fear that the Prince of Transylvania might come to the rescue of his kinsmen of Hungary, and that in his wake would follow the Crescent and the horsetail standards of the Sultan. The interference in Hungary, for example, of Gabriel Bethlen proved entirely on the side of religious and constitutional liberty. In 1621 and 1624 Gabriel Bethlen, after invasions of Hungary, forced Ferdinand II not only to grant advantages to the Principality of Transylvania, but to reaffirm the religious and constitutional freedom of Hungary as expressed in the Treaty of Vienna. The same policy was pursued by his astute successor George Rákóczi I (1630–48). He too advanced with an army far into Hungary, and extorted from the reluctant Ferdinand III the Treaty of Linz (1645). By this arrangement the substance of the peace of Vienna was preserved, the autonomy both of Transylvania and Hungary, and the absolute equality of Protestants and Catholics in the latter kingdom, were guaranteed. Thus, until the mid-seventeenth century, Transylvania and its Princes had been the trustees and executors of the Treaty of Vienna. Now their influence ceased, for Prince George Rákóczi II ruined Transylvania by a policy of reckless foreign adventure (1648–58). Under his rule—and after his deposition by the Turk (1658)—Transylvania practically sank into the position of a Turkish dependency, until she actually became an Austrian one in 1691.

During the first half of the seventeenth century the moral, and often the material, support of Transylvania had been of the greatest service to Hungary, and yet there was one reason why many good Hungarians regarded her with suspicion. She was the home of heresy and of Calvinism, and, though many Hungarians were Protestant, it could not be denied that the old historic faith—inseparably associated with national glory and with the medieval constitution—was the Catholic one. Good Catholics therefore hesitated, patriotism pulled them towards Transylvania, religion towards the Habsburg, and the man, who represented and developed this last tendency more than any other, was the famous Peter Pázmány, Archbishop of Esztergom and Primate of Hungary from 1616 to 1636. He believed that heresy was a great danger, and that Catholicism under the Habsburg was better than toleration under the Turk. Hence he made a fixed resolve to Catholicize Hungary, but so far as possible by using persuasion and not force, and also without in any way impairing the political autonomy of Hungary. Religious union would end political discord, and the nation, if only firm and united, would be well able to maintain an independent national church and constitution and resist either Turk or Habsburg with equal ease. Pázmány was a great orator and a great diplomatist and gradually won back to Catholicism the chief magnates, who in turn influenced their serfs or dependants. At the time of his death he had practically achieved his work, for the Catholic party had become very strong in Hungary, though the majority of gentry still remained Calvinist. He had solved what appeared to be insoluble, and had shown that Hungary might be Catholic without being Habsburg, and that the old faith might serve to buttress the old liberties. On the whole Pázmány appears to have been in the right, for it was too early to expect a nation, which held two or even three different religious beliefs, to form one political union. But his experiment was a highly dangerous one, for, by separating the Catholic magnates from the Protestant gentry, he threatened to lay both at the feet of the alien king. Enthusiasm for Catholicism, however, stimulated zeal against the Turk, and the magnates, who were ever the first in border warfare, found congenial work in exercising their crusading zeal against the "dogheaded" Turks. Perhaps the best example of the tendencies of the age, and of the triumph of Pázmány's conceptions, is seen in Nicholas Zrinyi, the famous Ban of Croatia. His celebrated ancestor, Nicholas Zrinyi the elder, had won a great name for himself by defending Szigetvár with a handful of men against a Turkish host of a hundred thousand men led by the greatest of her Sultans, and finally had sallied forth—adorned as for a bridal—and died beneath the blows of a hundred scimitars (1566). He gave the finest concrete example of patriotism in that age, and his glorious death brought a thrill to many hearts. But his descendant was to do more for Hungary. Nicholas Zrinyi the younger too was a valiant warrior against the Turks, but he was something more —an impassioned national poet. He gave not only a concrete example of bravery, he breathed a soul and an inspiration into a whole people. His epic poem the *Zrinyiász* (1646), shows the conception of Hungarian patriotism which was based on Pázmány's ideas. The Turk is the infidel whom it is holy to kill, but before the object of this pious crusade can be effected, the Hungarian must return to the Catholic fold.

Zrinyi's ideas show the purely patriotic and national feeling of Hungary in the mid-seventeenth century. From 1606 till 1670 bickerings between the nation and its ruler had been constant, but continental warfare and the threatening attitude of Transylvania had absorbed too much of the Habsburg's attention to allow him seriously to endanger the constitution. As before mentioned, even so late as 1645 the influence of Prince George Rákóczi I forced Ferdinand III by the Peace of Linz to concede full autonomy to Transylvania and full toleration and recognition of parliamentary liberty to Hungary, in short to reaffirm the Vienna Treaty of forty years back in its most important provisions. But George Rákóczi II ruined Transylvania by a gambler's throw for the crown of Poland, and Ferdinand made peace with Europe at Westphalia in 1648. Henceforward the Austrian rulers, who had been absorbed in the West for over forty years, had at length time and energy to force their ideas upon Hungary. Even after the changes introduced by Bocskay there was undoubtedly a case for the reform of her constitution, much of the machinery was dangerously medieval, in particular the *jus resistendi* and the elective character of the crown. Moreover the ideas of the Habsburgs had become largely military, it now seemed to them that liberty was no compensation for inefficiency, and that the national and county assemblies of Hungary were simply obsolete engines of obstruction. Absolutist ideas were at their height, the French monarchy was now the most splendid and brilliant in the world, and it owed, or seemed to owe, all its glory to military efficiency and to royal absolutism. Moreover the case for autocracy was infinitely strengthened by that bigoted devotion to Catholicism and by that religious intolerance which inspired all the Habsburgs of the seventeenth century. In the Thirty Years' War the Emperor

Ferdinand II had destroyed the political liberties and the religious independence of Bohemia, and the company of Jesus had finished the work of the army of Caesar. In 1658 Leopold I became Emperor, Archduke of Austria, and King of Hungary, and, since he was an avowed pupil of the Jesuits and a confessed admirer of France, his influence and aims were to be feared. A war with the Turks did not lead to his further popularity for, despite the bravery of the poet-hero Nicholas Zrinyi and Montecuculli's great victory at St Gothard (1664), which broke the Turkish military prestige, Leopold made a disastrous peace against the wishes of Hungarians. This negotiation seems to have set the final seal on the determination of Hungarians to cast off the Austrian yoke. Zrinyi had once told Leopold that the three evils of Hungary were Turkish raids, religious persecutions, and German mercenaries. From the first danger Leopold had clearly failed to free her, for he had actually surrendered territory to the Turk. For the rest Hungary would be more free from religious intolerance under Ottoman rule, and Turkish janizaries were not likely to be any more cruel or licentious than German mercenaries. We cannot therefore be surprised that her nobles began to dream that Hungary might again shake off Habsburg rule, and become independent in some such way as Transylvania.

Nicholas Zrinyi, the clearest head and strongest hand among the Hungarian nobles, was killed in a boar-hunt in 1664. Other nobles—his brother, Peter Zrinyi, the new Ban of Croatia, Francis Frangepan, Stephen Tököli, and Francis Nádasdy—a confidant of Leopold—began to plot against Habsburg rule. The conspiracy really began in 1666 at the wedding of the beautiful and renowned Ilonka Zrinyi to Francis I Rákóczi, and, as on another such occasion

"at that bride-ale
was many men's bale."

The conspirators sought aid from Louis of France, from the Sultan, from Poland and from Transylvania, but their plot was so widespread that it could hardly escape detection. In 1670 Leopold, apprized in time, sent an army into Hungary, seized the chief conspirators, and, after a secret court martial, executed the three counts—Zrinyi, Nádasdy and Frangepan (1671). The other conspirator, Stephen Tököli, was already dead—but he bequeathed his ardent desire for Hungarian independence to his famous son, Emeric. Meanwhile a savage vengeance was taken, hundreds of Hungarian nobles were imprisoned, and a regular reign of terror ensued.

Leopold is already said to have sworn to make Hungary all Catholic and submissive to the Virgin, and to establish the *Regnum Marianum*. But he had sworn at his accession to maintain the liberties and constitution of Hungary and it took some time for his advisers to absolve him of his oath. Finally he allowed himself to be persuaded by Bishop Kollonics, and decided to treat Hungary as his ancestor had treated Bohemia, to establish absolutism and to convert the country to Catholicism by the utmost execution of religious pressure and of military force. By an edict of 1673 he abolished the constitution of Hungary, treated it as a conquered country, and left the execution of his designs to his chief adviser Kollonics. That worthy "did not his work negligently" and the Kollonics *régime* is synonymous with brutal persecution and terrorization. Protestant churches were broken down and defiled, ministers imprisoned or sent to the galleys, and the treatment of political or religious dissidents such that—whatever be our views as to the conspirators of 1670—we can hardly doubt that the edict of 1673 forced the insurgents to revolution in their own despite. The King left them no shred of constitutional or religious liberty, and, in such case, the *jus resistendi* might fairly be invoked as a plea for legalized revolt. As usual the chief hope of the rebels (Kuruczes or Crusaders as they were called) lay in aid from the Turks and Transylvania. Their leader, Emeric, son of Stephen Tököli, had all the high courage and spirit of the Hungarian champions of independence in the past, though he lacked the calm statesmanship of Martinuzzi or the disinterested patriotism of Bocskay. Tököli, like Bocskay, aimed at winning religious and constitutional independence for Hungary, but was inspired by far less pure and more personal ideals. He wished certainly to be Prince of Transylvania (and thus alarmed its reigning Prince) and his ambition soon reached to the crown of Hungary. When he raised the standard of revolt in 1677 he obtained money from Louis XIV and men from Transylvania, and both at a later stage from the Sultan. His early successes coincided with an ominous preparation for war on behalf of the Turks. Leopold therefore became frightened and in 1681 summoned the Hungarian Parliament at Oedenburg (Sopron), proposed a general amnesty, agreed to withdraw the German garrisons from Hungary, to grant a limited toleration to religious dissidents, and once more to appoint a Palatine—that official whose ascendancy always marked the power of the Hungarian nobility. The concessions were great, not indeed the most that an ardent Hungarian could hope, but all perhaps that he could reasonably expect. Yet Tököli from ambition or pride rejected them all, claimed the crown of Hungary and renewed the war. But Leopold's concessions had done their work ; Eszterházy, the newly appointed Palatine, won many Hungarians back to allegiance to Leopold, and Tököli eventually damaged his cause by allying himself with the infidel Turk. None the less in 1683 he seemed on the point of success, he had overrun almost all Upper (i.e. most of non-Turkish) Hungary and even penetrated to the gates of Pozsony (Pressburg). Meanwhile the greatest effort at Ottoman conquest since the days of Solyman was being made, an enormous Turkish army was advancing up the valley of the Danube, and in the summer of 1683 the horsetail standards were planted once more beneath the walls of Vienna.

At this crisis of his fate even the sublime religious faith of Leopold might be forgiven for faltering. In fact he was to be rescued at this crisis by an intervention which he might well regard as miraculous, for he was to pass from the depths of despair to the most brilliant of victories. Reinforcements hurried up from Germany to the relief of hard-pressed Vienna, and finally the lightning march of the heroic John Sobieski, King of Poland, effected its relief and scattered the Turks in flight. It was not the first time that the Turks had retreated from the walls of Vienna, now they were soon to be driven from Buda too, and to be hunted from the Alföld like deer. During the next few years the Turks were continually defeated by German armies, who had been schooled in battle against the French, and who were directed by great leaders. In 1686 Duke Charles of Lorraine captured the rocky citadel of Buda and drove the last Turkish pasha from the capital of Hungary. When the main army of

Turks was routed it fared ill with its light squadron under Tököli; beaten at Eperjes he was sent by the Sultan in chains to Adrianople, and never again recovered his full prestige. The heroic Ilonka Zrinyi, widow of Rákóczi and now wife of Tököli, held out at Munkács till the end of 1687, but that year was to witness the greatest blow yet given to Turkish military renown. At Harsány the Duke of Lorraine, whose calm judgment and steadfast assurance make him the Marlborough of this war, won the greatest of his victories. It was just over a century and a half from the defeat of Mohács and in its neighbourhood that this great battle was fought. The result was as decisive, the corpses once more as numerous (though now the dead were Turkish), and again the prize of victory was the lordship over the Alföld. On the first famous field it had been Hungarians who had fought and died, now it was largely by German arms and generals that their great defeat was avenged.

It was perhaps the grimmest tragedy of Hungarian history that, at the moment of those victories over the infidel, of which Zrinyi had dreamed, many Hungarians, whose whole being and thoughts were inspired by military ideas, stood either sullenly aloof, or actually joined Tököli in his vain efforts to stay the progress of the triumphant Emperor. When the Alföld, the home of the Magyar, was once more being won for Christendom and for Hungary, many of her nobles either drew sword against their King, or let their weapons hang idly rusting upon the walls of their dining-halls. Not all indeed did this, the influence of Eszterházy, the Palatine, brought a number into the fighting ranks, but many remained inactive. They instinctively recognised and feared that the triumph of the Cross carried with it the triumph of the crown, and that, if the Turks had to surrender to Christ the things which were of Heaven, Hungarians must surrender to Caesar the things which were of earth. Leopold the cold and inflexible had succeeded where the ardent and heroic Hunyadis and Zrinyis had failed, and, when he summoned the Parliament of 1687 he could meet it with the air of a conqueror. Early in the year he had set up at Eperjes in Upper Hungary a tribunal under General Caraffa who treated partisans of Tököli with the same measure of severity as Jeffreys in England treated those of Monmouth. Blood flowed in abundance, and in the Szepes (Zips) district Caraffa sent scores of Saxons to the block, and legislated from the scaffold.

But bigoted as was Leopold and brutal as were his soldiers, he was capable of learning from experience, and his proposals at the Parliament of 1687 were not altogether unreasonable from his own point of view. He had at least learnt something from the risings of the last decade, and was prepared to re-establish the constitution under conditions. He insisted that the kingship should no longer be elective, but should be made hereditary in the Habsburg line, and that the famous *jus resistendi* (on which Hungarian rebels based the legality of their resistance) should finally be abolished. The late events had rendered this measure absolutely necessary ; both these privileges had sometimes been abused, and they were clearly traces of the semi-barbarous independence of feudalism. The Parliament contented itself with vigorous protests against the Blood Tribunal, but was in no condition to resist his other demands, for Leopold's soldiers were flushed with victory and overwhelming in number. These two conditions were therefore granted without much opposition, Hungary ceased to be an elective monarchy after nearly seven hundred years, and abrogated the most dangerous feudal privilege of *Bulla Aurea*. The question of religious toleration was a more real and serious one, for Leopold clung to his idea of a *Regnum Marianum*, and would grant only a limited toleration to Lutherans and Calvinists, and even that subject to revocation by the royal will. This last provision necessarily prevented the settlement from being permanent, but none the less it does mark a certain stage of evolution. Leopold had realised that there was such a thing as a national state and national feeling in Hungary, and his recognition of the old constitution, despite the constant violations to which he subjected it, was a distinct advance. In 1673 he had claimed to govern in Hungary as an absolute autocrat setting aside at his pleasure every old law or limitation on his will; in 1687 he implicitly admitted the existence of the old constitution, at the price of the abolition of the *jus resistendi* and of the right of election.

The future fate of the Hungarian constitution largely depended on the issues of the Turkish war. It seemed in 1689 as if the Ottoman position were hopeless and the ruin of Turkey assured, and this meant perhaps the downfall of Hungary. Leopold's armies had won back all Hungary, crossed the Danube and penetrated far into the vale of the Morava, capturing both Belgrade and Niš, the new and the old capitals of Servia. But at this crisis fortune, or rather Louis XIV, intervened. Charles of Lorraine with a large army was recalled to defend the Rhine frontier against France; and in Mustapha Kiuprili— the new Grand Vizier of the Sultan—the Turks found a leader of a famous family, whose energy and courage were equal to the crisis. He realised at once that the intolerance of Leopold was worth more than an army to Turkey, and he set to work to stir up disaffection in Transylvania—that home of religious liberty, whence had so often issued the deliverance of Hungary. Michael Apafy, Prince of Transylvania, had already submitted to the authority of Leopold, and therefore the Sultan released Tököli, named him its Prince, and sent him to effect a diversion in Transylvania (1690). With his usual vicissitudes of fortune Tököli contrived to be at one time victorious, at another defeated. But his presence produced a very beneficial effect upon Leopold, for he granted to Transylvania in 1691 the celebrated *Diploma Leopoldinum*. This document guaranteed the free exercise of their religion to the adherents of all four creeds—Calvinistic, Lutheran, Catholic, and Unitarian, and their full admission to all political offices. He also promised to summon the Transylvanian Parliament or Diet regularly, and only to employ Transylvanian officials for governmental purposes. This agreement was subsequently broken several times, but it sufficed to quiet Transylvania for the nonce, and this last and most interesting of its decrees of toleration ends the picturesque and romantic history of this little principality among the rocks.

Meanwhile, profiting by Tököli's diversion, the Turks had recovered Belgrade, and in 1691 had set out to win back the Alföld. But they now met with the limit of their successes. At Szalantkem, in the extreme south of Hungary, the Turks were routed, and Kiuprili their heroic Grand Vizier was slain. The war dwindled in interest and became chequered in character till 1697, when Prince Eugène defeated a great Turkish army at Zenta led by the Sultan in person. In 1699 the Peace of Karlovicz concluded the war. As between the Emperor and the

Turk, the terms were that the former retained substantially the Hungarian kingdom as it now stands, save for the "Banat" (the territory enclosed by the Tisza (Theiss) and the Maros). Transylvania withdrew from its nominal allegiance to Turkey, and Leopold's claim to it was recognised. Lastly, Tököli was banished to Nicomedia. The subsequent Turkish war of 1715–18 may most fitly be described here ; in 1715 the Turks broke the peace of Karlovicz, but retribution was waiting for them from the sword of Eugène. In the campaign of 1716–17 the Prince won great victories which he crowned with the capture of Belgrade, perhaps the greatest exploit of his military career. On this followed the Peace of Passarovicz (1718), wherein the Turks ceded to the Emperor the "Banat" and practically the whole of Hungary as it now stands. Portions of Bosnia and most of Servia were also ceded, but these were recovered by the Turks at the peace of Belgrade in 1739.

While this brilliantly successful foreign policy rendered the frontiers of Hungary secure, the internal policy of the Habsburgs was disastrous and unfortunate. It has already been said that the Hungarians had not rejoiced at the Turkish defeats, recognising that the recovery of the Alföld might mean the loss of the constitution. Discontent with the Austrian rule and with Leopold's perfidy had been widespread, and had extended far beneath the surface. Hitherto the chief champions of Hungarian liberties—which might well be reckoned as class-privileges rather than as national possessions—had been the nobles, the *populus* or "nation" in the technical sense, not the crushed, suffering and infinitely numerous poor of the land. *Aurea libertas*, national pride and patriotism, religious privileges, all these had hitherto been the monopoly of nobles. Now, however, a more ominous sign appeared, the *misera plebs contribuens*— the peasants as a whole—began to show unmistakable signs of discontent, and it soon appeared that the people in the true sense resembled the "nation" in the false one, in being ready to die for faith and freedom. The taxation of the war-period was undoubtedly enormous and out of all proportion to justice, and was borne chiefly by these poor serfs of the land. Worse even than this, at the moment their pockets were rifled, their consciences were outraged by deliberate attacks upon that

Calvinistic faith which so many of them held. The combination of Jesuit and tax-gatherer was too much for them, and it needed only an excuse and an opportunity to stir them to armed rebellion. They found both under the leadership of Rákóczi, the prince of hussars, the last and the most famous of the long line of Hungarian rebels.

The rising of Francis II Rákóczi has often—and that too in very recent times—been misinterpreted. It was in origin a revolt of peasants, and as most of them were Calvinists, its chief demand was for religious toleration. In its later stages it became more aristocratic and political in character, but it never lost some of the traces of its origin. Francis Rákóczi himself embodied to both peasants and nobles the ideal of Hungarian chivalry. He was the descendant of two famous Transylvanian princes, and in his veins ran the blood of the heroic Zrinyis. He was a fervent Catholic but a sincere champion of toleration ; despite his aristocratic birth he had ardent sympathies for the peasant, and though ambitious was far more disinterested than Tököli. As an organiser and statesman he showed both capacity and firmness, but unfortunately for his cause he had no striking military qualities. He was an abler man and came far nearer to success than did Prince Charles Edward a generation later, and he resembled that illustrious pretender in his magical power of inspiring the masses of his followers with enthusiasm. The " Kurucz Songs," the ballads and airs sung by his soldiers around their camp fires, which legend has ascribed to the wandering gipsy Czinka Panna, are full of the most poignant and touching strains, and have a pathos as tender and a melody more exquisite than the Jacobite songs. It is from such wondrous tributes as these, such unforced and artless testimonies that we can derive the signs of a people's love for one who died a lonely and powerless exile.

Rákóczi raised the standard of revolt in 1703 and at first met with great success. Peasants flocked to him in thousands, nobles in scores, from Louis XIV came officers, subsidies and even French regiments. Meanwhile the Imperialist armies were far away, fighting in Bavaria, in Flanders and in Italy. With his gallant irregulars Rákóczi soon won successes, and at one time the boldest of his riders penetrated almost to the gates of Vienna.

But Blenheim was as fatal a blow to Rákóczi as it was to Louis Quatorze, for the retreat of French armies from Germany meant the advance of Imperialist ones into Hungary. Rákóczi could not hold his scattered army together, and his own military gifts were no match for the methodical professional strategy of the Imperialist general. In 1705 Rákóczi was badly defeated by Heister at Nagy-Szombat, and in the same year Leopold died advising his successor the Emperor Joseph I to open negotiations with the insurgents. But the great victories over France in 1706 caused Joseph to refuse Rákóczi's demand for the restoration of the constitutional rights of his country and of his own title as Prince of Transylvania, in return for the insurgents accepting the hereditary succession of the Habsburgs. Rákóczi replied by convening the famous meeting of nobles at the Parliament of Ónod (1707). At this meeting the aristocratic influence was predominant, and we see evident signs that the leaders aimed at establishing a sort of aristocratic republic with nobles as powerful and a ruler as subservient as in Poland. The scenes were violent, Rákóczi himself spoke with passion, and blood was shed. The final outcome was a solemn renunciation of all allegiance to the Habsburg and a proclamation of the independence of Hungary. The Emperor Joseph I replied to this by summoning a rival Parliament of his own at Pozsony (Pressburg), and maintained an attitude which was, under the circumstances, fairly conciliatory. He, however, obstinately refused to listen to the suggestions of foreign powers—especially of Lord Stepney, the English ambassador—who proposed to mediate between Joseph and his subjects. The war dragged on and in 1708 Heister again defeated Rákóczi at Trencsén, and this time his victory was decisive. Rákóczi continued to denounce the Habsburg furiously and to proclaim the independence of Hungary, but his power was really destroyed. Joseph died in 1711 and was succeeded by his moderate and well-meaning brother, the Emperor Charles VI (Charles III of Hungary), and in the same year terms of peace were arranged. The rebellious nobles assembled at Szatmár, and after long discussion finally accepted the terms offered by Charles in the agreement known as the Peace of Szatmár (1711), which is one of the most important of all contracts arrived at between Austria and Hungary. The arrangement was, on the face of it, more of a contract between equals than could well have been expected, and it marks a very definite advance in the recognition by the Habsburg of the separate position of Hungary. It is the conclusion of nearly a century of perpetual dispute, during half of which at least the old Hungarian constitution had been in constant danger of extinction. But the revolts of Tököli and Rákóczi had shown that Austria could not be safe from internal risings, unless she made genuine concessions to Hungary. These Charles formally made; he promised a general amnesty, the revival of the guarantees of religious freedom, the maintenance of the immunities and liberties of Hungary. Rákóczi declined to accept these terms, and retired first to France and then to the Bosphorus, where he died a lonely exile in 1735, the most picturesque and romantic of Hungarian pretenders.

The Treaty of Szatmár was after all only one step, though far the most important one, in the readjustment of the relations between the Habsburg and Hungary. It was the beginning of an era of good feeling between the two, of trust on the one side and of scrupulous fairness on the other. Charles III evidently intended to be a constitutional monarch, he signed a solemn *diploma inaugurale* to that effect, allowed Parliament in 1715 to embody it in a law and formally promised to maintain the old laws, rights and liberties of Hungary. In return for these concessions to her Charles secured others for himself in the famous Pragmatic Sanction (1723). Hereditary succession in the male Habsburg line had been secured by Leopold in 1687, now the Parliamentary Estates of Hungary transmitted the right of succession in the realm and crown of Hungary "to the female sex of the most illustrious House of Austria." By virtue of this act Maria Teresa was eventually enabled to become Queen of Hungary (1740).

From 1715 onwards reforms were rapidly pushed forward, for with a sovereign whom Hungary trusted reorganisation was easy and indeed inevitable. The whole frame of society was still dangerously medieval, and changes in the political and military system were rapidly effected. The feudal type of militarism still prevailed, and in Hungary in cases of necessity the nobles led out their *banderia,* or the King summoned the fyrd or *generalis insurrectio.* Both methods were hopelessly antiquated, it was not by such means Hungary had been reconquered or could be defended from the Turk. Charles now demanded and obtained of Parliament permission to raise and to maintain a small permanent professional or standing army in Hungary itself. Meanwhile he pursued a policy of rigid military centralisation, the districts known as "the Military Frontiers" were withdrawn from any control by the Hungarian Parliament and were administered and garrisoned under the direction of the military council at Vienna. The same centralising tendencies appear in matters more purely political, and the Hungarian Chancellery was stationed at Vienna and subjected to the control of the King. The power of the Palatine, the official elected by Parliament, who had always been the chosen leader of the aristocracy against the King, was whittled down till it became quite insignificant. In fact, the *consilium locumtenentiale*, or council of lieutenancy, which was stationed in Hungary, practically superseded him. As its very name implies this council also became very dependent on the King. Everywhere more modern and bureaucratic methods and more administrative efficiency were adopted with a resultant increase of power and authority to the crown.

Under Charles III then, the independent position of Hungary began to be undermined, not indeed by open force or even perhaps by secret design, but by a slow process of absorption and assimilation. When his daughter Maria Teresa became Queen (1740) the whole movement becomes much more evident. Her pathetic appeal to the Hungarian Parliament for aid (1741) produced not only the magnificent response of *vitam et sanguinem* from her nobles, it awoke in them a passionate loyalty such as no Habsburg ruler, before or since, has ever enjoyed in Hungary. Under her gentle sway the Hungarians insensibly adapted and modernised their medieval polity and society. Parliament and Palatine declined still further in importance; only in the counties in the *congregationes*, where sat the stubborn guardians of ancestral custom, were to be found fifty citadels of liberty. When Joseph II ascended the throne (1780) he soon proved the strength of these walls and the unyielding temper of these garrisons. Instead of trusting to the tendencies of the time and to a gradual evolution he attempted a complete and drastic reform of every medieval feature in Hungary's constitution. During the ten years of his reign every resource of his energy, every aid of force or of reason, was used by him in order to overthrow the old institutions of Hungary. His failure was absolute and the tragedy of his defeat so extreme that even his enemies have lamented the fall of this most extreme of doctrinaires, of this most well-meaning and most gentle of tyrants. The phenomenon of the successful resistance offered by a prejudiced and retrograde patriotism to his cosmopolitan policy of enlightenment is striking enough in itself, but it becomes still more wonderful when we remember the great advantages and the immense resources which Joseph possessed. One of the great writers of Hungary devoted one of the most brilliant of his novels to explaining this phenomenon, and Professor Marczali's book does for history what Jókai did for romance[1].

Here this hasty sketch of some of the broad features of Hungarian history may well end. It has been based on the works of writers of very different schools and represents a genuine attempt to hold the balance with an equal hand. I should be glad if I could think that my efforts to deal with the history of Hungary had been as successful as those of Dr Yolland in dealing with its language. Of both Essay and translation, however, readers will judge, but those who know Hungary best will be aware of the enormous difficulties in the way of giving the English reader an adequate idea of her tongue or of her history.

From the reign of Charles III onward all the important eighteenth-century developments—including of course the eternal question of the relations of the Habsburg to Hungary—are treated of in the work of Professor Marczali. Nor is the work valuable alone for the light it throws upon Hungary, it abounds in comparisons and in analogies with parallel developments in other lands. The comparison of the commercial and economic relations between Austria and Hungary to those of England and her colonies (pp. 94—99) is of high interest at the present

---

[1] *Maurus Jókai*, *Rab Ráby*, German edition, Pressburg and Leipzig, 1880. In 1909 an English edition (much abridged) was published under the title *The strange story of Rab Ráby*. Incredible as the details of the story may seem, they are based on facts, and the hero of the story is a strictly historical personage.

moment. Elsewhere we can find pictures of a system of primitive natural economy, or of a state of society largely medieval and barbarous, but we seldom see them existing side by side with more modern institutions, or have the opportunity of observing the reflex effect of one upon the other. The account of the peasants, of their folk-lore and of their superstitions (pp. 179—81, p. 182, n. 1), the picture of the true conservative *táblabirák* (pp. 135—42), of university life in the Calvinist Colleges (pp. 292—5), or the dramatic incident of the seizure of Agnes Bánffy by the orders of Maria Teresa (pp. 261—3), supply us with contrasts and extremes of barbarism and civilisation for which we should look in vain in any other European country in the eighteenth century.

One more word may be said, all the fundamental elements, on which Hungarian society and institutions are now based, are present in the eighteenth century, but at the same time we are beyond the controversies of party and of the present. The problems may appear similar to those of modern Hungary, but they are by no means identical; in some of the most important questions of to-day, as for instance in that of nationality, ideas were different and tendencies were more unconscious, and the same remark applies to almost every other question. Knowledge of Hungary in the eighteenth century is essential to the understanding of her in the twentieth, but the knowledge must be such as reconciles but does not confound the present and the past. It is essential to emancipate ourselves, not only from the influence of partisan controversy, but from the influence of history that is merely political. For, as the true science of history is to establish an organic evolution from the past, the real art of it is to discover when that connection ceases and where a spiritual revolution begins. For that purpose we need to know not only the history of parties and the form of political institutions, but that of society, of beliefs, of the culture and the thought of the past. Professor Marczali's book supplies us with these materials, and enables us to gauge the power and the immobility of prejudice, the stir and the force of aspiration, in a word to estimate the strength of all those deeper currents which have moulded the course of Hungarian history.

HAROLD W. V. TEMPERLEY.

INTRODUCTION.

I.

HUNGARY FROM 1711—1740.

FROM the time of the occupation of the country by the Magyars until the Peace of Szatmár (1711)—a period of over eight hundred years—the history of Hungary is pre-eminently a military one. The political tranquillity of the eighteenth century contrasts so strikingly with the glorious and passionate struggles of the previous ages that this contrast in itself would suffice to give to this particular period a distinctive character of its own.

The period is inaugurated by two important events, which—while accounting for the tranquil course of development and the results produced by a century of undisturbed activity—explain also the dangers latent in this tranquillity. These two events—the expulsion of the Turks, and the struggle for Hungarian independence of Austria—comprise all the factors which moulded the history of Hungary until 1848. As soon as the lull of the preceding storms permitted an adjustment of the relations between the great political and social forces, they remained unchanged for a whole century until the period of fresh upheavals.

Of these two events, the first, both in order of time and—in our opinion—in respect of importance, was the expulsion of the Turks from Hungary. The whole of the historical literature of Hungary regards it as a fact of practically second-rate interest, and does not consider it to be a fresh turning-point in the

history of the country. Under the prevailing influence of
present-day questions, Hungarian historians have been attracted
by the affinity of ideas and sentiments more particularly towards the sublime efforts to maintain ancient liberties and to
secure the rights of a new faith.

It is in these that the whole power of the ruling class of
Hungary manifests and exhausts itself. And these exertions
prevent Hungary from fulfilling the mission she was once called
upon to undertake, of being the vanguard and pioneer of Europe
on the borders of the East. It was a tragical case of the irony
of fate that the liberation of the Hungarian soil was accomplished
by foreign forces and that the large majority of the successors
of the Hunyadis and Zrinyis based their hopes on the victory,
not of the cross, but of the crescent.

Consequently, however enormous the political and social
effects produced thereby, the soul of the people was not stirred
by the liberation of the country and the restoration of her
territorial integrity : for the inner feelings of a people are moved
and stirred into action only by events in which they play a
part. Contemporaries speak in tones either of indifference or
of grief of the Peace of Karlovicz, which realised all that had
been merely the dream of Gabriel Bethlen, Peter Pázmány and
Nicholas Zrinyi. It was considered of importance and as epoch-
making for the Turks rather than for Hungary. The fact that
it brought the Hungarian Lowlands (Alföld) under Christian
rule is scarcely mentioned at all. Isaac Babocsai, the notary
of Tarczal, dwells mainly on the grievances brought thereby
upon his poor fatherland. Even the stout royalist Michael
Cserei considered the point of chief importance to be the fact
that this was the first occasion on which Turks resigned their
rights to provinces and towns where they had mosques, and
deplored the fate of Transylvania, for which no change could
be more unfortunate than its union with Hungary. Not the
event itself, but the auspices under which it took place, decided
the opinion of contemporaries.

The power, feelings and thoughts of the Hungarian nation
were monopolised by another life and death struggle. " The
old wounds of our glorious country were re-opened. Never was

there any event that so completely alienated the Hungarians from the Roman Emperor and the whole Austrian Government,—so completely, indeed, that the animosity of the Hungarians towards the Emperor has not yet ceased in this year of grace 1710, nay is actually increasing from day to day[1]."

The victory over the Turks merely served as a pretext and an opportunity for a foreign religious and political system to include Hungary, which it regarded as a conquest, in its sphere of authority, and deprive her of her independence. An eight years' war—(1703-11), this time, however, a civil war—again bled and wasted the country, and was ended only by the military and diplomatic overthrow of the national revolution, an event which coincided in time with the important victories of the Habsburg House all over Europe. This produced the compromise between king and nation concluded in 1711, which proved more enduring than the long series of its predecessors. Just as the treaties of Karlovicz, Passarovicz and Belgrade established the territorial unity and tranquillity of the country, so the Peace of Szatmár settled her internal organisation and constitution.

II.

THE RULING CLASS OF HUNGARY. THE MAGNATES AND THE GENTRY.

As the state of the country became more settled, it grew daily more evident that her constitution and internal organisation were not menaced by any serious danger—and still less her nationality. The conditions and men of the age of Leopold had given place to others. In consequence of the combined efforts of the prelates and nobility[2], the national form of government

---

[1] Cserei, Michael, *Nemzeti Könyvtár* (National Library), p. 50.

[2] The Hungarian nobility and the classes into which they are divided are treated of more fully later on. Here it is enough to say that the Magnates correspond roughly to the Lords, that besides the gentry (a very numerous class) there were a large number of peasant-nobles owning but a single holding each, and also many nobles with no landed property at all.

held its own against the foreign absolutist and Germanising
system, not only in the country itself but also in the territories
newly recovered.   It is true that such strong bulwarks of the
liberty of the estates as the election of kings and the right of
armed resistance had ceased to exist (1687).   The system of
permanent taxation, the standing army, the Pragmatic Sanction,
the *locumtenentiale* council and the vacancy of the office of Count
Palatine, all seemed to aim at making the power of the king
unlimited.   Yet all these measures had no tangible results.   Not
only did the Hungarian organism not yield an inch before the
imperial system : it actually gained ground upon it.   We must,
indeed, acknowledge that this fact was due in part to the
religious loyalty with which king Charles III (as Emperor,
Charles VI) observed the terms of his coronation oath.   There can
be no doubt, too, that the course of events was influenced by
his foreign policy, the exigencies of which rendered peace at
home desirable.   But this had been, more or less, the state of
things in the seventeenth century too.   That the country was
now more settled was due in particular to the new element, the
Hungarian "dynastic party."   After the Peace of Szatmár, the
Pálffy, Eszterházy, Erdödy, Károlyi and Batthyány families
began to assume increasing prominence.   Most of the high
temporal and spiritual offices were in their hands, and their
estates were continually being increased.   In the counties they
took the lead either as hereditary high sheriffs or as bishops.   At
the Court they overshadowed everybody else by their pomp and
wealth[1].   They felt the breath of the spirit of foreign countries ;
they were influenced by the favour of the Court: but they
remained Hungarians, as is proved by their correspondence, by
their testaments, and by their whole lives.

    The Hungarian nobility had reached a very important
turning-point in their evolution.   The seventeenth century in
Hungary was still pre-eminently an age of chivalry, both in a
bad and a good sense.   Its symptoms were : frequent changes of
parties, the grossest sensuality, and a contempt for the law, since
the Magnates were above all privileged knights.   In their fortified

---

[1] Cf. Cserei, Michael, *ibid.* (1694–99).   The person of Count Czobor in particular
was celebrated in a veritable cycle of legends.

castles, surrounded by their henchmen, they ruled practically as independent princes. They were engaged in the affairs of their estates, or at most of their counties. However paradoxical the statement may seem, the country was never so badly off for great statesmen of distinguished birth : only the eminent personality of Nicholas Zrinyi was capable of rising higher and acting from a national point of view. The transitional stage is then represented by the Eszterházys, whose resolute political and religious activity shows unmistakable signs of the influence of the great Peter Pázmány.

After the Peace of Szatmár there was only one law and one army in the country. Neither was foreign to such an extent as to compel practically all classes of the country to entertain the idea of resistance, or sufficiently tainted with the spirit of the Hungarian oligarchy to allow of rebels thinking they might resist with impunity. The magnates left their fortified castles and descended to the plains. Gradual dilapidation was the fate of their dark " eagles' nests," below which, in the valleys, rose stately manor-houses, the homes of luxury and enjoyment, in the centre of extensive gardens laid out in French or Dutch style. As early as 1683 the castle of the Count Palatine Eszterházy at Kismarton, which represents the transitional stage between the fortified residence and the manor-house, was erected. Immediately after the Peace of Szatmár, in 1714, the superb manor of Cseklész was begun : that of Edelény was built between 1720 and 1727, those of the Pálffys at Nagy-Gurab and Király-falva in 1725, and that of the Károlyis at Erdöd in 1730. Consequently the aristocracy renounced all attempts at resistance not only by law but in actual fact. The defence of the country was entrusted by them to the king and his army, and the most the aristocrats did was to endeavour to secure the predominance in the latter. The great merits of John Pálffy are familiar to everybody[1]. The greatness of the Festetics family was

[1] The royal deed of grant concerning Makovicza (once a Rákóczi estate) says : " Augustae domui—statim ab ineunte aetate sua pro locorum et temporum varietate atque occasionum exigentia, tum Pacis, quam difficillimi Belli Gallici et Turcici, novissimeque consopitorum intestinorum Rakócziano-Bercsenianorum motuum et disturbiorum temporibus, summa virtute—tanquam Fortes Miles conspicuusque Heros pro Deo, Rege et Patria, adeoque pro aris et focis, domi forisque strenue dimicando,

established by an ancestor of theirs who was a general at that time.
The activity of the aristocracy, however, displayed itself more
particularly in the field of politics. The great lords of those
days stand midway between the feudal lords of the Middle
Ages—whose birth was in itself a sufficient guarantee of their
participating in the rule of the country—and the modern aristocracy, whose power of acting a part in the government is due
more especially to their wealth and social privileges. Their birth,
indeed, was sufficient to entitle them to aspire to power, but it
was their education which fitted them for government. They
may justly be compared to the contemporary English aristocracy, which after a long series of civil disturbances took
some time to become reconciled to a foreign ruler. The chief
difference between the state of things in the two countries is
that, whereas in England the accession of the foreign dynasty
meant the triumph of Protestantism, in Hungary it involved
the victory of Catholicism; consequently, whereas in England
it was the temporal peers who secured the predominance, in
Hungary the spiritual peers won the ascendancy. The latter
joined hands with the Court, but by so doing succeeded in
reconciling the dynasty to the interests of the Hungarian nation
and its constitution.

Most conspicuous was the power of the magnates, those few
many-acred families; but the sphere of activity of the gentry
had its significance. The latter too laid down their arms
or took service in the Emperor's army. Besides looking after
their estates, they also engaged in the administration of the
counties, which, as the bulwark of defence protecting the interests
of nobility and nationality, maintained their importance even
when those causes which rendered them institutions of such
significance during the Turkish wars had ceased to exist. This
importance has been recognised by historical and political tradition. In my opinion, however, the county had other significant
spheres of authority in the eighteenth century. It prevented the

cum raro fidelitatis exemplo immortalique nominis sui laude et memoria gloriose
exhibuit et impendit." June 3, 1720. Preserved in the National Archives. The
expressions used in the diploma granted to Count Joseph Eszterházy are word for
word the same.

individual members of the gentry from appearing as mere atoms in their connection with the Court or even the wealthy and powerful magnates. In Poland the nobility became gradually divided into *slahcic*-es (peasant-nobles)—dependent upon the favour of miniature kings—and into *pands* (barons), but although the fundamental elements of such a development were also to hand, in Hungary this evolution was prevented by the county system. In Transylvania, where the county institution was not so fully developed, the conditions were actually far more similar to those in vogue in Poland. As the institution representing the whole gentry, the county stood in the way not only of foreign Turkish and German influences, but of the preponderance of the magnates and peasant-nobles of Hungary. It thus supported the moderate elements in their struggle to maintain the balance between extremes. At its head stood a magnate or prelate acting as high sheriff, it also contained numerous violent peasant-proprietors, but the chief influence was in the hands of the gentry, possessing estates of medium size and representing national and county interests alike, from whose ranks the county court assessors and sheriffs were recruited.

To the county life is due the fact that from this period the chief occupation of the gentry became legal science. It was in the law, stated in Verböczi's " *Tripartitum opus iuris consuetudinarii Inclyti regni Hungariae*" (1514), and in the later Acts supplementing it, that they found the surest basis for their political position and for the security of their property. The exercise of judicial functions in most cases gave the gentry an opportunity of rising to high offices in the State. In general, the distinction between magnates and gentry was still very unsettled, new families were constantly rising into prominence beside the older ones, either by royal favour or as a reward for their particular merits.

In our days a great writer has compared the French nobility before the Revolution to an army degenerated by a long period of peace. Their fall was inevitable, for they were no longer capable of doing their duty and yet imposed burdens on others. Such a comparison shows the capability of the Hungarian nobility to govern and the necessity for their government, for if ever there was a nobility which deserved the name of

army, such was indeed the Hungarian nobility. Ever since
it was established, it had not ceased to extend and defend its
country at the price of its own blood. Although in Hungary
itself a long period of peace had now begun, the Hungarian
nobility still continued to serve their monarch in every battle-
field of Europe. Ten years after the Peace of Szatmár they
actually complained that no member of the gentry was admitted
to the army, and that the number of Hungarian regiments was
being reduced[1]. Civil administration, the estates, the church
and education—in a word, every weapon of power and influence
was in their hands : they had their reward, for the country was
theirs, but they did their duty well. The *perpetuus miles* was
unable to replace the *posse comitatus*, and the *contributio* was
supplemented by voluntary donations. In France, the administration of the country was in the hands of an army of civil
officers, in Hungary of the landed gentry. In France, literature
was in the hands of laymen and *roturiers* ; in Hungary it was
controlled by the Church, which was itself a part of the nobility.
In France, the king controlled everything ; in Hungary, parliament also had a voice in the decision of affairs of State. In a
word, in France the privileged classes were a Gothic ornament
which had become superfluous ; in Hungary they were the
column supporting the whole edifice. In France these classes
were rendered unnecessary by the parallel development of the
royal power and of the *bourgeoisie* ; in Hungary they replaced
both and ruled because they rendered service to the country.

At the conclusion of this short sketch, which has touched
upon the various events, only in so far as they served as the
material for building up the future, as a necessary consequence
of what has gone before, the question must naturally arise :—
what was the reason that the Hungarian nobility maintained
this social, political and intellectual superiority in an age when
monarchical absolutism got the upper hand all over the continent?

This fundamental idea, which was general throughout Europe,
made its influence felt in Hungary just as much as elsewhere.

---

[1] Letter written by Francis Szluha (prothonotary) to the Count Palatine Nicholas
Pálffy (Feb. 23, 1722) : cf. F. Salamon, *A. m. kir. szék betöltése es a pragm. sanctio
története*, p. 135.

Whether consciously or unconsciously, Leopold I and his sons followed in the steps of their enemy Louis XIV, while Maria Teresa and her sons were just as powerfully influenced by the political organisation of their great enemy the King of Prussia. Yet, whereas everywhere else on the Continent princes were enthroned on the ruins of aristocracies and revolutions were arising, in Hungary, despite every attempt to overcome them, the nobility stood unbroken, and did not resign their rights until 1848—and that too in a spirit of self-sacrifice unparalleled in the history of the world.

Ranke himself in one place declares that the medieval constitutions remained intact in Protestant countries as contrasted with Catholic states, where absolutism prevailed. This is true so far as England and France are respectively concerned, but is incorrect with regard to other countries. The kingdoms of Prussia, Denmark and Sweden, which were pre-eminently Protestant countries, soon fell under the yoke of absolutism. In Hungary the Catholic majority did not prove at all dangerous to the Constitution. Nor has the degree of development anything to do with the matter. In Russia, a country on a far lower level of culture than Hungary, arose a species of unlimited monarchy similar to the others—though it admittedly owed much to the aid of foreigners.

Nor can we accept the somewhat chauvinistic view that the reason why the Hungarian nobility could not be overcome was that they were more energetic in their defence of their liberties than the others, and that the spirit of the nation itself stood in the way of oppression. History itself contradicts this supposition. The German historians of the twelfth century reproach the Hungarians with blind subservience to their sovereigns, just as later historians do with feudal licence in the eighteenth and nineteenth centuries. According to Otto of Freising, the great medieval historian, who journeyed through Hungary in 1147, the Hungarians "are so subservient to their master that they consider it a crime, I will not say to anger him by open contradiction, but to affront him even by secret whisperings[1]." Naturally this submissiveness to the king appeared in his eyes as an

[1] Otto Freising. Episc. *Gesta Fridr. Imp.* I. 31.

absurdity, and a proof of the barbarism of Hungary—for at that time the Germans were distinctly feudal in character. But at any rate the statement proves that we must find some other reason for the non-effacement of the Hungarian nobility.

The great historians of France are particularly fond of showing how the power of the kingship was increased by its appearing as the representative of the national unity. The *bourgeoisie* and the commons simply put the dictatorship into the hands of the king, to be used in the interests of the country. The Prussian kingship also went through a similar evolution. Peter the Great too was a dictator who used violence even towards the people, though he worked in the interest of great national ideals. Even in Hungary there is no lack of examples of the kind. King Matthias Corvinus ruled almost as an absolute monarch, in spite of all constitutional forms ; the same may be said of Gabriel Bethlen, however defiant his parliaments might be : and the fact is that these rulers were not only powerful men, but men from whom the nation expected the realisation of its ideals. Consequently one of the principal causes contributing to the unlimited character of a monarchy is that, in the interests of its unity and position in foreign affairs, the nation should be ready to renounce its autonomous rights.

In its struggle for predominance, the kingship did not stand alone. Everywhere in Europe it found a sure and decisive support in the *bourgeois* elements, who, as a result of their wealth, intelligence and tractability, were able to turn the scale. In France, the kings raised the *noblesse de robe*, the officials and judges, to a level with the *noblesse d'épée*, the feudal nobility. In Prussia, the kings were supported by a *bourgeois* bureaucracy. In Sweden and Denmark, it was simply the loyalty of the *bourgeoisie* and peasantry that raised the kings above the heads of the senators.

In Hungary too there was no lack of towns. Burgesses were invited to attend at the parliaments, and the inhabitants of the towns were for the most part well-to-do and thrifty. The number of towns—as estates of the realm—increased. The Parliament of 1715 incorporated a whole series of royal free boroughs, extending the rights of political representation to them also[1]. In the constitutional struggles up to this time they had been for the most part royalist : even Debreczen redeemed its liberty from Rákóczi by a sum of money, and offered excuses for its action to the royal government[2]. The towns had, above all, to be circumspect. But, until the public feeling of the nation had raised Budapest to the position of a great city, the towns were almost inimical to the national spirit. They kept to themselves : and although composed of merchants and manufacturers, did not lead the way except in material respects. Albeit they were the seats of universities or university colleges, they had as little influence on the spirit of the students as if the monastic system of education had been still in vogue. Any member of the *bourgeois* class who rose above his fellows by his breeding and capabilities, attained to a position of eminence either abroad or in holy orders. There could be no question of unity or of common interests.

The explanation of this phenomenon is to be found in the fact that the towns were foreign in point of speech—and in spirit too, with the exception of those in the Szepesség (Szepes Zips District in Upper Hungary). Apart from Debreczen and Szatmár-Németi they were nearly all German and Slav. As passive factors in the work of resistance they stood in the midst of the turbulent county and political life of Hungary. If they joined any cause, the fact was sufficient in itself to make that cause suspicious. In Hungary, no unlimited monarchy could develop, because there was no *bourgeoisie*.

We are struck by another consideration if we examine the development of absolutism all over Europe.

Wherever we see this peculiar form of government, characteristic of the early period of the modern age, starting to develop, we find a dynasty whose fate had for centuries been bound up with that of the nation. In France, the classic home of absolutism, the formation of a nation practically coincides with the

---

[1] Debreczen, Szeged, Szatmár and Németi.

[2] "In these stormy days Debreczen did not for one moment forget that she was a royal free borough and as such was not exempted from the loyalty due to the crowned king of Hungary." Stephen Szücs, *A. sz. kir. Debreczen város története* (*Hist. of the royal free borough of Debreczen*), vol. III. p. 726. It is a pity we have not more such exhaustive monographs.

rule of the Capet dynasty. The kings of Castile, whose power was developed by Philip II, were descended from Pelayo (750). The Grand Dukes of Russia, the ancestors of Peter, took their origin from Rurik: and the rule of the Hohenzollerns, the youngest dynasty, coincides with the cultural advance of Brandenburg. Could the nation have any political interest—particularly in its relations with other nations—which was not at the same time that of the king?

In England, on the other hand, we see that in 1603 a foreign dynasty ascended the throne: and, ever since that date, England has been governed by foreign rulers. In Poland, the national dynasty of the Jagellos became extinct in the sixteenth century; and, as no other national dynasty could be founded, the Poles were compelled to protect themselves against foreign influence by *Pacta Conventa*, wrung from their elected kings. It seems therefore that an essential preliminary condition for an unlimited monarchy is that it should be established by an old dynasty capable of securing unity and the triumph of the nation in the face of foreign foes. So absolutism is not purely the work of court cabals and oppression: it has sprung into existence wherever the kingship has been engaged in performing duties of an entirely national character.

The fundamental bases of human states and societies are hidden deep in obscurity: and, as the poet says, "if the word were revealed to our intellects, who would presume to utter it?"

III.

The fears and presentiments of Michael Cserei and his contemporaries were not realised. In 1740 the country was undoubtedly more thickly populated and wealthier, more civilised and freer than it had been in 1711. Its condition did not indeed fulfil the ideals of political and religious liberty or of national independence: but we must not forget that the period in question had not been preceded by the glories of the Angevin kings and Matthias or even by the rule of a Gabriel Bethlen.

and a Nicholas Eszterházy—but had in fact seen the close of the Turkish conquests and of the destructive religious and national wars. The Hungarian nationality had stood on the brink of extinction, the constitution on that of annihilation : now they were both factors of importance in Europe. Even Tacitus considered the existence of an Empire at Rome capable of explanation, for "quotus quisque reliquus qui rem publicam vidisset?[1]" In Hungary the work of the parliaments, the glorious deeds of the Hungarian armies, and the growth of the population of the Hungarian Lowlands (Alföld), must have been a source of peculiar gratification to those who had witnessed the activity of Heister and Caraffa, had taken part in the battles of Trencsén and Zsibó and in the surrender at Majtény that followed the assembly of Ónod, and could still recall the days when Buda was the headquarters of a Turkish pasha.

A feeling of greater security and contentment did actually begin to spread by degrees over the whole land. It was felt that the expulsion of the Turks and the cessation of civil strife had rendered feasible the peaceful development of the country. Both royalists and independents were intent on making the best of the improved situation. In the words of Francis Szluha, a former adherent of Rákóczi, who was one of the principal orators of the Parliament of 1722, "under Charles III Hungary had sailed into smooth waters." Another orator, a prelate, declared that Charles was greater than Alexander the Great, for not only did he conquer but he strove to further the prosperity of his conquests. The political consequence of this feeling of gratitude and security was the acceptance of the Pragmatic Sanction[2].

And this conviction pervaded not only the so-called " ruling class "; it took possession of every grade of Hungarian society. In 1717 and 1718, during the Turkish wars, internal disturbances were still feared. With all the optimism characteristic of exiles, Rákóczi and Bercsényi persisted in waiting for an opportunity to return home. At the close of Charles's reign, the war with the Turks broke out afresh (1738). Its whole course was an unfortunate one; and it jeopardised all the conquests of Eugène.

[1] *Ann.* I. 3.   [2] v. Salamon, *loc. cit.* pp. 130—160.

Everybody could foresee that the death of the Emperor would give rise to disturbances all over Europe.   The son of Francis Rákóczi actually did set up a claim to the inheritance of his father, but even among the exiles it was considered a crime to attempt to disturb the harmony of the fatherland.   Our information on this point is not derived from official sources or from persons in power at the time : it is supplied by the opponents of the existing regime—magnanimous opponents[1], it must be admitted. The agreements come to between the king of Hungary and the magnates at Szatmár and in the parliaments, were preserved and extended, for, though perhaps unable to offer complete satisfaction to the conflicting interests, they at least succeeded in reconciling them.

No one can deny the decisive influence which this peaceful condition of affairs in Hungary, and her reconciliation with the dynasty, had upon the course of events throughout Europe during the reign of Maria Teresa.   But even in the days of Charles, the fact that the Hungarian nation had changed sides made its influence felt in maintaining the balance of power in our quarter of the globe.   In the sixteenth and seventeenth centuries the rivalry between the Bourbon and Habsburg Houses was the chief motive-force in the politics of Europe. The Emperor and Spain were faced by the united power of the French, the Turks, and the smaller Protestant states. Every important turning-point in history saw Europe sharply divided between these two systems.   On such occasions Hungary, as a country pre-eminently under Turkish and Protestant influence, had employed all the power at her command against the House of Habsburg.   The risings of a Bethlen, a George Rákóczy, and a Tököly, were all connected with the general policy of opposition and, as goes without saying, with the Turks. After the Peace of Karlovicz had resulted in paralysing the Turks, it was as the ally and instrument of the French that

---

[1] "God forbid that anyone should come to us now."   And later : "Heaven be praised, no one of any importance has come.   Those who have come are such as have escaped the gallows."   These quotations are from an absolutely authentic source, Clement Mikes, who by his loyalty and writings has rendered the exile of Francis Rákóczi II immortal.

Francis Rákóczi created a diversion against Austria in the Spanish war of succession. "Since those days Austria has rested on an entirely different basis. Of old it was German soldiers who carried on the Hungarian wars, and it was said that the rivers of Hungary had been dyed with German blood, now Hungarian soldiers appeared in German wars, forming the back-bone of the Imperial army. That country which had hitherto been a constant menace to the Imperial power now constituted its mainstay." This is the opinion of Ranke on the changes that had taken place[1].

This was the part played by official Hungary. Naturally enough—in fact where such radical changes take place, it cannot be otherwise—the great exile appeared on the horizon now and again, but his glory and influence were on the decline. We have seen how bitterly one of his leading supporters pronounced sentence on the hopes of his party. Distinguished individuals were indeed able to rise to positions of eminence in the French army; for some time the Protestant malcontents continued to emigrate into Prussia, but as a political factor this party had ceased to be of any importance[2].

At any rate the Hungarians had obtained full recognition as an independent nation. Foreign peoples in the East took them as their standard, changing their mode of life to such as should correspond to that of the Magyars. In his desire to bring his Russians into closer connection with the West, the Czar Peter the Great endeavoured to make their costumes Hungarian, and had Hungarian model dresses displayed to view in Moscow[3]. At first confined to the Court and civil servants, his decree relating thereto was later extended to the peasant class. In his Memoirs Frederick the Great recognises the epoch-making importance of the appearance of Hungarian light cavalry in the wars of Europe. Ziethen, the greatest cavalry

---

[1] Ranke, Leopold v., *Abhandlungen und Versuche*. I. *Die grossen Mächte*, p. 16.
[2] The first Prussian hussar regiments were composed almost exclusively of Hungarian Protestants. Even in the Seven Years' War there were a large number of Hungarian officers and soldiers in the Prussian army, and many men still fled over the frontier.
[3] Brückner, Alex., *Peter der Grosse*, p. 224.

leader of his age, admitted that he had learned his trade from
Gabriel Baranyi, a Hungarian[1].

It was through changes of this kind that Hungary passed
until the succession to the throne of the last of the Habsburgs,
the Empress-Queen Maria Teresa, which ushered in an age
of new interests and fresh struggles (1740). Hitherto Hungary
had been opposed by a dynasty, henceforward she had to deal
with provinces ruled over by the same crowned head—a result
of the Pragmatic Sanction.

[1] Carlyle, *Frederick the Great*, vol. III.

HUNGARY IN 1780

CHAPTER I.

ECONOMIC CONDITIONS.

THE enormous mass of material preserved facilitates the work of the student in giving a faithful picture of the Hungary of a century ago : but there is no lack of factors which obscure his vision and render objective criticism extremely difficult. There is scarcely any event of the public life of those days which is of purely historical interest: most of the ideas and interes. for which the Hungarian nation was struggling a century ago are still in force, albeit in a transformed state. At every step we feel that, even if not treating of the same stage of progress in which Hungary is found at present, we are dealing with those factors which brought into being the life and conditions of the Hungarian nation of to-day.

As is well known, on the initiative of Count Stephen Széchenyi, the first reforms aimed at transforming modern Hungary were carried out in the field of economics. And even if we do not accept the suggestion that all mental refinement and activity is merely the result of the material progress attained, there can be no doubt that the economic conditions of a nation always reflect and most faithfully explain its whole life and evolution.

Transformation in the field of economics is at all times in the greatest accordance with the laws of evolution, for it is not so subject to the action of certain great men or to the chances of foreign politics as are the constitutional, the military or even the literary conditions of a State. Consequently its treatment offers no difficulties in point of method, we have figures to refer to in everything, and, according to the old saying, figures not only rule everywhere in the world, but show how it is governed.

Our object, however, is not a statistical but an historical one. In treating of economic affairs nothing is easier than to commit the error of considering as a national trait what is merely the general characteristic of a certain economic condition. As we know, many general characteristics of this kind have actually been regarded in Hungary as specifically Hungarian. To do justice to our task as historian, we shall endeavour to put before our readers not only the actual state of things in the past, but the manner in which that state developed. And our final object must be, while giving a sketch of the various factors in this development, both in economic, political and intellectual life, to point out the organic connection between them all. To economists, legislators or publicists there may be some importance in isolated data, to the historian they cannot be of any account unless they form a part of the real life of the nation.

We shall see that the country as a whole changed comparatively little, but that the relations of the various districts of the country to one another underwent a perceptible change.

I. *System of taxation.*

We shall begin with the simplest part of the mechanism of Hungary during the eighteenth century—with the material burdens imposed on the citizens by the State. The Hungarian constitution was of a peculiar kind, and the temporal and spiritual nobility were exempted from the payment of direct taxes, their debt to the State being fulfilled by the maintenance of the *posse comitatus*. As for indirect taxes, the nobility was affected at most by the price of salt. Under the influence of the trend of affairs all over Europe, the royal Government did indeed endeavour to curtail these privileges, but in this case the estates resisted with all their might. During the Parliament of 1728–29, after considerable struggles, they succeeded in securing the recognition of the principle that " ne onus inhaereat fundo[1]." This principle was given the binding force of law by Act VIII

---

[1] The Government wanted to tax the grounds of the peasants in order to get a fixed assessment of the contribution. The Parliament declared, 1728, that it would be against the law, as the ground did not belong to the peasants, but was a property of the nobles, who could not be taxed.

of 1741 and was thereby made obligatory for all time. This was practically speaking the price paid for the powerful *posse comitatus* put into the field during that year. While rendering their country the last important services in war, the nobility desired at the same time to secure their privileges for all time. For Hungary the exemption of the nobles from taxation played the same part as the question of the *theorikon* had done in Athens of old; the latter constituted the corner-stone of the predominant democracy, the former that of the aristocracy. For the overthrow of both the advent of a Demosthenes was required.

It was the Parliament of 1715 which first voted permanent taxes for the maintenance of the sovereign's standing army[1]. These taxes were imposed exclusively on the royal free boroughs and on the *misera contribuens plebs*. In 1724 the amount to be contributed was fixed at 2,138,000 florins, to which sum, in 1728, 118,652 florins were added as meat allowance for the soldiers. The Parliament of 1728–29 raised the amount to 2,500,000 florins.

During the reign of Maria Teresa, in 1751, the estates of the realm bargained for a contribution of 3,200,000 florins, which sum, as a result of the huge expenses entailed by the Seven Years' War, was raised in 1765 to 3,900,000 florins, an amount that included the maintenance of the Royal Hungarian Body-guards[2]. As fresh strips of territory were re-annexed, the re-incorporated parts were taxed as well. Slavonia, annexed to Hungary in 1750–51, paid 89,337 florins; the 13 towns of Szepes (Zips) (recovered in 1772) paid 17,220 florins 50 denars (equal to 25 *portae* (v. note 5, p. 20)), besides which, in 1776, Lubló, Podolin and Gnezda paid an extra sum of 1,377 florins 40 denars (i.e. equal to 2 *portae*). Croatia and Upper Slavonia, which came back under

---

[1] All these data are taken from the report submitted by the Royal Hungarian Chancellery and dated June 30, 1785 (No. 8323).

[2] The Hungarian Noble Guard was created by Maria Teresa, in 1760, with the view of flattering the nation. Each county could recommend two young nobles to be members of the Guard. A palace was built for them in Vienna, but they accompanied the Court when it sojourned in Hungary and, being good horsemen, did also great service as couriers. Much greater was the importance of this Guard in furthering the intercourse of the Hungarian gentry with French literature, so that George Bessenyey, Abraham Barcsay, Alexander Báróczy were the founders of the "French school" in our literature. Somewhat later the celebrated poet Alexander Kisfaludy was also a member of this Guard.

the control of the Hungarian excise authorities in 1780, contributed 109,707 florins; and the three counties of Temes (which
were united in 1782) gave a sum of 372,000 florins as their quota.
Consequently the so-called *contributio* would have amounted in
all to 4,481,700 florins (in round figures), had not certain large
strips of the territory of the counties of Szörény and Krassó
been excorporated, the sum being thereby reduced to 4,392,911
florins $53\frac{9}{16}$ kreuzers[1].

To modern ideas this sum is a very trifling one. Even in
those days the statesmen of Vienna looked upon it as such ; and
the reason given for the fact that the interests of Hungary, in
respect of duties and commerce, were at all times subordinated
to those of the German Hereditary Provinces, was that the
burden borne by Hungary was far smaller than that imposed
on the former[2]. Joseph II himself shared this conviction, as
he often explained. But for the estates themselves on which
they were imposed, these burdens were by no means contemptible ones. The Parliaments of 1751 and 1765 gave a faithful
picture of the state of the country when they declared that it
was unable to bear any greater burden. It was not the sum that
was so enormous, the important point was that the peasants
had to pay in specie. Now there was such a scarcity of ready
money in the country, that in 1783 the county of Sáros expressed
the fear that the age of trade by barter would begin afresh[3].
And in the same year several counties suggested that the
military authorities should accept payment in kind[4].

The Parliament itself merely settled the sum total of the
taxes, which remained in force until the next session, the
amount falling to each several county was determined by special
commissions. As an ideal unit, the ancient *palatinalis porta*[5],

---

[1] The florin had 60 kreuzers or denars.

[2] This question is dealt with in detail by Count Charles Zinzendorf—later president
of the imperial head office for the control of State accounts—in his proposals dating
from 1770–72 (National Museum, Germ. fol. 266). Cf. also the despatches of the
Venetian ambassador (Vienna Imperial Archives).

[3] Chanc. Arch. acclusa 305 (1785).

[4] Chanc. Arch. No. 11,453 (Oct. 30, 1783).

[5] The *porta* was originally a feudal "gate" on which, according to Decree
No. 4 of Sigismund (1405, § 2), 30 denars were due. Act IV of 1474 (Matthias
Corvinus) distinguished the *porta* from the *fumus* or house, as it corresponded,

of the value of 688 florins 50 denars, was still maintained. The new distribution among the various counties was called the *rectificatio portarum*. There was trouble enough before an agreement could be come to, the various counties did all in their power to throw the burden on their neighbours, using their own poverty as an argument in their defence[1]. As early as 1737 Count Alexander Károlyi complained of the trouble the *portae* gave him[2]. The greatest difficulty was occasioned by the fact that there was no fixed basis for taxation : consequently artificial units (*dicas*) had to be invented for the assessment of the taxes to be paid by the various counties, parishes and individuals[3]. Yet we must admit that, despite its artificial nature, the test used for the assessment of taxes was fairly rational and is regarded as such even by an Englishman writing at the time[4]. The peasants themselves, their families, spring and autumn crops, all kinds of cattle, and hay were all taken as so many units or parts.

As, however, the money value of work or of the crops was not the same in all parts of the country, naturally enough the burdens imposed on the single *dicas* differed in the various counties. The main point considered was the ease with which money was obtained and the crops marketed. Consequently those counties and parishes, where the consumers were nearest at hand, had to pay relatively higher taxes than the others. In towns the extent of and income produced by industry and trade was the deciding factor. Yet in the case of the latter there was a safe and permanent basis for taxation—the house-tax. As parishes engaged in particular in industry and trade, the royal free boroughs were assessed after $548\frac{7}{8}$ *portae*, i.e. a little more than one-eleventh of the whole number ($6384\frac{3}{4}$).

not to a family, but to a plot of ground. Later on, in 1609, one *porta* was calculated to include four sessions or twelve houses of cottagers. In 1609 each *porta* paid four florins, in 1659 ten florins. Finally, the Parliament of 1723 determined the question of assessment, and the *portae* were subsequently distributed in a fair manner.

[1] The law of 1723 establishes the generous principle, that common burdens must be borne by everyone in proportion to his means.

[2] Letter to the Chancellor Count Louis Batthyányi, dated Nov. 14, 1737 (Nat. Museum).

[3] For this so-called *dica*, see Appendix No. 2.

[4] Townson, *Travels in Hungary* (London, 1797), pp. 135, 136.

Croatia enjoyed the special privilege, acquired under Wladislav II (1490–1516) and maintained right down to 1847 —of paying only half of the *contributio* assessed, as compared with the other countries[1].

In that age, when the requirements of the State were of more importance than the services it rendered to the citizens, when the continual increase of the army and of civil servants and the growing expenses of the Court alike entailed extra burdens on the taxpayers, while those involved by a feudal and hierarchical system had not yet come to an end, no single people was able to bear its burdens lightly. Even in France, the classic home of financiers, the state of things was the same. According to Machiavelli the amount of taxes imposed (c. 1520) was a trifling one, but was a heavy burden to the peasants, as the taxes had to be paid in specie. Just the same was the case in Hungary, as we know, some 250 years later. The correspondence of Colbert is full of complaints about bad taxpayers, and, though he decreed that the cattle and most indispensable tools of the agricultural labourers should not be seized by the bailiffs, at the same time he gave orders that this fact should by no means be brought to the notice of the peasants, otherwise they would pay no taxes at all[2]. This is also one of the characteristics accompanying a certain stage of economic development which cannot be considered as exclusively Hungarian. In Hungary too the complaints of the Government about the arrears of taxes were just as frequent as those of the people about the burdensome nature of the taxes. In Hungary, moreover, there was something "national" about the non-payment of taxes, which were used to hire an army of foreign oppressors and to maintain the Court of a foreign non-Magyar Capital. In the same days that we hear the stories of the enviable lot of peasants, sung by gentleman poets, there resounded the plaints of the peasants, whose food consisted only of sloes, wood-sorrel and wild pears and who could not drink wine because they were in debt :—

"Burdensome taxes and fines without number ;
Soldiers want quarters and cash must be found them."

[1] *Wlad. Decret.* I. (1491, of Slavonia), § 2.
[2] Ranke, Franz, *Geschichte* (1st ed.), vol. III. p. 227.

The possibility of a peasant revolt was continually in the foreground, the tables might yet be turned. The Hungarian peasant

> "Had pledged his soul; even that was not his own :
> In terror waited what each day would bring ;
> For daily losses were his hapless lot,
> And bailiffs feared he worse than Tartar hordes.
> Whole parishes fail to pay—sometimes a groat—
> The judges are threatened—irons or stripes their fee :
> The prisons fill sometimes to overflowing ;
> But all in vain, no money is forthcoming."

Yet in general we may remark that, except in certain bad years, distraint and the existence of large arrears were unknown in most parts of the country. It was only in the North-West counties, about 1780, that such things were at all common: and in the other counties the burdens cannot have been so very oppressive. Certain districts were continually compelled to suffer owing to the change in trade and in commercial conditions. Nothing could be done to remedy the conditions of taxation: the items voted by the Parliament of 1765 remained practically unchanged until the end of Joseph II's reign, and wherever the burdens of any particular parish were relieved, the amount involved was distributed over the whole county. Yet the economic conditions, which served as the basis of the system of taxation, were by no means of a permanent character.

If we make a general survey of the distribution of the *portae* between 1724 and 1780, we shall get the following picture[1] of the principal districts of Hungary:—The *portae* of the counties adjacent to Austria (Pozsony, Nyitra, Mosony, Sopron, Vas) were relatively very numerous. This was not only because they were then (as they still are) relatively the most thickly populated districts in the country—a fact more striking then than now—nor because they were so fertile ; but more importance was attached to the fact that it was an easy matter for their inhabitants to carry their corn, cattle and wine into Austria—an advantage of incalculable value as compared with the other counties, where pure wheat had to be used to feed swine

---

[1] For details v. Appendix.

as the farmers were unable to carry it away[1].   In their territory
was situated Pozsony, the seat of Government offices and magnates, Nagy-Szombat, the seat of the national university, Sopron,
Szent-György and Ruszt, far-famed for their wines, and a host
of smaller manufacturing and market towns.   The neighbourhood of Miava could compete with any district on the continent
in point of handicrafts.   The ordinary materials required in the
country were for the most part woven there.   If we consider
their present position, the burdens imposed on the counties of
Trencsén, Liptó, Turócz and Árva were, relatively speaking,
larger still.   But the population of these counties were diligently
engaged in industry; their wares found markets all over the
country; and even the gentlefolk wore "Pukova" cloth (from
Puchó in the county of Trencsén).   The primeval forests (the
products of which were floated down to the markets in rafts),
medicinal herbs, hemp and flax, all constituted sources of
income.   It was here that, even in later times, more gold and
silver was in circulation among the peasants than in any other
part of the country[2].   We are told that in 1786 no fewer than
3000 Slovak pedlars were wandering over the world[3].

In the Ore Mountains district a means of subsistence was
afforded by the mines and the numerous officials and miners
engaged in the same.   In 1787 Selmecz was still described, by
the royal commissary Baron Ladislas Prónay, as very flourishing.   Between 1740 and 1773 the takings of its mines were
estimated at nearly 70 millions—i.e. an average of almost $2\frac{1}{2}$
millions a year.   Though poor[4], Besztercze had one excellent
industry, for it manufactured numbers of sword-blades, and also
contained numerous house-painters[5].   As this district formed a
market which could be depended upon, the "portion" (*contributio*)
of the counties of Zólyom, Bars and Hont was also a large one.

A considerable part of the taxes was contributed, further, by
the counties of Szepes and Sáros, where there was a flourishing

---

[1] Chanc. Arch. No. 9955 (1783), of the county of Somogy.
[2] For details cf. *Manch Hermaeon, von den Reformen Kaiser Josephs*, p. 314.
[3] Csaplovics, *Gemälde von Ungarn*, vol. II. p. 92.
[4] Baron Prónay, *Helyt. lev.* (Archives of *cons. locumten.*), No. 13,594 (1787).
[5] Korabinszky, *Geogr. Hist. Lexikon von Ungarn*, 452 (Neusohl).

baize and linen industry. The greater part of the profitable export of wine to Poland fell to the share of Késmárk and Eperjes. Individual families acquired considerable wealth[1]. The whole county of Sáros was covered with manor-houses and pleasure gardens. In a word, these districts acquired an important position as active factors in the economic system of Hungary, partly owing to the gifts of nature, partly to their industry, which had not yet felt the influence of foreign competition.

The mining districts of the counties of Máramaros and Szatmár were of smaller extent; but even they made their effect felt in the comparatively large number of *portae*.

Generally speaking, the main source of wealth of the country was at that time to be found in the Little Alföld and in the hills and valleys that flank Hungary to the North. These counties and towns were of the first importance, not only as producers but also as consumers. The districts under the control of the commissaries of Pozsony, Beszterczebánya and Kassa, together with that part of Sopron belonging thereto, were paying just half of the aggregate taxes of the country.

It is interesting to compare with the above the conditions of taxation of the Lowlands (Alföld) and the southern parts of the Trans-Danubian district. To-day, it is here that we find the economic centre of gravity in Hungary, but in those days it consisted for the most part of unpeopled marshland or forest-covered country. The main source of income was cattle-breeding which did not, and in fact could not, support more than a comparatively scanty population. It was carried on by the great lords and landowners on their estates rather than by the peasant. But the work of colonisation was begun, and the state of the highroads was improved. After 1740 the fear of the Turks ceased to exist. We find a rapid development that reminds us of the state of things in modern America. In 1723, the taxes paid by the county of Pest did not amount to one-third of those contributed by the county of Pozsony; in 1780 they amounted to more than half those of the latter, and in 1847 were considerably

---

[1] In 1744 Alexander Pulszky of Eperjes gave the town of Miskolcz a loan of 40,000 florins: cf. Fényes, E. M., *Geogr. Dict.* vol. III. p. 103.

larger. In 1733, the county of Bács-Bodrog was paying only one-sixth of the amount contributed by the county of Nyitra: in 1780 its assessment was two-fifths of that of the latter, and in 1847 it actually had 66 more *portae*. In 1724, though they had already considerably increased, the taxes paid by the county of Tolna were only half those contributed by the county of Liptó: in 1780 they surpassed the same in amount[1]. Such comparisons could be continued *ad infinitum*.

Besides the war taxes, the country people were paying domestic taxes too—though the nobility were also bound to take their share of this burden by ancient laws which were, however, not observed. The house taxes—to cover the expenses of the county self-government and of the municipalities—generally amounted to one-fourth or one-third of the war taxes. In large counties it was naturally less than in smaller and poorer ones: for the staff of officials was practically the same in number everywhere and the expenses involved by them were practically the same in all counties. In the county of Somogy every *dica* (there were 127,571⅔ in all) paid 1 florin 33 kreuzers to the military chest and 37 kreuzers in house taxes[2].

The capacity of certain districts to discharge their obligations depended then as now to no small extent upon the character of the crops, the facility or impossibility of traffic with the consuming markets and the ravages of the elements etc. But in general, as we have already pointed out, there were comparatively few arrears of taxes. At the end of the military year 1778–79 (calculated from Nov. 1 to Oct. 31) the arrears amounted to 132,619 florins only: but as in other places 239,483 florins more than was due had been collected, there was actually a surplus of 106,864 florins. In the following years, however, the arrears continually increased in amount; at the close of 1784 they had risen to 500,000 florins: and it was not until 1787 that they began to decrease again.

---

[1] The Emperor Joseph actually thought that the burden imposed on the county of Tolna was disproportionately large. In 1785 he wrote (*Verbesserungs-Anstalten*, p. 36): "Wird auch in Ueberlegung zu nehmen sein, ob nicht der Tolnenser Komitat mit Porten zu sehr beschwert und ueberladen ist, da der Verlauf seiner Feilschaften nach Ofen und Pest sehr gering ist."

[2] National Museum, Lat. MS., 4°, 460.

As to which counties paid regularly and which did not, in this respect there was a certain amount of consistency. The counties most often behindhand were Pozsony, Nyitra and Trencsén, and in general the same is true of the tax-commissaries' districts of Pozsony, Kassa and Beszterczebánya. But even here the towns paid better than the counties. Of the whole amount of arrears (472,034 florins) outstanding at the close of 1782, no less than 84 °/₀ (395,000 florins) represented the arrears owing ·by these three districts. The districts of Sopron, Pécs, Buda, Debreczen and Szerém, which paid an equal amount of taxes, were only 60,000 florins in arrear. Of the provinces just incorporated, the three counties of Temes did not owe a single kreuzer, while the counties of Szerém were very little in arrear. Croatia on the other hand was always a bad payer. The counties that did not pay were naturally subjected to distraint: the number of seizures for debt increased every year and actually exceeded 700 annually.

It is clear therefore that the arrears of taxes were at that time most frequent in those counties whose economic importance has either not increased or has declined since that period. In the Alföld and in the counties flanking Lake Balaton there were not even any scattered instances of arrears or of seizures for debt. In the Pest receiver's district, which consisted of the counties of Pest, Nógrád, Esztergom, Fehér, Csongrád, Csanád, Békés, and Arad, of the Jász-Kún district and of the towns situated in their territories, the arrears amounted to no more than 8474 florins, of which sum 6900 florins fell to Nógrád county alone, and to that of Esztergom 1574 florins: the counties of Zala, Somogy, Tolna, Baranya and Sopron were entirely free from arrears; and even the arrears of the counties of Vas and Veszprém amounted to no more than 10,489 florins. On the other hand the arrears of the county of Gömör[1] were 51,000, those of the county of Pozsony 49,000, those of Nyitra 43,000, and those of Mosony county 46,000 florins.

Not only were the natural conditions in favour of the progress of the re-incorporated counties, the payment of their taxes, too, was rendered to a certain extent easier. On the

[1] Here the receiver of taxes found himself 45,000 florins in arrear.

southern frontier of the kingdom there was still stationed a
considerable body of soldiers, particularly cavalry: and the
requisition of supplies for them enabled the said counties to
pay a good part of their taxes in kind. According to the
military *regulamentum* in force since 1751, the articles of food
and the fodder supplied were deducted from the taxes. Yet
even though the said *regulamentum* fixed the price of wheat,
hay and oats at the lowest figure possible, many foreigners were
astonished at the patience of the Hungarians in maintaining so
large an army[1]. But in default of other consumers, the presence
of foreign soldiers was a relief. Many counties actually requested
that cavalry should be quartered within their borders. The
payment of the *contributio* in kind was in vogue in those districts which were economically least advanced, it being so to
speak the natural consequence of a system of primitive economy.
Of the annual assessment of 120,000 florins, the lower Slavonian
counties paid only 20,000 in specie, and the county of Somogy
only 15,660 out of an aggregate of 70,261 florins. In the
mining and industrial districts, on the other hand, the proportion
of the taxes paid in kind hardly represented 1—2 % of the
whole. There the higher price of comestibles would have
rendered the maintenance of a large body of soldiers anything
but advisable: and the political conditions were such as to
render their presence quite unnecessary.

The interests of the producers were further served by the
measures for the collection of three quarters of the annual taxes
of the counties before the close of the winter semester. It was
at this period that the peasants received money for their produce
and cattle.

One merit the older system of taxation certainly possessed :
it did not impose heavy burdens to prevent the colonisation and
prosperity of the Hungarian Lowlands (Alföld). The Austrian
customs duties were most severe in the case of wine, not in
those of corn and horned cattle. The road between Károlyváros
and Fiume was opened. As a result of the War of Independence
in North America, a new product of the Alföld, tobacco,

---

[1] *Gespräche im Reiche der Todten zwischen Ihren Majestäten Franz I und Maria
Theresia* (Wien, 1781), p. 82.

became an important article of export. Ever since 1735, when the idea was first broached by Count Joseph Eszterházy, who was Ban of Croatia at the time, the project of rendering the river Save an important channel of communication had been continually before the Government[1]. During the reign of Maria Teresa and still more during that of Joseph, industrious settlers poured in by thousands and were granted every possible encouragement. In a word, even if it had not yet thrown off the effects of the devastations of two centuries, the Alföld was active again and every element of its later prosperity was beginning to make its presence felt.

On the other hand, it was just at this period that the first symptoms of the decadence of the North-West districts began to appear, and the work of decay was to some extent furthered by the Government itself. In other respects, a new epoch in the development of Hungarian history in general was ushered in by the measures taken by Joseph II to make Budapest the headquarters of all the principal offices in the country. This policy of centralisation was the continuation of the work of Maria Teresa, who had already removed the national university to Buda, where, since their reorganisation, the supreme tribunals of the country had been fixed. The Diet of 1764–65 had already urged that its seat should be transferred to Buda, the *meditullium regni*. Here we are interested only in the effect these measures had on the *contributio*. In consequence of the transfer involved, the number of *portae* of the counties flanking Pozsony decreased by about 48½, while those of the counties adjoining Buda increased by a similar number[2]."

But the causes of the trouble were far more deeply seated. When, in 1785, Joseph II divided the kingdom into 10 districts, he called upon Joseph Ürményi, one of the most eminent statesmen of the day, who was royal commissary of the Nyitra district, to investigate the causes of the impoverishment of that part of the country. The reply of Ürményi is contained in a masterly memorandum[3], and later on, in his report for the year 1787, he returned once more to an investigation of this question[4].

---

[1] (Kolinovics) *Posthuma Memoria Com. Jos. Esterházy* (1754), p. 99.
[2] Chanc. Arch. No. 12,495 (1784).   [3] Chanc. Arch. No. 15,047 (1785).
[4] Archives of the *cons. locumten.* No. 19,285 (1787).

In his opinion, the causes of the decadence were as follows:

1. The export of Hungarian wine to Silesia had ceased. In fact even the counties of Pozsony and Sopron preferred to import cheap Austrian wines.

2. Previously, the county of Nyitra had supplied the mountain districts with corn. Ever since the occupation of Galicia (1772), those districts had satisfied their demand by buying corn from the latter country.

3. The large numbers of Jews in the county were ruining the country people with drinks supplied in the inns.

4. The county of Trencsén had contracted heavy debts: those of the various parishes amounted to 70,000 florins.

5. The manner in which the people earned their living being such that they got their money in summer, the collection of three quarters of the taxes in winter was disastrous and furthered usury.

From other sources we learn that even the mining districts had their troubles. The output of the mines began to decrease in volume. The mining towns were visited by a quick succession of natural calamities, from which Körmöcz was the greatest sufferer. Korpona was now dependent for its sustenance mainly on its trade in wine and fruit[1].

Ever since Poland had been split up and Prussia had closed its doors by imposing heavy import duties, the great demand in northern Europe for the wines of the " Hegyalja" (district of Tokaj) had ceased. This fact was felt not only in the county of Zemplén (as producer) but by the towns of Eperjes, Bártfa, Késmárk and Löcse, which traded in the wine.

The linen industry of the counties of Szepes and Sáros was still in existence, but it had ceased to be profitable. Foreign traders—in particular Greeks and Servians—bought up the hardly-wrought products of the poor peasants for a mere song and made immense fortunes thereby[2].

However there was a still more significant and more general cause of the trouble, into an investigation of which neither

---

[1] Cf. the report of Baron Prónay already cited. For the rest the chief source is Chanc. Arch. No. 16,285, (1785), "Extractus Causalitatum accumulatarum Contributionalium restantiarum."

[2] Schwartner, *Statist.* (2nd ed.), vol. I. pp. 364—368.

Ürményi nor any of the other authorities entered. Schwartner was the only man to recognise this cause, but even he does not venture to explain it.

In the first half of the eighteenth century, these manufacturing districts of Hungary differed very little from the adjoining countries of Moravia and Bohemia, either in point of speech or of the conditions of labour. At the outset, Maria Teresa treated both to the same measure of encouragement. Her husband, Francis I, established a flourishing china and majolica factory at Holics. Large textile and leather factories arose at Pozsony, Sassin, Magyar-Óvár and Nezsider, for the most part by the aid of the dynasty. The cotton factory established at Cseklész in 1766 started work with a capital of 60,000 florins. Here were to be found all the preliminary conditions, not merely of an industry in its infancy, but of one developing in all points in accordance with the ideals of the eighteenth century.

During the latter years of her reign, the great Queen manifestly preferred to encourage the industry of the Hereditary Provinces—particularly after the Parliament of 1765, when she was obliged to reconcile herself to the fact that the Hungarian nobility would not undertake to pay taxes. Under Joseph II an entire change took place. He categorically declared that until a radical reform was made in the matter of the *contributio*, i.e. so long as the nobility were exempt from taxation, there would be no question of an encouragement of Hungarian industry, particularly where it might compete with that of the Hereditary Provinces. The regulations Joseph issued, after his protective duties had rendered the Austrian manufacturing industries capable of competing with those of France and England, so completely strengthened the cause of Austrian industry that its Hungarian rival was no longer able to stand in its way. Better lines of communication were opened out. The number of those who wore fine foreign cloth and despised home products was continually on the increase. The whole nobility of Hungary proper and of Transylvania and the wealthier commoners purchased their clothes in Vienna[1]. The industrial population of

---

[1] This is proved not only by the complaints of poets and writers but still more strikingly by the returns of the customs

the counties of Pozsony, Nyitra and Trencsén saw that the sale of their wares was decreasing. Another important point is that the wares of the North-West had previously found a ready market in the Alföld, but under Joseph II large numbers of foreign master-workmen began to settle there, so that even here too the general public were able to provide for themselves at home. As for the gentlefolk they no longer wore any but foreign cloth.

As a consequence of all these causes, the barren soil was no longer able to provide a sustenance for the remarkably dense population. The people began to emigrate in large numbers towards the fertile districts of the South. For the districts now under discussion the censuses between 1787 and 1847 show not only a decrease in the number of *portae* but at the same time a decline, or at the most a very slight increase, of population. That of the Alföld and of the districts lately occupied by the Turks increased in places to a most extraordinary extent. The change is particularly striking if we look at the towns of the two districts. For purposes of comparison, we annex the figures relating to the population of a few counties as presented by the censuses of 1787 and 1847 respectively[1].

In 1787 the aggregate populations of the two groups of twelve counties were practically the same: in fact that of the North-West counties was somewhat larger. By 1847 that of the southern counties exceeded the latter by some 900,000. During this period of 60 years, the population of the Alföld and Trans-Danubian counties was practically doubled; while that of the lesser Alföld and the mountain districts scarcely increased by one-fourth, and of the increase (353,000) more than half (185,000) fell to the counties of Pozsony, Nyitra and Sopron, i.e. to the flat country.

This comparison is important also for the light it throws on the nationalistic question. The counties of the Alföld and the Trans-Danubian district included in the list are the most purely Magyar ones: on the other hand, those of the North-West, with the bare exceptions of Sopron, Pozsony and Nyitra, are inhabited almost exclusively by Slovaks and

[1] See note 1 on next page.

Germans[2]. Consequently it may be said that the natural and economical conditions themselves have prepared the way for the predominance of the Magyar elements.

To-day, when in deciding every question the political point of view is the first to be taken into consideration, it may be asked whether the burdening of the non-Magyar territories to

[1] We have indeed official statistics relating to 1780 and 1782: but these are neither complete nor trustworthy. And in any case the two sets of figures included in our lists are sufficient for the purpose.

	Population		*No. of Portae*		
*County**	1787	1847	1723	1780	1847
Jász-Kúnság ...	95,458	195,233	67½	83	125
Heves	180,856	296,816	95½	123½	148
Csongrád ...	69,139	137,883	39	58¾	170
Szabolcs	198,625	220,719	92½	73¾	70
Hajdúvárosok ... ('Hajdú" towns)	28,476	65,521	35¼	37¾	31½
Somogy	165,932	231,359	90	102	123
Tolna	133,734	197,381	27¼	62	128
Fejér	110,317	184,393	56	87	111
Csanád	25,792	75,372	15	21	39
Békés	71,638	155,056	20	39	84
Pest	319,794	590,900	137¼	249	326
Bács-Bodrog ...	228,208	493,186	66	159	386
Totals	1,537,969	2,844,819	741¼	1095¾	1741½

	Population		*No. of Portae*		
*County**	1787	1847	1723	1780	1847
Árva	74,515	84,156	71½	63	54
Zólyom	69,663	88,130	106¾	103½	73
Trencsén ...	223,340	280,324	224¼	203	132
Liptó	67,922	76,548	64¾	51	34
Turócz	37,606	44,213	46½	46	24
Nyitra	294,685	364,351	350½	313¾	229
Sáros	143,280	197,878	166¼	116	89
Bars	107,671	130,248	160¼	149¼	98
Hont	125,576	110,128	175½	173	86¾
Pozsony	231,216	295,048	441¾	392¾	269½
Mosony	53,600	61,862	153¼	162	120
Sopron	159,989	210,016	387¾	349½	225
Totals	1,589,063	1,942,902	2349	2122¾	1434¼

*Including the royal free boroughs situated in the territory of the respective county.

[2] Cf. Keleti, Károly, *Magyarország népességének szaporodása és fogyása* (1870–75). Report of the Academy of Sciences, 1879. Tables on pp. 10, 11.

the advantage of the purely Magyar districts was not a piece of conscious calculation? We desire to anticipate this question by answering it at once.

Hungary in the eighteenth century, as we may confidently assert, did not know of any nationalistic question, in the modern sense. The ruling class—the nobility and the prelates, members of the *sacra corona*—constituted a solid unity, without respect of tongues. The Croatian nobles were just as fully members of the Hungarian " Sacred Crown " as either the Slovak or Magyar-speaking nobles. All attempts, made with more or less energy, to Magyarise foreign-speaking inhabitants of the country, were merely to facilitate religious conversion, and were originated mostly by members of the clerical order, who had scarcely the remotest idea that they were thereby rendering a service to the national cause.

As members of the " Sacred Crown," the nobility and the towns passed resolutions in the name of, and controlled the destinies of, those too who were merely subordinates and be-longed to the *misera contribuens plebs*. Here too nationality implied no difference at all. The peasants of Magyar town-ships were just as much outside the pale of the constitution as those of Slovak ones. On the other hand there were whole villages of Slovak or Wallachian nobles, just as there were of Magyars. Not only had the proprietor the right of con-trolling his serfs, in his own interests it was imperative that the lot of the latter should be as favourable and their bur-dens as light as possible. The property of the serfs being in reality owned by the noble, the taxation of the former made its effect felt indirectly on the latter. Such was the general conception of the matter, and such was the interpretation given to the same, particularly by the Parliament of 1764. The counties did indeed endeavour to throw a larger share of the burdens of taxation on their neighbours, but this was not done because the latter were non-Magyar, but rather to relieve their serfs, i.e. indirectly, their own estates. In those days the North-West counties were in fact wealthier than the almost uninhabited regions of the Alföld and the Trans-Danubian district. While in the North-West the number of *dicas* was increased by the fact that the peasants were numerous and that there were many parishes engaged in industry, in the latter the chief branch of produce still consisted of agriculture, for the stud-farms and cattle ranches belonged to the gentry, who paid no taxes.

It was the North-West Highlands and the lesser Alföld that were owned by the persons best able to defend their own interests and those of their dependants. It was here that the old and powerful families of magnates, the Eszterházys, Pálffys, Batthyánys, Illésházys, and Kohárys, who kept firm hold on the government of the country, rose into prominence: and it was here that their estates were situated. At the same time the most numerous estates of the principal prelates, in particular of the Primate (Archbishop of Esztergom) himself, were situated in this part of the country. In the Alföld and in the southern half of the Trans-Danubian district, the lords of the manor were for the most part gentry or families just rising into prominence[1]. The three counties of Temes, and the North-East part of the country, inhabited by Wallachians and Ruthenes, were almost entirely owned by the Treasury or by adopted foreigners (*indigena*).

The figures given below will illustrate the distribution of property[2], and may perhaps succeed in throwing some light on this part of Hungarian history, which has been so completely neglected. It is true that we can only offer a comparison of the *numbers* of the various estates, not treating separately of their extent.

In the lesser Alföld, 58 °/₀ of the aggregate number of estates were in the hands of prelates and magnates, only 9 °/₀ in those of the gentry (individual landowners), 24 °/₀ in those of *compossessores*, and 6 °/₀ belonged to the Treasury or to the royal family. In the districts inhabited principally by Slovaks, 41 °/₀ of the aggregate number of estates were owned by prelates and

---

[1] In 1759 an official Memorandum (Treasury Archives) says of the "Banat":—
" Hier ist der Fürst nicht nur Landesherr, sondern auch alleiniger Gutsherr."

[2] The data forming the basis of the above calculation are to be found in the " Catastrum omnium locorum populosorum Inclyti Regni Hungariae " drawn up on the basis of the official statistics for 1787—to all appearances for the Palatine Archduke Alexander Leopold. It contains the names of 11,298 places, and after each the name of the proprietor. It has not yet been published. Mus. oct. Lat. 46.

magnates, 17 °/₀ by the Treasury, 29 °/₀ by the gentry, and 2 °/₀ by *compossessores.*

On the other hand, in the northern half of the Alföld, only 34 °/₀ of the estates were in the hands of magnates and prelates ; 31 °/₀ were owned by the gentry, and 28 °/₀ by *compossessores* (mostly of the gentry order). As already stated, the southern half of the Alföld was still almost entirely Treasury property. Consequently it is clear that just that part of the country was most heavily taxed which was chiefly owned by men whose voice in public affairs could be and was most effective. For in the eighteenth century in Hungary—the age of the predominance of the spiritual and temporal magnates—the gentry were quite unable to compete with the latter in point of political importance and in respect of services rendered to their country.

Consequently, if the burdens imposed on these older counties at the time when the distribution of the *portae* was rectified seem to have been excessive, this system undoubtedly had plenty of supporters. And the fact that the conditions remained practically the same all through the eighteenth century, merely shows that there was no significant change in the economic basis either. It was not long since 32 counties had borne the burdens of taxation of the whole country[1].

And now we come to a more general, more lofty, point of view.

All history is a clear manifestation of the truth of the saying of the Evangelist—"whosoever will be chief among you, let him be your servant" (Matthew xx. 27). In the eighteenth century, the prelates and magnates not only governed the country by their counsels and their swords, it was their estates and their feudatories that bore the material burdens of the land.

We may safely assert that the chief event in the history of Hungary during the eighteenth century was the repopulating and the securing of the welfare of the Alföld. And a necessary result of this process was that the principal burden of service

---

[1] Assessment of 1659. Kollonics, *Einrichtungswerk des Königreichs Ungarn,* 1689. MS. in Academy.

and the chief reward, in the possession of power, fell to the lot of the Magyar-speaking gentry.

For, with the exception of the "Banat," the newly acquired territory became purely Magyar in character. The German and Slovak settlements, which, even towards the close of the eighteenth century, gave such a varied character to the ethnographical chart of the interior of Hungary, were of necessity gradually absorbed by the dominant race.

Among the settlers, a prominent place, both in point of numbers and importance, was assigned to those who descended into the plains from the North-West counties, which had suffered severely from the general trend of economic development. The stagnation in the increase of population in the latter counties was not due to any lack of propagation: on the other hand, Hungary was still in the fortunate position of serving as an America not only for foreigners, but for natives too. The hard-working and energetic inhabitants of the Slovak-German Highlands swarming southwards, and speedily acquiring a knowledge of the Magyar tongue and adopting Hungarian habits, constituted a remarkably important and still active element in the modern development of the country.

II. *Customs Duties.*

From the battle of Mohács, 1526, until the Peace of Szatmár, 1711, the country was continuously in arms. There was no break, indeed, in the sessions of Parliament, for the country had to be defended, not only against the Turks, but against the Germans too : but, apart from the securing of the integrity of the constitution, and of liberty of conscience, practically the only work the Parliaments had to do was to prepare for wars and to provide the means for carrying them on. Consequently the State was unable to exercise any direct influence on the work of rendering production and manufacturing industry capable of competing with those of other countries, at a time when all over Europe national industry was being developed and strengthened on the basis of the mercantilist system. Whenever Parliament did concern itself with economic affairs, it was

almost always in direct connection with some war; e.g. a whole
series of Acts forbade the export of *saltpetre*. And Act XLIII
of 1609 forbade the export of wine, one of the chief products
of the country, without even giving a reason for such action.
The only thing that occurs frequently is permission to drive
cattle towards Buccari. More energetic and more general demands were only to be heard when the collectors of customs or
one of the Hereditary Provinces trespassed upon the privileges of
the nobility.

The restoration of peace involved the necessity of ordering
the affairs of the country and keeping it up to the mark in
economic respects too. Act LIX of 1715 appointed a *commissio in oeconomicis*. It may be remarked that this is the first
occasion on which this general conception is to be found in
Hungarian legislation, for up to this point Parliament had
always legislated only on specific articles. From this time the
unrestricted export of wine, corn, and horned cattle was continually demanded with ever-increasing persistency. The
Parliament of 1723, which instructed the *consilium locumtenentiale* to elaborate an economic system, was the first of which we
can definitely assert that it was guided by strictly economic
principles. It did all in its power to further exports[1], while on
the other hand it endeavoured to restrict imports to bare necessaries[2], e.g. it forbade the import of iron, since there was plenty
of that material in the country[3]. It provided for the settlement
in the country of foreign master-workmen and for the prevention
of the adulteration of wine[4]. In a word, although somewhat
empirical and primitive in character, we have here the beginnings of a Hungarian mercantilist policy consciously inspired by
definite aims.

It was, however, unable to get beyond the initial stages.
The same demands are put forward by all subsequent Parliaments, practically up to 1848. We have seen that during the

[1] Acts LXXVIII and CXIX of 1723.
[2] Act CXVI declares in principle that His Majesty shall take measures "ne merces
Publico damnosae vel inutiles introducantur. Ac ut naturalia quoque in sortem
mercium inducendorum a questoribus acceptentur."
[3] Act CXXI.
[4] Acts CXVII and CXVIII.

reign of Maria Teresa the Government employed its whole economic influence and used all its authority in favour of the Austrian or Hereditary Provinces. We can imagine such a state of things—in fact we should consider it perfectly fair that the Hungarian products should be allowed free access to the Hereditary Provinces while the better developed Austro-Bohemian manufacturing industry predominated in Hungary too. In its relations with Austria, Hungary was reduced to the position of a colony, as is shown by the fact that the raw products of Hungary were reserved exclusively for the use of Austria, while the Austrian markets were not thrown open to them unless no similar product in the Hereditary Provinces was capable of competing with them. Hungarian corn was produced more cheaply than its Austrian rival, consequently it had to be excluded by means of protective duties and not allowed to enter, except in cases of famine or when prices ranged very high. The Hungarian wine was so good and so cheap that, if allowed to enter the markets of Austria, no one would buy the wines of Lower Austria, which had the greatest difficulty in making any headway at all, consequently energetic measures prohibited the import of Hungarian wine. The only article in connection with which there was a certain amount of free trade was cattle; for here the greater part of the Hereditary Provinces were entirely dependent on Hungary for their supply.

The first question that must naturally arise is, how was it possible that Hungary should be reduced to a position of such subordination to the Austrian or Hereditary Provinces?

The answer is, up to 1776, when she acquired Fiume, Hungary had no connection with the sea, still less with foreign countries. Westwards, it is true, Buccari was a free port, but the cattle driven there were taken for the most part through Styria—and constituted almost the only important article of export. Hungarian products—with the exception of wine, the chief markets for which, in the seventeenth century, were Poland and Northern Europe—could be exported westwards only. The more thickly populated countries lying to the West absorbed the superfluous Hungarian products from cattle-breeding and agriculture, and could make use of Hungarian wool and copper.

Hungary, without the markets of the Austrian Hereditary Provinces, must have gone to rack and ruin! On every other side she was surrounded by peoples whose raw products were even more abundant than her own, and by countries whose population and needs were even less than those of Hungary herself. Until Fiume was annexed to Hungary, and until the road to that port led through Hungarian territory, the Hereditary Provinces were able to shut off Hungary effectively from Western Europe: while these Provinces themselves, as a result of their geographical situation, did not depend for their commerce by sea or towards the East on any Hungarian road or waterway, so that there could be no question of retaliation. It was not until 1783 that the first boat from Vienna went down the Danube to the Black Sea. This fact explains the helpless position of Hungary, even from a purely commercial point of view[1].

This opportunity was made the most of by the Government. The customs and *harminczad*[2] tariffs (introduced in 1754 and subsequently renewed) all served the purpose of rendering Hungary incapable of competing with the Hereditary Provinces. It is true that the separate Hungarian *harminczad* was not abolished; but the instructions for employing the same were elaborated in Vienna, and the monarch in all cases accepted the views of the imperial Treasury as opposed to those of the Hungarian Treasury and Chancellery. Only we must not imagine that the Hungarian authorities did not recognise the evil or did not desire to remedy it. The appeals they submitted to the throne were for the most part to the point and were always patriotic in spirit. We must not forget that, until 1780, the whole southern or military frontier of the country was directly controlled by the imperial Treasury, and that, as a consequence, the German Government kept its power in financial matters, even

---

[1] According to a certain system of national economy, in international trade producer and consumer are interdependent. "But in political economy, the advantage is with the party supplying the capital, who acts as middleman and, while importing for the most part raw products, exports manufactured articles." Roscher, *Kolonien, Kolonialpolitik und Auswanderung* (2nd ed., Leipzig, 1856), p. 130. Fiume was annexed to Hungary in 1776.

[2] The *harminczad* was an *ad valorem* duty of $3\frac{1}{3}$ % on all goods, whether exported or imported. It was introduced as early as the thirteenth century, and had changed very little since that time.

when its influence in constitutional and military affairs was on the decline. Transylvania, Galicia and the "Banat" were all separate customs-territories. The lessons taught them in their own and more particularly by other countries had made the statesmen of Vienna familiar with the laws of commerce, though it must be admitted that they were rather too fond of a profitable balance-sheet.

The system of customs duties was finally settled at the meeting of the State Council held on June 30, 1769. The tariff was the same for the whole monarchy—insignificant export duties, still more insignificant duties on goods passing through the country for re-export: in the case of imports, trifling duties on raw products or such as were particularly required by manufacturers, though those imposed on articles of luxury were all the more severe[1]. In a word, the people of Vienna could with justice boast that, while their commerce was based on systematic principles, in Hungary the significance of the tariff was merely a question of revenue[2].

As regards the relations with foreign countries, there can be no doubt that this system did much to further the development of Austrian industry[3]. Articles coming from abroad had to pay duties of 10—30 %; while inland products paid only 5 %. The classification of the former depended upon the extent to which the same were required. The export duties ranged from $1\frac{1}{2}$ to 3 %.

Let us see how the new machinery worked in Hungary. The Parliament of 1764 frankly declared that Austria practically lived on Hungary and must be well aware of the fact. The German councillors themselves were convinced that such was the case and made no secret of their conviction, in fact it was the consciousness of the services thus rendered by Hungary that prevailed on them to urge continuously that her resources should be nursed and further developed. Let us see what were the views,

[1] Hock, C. von, *Der österreichische Staatsrath* (Wien, 1879), p. 93.

[2] "Gedanken über den Finanz-Plan" (Mus. 466 k). "Es ist das bisher in den deutschen Landen eingeführte Mauthsystem auf Commercial-Grundsätzen gebaut, das in dem Königreich Ungarn bestehende aber blos auf Finanz-Principien bestanden."

[3] This point is made in a masterly memorandum of Count Charles Zinzendorf (1784), to which we shall have occasion to refer again.

in 1778, of the persons best entitled to deal with the question—
the Hungarian merchants[1].

They start by showing that foreign articles pay heavier
duties in Hungary than in Austria. The import duties on a
quintal (112 lbs.) of sugar were, in Austria 20 florins, in Hungary 21 florins 43½ kreuzers; on a barrel of herrings, 4·24 and
5·29 florins, and so on. Silk and other raw materials required,
coming from abroad, could not even be imported directly into
the country, but had to be obtained from Austrian middlemen,
so heavy were the charges on direct imports[2]. And, although
foreign articles imported viâ Vienna had to pay not only the
import duties of the Hereditary Provinces but transit duties
and then the Hungarian *harminczad*, in most cases all these
charges combined amounted to less than the duties imposed on
direct imports into Hungary. Non-European wares, such as
sugar, spice, coffee and so forth, imported from the Hereditary
Provinces into Transylvania or Galicia paid no duties in Hungary. On the other hand, owing to the heavy duties, foreign
goods could not be imported into Austria viâ Hungary. The
direct duties on iron were raised to such an extent that Hungary
was compelled to meet the demands for this article by buying
it in Vienna. The heavy duties imposed on wool, tallow and
potash restricted the export of those articles. Even the Poles
had advantages over the Hungarians, for, while the former
paid only 2 florins on a quintal of wax, the latter were paying
6 florins 30 kreuzers. If a Hungarian merchant returned Austrian
manufactured goods as unsatisfactory, he was obliged to pay
the heavy import duties in force in Austria. As a consequence
of all these facts, they were unable to compete at all with the
Vienna merchants and were compelled to purchase everything
from middlemen.

The Hungarian merchants very humbly prayed the monarch
and the *consilium locumtenentiale* to put an end at any rate to
the most crying grievances. Far more resolute was the position

---

[1] The appeal of these merchants (Chanc. Arch. No. 2165 (1781)) from the towns
of Györ, Buda, Pest, Pécs, Károlyváros, Zágráb, Pozsony, Nagy-Szombat, Ujvidék,
Temesvár, Selmecz, Debreczen, Eperjes, Besztercze-Bánya, Kassa and Nagy-Sziget
was written in German and was addressed to Maria Teresa.

[2] E.g. on a quintal of indigo, 47 florins 50 kreuzers.

taken up by an *Austrian* merchant, whose patriotic purpose was to encourage Hungarian exports.

In an anonymous work, which appeared in Latin, this man explained how the export trade of the country could be furthered "and the active commerce of Hungary and of the other Hereditary Provinces promoted[1]." He enumerates the measures taken by the Austrian board of commerce to improve trade, and shows how, after 1778, things had been allowed to go their own way, a course that was for a time perhaps more advantageous. But as private persons could not avert all evils, the State ought to interfere. Above all it was imperative to introduce better and more severe commercial laws and to reduce freight charges. In the case of ordinary Eger wine, a barrel of which cost 3 florins, the *portorium* in the Hereditary Provinces alone was 15—20 kreuzers. Hungarian wine could not be kept for longer than three days in any town, otherwise a consumption duty (excise) of 2 florins per barrel had to be paid. The export of tobacco was also very difficult—although the duties themselves were trifling—for 100 florins had to be deposited and 3 florins in fees paid every day to the excise officers, for every quintal, the value of which was in many cases no more than 6 florins. Hungarian corn, which could only be carried viâ Triest, had to pay 20 % of its value. But worst of all was the restriction of the export of wine. Everyone who desired to take Hungarian wine abroad had to take an equal quantity of Austrian wine with him[2]. The only people who profited by this measure were the French. The author understands restrictions being put on the export of hare-skins, wool and similar articles, for they were wanted by factories at home in order to be able to manufacture cheaply. But he was at a loss to understand why restrictions were placed on the export of tallow.

He points out, indeed, that the Hungarians did not contribute

[1] "Propositio ex animo patriae studioso profecta, quanam ratione domestica producta in exteras regiones exportari et in Hungaria aliisve ditionibus activum commercium promoveri possint." Posonii et Budae, 1782. The author was Joseph Weinbrenner, a prominent merchant in Vienna.

[2] This classical example of economic oppression is often referred to in travels and in the economic books of the period. Cf. Nicolai and *Briefe eines Franzosen*, also Gregorius Berzeviczy, *De Commercio et industria Hungariae* (Löcse, 1797).

to the common exchequer so much as they should have done: but it is very rarely that we find an Austrian German writing impartially and without any feeling of jealousy about Hungary[1]. The Hungarians, he says, were furthering the interests of trade, but could they be expected to renounce their ancient institutions for a trifling profit? If the restrictions on exports were removed, the nobility would gladly pay taxes. "And if it is true that the Hungarians do not contribute in due proportion to the common expenses, we must not forget that we should be very wrong in making it look as if the interests of Hungary were at variance with those of the other Provinces. On the other hand, we must always remember with gratitude how much blood the Hungarians have spent in our defence[2]." And this was of more importance. If the raw products of Hungary found a ready sale, the Hereditary Provinces would profit most thereby. After the large export of corn of 1772, more money was brought from Hungary to the markets of Vienna than ever before or since. The author added a hope that Joseph II would adopt his views and thereby enhance the power of his empire. Joseph II did not do so, but all the suggestions offered by the author were eventually adopted.

There would be no end to the story were we to enumerate all the means resorted to with a view to restricting Hungarian industry and production, and to centralising the trade of the country in Vienna. When commercial treaties were made with foreign countries, it generally happened that the Austrians, in protecting their industry, injured the interests of the foreigners, who then revenged themselves on Hungarian goods. Where the interests of Hungarian trade did not come into collision with even any minor Austrian interest, the Government did actually take steps to further the export of Hungarian goods. When, in 1780, a new commercial treaty was concluded with Russia, the latter reduced the import duty on Tokaj wine from 60 to 9 *roubles* an *antal* (60 *litres*). Prince Kaunitz, as imperial Chancellor, on many occasions informed the Hungarian Chancellery that

---

[1] "Germano Austriacarum Provinciarum Incolae de strenuis Hungaris raro absque partium studio et rarius adhuc absque invidia loquantur." Weinbrenner, *loc. cit.*
[2] *Ibid.* p. 177.

Hungarian wine might be exported to Sweden or again to England. When the United States of North America were founded, the emperor Joseph II sent a delegate to America with a view to negotiating for a commercial treaty, and on this occasion called upon the Hungarian Chancellery to communicate a list of the main products and manufactured goods of Hungary to the said delegate[1]. The answer to this summons was given by Francis Győry, Aulic Councillor, whose reply proves how dangerous the Hungarian councillors felt the state of affairs and the prevailing conditions to be for Hungary.

To compile a list of Hungarian manufactured articles—he says—would not be worth our while, nor would it be in place[2]. In a few royal free boroughs, indeed, there were craftsmen who supplied the everyday needs of their fellows and managed to earn a livelihood, but they were unable to manufacture in large quantities in advance, for they had neither the capital nor the credit. They imported everything from Vienna. There were scarcely any factories in the country. For this fact no one could make the inactivity of the nation responsible, it was due to the system of customs duties and the enormous charges for export[3]. There had been numerous leather factories, and cloth too had been manufactured ; but all this had become a thing of the past, owing to the competition of the Hereditary Provinces. Consequently, practically the only article they could export to America would be preserved meat.

The *consilium locumtenentiale* and the Governor of Fiume too had many opportunities of expressing opinions on this question. They both saw that the prevailing system rendered the development of Hungarian industry impossible and enabled Austria to dictate the prices of all raw products. They were just as well able to calculate the effects of the tariff imposed on each several article as those councillors who had determined the said tariff, and had refused to abolish it despite the appeals with which they were besieged. They saw the material decadence of the country, and were not astonished by the commercial

---

[1] Chanc. Arch. No. 3720 (March 20, 1782).
[2] " Nec operae pretium, nec conveniens foret." Chanc. Arch. No. 3879 (1783).
[3] " Ob systema vectigalis et ob majus exituale portorium." *Ibid.*

balance-sheet, which was always "active"—i.e. the exports represented a larger sum than the imports! In time, it seems, they grew to accept this state of things, as a decree of fate, in a spirit of utter indifference.

Yet Hungary, having survived three centuries of devastation by Turks, Tartars and Germans, did not break dòwn under the systematic bleeding carried out during this century.

III.   *Agriculture and Cattle-breeding.*

Count Francis Györy concluded his report referred to above by saying that, if his Majesty did not take urgent measures to remedy the evil, the masses in Hungary would be unable to pay their taxes, owing to the lack of ready money. Yet nature had bestowed everything in plenty, and the people had everything except money[1].

His Majesty, Joseph II, did not take any such measures; in fact he still further developed the financial and economic system handed down to him; yet the ruin predicted did not follow as a consequence of this policy, and Hungary advanced much more rapidly and continuously than the Provinces which were her parasites. On this point all our sources, whether official or non-official, are agreed. If Hungary was treated as a colony, she possessed a goodly share of that inexhaustible vitality characteristic of colonies only.

Writing in 1769, the Venetian ambassador could not find words to express the advance being made by this country, and made use of expressions generally applied to-day only to the valley of the Mississippi or to California. The advance made by the kingdom during the last 25 years, in point of population and civilisation, was incredible; several simple villages had become populous towns, and many crafts, of which there had not been a trace before, were in a flourishing condition.

---

[1] "Clima regnorum istorum adeo est clemens, ut jure dici possit, illis non tantum pene nihil deesse, sed abundare omnibus, si sola parati aeris species excipiatur. Totius enim penuria tanta laboratur ac quasi in dies ita angetur, ut nisi Providentia M. V. cras hodie commercium relevet, jam praevideatur, plebem quae frugibus etc. partim abundat, sed distrahere non potest, in Abundantia sua pauper, Contributionis Pecuniariae obligationem ferre non potest, plane esse collapsuram."

Sericulture had begun in earnest; and there was no doubt that the population would increase still more rapidly[1].

All this is true in particular of the districts formerly occupied by the Turks. An area of more than 11,000 square miles, which had hitherto been left almost waste, was now brought under cultivation. It was thinly populated by people who swarmed together from all parts: and this district began to resemble the varied character of colonies, not only economically but in point of nationality also. The inhabitants did not settle down permanently at once, but for some time kept wandering from place to place[2]. Under such circumstances, the conditions of life being so easy, it was only natural that, even without including the immigrants, the increase of population should be enormous, indeed, even to-day the birth-rate of this district is higher than that of any other[3].

There were two methods of occupation. The proprietor either established farms, on which the chief importance was attached to cattle-breeding; or he collected serfs from all parts of the country to cultivate his fields and form villages. The former method was in vogue in particular in the district between the Danube and the Tisza, where the sandy soil was more favourable to cattle-breeding than to the cultivation of cereals: the classical example of the other method is the county of Békés colonised by Baron Harruckern and his heirs. The imperial Treasury, which owned the whole of the " Banat," was particularly zealous in the work of colonising. The work was not immediately profitable, but the Treasury prudently took measures for increasing the wealth of the State indirectly, by having the soil cultivated and the district in question more thickly populated.

In this part of the country agriculture began to develop again from the most primitive beginnings. As the population was not dense and the area was enormous, the chief source of income was cattle-breeding. The latter had many advantages. Little supervision was required, scarcely any investment was

---

[1] Renier, Paolo, ed. *Arneth*, vol. I. h, p. 320.

[2] Among the papers of the Royal Hungarian Chancellery are to be found innumerable petitions of newly established villages for the granting of new sites.

[3] Cf. Keleti, *l. c.* This is particularly true of the counties of Békés, Csanád and Somogy, where there is one birth a year to every 16—19 inhabitants.

needed, its products were very easily turned into money, for cattle were transported without any difficulty. It is true that the least possible care was bestowed on the animals, which were left outside on the farms winter and summer ; such a thing as fattening had never been heard of; and no hygienic measures at all were taken; but even then the profit made was substantial enough. Absolutely no capital was required, and the lord of the manor paid no taxes, however many thousands of oxen or horses he might have. It is true that, owing to the deficient care bestowed on them, the cattle were being constantly visited by the cattle-plague, and that the horseherds (*csikós*) and cowherds (*gulyás*) could not be controlled : but it must not be forgotten that every penny produced by the once profitless waste or prairie (*puszta*) was a clear gain, not only to the individual landowners, but an addition to the national wealth.

During the whole course of the eighteenth century, cattle-breeding undoubtedly formed the main staple of the active trade of the country[1].

It must be noted that in the case of fattened swine, the imports exceeded the exports, the balance being in favour of Hungary only in the case of lean swine and sucking-pigs, a fact that shows that Hungary in those days was in practically the same position in relation to the Austrian Provinces as the Provinces of the Lower Danube are to-day in relation to

---

[1] The tables referring hereto are to be found in the Chanc. Archives, Nos. 6035 (1783) and 9142 (1784).

The value of the horned cattle exported was :

in 1780,	2,591,000 florins,
in 1781,	2,230,000 florins,
and in 1783,	3,636,000 florins ;

that of the sheep exported was :

in 1780,	482,000 florins,
in 1781,	466,000 florins,
and in 1783,	544,000 florins ;

that of swine exported was :

in 1780,	752,000 florins,
in 1781,	718,000 florins,
and in 1783,	780,000 florins.

The value of the wool exported was :

in 1780,	1,340,000 florins,
in 1781,	1,976,000 florins,
and in 1783,	2,820,000 florins.

Hungary. The export of horses was very small, ranging in value between 40,000 and 50,000 florins.

The four articles of export just mentioned represent one-half of the aggregate exports—particularly if we include the other raw products connected therewith, raw hides, etc. I believe this one fact is sufficient to demonstrate the extreme poverty of the country in those days. For in a country consisting of *latifundia*, such as Hungary was then, cattle-breeding must be exclusively under the control of many-acred landowners; and, as a consequence, the profit derived therefrom must be concentrated in a very few hands. One or two great lords, a few officials, large numbers of herdsmen and menials—such was the population of the Alföld in those days. And the picture presented by scattered dwellings miles distant from one another, half-wild herdsmen completely isolated from the outer world, and incalculable masses of cattle and horses, became so ingrafted in men's minds both at home and abroad as the true picture of the Hungarian Alföld that, even after the conditions had entirely changed, it was no easy matter to break away from this tradition.

Of Italy it was said of old that it was ruined by *latifundia*. In Hungary, on the other hand, it was the latter which prepared the way for a higher development. The difference lies in the fact that, whereas in ancient Rome the huge estates grew into existence on the ruins of a numerous and honest peasantry, in Hungary it was the *latifundia* which raised the greater part of the Alföld out of its previous chaos. The great proprietors alone possessed the material resources and political influence to enable them to make the first indispensable investments. Even trade with foreign countries would have presented insuperable difficulties, owing to the defective nature of the means of transport, had not the purchasers been able to acquire large quantities of the articles they required at once, and the name of the vendor offered a certain guarantee of good faith. For the " new country " the land-owning magnates and, to a certain extent, the Treasury, were practically as important factors as were the first large trading companies in giving the over-seas colonies a place in the commerce of the world. Nor must we lose sight of the fact that the system of customs duties had, as it were, predestined Hungary to the breeding of cattle.

The transition from cattle-farming to a cultivation of the soil, which, though primitive in character, required a greater density of population, was slow and gradual. There was, indeed, no lack of abuses. So far as the "Banat" in particular was concerned, for a long time the belief prevailed that it was adapted for cattle-breeding only : and the "Banat" as one of the granaries of Europe is a discovery of quite recent times. As late as 1785 very loud complaints were heard that only very little space was left open in that district for pastures. The Emperor himself considered that these complaints were quite justified[1]. Count Anton Jankovics, royal commissary, who was particularly well acquainted with the conditions prevailing in the southern part of Hungary, was himself of opinion that in the "Banat" cattle-breeding was more profitable than the cultivation of the soil. He recommended that the third field marked out in the several areas, belonging to each village, should be left open as pasture-land. On the other hand, the *consilium locumtenentiale* believed that the days were over when cattle-breeding could be the most profitable branch of agriculture for that district, which happened also to be adapted for the cultivation of the soil[2]. When the Emperor travelled through the "Banat," he himself warned the Chancellery that the new landlords of that district wished to force their serfs to depart from it with a view to acquiring larger areas for purposes of cattle-breeding[3]. It was only the Francis canal (1794), with other facilities for communication, and with the considerable work of colonisation carried out by the Government, that converted the district between the Maros, the Danube and the Tisza into a granary of wheat.

In the newly acquired territory, at every step it became evident that the system of agriculture followed had consisted in

[1] Chanc. Arch. No. 6096 (1785).

[2] An extensive work dealing with the regulation of the pasture-lands of the "Banat," is to be found in the Chanc. Arch. No. 8983 (1785).

[3] Rescript of Joseph II to Count Charles Pálffy, Deputy Chancellor, dated Temesvár, May 26, 1783, Chanc. Arch. No. 5257 (1783). According to Reviczky (*Status Regni Hung.*), the large increase of population in this district was absolutely disastrous, as it rendered cattle-breeding impossible.

merely collecting the treasures latent for so long a period in the bowels of the earth, without giving the soil anything in return. We have an exhaustive account of the economic conditions prevailing in the Alföld at that time from the pen of Samuel Thessedik, the famous Lutheran pastor of Szarvas, a man who by his studies had made himself familiar with the methods of farming in more populous countries of Europe too and who did his level best to improve the standard of his own people[1]. Though he is not quite objective and, like every radical innovator, took a perhaps somewhat too pessimistic view of the conditions of former times, his work may still be used as an authority, as it was by later writers in the eighteenth century.

According to the general custom prevailing among writers of the day, Thessedik did not content himself with pointing out the means for advancing the material welfare of the people, but had a plan ready to hand which must unerringly lead to their absolute bliss and perfect happiness, the realisation of which he naturally expected the omnipotent sovereign to undertake. What he taught would to-day be called "state socialism." But, just because his work covers every field, it has preserved for us many details of the mode of life and method of farming then in vogue in the Alföld, which would otherwise have been hidden from posterity.

This warm-hearted and learned friend of the people was distressed to see the constant decline in the productive force of the soil, due to a lack of rational farming. In the pastures, the healthy grass was being gradually eradicated by useless or poisonous weeds, this fact being constantly the cause of cattle-plague, to the detriment of cattle-breeding. He had seen a fine stretch of flat meadow, some 800 acres in extent, entirely overgrown with noxious weeds, called very expressively soldiers' grass, which were difficult to extirpate. The days were over when the cattle grew up, so to say, side by side with the grass, all wild ; and now the treasures thus robbed from nature ought to be replaced by careful cultivation. The Hungarian cattle and horses could not be compared with those of foreign countries,

---

[1] *Der Landmann in Ungarn; was er ist und was er sein könnte.* Gedruckt auf Kosten des Verfassers, 1784. It has been translated into Hungarian.

either for strength or outward form. Everybody had confidently believed that not even the wasteful process, which had been followed, could exhaust the productive resources of the soil[1].

This carelessness and a wasteful system of farming was still more in evidence in the cultivation of the soil. In many places on the left bank of the Tisza the land was ploughed once only. The finest fields were overgrown with wild oats and wild rape. When in 1781 a certain great proprietor, at the annual distribution of plots, had wished to leave certain fields fallow, only two out of some 600—700 peasants could be found to agree to the proposal. For fallow fields had to be ploughed several times, and the labourers' cattle were not capable of hard work. Of course no one thought of manuring.

Thessedik relates how the first colonisation and cultivation of the soil, after the expulsion of the Turks, was carried out by Baron Harruckern. His words are authentic, for he himself was pastor to more than one such colony. In the course of a few years, fifteen almost wholly new parishes, settled on the waste and neglected estates, had assumed proportions that were incredible to anyone who had not seen them. Where, 50—60 years before, smoky mud-huts, Turkish baths, Armenian stables or farm-houses had stood, were to be found villages containing from 500—1000 houses and 5000—8000 inhabitants. Fifty years before, a few thousand people had been living, where 60,000 —70,000 now dwelt, on the estates of the Harruckerns.

Very little work had been required to make a good profit out of the soil which had lain uncultivated for centuries, while it had been drenched with Christian and Turkish blood. After being once ploughed it produced splendid wheat. The peasants' cattle had grazed on grass which covered all but the tops of their horns! At the beginning of the period of colonisation in particular, the peasants had been able to plough and reap where they listed, such was the abundance of fields and meadows. They soon became so well-to-do that this district was, and still is, called the "Hungarian Canaan."

Now this prosperity was beginning gradually to decline. The parishes were still 8—12 miles distant from each other;

---

[1] Thessedik, pp. 52, 53 and *passim*.

but the peasants and the Armenians (tenants of the *pusztas*) were already treading on one another's heels. The farmers, who had for many years been able to produce pure wheat from the rich and unexhausted soil after once ploughing it, still persisted in ploughing their already exhausted lands once only; but instead of wheat and barley, they reaped wild oats, wild rape, thistles, and tares. They could not make a living. If the year was a dry one, man and beast suffered alike. Formerly the beds of the rivers had been deeper; now they were continuously growing shallower, the result being frequent floods, which ruined the pastures. The inhabitants of the large villages complained bitterly ; for the greater the increase of the population, the farther had they to go to rent farms and fields[1].

We have here a description of the period when a system of extensive farming was no longer feasible, though the people were not yet advanced enough to pursue a system which should make up for the growing deficiency of virgin soil and restore its fertility, hitherto thought inexhaustible, by more intensive cultivation. Other sources, including official ones, present almost the same picture as Thessedik. We see the interests of the tenant-farmers in collision with those of the villages. Owing to a lack of pasture-land, the peasants could not keep cattle enough, while the Armenians actually pastured the lean cattle of strangers. The Government did all in its power to provide that the profits should accrue to whole parishes, not to single individuals[2]. In a word, though everything was transitional, the transition did not last very long. The county of Békés, in which Thessedik was particularly concerned, very soon secured a prominent position among the counties of Hungary on account of the industry and diligence of its inhabitants. This fact, however, is due in no small measure to the exertions of that Hungarian, who first warned his countrymen of the dangers involved by an exhaustion of the soil and taught them how to avoid it.

In other parts of the country, too, we see that agriculture was of a very primitive character. Up to 1764, the area of land

---

[1] Thessedik, pp. 95—99.

[2] Cf. the document No. 12,203 (1785) in the Chanc. Archives, which refers to Békés county.

belonging to the town of Karczag was remarkably extensive.
But from that date so many settlers came in that the land had
to be measured out and divided on the three-field system[1],
and when the land was split up into these divisions there was
trouble[2]. At Szent-Márton-Káta, too, it was discovered that
the land available for agriculture was getting too limited, the
landowners were trespassing on the common-land[3]. In the
Trans-Danubian district there were still places where the land
was divided on the two-field system only ; such were the estates
of the Abbot of Zselicz in the county of Somogy[4]. In the
" Banat," manure and harrows were unknown quantities[5] ; and
in the North-East counties, the division of ploughed fields into
three fields was absolutely unknown, and the use of manure was
quite exceptional[6].

That the soil was scantily settled and poorly cultivated is
proved by a very competent judge, who says that even in the
heart of the country the peasants (particularly the owners of
a whole " session") had much more land than they were able
to cultivate effectively[7]. According to this authority, even the
peasants were often obliged to obtain outside labour at harvest-
time, and consequently the sessions ought to be divided into
halves and quarters, and in general every effort should be made to
further the distribution of the land among the younger peasants.
There were loud complaints made in the " Banat" too that the
one object of the farmers was to occupy as much land as possible
without even thinking of providing the necessary capital or of
cultivating the soil to a proper degree.

[1] Chanc. Arch. No. 4761 (1784).
[2] Chanc. Arch. No. 10,021 (1784). The parish of Hirip in the county of Szatmár
also complained that its land was divided on the three-field system. Chanc. Arch.
No. 9610 (1783).
[3] Chanc. Arch. No. 10,705 (1784). [4] Chanc. Arch. No. 11,282 (1783).
[5] Hermann, Reisen, p. 268.
[6] Cf. the instructions issued by the royal commissary, Baron Simon Révay (Chanc.
Arch. No. 9958 (1785)):—"Multum frumenti accederet, si territoria in tres dividerentur
(cum nunc duae tantum sint) calcaturas. Tertiam quippe calcaturam Fagopyro
seminare possent, accedente simatura, quae hic valde rara." The same complaints
are found in the commissary's report to the consilium locumtenentiale, No. 7152
(Feb. 7, 1787).
[7] Report of the royal commissary, Paul Almási, to the consilium locumtenentiale,
on the Pest district, No. 33,668 (Sept. 8, 1787). For explanation of " session "
v. Appendix II.

These conditions are not characteristic of Hungary or of this particular period only; they are to be met with everywhere where settlers, finding waste or virgin soil, endeavour to get a speedy profit from their labour.

The remarks to be found in official or private reports concerning the defective character of the cultivation of the soil, of threshing—which is generally an exception to the old method of treading out corn with horses—and of the storing of corn in caves, refer to features which are truly Biblical in their primitive character.

In certain districts of Slavonia, however, where the villages had to be forbidden to divide up their land afresh every year[1], we do actually find conditions that remind us more than anything else of the state of things in primitive days. Here we find copies of the Russian *mir*, and in general of the first settlements and village-formations.

The primitive character of the agriculture is shown not only by the manner of cultivation, but by the products themselves. Autumn crops, the high-water mark of peasant farming, were very rare. The main product of the eastern half of the country was maize, which required very little investment of capital. Another advantage which this product offered was that it was not included in the old laws among those which had to pay tithes[2]. Even in other parts of the country mangcorn, and rye, not pure wheat, were the chief products. We find evidence of this fact particularly in the returns of the Treasury and Church estates; yet the latter could surely have better afforded to invest in wheat seeds than the peasants[3]. It was left for the Emperor himself to point out to the Government that the production of mangcorn should be, so far as possible, restricted, and pure wheat grown in its place. Potato-growing was still practically unknown. Taught by the famine of 1772, the Government interfered and ordered that potatoes too should be grown, and Joseph II, in particular, ordered

---

[1] Chanc. Arch. No. 2055 (1782).

[2] Matthias, Decr. v. (1481), § 1; Wladislav II, Decr. III. (1498), § 51.

[3] According to returns of 1783 the Treasury estates supplied about fourteen times as much mangcorn to the army as wheat. Chanc. Arch. No. 1160 (1783).

the royal commissaries of the ten districts to provide for the planting of this vegetable. At the opening of his reign (1780), potatoes were so little cultivated that Thessedik and Luca, who compiled all possible data, did not even include them among the products of Hungary. On the occasion of the great famine that ravaged the northern counties in 1782, though we are told that the people lived on the bark of trees, no mention is made of potatoes[1]. According to Schwartner, it was in 1788 that the *solanum tuberosum* was for the first time cultivated in the counties of Szabolcs, Bihar, Arad and Pozsega[2].

We may safely consider the cultivation of cereals to have been the chief source of income of the peasants themselves; the amount of the serfs' arable land was always considerably larger in proportion than that of the allodial grounds. The proportion changed so soon as the lords of the manor began to convert their *pusztas* into ploughed fields. On the other hand, the production of marketable plants was for the most part confined to the gardens of landowners and of tenants. Peasants did not go in very much for growing tobacco, though that plant found a new home in Hungary in the eighteenth century. Rape, however, which is to-day an important article of commerce in Hungary, was not cultivated at all in the eighteenth century.

By order of the Government, returns were prepared of the extent of arable land, meadows and vineyards, in so far as the latter were in the possession of serfs. Even if we take into consideration the fact that the proportion of allodial estates was much larger in the Alföld than in the North-West, it is surprising to see how much less, in proportion, was the amount of land under cultivation in the districts recovered from the Turks than in the older estates. The arable land in the county of Árva was just as much in area as that in the county of Heves, which is three times as large. In the county of Mosony there was three times as much arable land as in the county of Fejér; and in the county of Komárom almost twice as much as in the county of Szabolcs.

---

[1] Reports of the counties of Árva and Liptó to the *consilium locumtenentiale* in 1782.

[2] *Statistik*, vol. I. p. 293.

The production of the various kinds of cereals was as follows (here too only peasant-land is included): wheat, 3,906,259 ; rye, 3,137,822 ; barley, 2,034,612 ; oats, 3,503,962 (the figures refer to Pozsony bushels, and are taken from the returns mentioned above).

These figures refer only to the older territory, not including the "Banat." But in any case the proportionately trifling production of wheat is a striking feature.

As the returns show, the export of cereals and marketable plants was insignificant enough[1].

In 1780 and 1781 the export of flour was still very insignificant: but in 1783 it represented a value of 1,054,000 florins. Yet even if we include the latter, the aggregate value of cereals and vegetable products exported in 1783 (in which year the export of the same was at its highest) was very little in excess of that of the export of horned cattle.

Of agricultural products, grapes and wine are those which are most closely connected with small holdings. Consequently any considerable rise in the production of these articles is always the surest sign of a density of population. It is in respect of wine-growing that the map of ancient Hungary most resembles that of the Hungary of to-day, for the famous wine-growing

[1] Value of wheat exported :

in 1780	765,000 florins,
in 1781	615,000 florins,
in 1783	999,922 florins.

Value of mixed rye and wheat exported :

in 1780	379,000 florins,
in 1781	428,000 florins,
in 1783	649,000 florins.

Value of barley exported :

in 1780	123,000 florins,
in 1781	208,000 florins,
in 1783	237,000 florins.

Value of oats exported :

in 1780	152,000 florins,
in 1781	221,000 florins,
in 1783	356,000 florins.

Value of tobacco exported :

in 1780	897,000 florins,
in 1781	818,000 florins,
in 1783	940,000 florins.

districts are still the same. By reason of their character, the
Alföld (the re-occupied part of the country) was not adapted
to the cultivation of this branch of agriculture. Immediately
after the re-occupation, in the neighbourhood of Arad, wine-
growing was begun on a large scale and prospered; and for
this result the verdict of his contemporaries assigns the chief
credit to George Edelspacher, a landowner of Gyorok[1].

Towards the close of the eighteenth century, the complaint
was general that the great demand for Hungarian wines abroad
had ceased. The chief sufferers were the Hegyalja or Tokaj
district and that of Sopron. The occupation of Silesia by the
Prussians was considered as sealing the fate of the Hungarian
wine trade.

Another great blow was the forced advance of wine-growing
in Lower Austria; for these wines began to compete with home
products in Hungary itself and received most effective support
from the Government. In many places the vineyards were
again converted into arable land. But the finest wines (of
the first press) still succeeded in maintaining their supremacy[2].
The only point about which foreigners complained was that the
Viennese merchants adulterated them[3].

[1] Fényes, Elek, *Magyarország geogr. szótára* (*Geogr. Lexicon of Hungary*).
Article on "Gyorok."

[2] The will of Frederick the Great is sufficient proof of this. Even in England no
legacy was complete without a gift of Hungarian wine.

[3] Berzeviczy, *de Comm*. p. 25; the statistics of viticulture follow.

Value of wine exported:

in 1780	1,318,000 florins,
in 1781	1,153,000 florins,
in 1783	1,047,000 florins.

In the case of this article, however, there was already a large import, which was
continually on the increase, while the export, as we see, was declining.

Value of wine imported:

in 1780	448,000 florins,
in 1781	461,000 florins,
in 1783	506,000 florins.

A certain foreign traveller accused the regulations restricting the export of
Hungarian wine not only of causing a material stagnation of the country but of
producing the physical and mental ruin of the inhabitants. He declared that the
people, oppressed by the drudgery of feudal slavery, were drowning their bitterness
in wine, which was excessively cheap, and that their drunkenness reminded him
of the American Indians. This foreigner apparently was very superficial in his
judgments. We have no reason to believe that the Hungarian peasants, who are

In addition to these main products, the peasants were engaged in minor branches of farming. Dairy-farming—in connection with cattle-breeding—was only just beginning to assume an importance in Hungary: hitherto it had been an unknown quantity[1]. Foreigners were struck by the fact that the serfs did not themselves consume any articles that they could sell. Consequently, however abundant the crops of fruit and vegetables, these men practically never tasted them[2].

The cultivation of garden produce, as well as the care of the poultry, was the work of the women. Large quantities of fowls were exported to Vienna and Lower Austria[3], despite the interference of the landlords in these affairs, which always involved a loss[4]. The profit derived from the fowls was used by the housewives to pay for minor articles—salt and candles.

In addition to the older modes of occupation, the cultivation of rice and of silkworms were furthered by numerous decrees issued by Government after the close of the reign of Maria Teresa. Owing to the climatic conditions, rice could only be cultivated in one part of the "Banat," where a certain landowner was directly ordered to produce it. Consequently, only very few landowners were able to participate in the profit its cultivation assured. Quite different would have been the result of sericulture had its adoption in Hungary been entirely successful. The profits resulting therefrom would, for the most part, have accrued to the peasants; for sericulture requires, above all, work and care, not capital or land. A certain amount of success was obtained in the southern parts of Hungary, and in particular in Slavonia, where, as the returns show, the number of mulberry trees and the production of raw silk increased from year to year.

still more sober than any other inhabitants of the same zone, were given to such excessive indulgence in the delights of Bacchus. But it is so easy to generalise when treating of a foreign "barbarian" people! *Briefe eines Franzosen*, vol. I. p. 49.

[1] Reviczky, p. 162.

[2] Cf. Lehmann, *Reise von Pressburg nach Hermannstadt*, p. 73. Thessedik makes a similar statement.

[3] Reviczky, *Status R. Hung.*

[4] The people of Rhéde, in the county of Veszprém, complained that the proprietor did not allow the chicken-dealers, who used to come from the Austrian frontier with high waggons full of hen-roosts, to visit the village, so that their wives could not buy any more salt or candles. Chanc. Arch. No. 9688 (1785).

But, owing to the very fact that sericulture required such concentrated attention, it could not be engaged in by peasants
who had to look after their fields, but only by poor cottagers[1].
Another obstacle in the way of its advance, as several counties
pointed out, was that the inhabitants refused to renounce smoking
in their kitchens "for the sake of caterpillars," and that extra
rooms with a smokefree atmosphere were few[2]. Despite all the
support given by the highest authorities, sericulture remained
unpopular and had, at that time, absolutely no influence on the
life of the people of Hungary.

The great trouble taken by Government to render sericulture popular is in glaring contrast with the insignificant
results achieved[3]. We may safely say that at this period no
other branch of the economic life of Hungary was the subject
of so many official documents as was sericulture. And the
whole affair is characteristic of the methods of the Government.
Everything had to be done to promote sericulture in Hungary,
for Vienna and the Hereditary Provinces would thus be able to
secure the raw material required by their manufacturers at a
cheaper rate in Hungary than in Italy or the East. Further,
it was after all better that the profit on this article should go
to Hungary than to some entirely foreign country, which did
not pay any taxes at all. But at the same time every care was
taken that Hungary should not get further than the production
of the raw article.

When, in 1783, an artisan well instructed in the matter,
desiring to establish a silk-spinning mill at Györ, appealed

---

[1] Cottagers (*inquilini*) are peasants who own a cottage but not land.

[2] v. the answer of the county of Abauj to the summons of the *consilium locumtenentiale* to further sericulture and send in returns (Chanc. Arch. No. 6853 (1783)):
" Novimus genium et indolem populi nostri, qui nulla aut longa et incerta spe utilitatis
visa, mavult aliis potius et certioribus quaerendis vitae mediis semet impendere."

[3] The amount of raw silk produced in Hungary, Croatia and Slavonia was:

in 1764 ...	o	hundredweight	80	lb.
in 1765 ...	1	,,	83	,,
in 1770 ...	18	,,	—	,,
in 1775 ...	21	,,	83	,,
in 1780 ...	76	,,	37	,,
in 1782 ...	77	,,	82	,,
in 1784 ...	128	,,	29	,,

Chanc. Arch. No. 5150 (1785).

for a very trifling subsidy, the Hungarian Government supported his appeal: but the Emperor wrote in the margin of the petition, "stantibus circumstantiis nequeo quidquam ex aerario pro promovenda fabricatione in Hungaria conferre; cessante autem causa, cessabit etiam effectus[1]."

The carrying out of this principle sealed the fate of Hungarian industry while it was still in the womb, and the sentence of death was passed on it in the interests of Austrian industry, which had risen to importance by the aid of State grants, and was still dependent upon them.

IV. *Industry and Commerce.*

The mournful phrases just written form the most fitting introduction to a sketch of the state of Hungarian industry in the late eighteenth century.

During the reigns of the earlier Kings of Hungary, a great part of the settlers had been craftsmen. They were foreigners who practised the crafts in question, but they practised them to the profit and advantage of the country in which they had settled; and they very soon became good Hungarian patriots. And these settlements became more and more numerous and general after the great national disasters which Hungary suffered as a result of her being exposed to the attacks of the wild hordes of the East. The greatest devastation, the result of the inroads of the Tartars (1241), was followed by the age of the greatest influx of foreign immigrants.

A still more overwhelming blow to the material welfare of the country was dealt by the two centuries of Turkish wars and devastation. We can imagine how, after the recovery of Buda or the Peace of Karlovicz (1699), a king Béla IV might have diverted the stream of Huguenot refugees into Hungary—those men who took the natural ability of their race into Northern and Central Europe, and either founded or gave a fresh impulse to the industry alike of Prussia, England and Holland.

There was no lack of immigrants. The southern borders of the country were occupied by wild, barbarian Servian settlers

---

[1] Marginal note written by Joseph II. Chanc. Arch. No. 5770 (1783).

engaged in tending sheep, who continually advanced into the interior; in the West and centre of Hungary, honest, hard-working agricultural labourers were settled. The population of Buda, which was beginning to be rebuilt, was composed of the "scum of the Serbs (Rascians)" and of Swabian vinedressers.

In this respect the behaviour of the Kollonics Government towards Hungary resembled the colonial policy of England which resulted in the loss of the North American colonies. Did not the great Lord Chatham himself declare in the English Parliament that the colonists should not be allowed to manu-facture even a horse-shoe nail[1]? And in the age when the mercantile system was predominant, did not every colonising Government do everything in its power to prevent craftsmen and artisans settling and operating in its colonies?

But in following up this analogy we should wander very far from our subject. Hungary was after all only in part a colony. As for the North-West districts, we have seen that they did not lose their hard-working inhabitants, who had for centuries been engaged in industrial activity. Of old they had possessed quite as great, if not greater, skill in craftsmanship than the inhabitants of the neighbouring Austrian Provinces. During the Turkish wars they had remained isolated, and the old crafts-manship and manufacturing skill rooted in the sure but restricting forms of the medieval guilds, unable to compete with the huge factories springing up all over Europe, was reduced to the level of domestic industry. They were now the remains of an ancient superannuated civilization. Hitherto their isolated situation had protected them, but now they were unable to take the field against the advanced capitalism and labour of the neighbouring countries, which had been strengthened by the strenuous com-petition for European trade.

The ruins of the weaving and cloth industry, which still remained in existence in Hungary, did not receive their due share of patronage even from Maria Teresa. As powerful foreign factories had to be competed with, the State preferred to main-tain a few large factories, or to promote their establishment, to supporting the less important handicrafts already in existence.

[1] Roscher, *Kolonien* (2nd ed., Leipzig, 1856), p. 262.

As already mentioned, large factories endowed with extensive privileges were actually established during the reign of the great Queen—at Cseklész, Nezsider, Mosony and Sassin, but the owners, like most of the workmen, were foreigners, who did more to suppress the Hungarian industrial class than to raise the standard of work.

According to the census of 1782, in the royal free boroughs in the whole country, there were 17,074 master-workmen, 14,612 journeymen, and 6102 apprentices engaged in industry. There were, therefore, almost as many independent tradesmen as there were assistants. This single fact clearly proves that there was an almost entire lack of large establishments and a great predominance of small tradesmen[1].

The eighteenth century was the age when the State began to prepare an inventory of its resources. From all directions, individuals and corporations were constantly pointing out where and how to further the welfare of the people and thus increase the revenues of the State: and, though unable to protect the interests of home industry, the Hungarian authorities prepared returns and drew up tables dealing with the same.

As early as 1783, the *consilium locumtenentiale* enunciated the patent truth that, in the trade with foreign countries, almost every "active" article (i.e. articles the export of which exceeded the import) was a raw product, while nearly all "passive" articles were manufactures. It pointed out further that the raw materials for the manufacture of those articles (for which most money left the country) were supplied in large quantities by Hungary herself[2]. It called upon the authorities everywhere to report as to which branch (or branches) of industry was (or were) established within their sphere of jurisdiction, and how the same could best be furthered. After the reports had been sent in, the council submitted them, together with their own remarks and views, to his Majesty, by way of the Chancellery.

The first complaint made was that large quantities of linen and common cloth were actually being imported from Turkey. The people of the county of Bács could not do without cheap

[1] Cf. the data of the census (*conscriptio*) of 1782. Chanc. Arch. No. 5841 (1784).
[2] Chanc. Arch. No. 6035 (1783).

frieze and linen of the kind. As, however, similar cloth was being manufactured in the neighbourhood of Eperjes and Kassa, it was hoped that these imports would be stopped without delay.

Kordovan and moroccan leather were also being imported in large quantities from Turkey. Here, however, there was nothing to be done, as, if the manufacture of kordovan leather were to be given a place in Hungarian industry, a large number of goats would have to be kept, and that would be very detrimental to the forests.

There was an abundance of dyers' requisites in the country : only indigo was entirely lacking, and without the latter the dyeing industry could not make much advance[1].

As for the tanning industry, it was impossible that the country should suffer any loss, for in one year no less than 240,000 hides had been prepared. But the towns interested desired to secure the future of this important branch of industry by the following measures :—

(1) The Greek and Jewish merchants should be forbidden to sell the raw hides or to export them out of the country. (2) A similar prohibition should be put on the export of oak apples too, that the industry might be furthered by the possibility of obtaining this important auxiliary at a cheap rate. (3) A request was made that Austrian articles should be charged with the same (export) duties as the Hungarian articles had to pay on entering the Hereditary Provinces[2]. (4) Part of the military stores should be furnished by Hungary. And, finally, (5) it was imperative that foreign craftsmen and skilled workmen should be imported to develop the industry of the country.

---

[1] Attempts were continually being made to acclimatise indigo in Hungary or to find a substitute for it. Many experiments to this end were made, in particular by a physician of Késmárk named Pfeifer, during the reign of Joseph II.

[2] The enormous difference between the two countries is strikingly demonstrated by an appeal made by the Hungarian tanners and curriers in 1783, Chanc. Arch. No. 11,688 (1783). So far as the articles of the latter were concerned, the *raw material* paid on the average 50 times as much duty if imported from Austria as it did when exported to that country. On the other hand, manufactured leather paid 25 times as much duty when imported from Hungary to Austria as it did when exported from the latter country into the former. In the case of tanners' articles the difference was not so enormous, on the average 25—40 °/₀—naturally in favour of Austria.

We see here a combination of narrow-minded, genuinely "guild-like" motives (1, 2), and of more general ones which were of importance to the public at large. And while recommending the last three points to the kind indulgence of the monarch, the *consilium locumtenentiale* left the first two out of consideration.

The *consilium locumtenentiale* made special mention of eleven main branches of industry, the raw materials required in which were at hand in the country, or the importance of which rendered them worthy of adoption.

Of these branches, cloth-making was being practised by 1423 masters with 336 calender mills. Only the lowest classes were wearing Hungarian cloth, the others preferred foreign materials. The factory at Mosony was the only one which produced materials suitable for the upper classes. A certain proportion of the cloth supplied to the army was purchased in Hungary[1]: this was the result of the provisions of Act XXIV of 1764–65. This branch of industry could without any difficulty be furthered privately too, under State supervision. Every facility was offered by the counties of Nyitra and Trencsén[2]. The cotton industry, however, could not be dealt with at present: for the raw material required in the same was not at hand in the country.

The silk industry would make a considerable advance, if the dyeing industry were perfected. At present the mills at Buda and Pest did not use up even the produce of the country itself, which could not supply more than a small part of the demand[3].

The paper industry was quite unable to make headway against that of Austria.

The trade in glass had hitherto been a "passive" one: but the latest returns showed a balance in favour of the exports. Consequently there was no need to enter into a more detailed discussion of this question.

The wood industry was "passive." But as there was a plentiful supply of excellent raw material, the increase of

---

[1] Radvány lodged an appeal to be allowed to continue to supply the army with cloth. Chanc. Arch. No. 1021 (1782).

[2] A document preserved in the Chanc. Arch. No. 10 (1781) gives us interesting details concerning the extensive industry of Miava and district.

[3] According to Reviczky, even women of the lower classes wore silk dresses.

the exports depended solely on the exertions of the parties interested.

As for the iron industry, there was a lack of raw materials, and though all that was manufactured was sold, much more was imported from Styria. The spirit (brandy) industry was also " passive."

The only branch of industry which was "active" was that of copper founding. Yet a hundred times more copper was exported in a raw state than in a manufactured one.

The returns prepared by the Council, however, treated most exhaustively of flax and hemp spinning, returning to this subject over and over again. The greater part of the population of the county of Szepes were engaged in this industry. The county authorities considered it imperative that a book treating of this craft should be distributed among the people, seeing that in that county the women too could read and write. As it was, a large amount of money was still being sent to Poland to pay for linen : and only the lower classes wore home-made cloth, while the *bourgeoisie* preferred foreign materials. The other counties too recognised the importance of this question. Sopron was willing to offer a reward to the best spinners, and the county of Körös was ready to grant exemption from taxation to those who excelled in this trade, and thought it desirable that in- struction in it should be given to children too. The proud district of Jászkunság, on the other hand, wanted to make it an employment for the county prisoners[1].

According to another report of the *consilium locumtenentiale*[2], the counties of Pozsony and Nyitra produced the most flax and hemp, and actually exported linen. The counties of Sopron and Varasd supplied their needs by importation from Austria. The counties of Bács, Bihar, Borsod and Zemplén complained that it was useless for them to produce these articles, as they could not sell them. In general, the country exported not only coarse but fine linen ; and large quantities of the raw material (flax) were also exported. According to the unanimous opinion of the counties, the Governor of Fiume and the *consilium locum-*

---

[1] Chanc. Arch. No. 5236 (1785) of *cons. locumten.* March 18.
[2] No. 1628 (1784).

tenentiale, the establishment of factories, which would be an easy matter, would remedy the evil. The moment the factories were there, the price of the material would rise and production advance. The most suitable place for this purpose was Kassa, where capital enough had already been collected; only it would be necessary to grant exemption from taxation for a time.

As concerning the reports submitted, particularly those of Szepes, the opinion of the Council was that the Government should summon from Silesia, as the chief linen-producing country, an expert at a good salary, who should impart instruction with reference to the finer and more expensive articles in the counties of Szepes and Sáros, where spinning was extensively practised by the inhabitants.

As we see, every fundamental condition for the development of the manufacture of a very important article of trade was to be found here. There was plenty of raw material, and the inhabitants too were adepts at this branch of industry everywhere, and not in scattered localities. When the Emperor Joseph II was informed that a certain mining town was becoming rapidly impoverished, the first idea that occurred to him was to alleviate its lot by furthering the linen and lace industries[1]. In very truth this seed, if not trodden under foot, was capable of producing a majestic tree. Very little support indeed was asked for it, for what would the expense entailed by calling in a Silesian weaver, or by a few years of exemption from taxation, be in comparison with the enormous State grants which the Austrian industries, in particular that of weaving, were continuously receiving[2]?

When the Chancellery submitted the proposal in question to His Majesty, the answer was as follows: "*Until Hungary is placed in a position equal to that of the other Hereditary Provinces, the Treasury cannot support any handicraft which would curtail the means of subsistence of the Hereditary Provinces[3].*"

---

[1] Chanc. Arch. No. 2693 (1784): Of the town of Selmecz. In the sixteenth century lace-making was very extensively cultivated there: but the town council forbade girls to engage in it—for moral reasons.

[2] In 1781 alone the Emperor distributed 100,000 florins among the spinners of Moravia. Hermann, *Reisen*, p. 236.

[3] Chanc. Arch. No. 8523 (1785), Ad. 10: "In so lange nicht Hungarn in eine proportionirte Gleichheit mit den übrigen Erbländern gesetzt wird, kann daselbst

Hungary, which in economic respects was a colony, had to pay dearly for not being entirely such in political respects.

The history of the mercantilist system offers an analogy to this kind of treatment elsewhere. When the English Parliament complained to William III that the Irish wool factories were developing, the King replied as follows: "I will do all that in me is to discourage the woollen manufacture of Ireland[1]."

The customs returns demonstrate the position which Hungarian industry and consumption occupied in their relations with foreign countries[2].

keine Manufactur ab aerario unterstützt werden, welche den übrigen erbländischen Provinzen am Nahrungsstande Abbruch thut, weil in Hungarn die Lebensmitteln viel wohlfeiler sind. Jedoch bleibt einer jeden Grundherrschaft unbenommen auf eigene Unkosten derlei Fabriken anzulegen. Joseph."

[1] Roscher, *Kolonien*, p. 255. Cf. Macaulay, *History of England*, vol. VIII. p. 51. According to the great historian, the Irish factories in question must in any case have gone bankrupt, even without the help of the English Parliament.

[2] The trade in the principal articles was as follows:

Value of cotton materials imported:

in 1780	612,370 florins,
in 1781	579,478 florins,
in 1783	478,000 florins.

Value of sundry manufactured articles imported:

in 1780	237,000 florins,
in 1781	246,000 florins,
in 1783	219,000 florins.

Value of iron and hardware* imported:

in 1780	343,000 florins,
in 1781	266,000 florins,
in 1783	386,000 florins.

Value of wooden wares imported:

in 1780	300,000 florins,
in 1781	327,000 florins,
in 1783	322,000 florins.

Value of silk imported:

in 1780	783,000 florins,
in 1781	751,000 florins,
in 1783	877,000 florins.

Value of cloth and other woollen goods imported:

in 1780	1,883,000 florins,
in 1781	2,061,000 florins,
in 1783	1,688,000 florins.

Value of fine and coarse linen imported:

in 1780	1,334,000 florins,
in 1781	1,646,000 florins,
in 1783	1,323,000 florins.

* The export and import of firearms and scythes are to be found in separate returns.

The value of copper exported in a manufactured state ranged at about 13,000 florins, while the import of similar articles scarcely reached 4000 florins. But, as we have seen, this was the only "active" branch of industry. On the other hand, the value of the copper exported in a raw state fluctuated between 633,000 and 1,140,000 florins.

In dealing with the history of Hungarian industry, the importance of foreign trade is probably by no means so great as the amount of internal trade secured and the extent to which it furthered wealth and comfort at home.

There can be no doubt that, during the reign of Maria Teresa, the advance of civilization and the growing necessities of the population were accompanied by a remarkable increase in the number of craftsmen. However trifling the industry was in 1780, its progress since 1740, particularly in the South and North-East, must be described as simply enormous. A very well-informed Hungarian has preserved for us a few features of the Hungary before Maria Teresa, which bear directly upon this subject. There were very few noblemen's houses in the country which were not built of wood, and glass windows were rarities even in towns[1]. These facts make it easy for us to imagine how simple and unpretentious must have been the clothes and food of the people at large. There is nothing contradictory in the fact—which merely serves to complete the economic picture—that the number of servants was enormous, that hospitality was the order of the day, and that clothes sparkled with gold and jewels[2]. According to a calculation, which is probably not an exaggeration, no less than three million florins of unused capital were lying idle in *agraffes* (clasps of mantles) alone[3]. A contemporary poem has it that in the older families buttons were passed on from father to son[4]. In a State

---

[1] "Habitacula Nobilium in pagis vilissima vix aliqua murata domus, sed ligneae. Fenestrae vitreae in pagis nullae, in oppidis rarissimae, sed ex vesicis animalium adornatae." Anton Szirmay, *Fragmenta Hist. Secr. sui temporis* (Mus. Lat. 4°, 374), Appendix, p. 224.

[2] When Joseph Ürményi was installed as High Sheriff of the county of Bihar, the royal commissary, Count Anton Karolyi appeared in a costume valued at 100,000 florins. *Magyar Hirmondó*, 1782, p. 406.

[3] Chanc. Arch. No. 7781 (1783).

[4] v. the "Speculum" in Appendix IV.

document of vast importance which he submitted to Maria Teresa in 1757, Count Nicholas Pálffy took as his starting-point of reform the regeneration of the mode of living of the Hungarian nobility[1]. It is true that the growing luxury made Hungary a good customer of foreign countries : but the better mode of living everywhere brought into being at least the most primitive forms of industry. The number of guilds formed during the reign of Maria Teresa must be described as very large. The greatest number were naturally enough created in the newly re-conquered districts : and most of these were destined to supply the needs of field labourers. In an insignificant place like Kis-Komárom, guilds of weavers, shoemakers, furriers, market tailors, Hungarian and German bootmakers, cartwrights, rope-makers and coopers came into existence[2].

Yet complaints were still general, and every Hungarian felt that there was no industry in the country and that the evil must be remedied. The Parliament of 1723 ordained that foreign craftsmen should be settled in the country. Then, by order of the Chancellery, the *consilium locumtenentiale* collected data from the various authorities as to what craftsmen were required in the several places where there was need of such, and where were the most suitable spots for such immigrants to settle. The data were sent in, and the final report of the Council offers a fairly faithful picture—not perhaps of the position of the Hungarian industry of the day—but at any rate of the extent to which the tradesmen of Hungary supplied the local wants; it also shows where new settlers were considered indispensable.

Most of the towns were desirous of receiving cloth-weavers in their midst, thus giving expression to the general want[3]. A few towns wished to become the homes of the manufacture of the articles indispensable to the luxury of the age with its increased standard of living; others again offered themselves as suitable to even the most primitive crafts, e.g. the town of Buda asked for stonemasons and skilled workers in stucco, upholsterers, pastry-cooks, makers of silk stockings, etc.; Sopron

[1] In the family archives of the Pálffy family at Malaczka.
[2] Chanc. Arch. No. 4400 (1781).
[3] Székes-Fehérvár, Bártfa, Breznóbánya, Debreczen, Köszeg, Györ, Ujvidék, Pécs, Szent-György, Temesvár, Zólyom, Kaproncza, Varasd, Zágráb, Szatmár-Németi.

begged for an *aquilex* (hydraulic-engineer); Károlyváros, Korpona and several others for watchmakers—Korpona for bakers too. The town of Zombor, on the other hand, was ready to welcome any kind of master-workmen[1]. So far only royal free boroughs—the privileged haunts of arts and crafts—have been mentioned, and if in these there was so great a lack of industry, it is easy to imagine what a large industrial market would be afforded by the smaller townships. The standard of comfort could not keep pace with the general well-being and growing wealth of the land to such an extent as to make industry a profitable business in country places. In general it was remarked that the craftsmen in the market towns looked upon their crafts as a secondary business only, regarding their main occupation as agriculture. The poorer among them went harvesting in summer, practising their crafts in winter only[2].

As late as 1785 the Chancellery complained that a great part of the newly settled artisans regarded industry as a merely secondary occupation, since their chief business also was agriculture[3]. The German artisans of Szabadka were charged with preferring hunting to work[4].

But this was only one half of the country—that part which had been colonised. In the other half, the permanent character of the population and the decadence of economic conditions were already making their influence felt. Several older towns of the North-West Highlands and the mining district had become veritable "rotten boroughs." Many of them, more or less sorrowfully and plaintively, declared that even their own craftsmen were unable to make a living, and had been forced to resort for the most part to agriculture and viticulture[5]. To

---

[1] The full list was as follows: Turner, glove-maker, miller, wheelwright, tinker, watchmaker, shoemaker, baker, stocking-weaver, candle-maker, coppersmith, saddler, engraver, glazier, cutler, currier, basket-maker, comb-maker, gardener, musician, maker of golden spurs, sieve-maker, potter, helmet-maker, hatter, German button-maker, silk-dyer, German tailor, silversmith, tobacco-roller, upholsterer, weaver, dyer, starch-maker, cloth-maker, brazier, bell-founder. The demands of the towns of Pozsega and Varasd were not much more modest.

[2] Report of Paul Almási to the *consilium locumtenentiale* (No. 33,668 (1787)).

[3] Chanc. Arch. No. 6514 (1785).

[4] Cf. Korabinszky: article on Marientheresienstadt.

[5] Felsöbánya, Bazin, Modor, Uj-Bánya, Nagy-Szombat, Pozsony, Eperjes, Trencsén, Nagy-Bánya, Kis-Szeben, Kassa, Komárom.

our greatest astonishment, among those towns which considered the settlement of the new rivals to be dangerous, we find Pest and Szeged too—the new emporiums. Yet we believe that this fact was due to a circumspect precaution, which, in the fear of a larger *contributio* being levied, painted a dark picture of the existing state of things, rather than that these two reports really reflected the actual situation. A pleasant contrast is offered by the little town of Bélabánya, which believed itself able to offer a home and a subsistence to a currier, a brick-maker, a glazier, a candle-maker, and even to a Servian merchant.

Even in those days there were people in the country who attributed the retarding of industrial development in especial to the guild system. In this place it is sufficient to state that in the history of Hungarian industry the guilds played the same part as the feudal system did in that of agriculture. They stood in the way of the highest degree of development, of which, however, the country would, in any case, have been incapable owing to lack of capital. At the same time they prevented the unsparing and unrestricted plundering of a public as yet unable to defend itself. The prices of the several agricultural products and the most indispensable manufactures were fixed according to quality: and the *limitatio*, the official list of prices, was strictly enforced by the various municipal authorities in their several spheres of jurisdiction.

The system of restriction was not only in force as regards industry, it made its influence felt still more in the case of the trade of the country. The emancipation and advance of the latter was in no small measure impeded by the fact that the merchants were for the most part foreigners. It is true that since the days of the kings of the Árpád dynasty, the majority of the crafts-men and artisans had been foreigners too, but the latter lived completely isolated in their guilds and corporations, and, though they were not easily Magyarised, no suspicion could be thrown on their work and on its profitable results. The merchants, on the other hand, were at all times in continuous intercourse with the owners of the land, were more ready to renounce their language and national customs, and were more scattered over the country: but most of them were foreigners not only in speech but in religion too. In addition the "Greeks," Armenians and Jews engaged in trade were treated by the Hungarians, and in particular by the nobility, with that aversion born of a combination of hatred, jealousy and contempt with which the landed aristocracy of birth has always regarded the power of money, ever since history began. The subordination of industry to the landed proprietors was manifest enough : the merchants were the only element which might develop into rivals, all the more dangerous in proportion as the new and expensive style of living exhausted the material resources of the nobility.

The "Greek" merchants in particular increased in numbers : and it was these who were the special objects of public hatred[1]. The greater part of them had originally been Turkish subjects who, by the treaty of 1739, had been permitted to trade in Hungary[2]. In point of nationality they were, for the most part, Macedonian Greeks and Wallachians, with a sprinkling of Servians (Rascians)[3]. Wherever there was the remotest chance of any trade, one or two of them settled. They were to be found in the capital town of every county. They were well-to-do, and clung to each other ; and when the Emperor Joseph issued his decree of toleration, wherever at least 10 or 20 families w e living, they begged for permission to build a church, as they were capable of maintaining the same. As members of the Greek Orthodox Church, they had to put up with a good deal of oppression. At Pest the *magistracy* (corporation) was for a long time unwilling to allow them to purchase houses ; they were put under the same disabilities at Kecskemét too : but in the end their endeavours overcame all obstacles. It was not only in the towns of the Alföld that the commerce was in their hands. They established themselves at Komárom, at Györ and even at Sopron. We have seen that the demands of the town of Bélabánya included the settlement of a Rascian merchant. Even at the opening of the century, according to an authentic tradition, there were very few market towns in the Trans-

---

[1] There is a particularly bitter satire on the Greeks of Miskolcz in the Museum (Hung. MS. 4°, 152).

[2] Chanc. Arch. No. 4427 (1782).

[3] Rascians—the name for Serb immigrants into Hungary.

Danubian district which had no Greek shopkeepers. Praise is lavished on their unpretentiousness, on their simplicity—often bordering upon niggardliness—on their common sense and comparative refinement[1].

Naturally enough, their trade consisted principally in buying up raw products of the soil, and selling Austrian manufactures and colonial wares. The fact is worth mentioning that in most *carta biancas* and bonds I have seen, Greeks appear as the creditors. As the system of credit was not yet on a sound basis, their life was still for the most part nomadic, reminding one to some extent of the age of caravans.

It was owing to the deficiency of credit and to lack of means of communication in particular, that the greater part of the trade of the country was carried on at the fairs. During the reign of Maria Teresa, we find complaints being lodged against the issue of an excessive number of licences for holding fairs. The county of Szepes declared that the right of holding fairs should be restricted, for numbers of craftsmen were wandering the whole year round from one fair to the other. The Chancellery however was of opinion that the fairs were needed and were of value in promoting trade; and the documents relating to the years 1780–86 prove that in no instance was an appeal for a licence to hold a fair rejected.

Of these fairs—the dimensions and popularity of which, in the unanimous opinion of economists, are in inverse proportion to the economic development of the country—the most important was for some time that of Debreczen, which served as an intermediate station for the trade of Hungary proper and Transylvania, on the one hand, and of the Alföld and Highlands (particularly the Szepes district), on the other. However, as the import of Austrian articles into the Alföld was from year to year increasing in dimensions, while on the other hand the production of the Alföld too was continually increasing, Pest, which had formerly been a comparatively insignificant market, gradually assumed importance as the staple of this barter trade.

---

[1] Lehmann, *Reise*, p. 67. This writer actually describes their method of travelling as caravan-like, particularly on the occasion of fairs at Pest and Vienna: "Die griechischen Handelsleute sind bekanntlich angenehme und bescheidene Menschen.'

Matthias Bél makes special mention only of the cattle market at Pest[1]. The German traveller, to whom we have had occasion to refer on several occasions, considered the three great fairs[2] to be of vast importance and compared them to the "Messen" of Leipzig and Frankfort. A lively picture of the trade of the town of Pest is offered by Paul Almási, the Hungarian who dealt probably more thoroughly than any of his contemporaries with the commercial conditions of the country[3]. By this time the corn .trade with Pozsony and Vienna was in the foreground. The other main articles of export were potash and tobacco. The greater part of the latter was purchased by the Imperial and Royal Abaldo (who had the monopoly of the *régie* of the Hereditary Provinces); and smaller quantities were sold to foreigners. Besides this, a large amount of wax and wool, and some clothes (to Turkey) were exported. According to the returns of the head *harminczad* (customs) office at Pest, in 1786 the value of exports was 385,833, and that of imports 775,578 florins. Two-thirds of the latter (475,623 florins) came from the Hereditary Provinces. The principal articles of import were cotton goods, coffee, small ware, iron, clothes, furs, pepper, cloth, woollen goods, sugar, linen, silk and ribbons.

The staple for the trade of Pest was Vienna, the imports from which city alone amounted to 718,451 florins, i.e. more than 90% of the whole. Galicia supplied goods of the value of 8927 florins, Turkey of 25,125; and those imported by sea amounted to 25,209 florins in value.

These returns alone show that the trade of the country was very considerable; but they do not include transit trade and the trade in cattle. According to experts, the whole trade of Pest amounted in the aggregate to about 3,766,592 florins in value[4]. "Taking all in all, therefore, Pest is already an important staple of commerce: and her position on the banks of the Danube seems to destine her by nature to be the centre

---

[1] *Notitia Ungariae Novae*, IV.

[2] Lehmann (1785), p. 115. He tells us that Swiss, Saxons, Frenchmen and Turks came to these fairs.

[3] *Cons. locumten.* No. 33,668 (1787).

[4] In the golden age of "tables," this extraordinary precision need cause no astonishment.

for the trade of Hungary with the Hereditary Provinces, with the sea-coast and with continental Turkey[1]."

The trade of Pest gives us a true picture of that of the whole country. The chief feature of all the fairs was the exchange of raw products for foreign manufactures. The fair at Debreczen still maintained its former importance : while the principal emporia of the Trans-Danubian district were Sopron and Győr. And in the South-West Károlyváros too rose to a position of importance as a result of the measures of Joseph II. In the "Banat" the most important fairs were those of Temesvár, where the principal article of commerce was horned cattle[2]; it was not till later, when the "Banat" began to produce iron and only when the Francis canal was opened, that the fairs of Török-Becse attained a celebrity all over Hungary.

A factor of extreme importance in the furtherance of the foreign trade of Hungary was the union of Fiume with the mother country (1776). The mere fact that this union was accomplished proves how much Maria Teresa had at heart the material prosperity of her loyal kingdom of Hungary[3]. But, although the Queen interested herself to such an extent in the development of that port, and though its first Governors were men of the greatest refinement and energy like Count Joseph Majláth and Paul Almási, the trade of Fiume did not do justice to the hopes attending its establishment.

The chief advantage accruing from the possession of a free port—as pointed out in the section dealing with "customs"—was certainly that Hungary was thereby brought into direct touch with the outside world without being dependent on the mediation of the paralysing customs system of Austria. The chief obstacle in the way of the development of this port was the fact that for the greater part of the country the connections with Triest were easier, safer and cheaper ; and the harbour of

[1] Townson, who was at Pest in 1793, considered the horse fair to be the most important already. He declared there was a large trade in oak apples and raw hides too.

[2] Lehmann, *Reise*, p. 151.

[3] The Emperor Joseph II himself recommended the union in 1775, when he was Crown Prince. He considered that Fiume and Buccari should be incorporated in Hungary on condition that a trading company be established in the former place. Cf. Arneth, *M. Theresia*, vol. IX. p. 466.

the latter town naturally enjoyed the particular favour of the Vienna Government[1]. The abundance of capital on the Austrian coast, and the lack of the same on the Hungarian sea-board, was also a factor that must not be ignored.

The fact that the political conditions themselves did very much to further the advance of Fiume immediately after the union (1776) was a piece of peculiar good fortune. The same year saw the outbreak of hostilities between the American colonies and England, which resulted in cutting off the supply of American tobacco to the European markets. Hungarian tobacco was at once exported viâ Fiume to replace the American. This improvement in trade, however, lasted only for a comparatively short time; as early as 1782 complaints were made that Hungarian tobacco had no sale, and, at the same time, America appeared on the scenes again as purveyor of tobacco to France[2]. So far as I know, this was the first instance of that American competition with the produce of Hungary which has extended to so many articles in the markets of Western Europe since that time.

Besides the trade in tobacco, the same war gave a certain impulse also to the export of preserved meat[3]. The preserving and exporting of meat was in the hands of a chartered company, which for some time was able to show splendid results. Joseph II expressed himself satisfied with the success achieved by this company[4]. The export of raw goods not required by the

[1] Cf. Weinbrenner, *passim*, and the numerous complaints and protests of the Governors of Fiume.

[2] *Magyar Hirmondó* (Hungarian Courier), 1782, p. 274.

[3] The affairs of the company for the export of preserved meat are dealt with in official documents dating from 1783 (Nos. 11,698 and 12,653).

In 1781, 259 oxen were pickled; in 1782, 2075 oxen and 469 pigs. Hitherto, the company had lost on every *expeditio* (to Marseilles). Yet it would probably be able to compete in time of war with Irish preserved meat, though the export of the latter was subsidised by the English Government, whereas Hungarian meat had to pay an export *harminczad* of 45 kreuzers. The Chancellery proposed that the export from Fiume too should be subsidised, whereupon the Emperor instructed the said Council to confer with the Austro-Bohemian Chancellery. At the conference the imperial Chancellor proposed that a subsidy should be granted to encourage export, but that such subsidy should be 15 kreuzers a hundredweight if exported viâ Fiume, and 30 kreuzers if exported viâ Triest. Here too the main object was the advance of the trade of Triest.

[4] Chanc. Arch. No. 3492 (1783).

Hereditary Provinces did not clash with his "principles." He actually reduced the duties by 50 %, in order to further the company's interests[1]. But here too, just as elsewhere, he imposed restrictions on the export of wool, hare-skins and other articles required in Austria.

Paul Almási—whose name we meet everywhere in the front rank where Hungarian trade is concerned—in his capacity of Governor, elaborated a detailed report of the state of the trade of Fiume and of the reforms required[2]. In a special rescript, the monarch declared how satisfied he was with the report and with the Governor.

Almási started by stating that the union of Fiume with Hungary had been of great advantage both to that port[3] and to the country. The principal articles of trade were corn and tobacco. The trade of the port was furthered by the local tobacco and *rosolis* (liqueur) factories as well as by the preserving of meat.

There could be no doubt, however, that Fiume could not compete with Triest, and probably would never be able to do so. It had been easy to transfer the trade of Venice at a moment's notice to Triest, but Fiume could not expect the monarchy to divert this trade to her in preference to Triest. In any case there was room for both ports, Triest would be the natural channel for the trade of Austria and the adjacent counties (of Hungary), and Fiume for that of Slavonia and the " Banat."

With the view of furthering the trade of Fiume, the charges for transport by the Károlyváros road were fixed in accordance with those in force on the Triest road. Efforts were being made to establish a watermen's guild for the navigation of the rivers. Almási considered it imperative in the interests of the advance of the export trade to import and plant foreign tobacco and flax seeds. He was also the first who desired to realise the project of wine export[4].

[1] Chanc. Arch. No. 6472 (1782).
[2] " Allgemeine Uebersicht was seit meinem Vorsitze im Litorali geschehen, und was annoch geschehen könnte." Chanc. Arch. No. 9160 (1784).
[3] Count Joseph Majláth, the first Hungarian Governor, was indeed received with great ovations. Mus. Lat. MS. 4°, 466.
[4] A great obstacle in the way was the lack of suitable cellars.

In addition to what had already been done, he considered the following measures necessary to the development and improvement of the town and its trade :

1. More extensive connections with the interior of the country must be established with a view to acquiring capital. Triest possessed a large amount of capital, yet it was subsidised in everything by Government. It was a pity that the Government itself, by the collection of endowments, was offering opportunities to Hungarian capitalists to invest their money elsewhere, and encouraging them to do so by prospects of a high interest[1]. Even if there were capital to hand, the control of Government was indispensable, so little developed was the spirit of speculation. Consequently, if a suitable joint-stock company were formed, the Government itself should send a delegate into the kingdom, armed with official instructions, to gather information concerning the best sources whence the principal articles of commerce could be obtained[2].

2. There was need of at least one new road leading to the coast. Owing to the difficulties of transport, the road already in existence was unable to deal with an extensive traffic.

As we can see, the demands made for Hungarian trade in this instance also were comparatively trifling ; what it required from the State was rather encouragement than an actual subsidy in any way comparable to those which Triest enjoyed in abundance.

But, in the eyes of the Emperor Joseph, here too the deciding point was a politico-constitutional one. Asked to settle the question of the independence of the commercial banking institute of Fiume, he decreed that everything should remain as it was until the whole commercial system of Hungary had been changed[3].

The Emperor's behaviour in the matter of the school of navigation was also characteristic of his point of view.

On Sept. 12, 1783, the Imperial Chancellery informed the Hungarian Chancellery that, in view of the fact that there was

[1] v. infra.
[2] These instructions were elaborated by Almási.
[3] Marginal note to Chanc. Arch. No. 6088 (July 5, 1783).

as yet very little Austrian shipping, and of the proximity of Fiume to Triest, His Majesty had decreed that there should henceforward be only one school of navigation, and that at Triest[1].

The answer of the Hungarian Chancellery was drawn up by Count Charles Zichy. He pointed out that the Triest Fund had indeed contributed 4000 florins to the school of navigation at Fiume, but this sum had already been repaid. The school had received 6000 florins out of the Hungarian and Croatian Funds, which bore all its expenses. The outlay of the *fundus literarius* on the school hitherto had amounted to 13,700 florins. This money would be lost if the school were closed. Owing to the distance and expense of travelling, Hungarian subjects could not go to Triest. In Triest there was no "Latin" (Grammar) school or faculty of arts to enable the students to prepare themselves in a proper manner. The town of Fiume itself badly needed the institute: and Hungarian trade would never be able to prosper without it. For all these reasons, and in particular that the sons of Hungary should not be deprived of the only opportunity they had of training themselves in the science of navigation, the Chancellery begged that the school should not be closed.

We must and do appreciate to the full the efforts made by Joseph II to further the interests of the Hereditary Provinces. We can even explain his system for favouring the latter in preference to Hungary. In the present instance, however, every impartial observer admits that not only was written law and the right of possession on the side of Hungary, but Hungarian interests of the very first importance were at stake. The question might be of importance to Triest too: but it involved the very existence, not merely of Fiume, but of the whole sea trade of Hungary.

The answer which the Emperor gave to the address of the Chancellery was simply this: "I abide by my resolution[2]."

A considerable obstacle in the way of the advance of the

---

[1] No. 9492 (1783).
[2] Chanc. Arch. No. 10 (1783): "Datae resolutioni meae inhaereo." No reason is given.

Hungarian coasting trade was the fact that it was almost exclusively an exporting one, for the boats that took Hungarian raw produce had great difficulty in finding in foreign ports articles suitable for exchange, owing to the Austrian customs system[1]. Consequently, the trade of Fiume consisted for the most part in the transport of goods to Triest and to a few neighbouring Italian ports.

In the eighteenth century, the classic age of material development, when every possible advantage offered by nature was exploited to the full, obviously enough there was no lack of plans of the most diverse character for raising the trade of Fiume to a level of unbounded greatness. In the age of common sense the huge ranges of mountains, created by nature as the watersheds of rivers and peoples, collapsed just as readily as the differences and divergencies created by history in the customs and development of nations.

Everybody is familiar with the plans and experiments of the celebrated Count Maurice Benyovszky (the fugitive convict from Kamtchatka and subsequent conqueror of Madagascar), the objects of which, it must be confessed, were sound enough[2]. In 1780 a French engineer of the name of Fr. Maire, acting on "the instructions of a great Hungarian genius," presented a plan for connecting Fiume with Károlyváros, by a channel and—naturally enough—the valley of the Danube with the Vistula and the Baltic Sea[3]. Plans and offers were continually being submitted for connecting the Hungarian coast not only with the valley of the Save but, indirectly, with Galicia and the districts adjoining the North Sea and the Baltic. The employment of the river Poprád, in particular, played a prominent part in all these plans: and there was an endless succession of foreign applicants with plans for carrying the scheme into effect[4].

[1] Chanc. Arch. No. 2849 (1783).

[2] Chanc. Arch. No. 6512 (1780). In the writer's opinion, "l'administration est plus propre à décourager que d'étendre le commerce." As Count Széchenyi wrote half a century later on the same subject, "Love is enhanced by hindrances, but not so trade."

[3] Chanc. Arch. No. 5726 (1781).

[4] There are several schemes of this character, both in the Hungarian and in the Imperial State Chancellery.

Naturally enough, all these plans led to nothing; but they all touched on one point, and that the greatest misfortune of all—communication by road between Fiume and the mother country was not only difficult but expensive too. However excellent the Caroline and Josephine Roads might be, they did little to further trade; for the cost of transport was very considerable, on an average one florin per hundredweight. Consequently, conferences were continually being held with a view to rendering the Kulpa navigable almost to its source, to regulating the channel of the Save, and the like. The project of a canal between the Drave and the Save was also broached. Benyovszky and his associates went bankrupt, the canal-scheme was shelved: and, notwithstanding all the roads, Hungary had to content itself with very artificial and expensive methods of communication between the coast and the interior.

Towards the close of the reign of King Charles III (Emperor Charles VI), the grandfather of Joseph II, it had still been a matter of doubt whether Fiume or Triest was to be the Queen of the Adriatic[1]. Everybody admitted that the harbour of the former place was better and safer. And in those days the interference of the State as a factor was still in its infancy. The advance of Triest during the reign of Maria Teresa was extraordinarily rapid: according to the policy of the Government, this place was destined to be the successor of Venice. The union of Fiume with Hungary had given hopes of a brighter future for both. But the Hungarian State did not possess a sufficient measure of commercial independence to be able to develop her port in conformity with her own interests.

The chief obstacle in the way of the prosperity of the Hungarian sea-coast was the lack of transport facilities. And if no greater facilities could be secured here, where so many interests were at stake and so many measures were taken, we can imagine what the conditions must have been in the interior of the country.

It will surprise no one to learn that the first regular roads were military ones, and that the supply and transport of food to the armies were the considerations that first influenced the

[1] Keyssler, *Reisen*, vol. I. (1733).

opening up of communications between the Danube and its tributaries. Commerce was merely one branch of the reorganised State life and culture, of which the army constituted the fundamental condition, with its mission of keeping back the Turks.

At any rate, the regulation of the channel of a river or the opening of a new road, naturally involved expense or at least labour. During the time of the Turkish invasions a great many laws referring thereto prove that the system of forced labour (*corvée*) was monopolised by the fortifying of castles and by the transport of commissariat stores. Later on, when the frontier was more distant and less insecure, the material resources of the country, in so far as the control of the same could be exercised by the Government, were exhausted by the army, by the government offices and by the civil list. Despite numerous experiments and endeavours, the establishment of a public fund for educational and other cultural purposes was out of the question.

It is rather the principle involved than any actual results achieved that constitutes the importance of the decree of Maria Teresa, which provided that $1\frac{1}{2}\%$ of the price of salt should be devoted towards regulating and rendering navigable the rivers[1]. The amount was fixed at 45,000 florins. The first task projected was to be the clearing of the Érsekújvár branch of the Danube. The work was begun in earnest, and a survey was made of the Garam (tributary), the rendering navigable of which was ordained by Act XIX passed by the Parliament of 1764–65. In the opening years of the reign of Joseph II, when there was a prospect of a war with Turkey, and afterwards when it was hoped to reap the profits of the commercial treaty of 1784 in those districts, important works were undertaken in the southern regions of the country. However we may remark, without going further, that very little was actually effected.

At this time the magnificent rivers of Hungary were pro bably more an obstacle than an assistance to the trade of the country. The beds of even the most frequented of them—the Danube and the Save—were still full of piles and sunken tree-trunks which rendered navigation almost impossible at low-water

[1] Chanc. Arch. Nos. 36 and 279 (1781).

6—2

or during gales. A boat carrying a load of 1000 centners could not navigate the Kulpa except in flood-time. Navigation on the Tisza, even from its mouth to Szeged, was rendered extremely difficult by the numerous shoals. There was an enormous shoal at the mouth of the Béga, and its channel was rendered unnavigable by the hemp-netting which the inhabitants steeped in the stream[1].

There were just as numerous complaints about the numbers of corn-mills which occupied those parts of the rivers best adapted for navigation[2]. They were placed anywhere: and the boats could scarcely avoid running into them. They were particularly numerous and dangerous on the Save[3]. On the Danube itself, below Pozsony, there were no fewer than 528 of them[4].

Towards the close of 1782 and in 1783, when there was every probability of a war with Turkey, the Emperor was deeply concerned about the opening up to navigation of the Drave, the Save and the Danube. Commands and rescripts dealing with this question followed one another in quick succession. The Emperor was continually urging the cutting out of tow-paths beside the Danube and the Drave. The counties did actually complete the work, employing forced labour and navvies. There could be no doubt that all these works of regulation and repairs being carried out for military purposes would do much to further peaceful trade also, and in this case it was not the Emperor or the Vienna Government that presented obstacles.

On July 29, 1784, the Emperor sent a rescript to the Hungarian Chancellor. The war council had been informed that *the county authorities had thrown into the river the trees cut out to make a tow-path*[5]. Naturally enough, as a result the

---

[1] "Briefe über die Schifffahrt und Handlung in Ungarn, Slavonien und Kroatien. Aus dem Italienischen" (Prague, 1783), pp. 4—30.

[2] Appointed royal commissary to investigate this matter, Baron Lawrence Orczi wrote:

> "Full many a mill will rue the evil fate
> That me towards Homonna doth precipitate."

N.B.: in Hungary there are still numerous floating mills.

[3] Report of Count Ladislas Erdödy to the *consilium locumtenentiale* (No. 8284 (June 20, 1785)).

[4] *Almanach für Ungarn.*   [5] Chanc. Arch. No. 8080 (1784). B. M.

work performed had done more harm than good. Some time previously, in 1783, when the work was well in hand, the Emperor had also informed the Chancellor by special rescript that, according to reports delivered by him, many of the county officials, who had estates or inns on the banks of the Drave, were doing all in their power to prevent the river being rendered navigable. At the same time he called upon the Chancellery to suggest what could be done to put an end to all these obstacles[1].

It seems incredible that the counties or individual authorities should have acted in this manner to the prejudice of their own trade. We must not, indeed, presume that they had any bad intentions, as the Emperor did. One fact, however, is indisputable: whether consciously or unconsciously, they felt that the completion of these channels, involving greater facilities of communication, would put an end to the happy isolation of the Hungarian nobility. The establishment of an export trade would tend to increase the extent of luxury: the money would in no case remain in the country, and Hungary would cease to be a " Canaan flowing with milk and honey."

Baron Lawrence Orczi, a gallant soldier and frank outspoken patriot, who was in the confidence of the monarch and had been selected to carry out the work of regulating the rivers of Hungary, has himself given expression to these fears in several verses,

> " Károlyi[i] drained the marshland of Ecsed,
> Exterminating myriads of tortoises ;
> Zsigrai rid the Sárvíz (Mud-Water) of cray-fish:
> Like wonders must Orczi work on the Tisza.
>
> Let's dig ditches then for uncertain wages,
> Expecting velvet in exchange for uncrushed hemp,
> Gold in return for sweet wine of Tokaj
> And foreign manufactures for Hungarian produce.
>
>   *   *   *   *   *   *   *
>
> Who knows what all these strange decrees will result in?
> From Moldavia oxen and horses shall be driven to Vienna,
> But cattle bred in Hungary may stay where they are.
> For they bring wealth to none but Noblemen[2]!"

[1] Chanc. Arch. No. 9521 (1783), dated Königgrätz, Sept. 24. B. M.
[2] Baron Lawrence Orczi, *Költeményes Holmi*, vol. II. p. 215. No attempt has been made to reproduce the rhythm or rhyme of the original.

The writer recognised the gravity of the situation and was fully alive to its consequences. The political and economic existence of the Hungarian nobility was at stake, and in those days the Hungarian nobility still stood for the Hungarian nation.

In another poem, or rather essay in rhyming prose, Baron Orczi compared with the existing conditions the state of things, which would inevitably follow the improvement of the means of communication.

> "Good God, of what use is all this labour,
> Which must involve the fatigue of thousands of peasants?
> Maybe venturesome navigation will produce much wealth:
> But methinks true happiness is of another sort.
>
> Maybe John Bull will sail to Tokaj
> And fill his galleys with the nectar sweet:
> But he will give us lace for our women-folk
> And set a heavy price on his gaudy wares.
>
> From us he will take all that's worth having,
> Alluring spendthrifts to buy showy trinkets:
> And in the end our serfs will despise the sickle,
> Turn sailors, and neglect the stubble.
>
> *   *   *   *   *   *   *
>
> Is deceitful trading a fit employment for Hungarians?
> Tell me, where will all this rivalry lead to?
>
> In the counties of Zemplén, Bereg, Ungvár, Szabolcs,
> There is money, food, and wine in the cellars:
> What more is needed? Why should the Hungarians
> Live a life of uncertainty to fill their purses fuller[1]?"

Not even the most logical essay could present more clearly the conflicting interests of the day than do these unpretentious verses. The political creed of the Hungarian nobility has never since been expressed with such direct and almost naïve self-consciousness. A country, thus victimised by surveyors and so mercantile in character, was no home for a Hungarian gentleman with his love of liberty and independence.

---

[1] *Költeményes Holmi*, vol. II. p. 186. Title of poem, "Tokajban való érkezés télen" ("Arrival in Tokaj in winter").

Let us seek, if we may, a corner of the world,
Whither no commissary or surveyor has yet set his foot,
Even in the North, amid eternal snows,
And let us build us there a modest dwelling[1]."

The new tendency was as yet only in its infancy, many years had to pass before the economic transformation of Hungary was accomplished, and the chief labourer in the interests of this transformation was no "double-faced courtier," but a Hungarian and a magnate—Count Stephen Széchenyi.

We must, however, admit that the old nobility and the administrative authorities of the counties did not regard the encouragement of trade as one of their most important duties. Yet in the latter poem, in which he spoke of emigration, Orczi talked of paying visits to Voltaire and Rousseau. What must have been the opinion of those who saw even in Orczi the Frenchman fond of innovations?

Considerable light is thrown on the question of the up-keep of roads and sluices by the history of the Mirhógát (Mirhó Weir), which is still in existence. As early as 1760, several Cumanian villages closed an outlet of the Tisza—the so-called " Mirhófok " —by a sluice 270 fathoms long, with a view to preventing inundations. In 1776, believing that its interests had thereby been damaged, the county of Heves protested and in nine days destroyed the sluice. To this fact was partly due the emigration of the Cumanians *en masse*. The county authorities subsequently postponed the reconstruction of the sluice until 1785, when the Emperor Joseph condemned the deputation of the county, headed by the High Sheriff, to pay compensation to the sufferers[2].

The highroads were, if possible, in a still worse condition than the rivers. The merchants of Lemberg, who applied to the imperial Chancellor for permission to take the shorter route to Triest viâ Hungary, gave a very lively description of the road leading through the whole country[3]. The Imperial Government was particularly interested in the matter ; for, if this trade route

---

[1] *Ibid.* p. 83. "Válasz " (Reply) to Barcsai.
[2] The documents relating to this affair are to be found in Chanc. Arch. No. 15,570 (1785).
[3] Chanc. Arch. No. 6413 (1782) and No. 1581 (1783).

could be developed, Triest would replace Dantzig as the principal port for Galicia[1].

According to the report of these merchants, three days were required to cover the distance between Hatvan and Csány in bad weather (eighteen statute miles). The bad road often necessitated a sojourn of a whole week at Szihalom. From that point to Kövesd every mile of road along the embankment meant a whole day's journey, and so on, in the same way, until they came to the frontier. This north-eastern road had always been notoriously bad; and, even in 1787, it was similarly described by Paul Almási, royal commissary. But, according to the merchants of Lemberg, that part of the road to Triest which lay between Buda and Kanizsa was in a similar state. And nowhere were the inns provided with even the bare necessaries of life[2].

The most important highroad in the country was that from Vienna viâ Budapest, Szeged and Temesvár, to Nagy-Szeben. Of this road we have the following account from the pen of a trustworthy traveller, "Between Pozsony and Nagy-Szeben, the roads are for the most part such as nature and carriage-wheels have made them. Beside the highroad between Pozsony and Buda, in many places there is a ditch: but that makes it all the worse. Below Pest, as far as Szeged, the road is entirely unmade. A mile this side of Szeged the highroad has been entirely taken up—this part should be avoided by everybody. From Szeged to the frontier of Transylvania the road is everywhere unmade. In Hungary the bridges are in better condition than in Transylvania, yet they are often responsible for detaining the post[3]."

From Buda, as the centre of the country, mail-coaches were despatched twice a week to Kassa, Tokaj-Debreczen, Temesvár, Eszék, Baranyavár, Pécs and Körmend. The business of the postal service, to judge by its returns, was on the increase. In

---

[1] Arch. *Cons. locumten.* No. 33,786.

[2] An inhabitant of this district, Szirmai—at an earlier period, it is true—wrote as follows of the roads: "Viae et pontes ex virgultis, saepe impermeabiles"; and of the inns: "Diversoria in Regno praeter majores urbes nulla, sed popinae vilissimae, eaeque tantum hinc inde."

[3] Lehmann, *Reise*, pp. 40, 41. Murray Keith, *Memoirs*, vol. II. pp. 307, 308.

1782, its net income amounted to 74,545 florins, 6517 florins more than that of the previous year[1].

The other factors in the furtherance of commerce were unknown in the country. There were no laws dealing with bills of exchange and no special courts for commercial cases. The branches of Vienna banks were not introduced until the days of Joseph II. Even Almási believed that the trade of Hungary and Fiume was in no need of bank-notes. The most elementary conditions of a system of credit were wanting. The rate of interest was higher than in the Hereditary Provinces. At the opening of Maria Teresa's reign there was no copper money in the country[2]: and even as late as 1785 complaints were heard of the lack of small coins—a fact that stands out in sharp contrast to the cheapness of articles of food[3].

All these features—difficulty of communication, bad roads, lack of inns, non-development of a system of credit—in combination with caravans and fairs, complete the commercial picture of the country. In addition to the large trade done by the caravans and fairs, a very important part was played everywhere by hawkers at this stage of economic development[4]. From the North, from the counties of Zólyom and Árva, Slovaks tramped through the country with linen, oil, and saffron: and many and loud were the complaints uttered against them by local tradesmen everywhere[5]. Itinerant tradesmen from the neighbourhood of Gottschee were also appearing on the scenes. On one occasion, in the county of Bihar, 15 carts of Russian sellers of *eikons* (holy pictures) were seen. The latter were even suspected of political intrigues[6].

---

[1] Chanc. Arch. No. 1343 (1783). If any particular service increased its charges, the business declined. E.g. in 1779 the mail-coaches between Vienna—Buda—Nagy-Szeben took 230 passengers, who paid fares of 15 kreuzers a mile. In 1782, on the other hand, when a mileage of 22½ kreuzers was charged, the number of passengers decreased to 102. Chanc. Arch. No. 4875 (1784).

[2] Szirmai, *ibid.*, Supplement, p. 224: " Cupreae pecuniae nullus usus."

[3] Lehmann, p. 69. So the complaint that in this cheap country there is a comparatively great deficiency of the smallest coins is not a recent one.

[4] Roscher, *Kolonien* (2nd ed., Leipzig, 1856), p. 103. This sharp-sighted scholar endeavours to explain the laws governing the economic development of colonies in general. Hungary is not even mentioned in his work. But, as we have seen, there were many features in common between it and an ordinary colony.

[5] Chanc. Arch. No. 854 (1783).   [6] *Ibid.* No. 926 (1783).

One of the greatest merits of Joseph II in economic matters was that he developed Austrian commerce and raised it to the level of those of the other European States. When the Viennese merchants protested against his new measures, he replied: "Why, it is I who am making merchants of you; hitherto you were only shopkeepers, the agents of foreigners." And how much lower was the level of Hungarian commerce than that of Austria! We have seen the opposition encountered by the monarch when he endeavoured to lay its first foundations. It was in vain that he put a series of schemes before the Chancellery. Just as the Hungarian nobles felt that the economic transformation was merely the forerunner of a political change, the starting-point of the monarch was that no improvement in economic conditions could be achieved unless a beginning were made with a reform of the political conditions. His judgment on the question ran as follows: "In Hungary neither the nobility nor the *bourgeoisie* possess any industry, nor have they any inkling of the conceptions of trade." This statement he proves quite clearly by the fact that neither of these classes had settled as yet in Fiume, or in any of the re-incorporated parts of the kingdom. So the new measures and fresh outlays should be kept for better and more enlightened times. The Danube, Save, Kulpa, Drave, Tisza, Szamos, Maros and Vág, which were already navigable in part, would be regulated superficially only. There should be no more commissaries and commissions, which only scribbled a lot of nonsense and involved useless expense[1].

When, in 1785, the whole administrative system of the country was transformed, Count Niczky, the president of the *consilium locumtenentiale*, was entrusted with the elaboration of a draft for carrying out the transformation. Section 10 of this draft

---

[1] "Nulla hucusque adhuc in Hungaria nec inter proceres nec inter cives viget Industria, nec Clarefactio ad Commercium tendentium Idearum, hoc abunde manifestatur, quod hucusque nec Flumine nec in aliis partibus Regno noviter incorporatis aliquis illorum illuc se stabiliverit, remaneant ergo haec novae dispositiones ad meliora et clariora tempora. (Names of rivers follow) jam aliunde in partem navigabiles solum ab ingentibus difficultatibus eliberentur et de reliquo et Commissarii et Commissiones nihil nisi scripturationes et expensas inutiles efficientes remaneant. Josephus." No. 5855 (June 29, 1783). The Latin style enables us to understand why the Emperor put an end to the "curialis stilus."

proposed, as one of the duties of the *consilium*, the supreme control of economics, factories, agriculture and industry. In rejecting the same, the Emperor pronounced sentence on the economic endeavours of past years in the following terms : " these rubrics are so little adapted to the constitution and conceptions of Hungary that they are very inopportune at the present moment : for a long period of years large quantities of paper and ink have been wasted without any essential results having been attained. People tried to polish and varnish where there was still need of a plane[1]."

During this period the trade with foreign countries was continuously "active." In Hungary the land was being rapidly brought under cultivation : but the inhabitants could not yet accustom themselves in like measure to the luxury offered by foreign industry and colonial wares[2].

---

[1] " Diese Rubriquen sind so wenig noch geeignet für die Landesverfassung und Begriffe Hungarns, dass man sehr zur Unzeit mit ihnen hervorgetreten ist, und nur eine grosse Papier- und Dinten-Versplitterung durch alle diese Jahre verursacht hat, ohne dass etwa wesentliches geschehen ist. Man wollte Firniss und Glanz geben, da wo erst der Hobel hätte wirken sollen." Chanc. Arch. No. 12,807 (1785).

[2] In 1778, the aggregate value

of exports was	14,262,800 florins
of imports ,, ...	10,390,328 ,,
Balance in favour of exports ...	3,872,472 ,,

In 1779, the aggregate value

of exports was	16,205,217 florins
of imports ,, ...	9,313,191 ,,
Balance in favour of exports ...	6,892,026 ,,

In 1780, the figures were :

exports	12,198,815 florins
imports	10,419,230 ,,
Balance in favour of exports ...	1,779,585 ,,

In 1781, the figures were :

exports	12,294,379 florins
imports	11,518,661 ,,
Balance in favour of exports ...	775,718 ,,

In 1782, the figures were :

exports	13,527,124 florins
imports	9,192,743 ,,
Balance in favour of exports ...	4,334,381 ,,

The produce of the mines, however, all went abroad : and
Hungarians living out of the country, even in those days, spent
their "balance" at Vienna and elsewhere ; while a large amount
of ready money left the country in the shape of interest on
loans. The mercantile balance-sheet, to which so much importance was attached, did not offer any trustworthy test of the
national wealth at this time. These figures show, besides, that
the exports and the surplus were greatest in 1779, when the
general naval war and that of the Bavarian succession too were
at their height. During the reign of Joseph II the exports
never exceeded the imports to such an extent.

The most important frontier of the country, from the commercial point of view too, was that between Hungary and
Austria. As we have seen, the coast was responsible for
barely one-fifteenth of the export and import trade. The
aggregate trade was distributed among the various frontier-
lines as follows :—in 1783 (one of the years when the export
trade was at its highest) the value of exports to Lower Austria
was 9,074,623 florins, more than half of the whole : while the
imports from that quarter represented a value of 6,053,000
florins, also more than half of that of the aggregate imports.
The value of exports to Styria was 1,374,000, that of imports
from that province 937,000 florins. Moravia, where there was
a market for wool, took goods to the value of 2,646,000, and
exported goods to the value of 727,000 florins. The figures
relating to the trade with Silesia were 1,139,000 (exports) and
342,000 florins (imports). The exports to these provinces,
which consumed, manufactured or forwarded to other quarters
the corn, wool, horned cattle, tobacco and wine of Hungary,
were far in excess of the value represented by the imports from
the same. Only on two frontiers was the trade "passive"—those
adjoining Turkey and Transylvania. The value of exports
to Turkey was 214,000, that of imports from Turkey 787,000
florins. The figures relating to the trade with Transylvania
were 428,161 (exports) and 977,345 florins (imports)[1].

We are able to control these data by the aid of the returns

[1] All these data are taken from the official annual returns preserved in the archives
of the Chancellery and of the Government. The untrustworthiness of these returns is,

of the Austrian customs authorities. As concerning these latter, in 1784 Count Charles Zinzendorf, president of the imperial and royal board of control, submitted a report to the Emperor. Zinzendorf himself was very sceptical as to the trustworthiness of the returns[1]. He was almost the only Austrian statesman of the day who thought it would be an advantage to do away with the customs barriers then existing between Hungary and the Hereditary Provinces of Austria[2].

According to the Hungarian returns, the aggregate value of goods imported from the Austrian Provinces in 1782 was 5,494,986 florins, while the value of exports to Hungary in the same year, according to the Austrian returns, was 9,166,628 florins—i.e. very nearly double. This fact alone shows us that the official returns are not trustworthy sources of information. Even according to the Austrian returns, the trade of Hungary with the Hereditary Provinces was "active": but the Austrian export trade is put at a far higher figure than in the Hungarian returns. On the other side (imports into Austria) there is no such enormous difference between the two returns[3].

Though he had not much faith in the returns, Zinzendorf came to the conclusion that the Hereditary Provinces did actually possess an industry (a fact which, according to him,

---

however illustrated by the following case: According to the returns of 1783 (Chanc. Arch. No. 9142 (1784)) the *transito* (i.e. re-export) trade was as follows:

Imports of *transito* goods from

the Hereditary Provinces	...	1,609,813
foreign countries ...	...	...	2,307,166
Total value (in florins) ...	...	...	3,916,979

On the other hand, the aggregate export of *transito* goods amounted to 3,497,281 florins only. Consequently more than 400,000 florins' worth of goods (one-ninth of the whole) passing "through" the country, did not pass "out"!

[1] This important report will be found in the Chanc. Arch. No. 5324 (March 31, 1784).

[2] Dispacci, March 3, 1781.

[3] According to the above returns, the trade of Transylvania was "passive":— imports 1,347,706, exports 600,497 florins: deficit 747,209 florins. Zinzendorf refuses to trust these figures too, for no one would give that country so much credit. He is all the more unwilling to believe in the returns, as in 1770 the imports were only 1,199,000 and the exports 990,400 florins, and the exports could not have decreased so enormously in so short a time.

so many people were unwilling to believe), and that Hungary was their best customer (to the extent of at least 3,500,000 florins a year): consequently, Austria could not close her balance-sheet with a deficit. Another conclusion of his was that the corn, cattle and vines of Hungary, by a moderate calculation, must bring in 10 millions a year. Consequently, it was these branches of economics that the monarch ought to make the objects of special care. If they were encouraged with success, factories would spring into existence without the aid of Government, and the industry of the country would develop.

What Zinzendorf recommended and demanded was practically—if we may use the expression—the personal economic policy pursued by Maria Teresa. Each of the two realms of which she was mistress should be allowed to develop within its confines what was its special feature, with which it could complement the resources of the other. But not even during the reign of Maria Teresa did this principle secure absolute predominance, for the economic interests were opposed by political ones.

V. *Conclusion.*

The data which have been given show the coexistence of two economic systems of an entirely different character and stage of development. One was the industrial and manufacturing system of the North-West districts, a remnant of an older civilization, which had developed in close connection with the mining industries of the mountain districts. The other was the rapidly developing agricultural system of the Southern and Central districts, which very speedily converted a waste and uninhabited region into one of the granaries of Europe.

A peculiar feature of this age is the fact that these two systems, which had developed side by side in older Hungary and had been complementary to one another, now became opposed. The former, which comprised industry and mining, began to decline—partly because the actual amount of ore decreased, partly because foreign competition produced a decline of industry in those North-West districts which had formerly been the most important in the country and had constituted a valuable factor in its national life. The industries of Hungary were being gradually out-distanced by those of the Austrian Hereditary Provinces, which owed their growing importance not only to their intrinsic merits and to the superior skill and numbers of the workers, but more particularly to the fostering care of the Government. At the opening of the eighteenth century, Hungary was almost entirely dependent on her own national industries; towards its close she was gradually becoming a mere market for the manufactures of the Austrian Provinces. Her industries, for a time at least, had, in respect of antiquity and organisation, if not of quality, been equal not only to those of Austria but to those of medieval Europe generally. The influence of the enormous pressure now brought to bear upon them gradually reduced them to the level of second-rate provincial cottage-industries. Previously they had been protected by their isolation, now, in the struggle for existence, they could not hold their own against more powerful rivals.

During the same period, agricultural production—the other great factor in the economic life of Hungary—was continuously developing in importance. In this connection the territory reconquered from the Turks was of particular significance: it was almost entirely devoted to agriculture, and yet consumed no considerable portion of its own produce. The first difficulties of settlement and cultivation were speedily overcome, and every new effort, in fact almost every fresh settler, within a short time perceptibly enhanced the rate of production. Even during the eighteenth century, this production went through several stages of development. At first, cattle-breeding was its most important branch. In a very short time, besides horned cattle, sheep-farming and the production of wool became an important source of revenue. Then the cultivation of the soil began to assume greater importance. Large tracts of land, which increased in extent from day to day, were soon devoted to wheat growing; just as in cattle-breeding, and more especially in sheep-farming, the more primitive methods gradually gave way to others marked by greater care and finish. The methods of cultivating the soil were constantly improving, and the amount of produce was continually increasing. Meslin was replaced by pure wheat, and tobacco was raised to the position of a principal product and article of export.

As we have seen, there was one branch of production which was not developed to any great extent—viz. viticulture. The matchless quality of Hungarian wine did not indeed permit of its being altogether excluded from the markets of the world, but it is quite certain that it made no new conquests, and had to struggle against foreign competition even at home. As by a decree of fate, this apparently adverse circumstance only served to further the general economic transformation, for this article was chiefly produced not in the new, but in the older, Hungary. The wine trade, and in particular the export trade, constituted the chief source of income, not of the magnates and nobles, but of the towns of the North-West Highlands and of the Little Alföld. Hence a decline in this trade depressed the latter districts yet further.

The fact that the progress in the North-West and South-East districts was not upon parallel lines in the eighteenth century had a particularly important influence upon the national development. There was not a development of the Hungarian industry and of its mineral wealth—and, as a direct consequence, an increase in the population of the North-West—which bore any proportion to the progress in agriculture and in the production of raw materials in the South-East. Had there been, Hungary might have become a model State from the economic point of view, and would to a certain extent have fulfilled the conditions which Fichte demanded for an ideal " isolated State." Its various parts, being interdependent, would have formed the mutual complements of the whole, and the consequent reaction against foreign influence would have been all the more powerful. But while, on the one hand, there was almost a glut of agricultural products, the number of consumers—who consisted chiefly of the artisan *bourgeoisie*—remained almost stationary or actually declined. Hence it found its chief market over the border, and—while Hungarian agriculture was making great progress, and promising yet more for the future—it was feeding the industrial workers, not of Hungary, but of Austria.

That such was the case, and that, owing to the influence of political and social forces, it could not be otherwise, was the economic destiny of the Hungary of the eighteenth century. The development and growth of this new agricultural and colonial Hungary of the South-East—a movement which threatened the economic existence of the North-West districts—was partially the work of the Government; on the other hand, the development itself does something to explain the attitude adopted by the Government. As the case stood, the new, though economically retrograde, branch of production appeared to possess great vitality; the older and more highly developed one seemed scarcely able to survive. Hence no one can blame the Government for following the elementary laws of economic policy and the dictates of Nature herself. That district in the country, which was now on the highroad to prosperity, was not merely reconquered but also recolonised territory. It was natural to treat as a colony, according to the rules of policy and economy, this large and fine territory, which Austria had helped to reconquer, and to extend the same conception to the North-West districts which had advanced far less rapidly—in fact, to the country as a whole. Political considerations also urged the ruler to this course. For, while the government and ruler must duly take account of a mature society and mature social conditions, the constitution and political affairs of a colony depend on the arbitrary will of the mother country.

In a colony production is cheap, but the wants are legion. While supplying the mother country plentifully with the raw materials which the latter uses herself or disposes of at a profit, a colony is the readiest and surest customer for the manufactures of that country. As, owing to their insignificant population, home consumption is quite unimportant, colonies depend entirely on foreign trade and cannot be their own masters; hence the mother country practically exercises a monopoly in fixing prices. These were the principles that in the eighteenth century guided the colonial policy of England in particular. Lord Sheffield, one of the greatest economists of his day in England and a contemporary of Joseph II, actually expressed himself in the following terms: " The only use of American colonies or West India islands is the monopoly of their consumption and the carriage of their produce[1]." These principles involved the loss of the North American colonies.

From the contents of the foregoing chapter, my readers will have been able to gather to what an extent the conditions of Hungary were in fact those of a colony, and, as a consequence, how far such a treatment was in conformity with the existing state of things. Further, they will have been able to compare the principles adopted by the Vienna Government towards Hungary with those of England to her colonies.

Before concluding, one essential difference between the policy of the Vienna Government and the colonial system followed by England must be indicated. Roscher sums up the principles of the mercantile system, as applied to colonies, as follows: (a) The object was that the colonies should, so far as possible, have no industries at all. They should, as it were, constitute the agricultural country districts, while the mother country should be the manufacturing and commercial Capital[2]. And again, (b) Every effort was made to further the production of raw materials in the colonies, to be exchanged for home manufactures. Naturally enough, the more the colonists produced, the greater would be the gain to the mother country, as purchaser and carrier ; or, to use a familiar expression, the less would be her dependence upon the raw materials of foreign countries[3].

We have seen how scrupulously the Austrian statesmen adhered to the first principle. It was their professed system, as the data we have given prove beyond the shadow of a doubt. The second principle was so consistently adhered to by England that, during the reign of Charles II, the planting of tobacco in the British Isles was forbidden, with the sole object of promoting its production in the colonies. At the opening of the eighteenth century, the State offered rewards to anyone importing ship-timber from the colonies into England, as well as to importers of indigo, hemp, flax, and raw silk ; and even in 1772, four years

---

[1] Roscher, *Kolonien* (2nd ed., Leipzig, 1856), p. 243.   [2] *Ibid.* p. 254.
[3] *Ibid.* p. 257.

before the secession of the American colonies, a bounty was offered on the colonial export of deal[1]. Consequently, if it desires to render its colonies industrially dependent on itself, the mother country must at least try to increase their capacity for production, even at times to her own disadvantage.

Austria did not act in this way towards Hungary. The Hungarian wine trade suffered severely in order that wine-growing might obtain a footing in Austria. The export of Hungarian corn and wool, even to Austria, was restricted by the imposition of heavy duties. In a word, Austria desired to develop, not only her own industry and commerce, but even her agriculture, to the prejudice of Hungary.

Her treatment of Hungary was not that of a mother country towards its colony, but of a jealous guardian entrusted with the care of a young ward of exceptional promise and intent on making the best use of his rapidly dwindling power. At the same time, Hungary did not comply in every respect with the conditions of a colony, she had an industry of her own which the mother country was now engaged in annihilating. In the work of colonisation, where such had taken place, the inhabitants and enterprise of North-West Hungary had had quite as large a share as had those of the Hereditary Provinces. Consequently, in economic respects, the position of Hungary was even worse than that of a colony.

The above sketch, almost involuntarily, displays the economic conditions of Hungary at this period to have been colonial, primitive, and in the earliest stage of development. But side by side with this new economic system, which seemed incapable of opposing serious resistance to Austria, there stood an old social system based on the traditions of a great historic past.

---

[1] Roscher, *Kolonien*, pp. 257—259. See also Beer, G. L., *Commercial Policy of England towards the American Colonies*, New York, 1893, for many other instances.

CHAPTER II.

THE SOCIAL SYSTEM.

THE settlement of the Magyars in Hungary (900) heralded the conclusion of the age of general migrations. To this settlement, to the occupation of the land, has been traced the formation and organisation of Hungarian, as of every other medieval, society. Many changes took place, new elements were built up on the older foundations of national life; but the essential features of society remained the same. In the assignment of social status, the important point continued to be whether the family in question belonged to the conquerors or conquered—other considerations being the district from which it came and the nationality to which it belonged. If distinctions of this sort were not maintained by descent or origin, they were established by a legal fiction. The conceptions of possession and right, if not every legal possession and claim whatever, were firmly rooted in the fact of conquest.

All over Europe, the Middle Ages were the period of the development of large orders or classes which organised themselves to defend their own interests, and in their struggle for predominance transformed the whole system of national life. The first and prevailing conceptions were not those of a State or even of a nation; men thought rather of establishing a nobility, a hierarchy or a *bourgeoisie*. These different conceptions, worked out to the minutest details, have, alike in their conflicts and in their connections with one another, completely permeated the life of the individuals belonging to these respective orders, and still form the basis of the social life of the European States.

The opening of the modern age was characterised by the fact that individual rulers or despots, inspired for the most part by classical traditions, ceased to attach themselves to the interests of one particular class or order, and sought to make their own persons the centre of power. The predominant factors of the Middle Ages—the Church, the chivalry, and the *bourgeoisie*—very soon lost their former exclusive authority. They were replaced by the modern State, whose strong, unified, and centralised government was preparing to assume and to perform their duties. The political importance of the several classes and orders declined in proportion as this conception of a unified State gained ground among the individuals composing each society. Tried by this test, the history of Hungary in the eighteenth century appears still purely medieval. The organising force did not yet reside in the State; the old society, constituted as a result of the conquest and the later conversion to Christianity, was still in existence; in its whole and in its parts it formed a complete unity, its one object being its own welfare, to which it subordinated everything else in the country. The importance of Joseph II in the history of the world consists in the fact that he represented the conception of the unified State, which perceived a disavowal of its own existence in the privileges, restraints and classes of medieval society. As its representative, he fought strenuously against the organisation that had previously predominated in his dominions, and sought the overthrow of the older Hungarian society as one of the principal objects in his life. His defeat was the greatest misfortune which he experienced, and the fact that his principles were carried out by other men and by other means, renders his failure all the more tragical.

The modern State developed out of the medieval, either in the form of an unlimited monarchy or as the result of a popular revolution. While the latter was based on customs and on written laws that were everywhere different, the former was ruled by abstract principles that were everywhere the same. The historical aspect of the struggle between these two forms of State, therefore, depends upon the extent to which the constitutional law and practice—developed by the several nations and countries—came into conflict with the new, universal principles. From this point of view then we must consider the condition, in which the Emperor Joseph II found Hungary on his accession in 1780, as medieval and as the work of great social forces that had predominated in that country for eight hundred years.

As in the case of every nation in Europe, here too, in the Middle Ages, national life consisted of two principal elements— of the nobility, who looked upon the king as their head, and of the Church, which was a part of God's kingdom on earth. The peculiar individuality of the Hungarian nation will at once become evident, if we investigate the activity and the achievements of these two orders, which predominated all over Europe. We must examine their internal organisation, as well as their efforts to organise or to control the other classes in the Hungarian State. But, before going further, we must emphasise the fact that both the nobility and the Church had been deeply affected by the developments of the Renascence and the Reformation, and that, for both alike, the eighteenth century was rather an age of restoration than one of peaceful and undisturbed rule.

I. *The Nobility.*

In the case of most nations of Europe, the origin of a hereditary noble order, privileged to bear arms and to exercise political rights, is generally traced to the act of conquest. The law of arms decided the question, the conquerors became the nobility, and the masses of the conquered were degraded to the position of serfs[1].

So far as the nations of Western Europe are concerned, the conquering nobility very soon became welded into one with the conquered serfs, at least as regards speech. Within a few centuries, the only distinction between Lombard and Italian, Frank and Gaul, Norman and Saxon, became one of class. In

---

[1] In England, "the nobles of this country are descended from the Normans, while the middle classes are the children of the Saxons." In France, "the advocates of the older system appeal to the never obsolete right of conquest, which conquest divided the nation into conquerors and conquered." Thierry, Augustin, *Conquête de l'Angleterre*, p. 803. Prévost-Paradol, *Essais sur l'Histoire Universelle*, vol. II. p. 478. Here, naturally enough, the important point is, not so much how the nobility came into existence, as how that nobility itself explained its origin.

Germany and Poland there never was any distinction in point of speech or origin, and it is here that we discern the first essential difference between the Hungarian nobility and those of other countries. The conquering Magyar nation remained distinct from the others in point of speech and manners. It was rather the equality that was ended, to the prejudice of its weaker and poorer members. Many of the Magyars ceased to belong to the privileged class, although—according to the old chronicle whose authenticity there is scarcely any reason to doubt—all were originally equally noble and free, as descended from the same father and mother, and as having all migrated from Scythia. On the other hand, following the custom in vogue among the Christian peoples of Western Europe, the kings endowed many foreigners also with the rights of nobility, who thus became members of the Magyar nation.

The Croatian nobility, in particular, occupied an important position among these latter. This nobility was also a member of the *Sacra Corona* and, by virtue of its noble rank, was directly Magyar[1]. Hungarian legal authorities have defined the admission of foreigners by saying that besides "natives" (*nativi*), foreigners too (*indigenae*) received Hungarian "citizenship" (*civitas*)[2].

Yet the Hungarian nobility remained essentially the same as it had ever been—the old free Magyardom. Every member of it, however great might be the differences in point of wealth and authority, was possessed of the same fundamental rights. The latter were not those of a medieval nobility, but the remnants of an ancestral public liberty[3]. Until the middle of

---

[1] Act LXI of 1741: "Praefatorum Regnorum Regno Hungariae adnexorum filii nativi, sub denominatione Hungarorum, quoad officia et beneficia Ecclesiastica et secularia, etiam complectantur." v. *Representatio Statuum et Ordinum Croatiae, Dalmatiae et Sclavoniae* (Varasd., July, 1773. Arch. *cons. locumten.*). Cp. *infra*, p. 110, n. 2.

[2] Ürményi, *Jus Publ.* ch. 4, § 2.

[3] Verböczi's *Jus* (I. 9) enumerates the four cardinal privileges of Hungarian nobles. 1. To pay no taxes and to owe service only in arms. 2. To have free ownership of their own domains. 3. To be subject to nobody except to the legally crowned king. 4. To have the power of offering legal resistance even to the king if he should attack the liberties and privileges warranted by the *Aurea Bulla* of Andreas II (1222). This 'jus resistendi' was abrogated by Art. 7 of the Law of 1687.

the thirteenth century, the name given to freemen in Hungary was *serviens*, i.e. a servant bearing arms. The title *nemes* (noble) did not become general until after the invasion of the Tartars (1241). The letters patent of the last kings of the Árpád dynasty which granted nobility, raised the person in question and his family to the rank of *serviens*, and endowed him with *aurea libertas*. Consequently it was not a question of privilege, but of liberation from servitude.

Just as the other aristocracies of Europe, this nobility too was in reality nothing more or less than an army encamped on the soil: only in Hungary a whole nation, not a privileged class, retained its military character. That is the reason why, during the reigns of the Arpád and Angevin kings, Hungary was in all probability able to put a larger army in the field than any other State in Europe.

Anyone qualified for, and able to undertake military service was more or less entitled to participate in the rights of the Hungarian nation. The unbroken succession of life and death struggles did not permit the Hungarian nobles to isolate themselves as did the other aristocracies. This fact accounts for the admission into the ranks of freemen of the Székelys in older days, and of the Cumanians after the Tartar invasion (1241). For the same reason, during the Turkish wars (1526–1718), others also were admitted as nobles: such as numbers of *hajdus*, i.e. the common soldiers serving under Bocskay (1606); inhabitants of certain privileged districts; and large numbers of people who were ennobled without grant of land (*donatio*). (These last were called *armalistae*, in Germany *Briefadel* as they had nothing but a bit of parchment to prove their nobility.)

As a consequence, the Hungarian nobility was a very numerous one. According to the census of 1787, there were more than 75,000 noble families, a number far in excess of that of the German, French or English nobility[1]. It is easy, there-

---

[1] According to Taine, the number of noble families in France in 1789 was not more than 26,000 or 28,000 ; and the population of France at that period was four times as large as that of Hungary. In 1806 the nobility of the whole of Prussia—the home of the "junkers"—did not comprise more than 20,000 families. On the other hand, at the same period, Prussian Poland alone contained 25,000 noble families. Cf. Zedlitz, *Preuss. Adelslexikon*, 1836.

fore, to explain why the nobles of those countries refused to regard the nobles of Hungary as their equals in rank, or as knights. For in those countries the nobility was in fact a privileged class, every member of which, at any rate in theory, was able to trace the ennoblement of his family back to some feat of arms by one of his ancestors. In Hungary, on the other hand, not only was that nobility esteemed most, which derived its right of possession from the common act of conquest[1], but the most important privileges were shared, not only by individuals, but by whole parishes or corporations, in many cases by whole districts or groups. In our opinion, this fact constitutes the fundamental difference between the Hungarian nobles and those of the other countries of Europe. Everywhere else the nobility was nothing more or less than a predominant class, in Hungary it was practically the ruling nation itself.

This fact had another consequence. In the history of other European countries, the feudal nobility disturbed the unity of nations and caused the disunion of whole countries; in Hungary the nobility helped to weld the country together and to preserve its unity. In other cases, the royal power, the representative of national unity, had to struggle against the particularising privileges of the nobles; in Hungary, the nobles were the most submissive servants of the national kings.

However, Hungary was so deeply influenced by the general currents of thought prevailing all over Europe, that none of her institutions were able to develop undisturbed and upon purely natural lines, and all had to struggle against the influence of general European conceptions. Consequently the privileged feudal nobility, which became predominant everywhere in the twelfth and thirteenth centuries, of necessity made its appearance also in Hungary. As early as 1146 we find traces of it in the victorious campaign of Geyza II against the Germans[2]. What Hungarians call the banderial system was nothing more or less than the feudal levy of Western Europe[3]. However, the system

[1] We find a certain measure of similarity on this point in the case of the present nobility of England, the chief pride of which is to be able to trace an ancestor among the Norman conquerors who came to England in 1066.

[2] Otto Frising., *Gesta Frid. Imper.* I. 32.

[3] The barons were obliged by law to go to war when summoned, together with

of public liberty was maintained side by side with it for a considerable time. Consequently, while all over Europe feudal levies or mercenary armies were fighting, Hungary had still a national army as well. This circumstance alone can explain the magnificent character of the wars of the fourteenth, fifteenth and sixteenth centuries.

Francis Salamon has explained how far the disaster at Mohács (1526) contributed to the rise of the new feudalised aristocracy. In our opinion, however, the advent of the latter was due not only to the greater danger caused by the Turkish conquest, which rendered local defence imperative, but more particularly to the fact that the nation at this period came under the rule of a foreign king.

During the whole of the older history of Hungary, the gentry had constituted the army of her kings. But the Habsburg House, which now acceded to power in Hungary, put its chief reliance in the magnates there, just as in its other Provinces. The great historical families of Hungary began to develop their power in the sixteenth century. Formerly, greatness could be acquired by royal favour or by national services. The names of the Garays, the Ujlakys and the Báthorys were familiar to everybody. But hitherto we may say that such cases had been quite exceptional[1]. It was only now that it became the rule that one half of the nobility should be continuously superior to the other in point of rank and authority; and it was not by mere chance that the hitherto almost unknown titles of count and hereditary baron now began to be frequent.

It was due to Verböczi's *Tripartitum* or Code of Hungarian Law, which was much influenced by the codifications of Western Europe, that this new aristocracy now became more completely separated from the serfs than the older order had been. In fact, it was this new class, the magnates, who really carried

their tenants or soldiers under their flag (*Banderium*). *Banderia* were also possessed by the king, the Palatine and the Bishops. This did not, of course, exclude the summoning of the nation or whole people in arms. The *banderium* corresponds to the English feudal levy, the latter or *generalis insurrectio* to the *fyrd*.

[1] Of importance in this respect is Act XXII of 1498, which ordained the maintenance of *banderia*. It is not the family or estate which is burdened, but ndividual magnates, designated by name.

on the war against the Turks. The gentry, on the other hand, who had not so many family and political interests at stake in the Turkish wars, took up arms rather against the Germans than against the Turks. Naturally there were many exceptions, for instance there were numerous families of gentry in the Trans-Danubian district. Yet for the most part there can be no disputing the assertion that the credit for the glorious border-struggles is due, first and foremost, to the great magnates, not to the warriors recruited from the gentry. It is not our business here to investigate the causes; for our purpose it is enough to establish the fact. The Zrinyis, Batthyánys, Pálffys, Eszterházys are everywhere to be found in the van. The district flanking the Tisza, where the older free gentry were most numerous, did not distinguish itself in the wars against the Turks after Dobó's time (1552). The political and military activity of this district and of the gentry as a whole was absorbed by other objects, by their struggles for the maintenance of the constitution and of liberty of conscience.

When the conception of an absolute kingly power first made its appearance, the royalist magnates had to choose between two alternatives. After the conspiracy of Wesselényi and the bloody end of Peter Zrinyi, Nádasdy and Frangepán (1671), there could be no longer any doubt that, when obliged to choose between conflicting duties, the Hungarian magnates preferred patriotism to subservience to the king. Though a late offshoot of the Hungarian nobility, they too clearly betray the fact that they were purely national in origin.

The Hungarian nobles were not merely predominant as were those of other countries, whose power was after all restricted by the Crown, by the Church, and by the *bourgeoisie*. In Hungary the nobility embraced everything, and imbued everything with its own spirit. Moreover, the services, to which it owed its position, were far greater and more exclusive than those of any other nobility in Europe.

It is true that, in every age and every country, the chief services rendered by the nobility, indeed those to which their very existence was due, have been military ones. But even here there was a difference between the Hungarian nobility and those of other countries. Elsewhere the magnates waged war for their own ends, oftener to the prejudice, than in defence, of the unity of the nation; in Hungary the nobility actually staked their property and lives to maintain the integrity of their country and their nation.

We must admit that the Hungarian nobility became divided against itself, according to whether the Turks or the Germans were regarded as the more likely to prejudice its rights and to endanger the welfare of the nation. But, as everyone knows and admits, even this disunion was occasioned by patriotic motives. Every letter of Hungarian history proves that the pro-Turkish party and the pro-German party in reality had one and the same object in view, viz. to secure the existence of the Hungarian nation.

Elsewhere it was the king who united the nation, and it was to the anointed sovereign that appeal was made for the redress of all grievances; in Hungary the kings were foreigners for a considerable period after the death of Matthias Corvinus (1490). Justifiably or not, it was always to be feared that, in the interests of his unlimited power, the king would confiscate the privileges of the nobility and destroy the liberty of the nation. Here, too, the nation must be identified with the nobility.

The other countries of Europe were fortunate enough to possess the remains of an older Roman town life or else to develop a *bourgeoisie* that very soon sprang into existence on similar lines. In Hungary, too, a *bourgeois* element arose— the towns were fostered by her kings, endowed with national privileges and given a species of representation in the national assembly. With few exceptions, however, the towns were the homes of German foreigners, maintaining a separate existence not only as a class but also as a nationality. Another peculiar misfortune was that it was just the characteristically Hungarian (Magyar) towns of the Lowlands (Alföld)—Pest, Szeged, Temesvár, Pécs, Buda—that were destroyed by the Turkish conquest. Those towns which survived subsequently took the side of the king rather than of the nation. Even had they remained national in character, in these centuries of unbroken warfare their peaceful character and occupation would have made their importance far less than that of the warlike nobility.

In other countries, the Church and its hierarchy constituted one of the chief antagonists of feudalism. It organised the whole country, upon its own lines, just as feudalism did. In Hungary, after the disaster at Mohács (1526), the hierarchy was unable to hold its own against the nobility, for the same reasons as prevented the towns from doing so. Not only was this the case, but the very foundations of its existence were shaken by the Reformation, which was making rapid progress in the greater part of the kingdom. Where the Catholic hierarchy succeeded in holding its own and in maintaining its property, power, and influence, it formed an integral part of the nobility. That the Church, as the lords spiritual, formed an estate of the realm, not differing essentially from that of the lords temporal in respect of public law, has always been a fact upon which Hungarian legists have laid stress[1].

The Hungarian nobility, therefore, had to organise, constitute, and maintain the government of the country under the greatest possible difficulties. In this work, they received very little aid— and that little of a dubious character—from either king or *bourgeoisie*. The blood shed on every field of battle and on the ramparts of every frontier-fortress was that of the nobility. It was the nobility that defended the rights and laws of the nation in Parliament. Finally, all that was done in the interests of culture and literature during the Turkish wars (1526–1718) is connected with the names of nobles. Balassa, Zrinyi, Koháry, the military leaders and heroes of the age, were at the same time its poets or its literary representatives. These two centuries of Hungarian history correspond in practically every respect to the "age of chivalry" of all the other nations of Europe[2].

It would be rash to say that the Hungarian nobility had

---

[1] Ürményi (*Jus Publ.*, Museum MS.) does indeed treat of the Church as a separate estate (*status*) but emphasises the fact that it was really only a part of the nobility.

[2] *Tripartitum*, I. 2: "*Quod tam Personae spirituales quam saeculares una eadem- que libertate utantur.* Et quamvis personae spirituales (medio quarum salutem humanam Dominus et Salvator noster administrari voluit) personis saecularibus digniores habentur, tamen omnes Domini Praelati et ecclesiarum Rectores ac Barones et caeteri magnates, atque Nobiles et Proceres Regni hujus Hungariae ratione nobilitatis et bonorum temporalium una eademque libertatis, exemptionis et im- munitatis Praerogativa gaudent, *nec habet Dominorum aliquis majus, nec nobilis quispiam minus de libertate.*"

declined in 1780. A bare generation separated the latter year from 1741, when the *posse comitatus* of Hungarian nobles had proved the mainstay alike of the nation and of the dynasty in the wars of the Austrian Succession. The army of the nobility had not yet ceased to exist. Even during the short war of 1778–79, the Hungarian magnates and counties had come to the aid of their king in the old way, without any Parliament being summoned. The nobles were still the apostles of Hungarian literature, the muse of Baron Orczi and his followers was characteristically aristocratic. The measures, taken by the Parliaments of 1741, 1751 and 1765, were precisely similar to those of a hundred years before. There was a development, not a decline of the power of the nobles. As we have seen, the *bourgeoisie*—the only rival that might have proved dangerous—had of recent years rather diminished in importance.

The other elements of the medieval state were present in Hungary too, just as in the other European countries, but the nobility always maintained its position as the factor responsible for the most important services. Consequently, anyone belonging to the nation (i.e. anyone possessed of any rights or privileges whatever—for, according to the legal conceptions of the Middle Ages, those who possessed no rights or privileges were not members of the nation[1]) could not enjoy his position as such unless he could establish a certain connection with the nobility. The King of Hungary was the head of the *Sacra Corona*, the members of which were the nobles, who derived their privileges from this fact[2]. As fictitious persons, the royal free boroughs possessed the privileges of nobles[3]. Also, we have seen that, as a political corporation, the Hungarian Church formed in every respect a part of the nobility.

[1] *Tripartitum*, II. 4: "Nomine autem et appellatione populi hoc in loco intellige: solummodo Dominos Praelatos, Barones, et alios Magnates, atque quoslibet Nobiles, sed non ignobiles." Here the term corresponds to the Roman patrician "populus." In Hungary too the non-nobles were "plebs."

[2] Ürményi, *Jus Publ.* ch. 11, § 1: "Corporis hujus politici, in jurisdictione Sacrae Coronae coadunatae Caput est Rex, membra vero Regni Nobiles." The *Sacra Corona* was in this aspect a corporation, of which all nobles individually, and certain free boroughs collectively, were members.

[3] Ürményi, *ibid.* ch. 15, § 2: "Liberae igitur et Regiae Civitates qua Communitates consideratae jure Nobilitati gaudent"; and cf. Niczky, *Staatskenntniss*, ch. 11.

Consequently, in its whole organisation, Hungarian society was a society of nobles. It contained, indeed, the other constituent elements of society—burgesses, peasants, and a hierarchy— but as a result of its political organisation the nobility was the predominant element. Moreover, another point, in which the Hungarian noble society differed from that of other countries in Europe, is that there nowhere existed so close a relation between the legal nation (i.e. that part of the nation possessing rights incorporated by law) and the nation as a whole (i.e. including all grades of society).

One of the last eminent historians of the French Revolution enumerates three great powers (the nobility, the Church, and the kingship) as existing in France before 1789, and explains their respective privileges by the services each had rendered to the State[1]. Judged by this test, the claims of the Hungarian nobility to reward can vie with those of the nobility of any country.

From a legal point of view, the Hungarian nobility did actually reap their reward in the laws. The whole country was composed of noble estates. In 1741 their exemption from taxation was secured practically for all time. Without the consent of the nobles no law could be passed, no constitutional change made. Further, in the field of the administration of justice, no noble could be judged except by a court of nobles; and the nobility possessed innumerable means of legal redress.

From the fourteenth century onwards, the several constituent elements of the Hungarian polity and society had, as we know, never been allowed to pursue an evolution that was natural and uninterrupted. The process of regular development was always being disturbed by some outside influence. Consequently the security of many laws relating to the Hungarian nobility was already fictitious rather than real. While Hungary was still passing through its age of chivalry, the theory of absolute kingship gained ground all over Europe and very soon made its influence felt in Hungary also. However, the advantages granted to the nobility, as a reward for their services to the nation, were still manifold and important.

[1] Taine, *La France contemporaine*, vol. I. pp. 4—10.

II.

The first and most direct advantage, accruing to the Hungarian magnates from the conquests made, was an enormous increase of their estates. It is true that the former owners or the patriots, who had more recently rendered signal services, did not receive back the whole of the conquered territory. The royal Treasury, by the help of the *neoacquistica commissio*, retained a considerable proportion of it. The leaders of the victorious foreign hosts, even the army contractors, could not be entirely excluded from a share in the spoil. The services rendered to the dynasty by numerous German princes and prelates of the Holy Roman Empire were rewarded by the presentation of estates in Hungary[1]. Yet many square miles of the reconquered territory—estates equal in extent to German principalities—were awarded to Hungarian nobles like the Grassalkovics, Jankovics, Festetics and Fekete families. Besides these, the estates of the older families of distinction, though they may have decreased in extent, yet owing to the relief from the constant dangers prevailing hitherto, they showed an enormous increase in value and revenues produced.

According to the statement of a Hungarian noble, the yearly income of Prince Eszterházy, the richest of the Hungarian magnates, exceeded 700,000 florins[2]. The value of the residuary estate of Count Louis Batthyány, the Count Palatine, left by him in 1765, was estimated at 9 millions, his yearly income at 450,000 florins. The yearly incomes of two other magnates exceeded 300,000 florins, the incomes of four others were over 200,000, and of four others again, over 150,000 florins[3]. According to the same authority, there were many nobles with

[1] The Treasury retained the greater part of the "Banat," and of the counties of Arad, Csanád, and Bács. Among the foreign generals who acquired landed property in Hungary was Prince Eugene of Savoy. Finally, the Hungarian estates of the Schönborn, Trautson, Limburg-Styrum, Eltz families etc. came to them from their German relatives in the Holy Roman Empire.

[2] G. E. v. R. (Gedeon Edler von Ráda = Gedeon Ráday?) in Bernouilli's collection of travels (vol. IX. p. 237).

[3] Of these the wealthiest were the Grassalkovics, Pálffy, Koháry, Károlyi, Erdödy and Festetics families.

fortunes of 50,000—60,000 florins. The yearly income of Count Czobor (who died the last of his line in 1741, and whose unparalleled extravagance threw him deeply into debt), was estimated at 1,000,000 florins. Any of these sums represented enormous wealth for a country where a bushel of wheat was to be had for half a florin, where the price of a pound of meat ranged between 1½ and 4 kreuzers, and where the serfs were all doing service in socage.

The magnate families were not only rich, they all occupied positions of distinction and enjoyed a monopoly of the chief offices in the State. In the eighteenth century the office of Count Palatine (the highest official after the King) was filled in turn by an Eszterházy, by two Pálffys, and by a Batthyány. The importance of this office was upheld by the laws, which aimed rather at increasing, than at curtailing, its prerogatives[1]. The Count Palatine was still the direct representative (Statt-halter) of the King, the *generalissimo* of the forces of the country, and the granter of benefices, though his former personal power was now restricted by the *consilium locumtenentiale*, by the King's Bench and by the military commander[2]. The same leading families monopolised the offices of Lord Chief Justice, Ban (Governor of Croatia) and Treasurer, all relics of the aristocratic republic of the Middle Ages, for which a place could hardly be found in the organisation of the modern State. After having been for a considerable time filled by a prelate, according to a medieval custom, the important office of the Chancellor was henceforth without exception held by temporal magnates[3]. The latter were the guardians of the Crown, the members of the King's Council and the leaders of the army[4]. When she established a new knightly order (St Stephen's Order, 1764), the Queen had especial regard to the magnates, from whose ranks even the majority of the bishops were recruited. By right of birth, they were all personally members of the national assembly: in

[1] Acts IX and XX of 1741.
[2] Niczky, *Staatskenntniss*, ch. 9.
[3] Nominally the Primate was the Lord High Chancellor.
[4] Among the latter we find, in the reign of Maria Teresa, an Eszterházy, a Pálffy, a Batthyány, a Károlyi, a Nádasdy, a Szécsenyi, an Erdödy, a Festetics, an Andrássy, etc. The guardians of the Crown are special officials of high dignity in Hungary.

fact those who were prevented from attending, women as well
as men, had the right of sending substitutes to represent them.
Though these substitutes could not vote, their mere presence
proved the intimate connection existing between the persons
whom they represented and the legislature of the State. Serving
as they did the interests of Crown and country alike, the magnates
won the gratitude and affection of both monarch and nation—
the ability to attain which is the surest token of a genuine
aristocracy[1].

Not only were the magnates the exclusive representatives of
the country at their own and foreign Courts, but they acted as
the personal substitutes of the King everywhere in the land.
They were the high sheriffs of the counties, and this sphere
of their authority was actually extended during the reign of
Maria Teresa, for the Queen took the initiative in depriving
ecclesiastical dignitaries of secular offices. The office of high
sheriff in each county, where it was not hereditary, was held
for life; and, though not out of the question, it was quite
exceptional for one of the gentry to rise to that dignity[2].

We see therefore that the magnates in Hungary were not
only the ruling class, both by the letter of the law and in
appearance, but that they actually fulfilled all the conditions
of such a class. In point of property and income they could
compete with ruling princes; their qualifications and education
enabled them to distinguish themselves in military and civil
offices alike, and they endeavoured, by their deeds and their
whole lives, to render themselves worthy of that to which
their birth had predestined them—pre-eminence at Court, in
the army, and in the Council of the State.

Yet, during the reign of Maria Teresa (1740–80), we cannot
fail to observe certain signs of a decadence of their political
power, or, at any rate, of the imminence of such a decadence.

---

[1] "Ye Magnates of Transylvania and our dear fatherland of Hungary, on whom,
as on a pillar, all the hopes and the happiness of our Hungarian people rest," are the
words addressed by the poet David Szabó de Barót to the Magnates (*Paraszti
Majorság*, Pozsony and Kassa, 1779, p. 4).

[2] Niczky, *Staatskenntniss*, ch. 9. Several counties had hereditary high sheriffs,
and the Illésházy family actually had the hereditary right to that office in two counties.

In the first place, Acts VII and IX of 1715 had already extended the *crimen laesae majestatis* to refer to the taking up of arms against the King, and to extend punishment beyond the offenders themselves, and to condemn their whole families to a forfeiture of their property. Hereby the Hungarian magnates were deprived of a means of protecting their own privileges and the rights of their country, to which they had often resorted during the seventeenth century. We cannot assert that this measure endangered the existence of the nobility as such, but there can be no doubt that it restricted the policy of the several magnate families to much narrower limits than those they had possessed in the sixteenth and seventeenth centuries.

In the second place, it was part of the King's policy to raise men belonging to the gentry to a position of wealth and dignity equal to that of the older and more prominent families of magnates. In this manner a kind of aristocracy of office rose into being side by side with the aristocracy of birth. In the nature of things, the members of this new aristocracy (a species of *novi homines*) owed their distinction primarily to the offices they held ; and in this manner the King's service was as it were set up in opposition to the personal and family authority derived from descent from an ancient and famous house[1].

In the third place, by constant residence in Vienna or in the neighbourhood of the Court, by having their sons educated in such surroundings, and by intermarriage with the leading Austrian families[2], the Hungarian magnates began to lose that strong national sentiment which had previously been their distinguishing feature. Though not yet an accomplished fact, we see the day approaching when the Hungarian aristocrats considered their national tongue and manners as strange and foreign[3]. The fact that they represented not merely a privileged

---

[1] According to the notes of a well-informed writer (Mus. Germ. 4°, 460) compiled in 1780 or in 1781, "hat die Selige Frau (3) dem hohen Adel unterdrückt und dem mittlern erhöhet als Grassalkovics, Fekete, Brunszvick, Bruckenthal, Jankovics, diese zu gefährlichsten Commissionen gebraucht."

[2] *Ibid.* "(2) Heirathen mit deutschen Familien betreffend." The first families to take this course were the Eszterházys, the Pálffys and the Batthyánys.

[3] As early as 1764, the Parliament found fault with a Count Erdödy for wearing German garb (*Mus. Jank. Coll.*).

class but the whole nation, had always constituted the mainstay and the surest foundation of the authority of the nobility in opposition to the kingly power. Now the nobility itself began to be disloyal to its own traditions. That Hungarian aristocracy —which had been a military one for so many centuries, and in the course of the eighteenth century had been transformed into an official and governing class—now assumed the character of a Court nobility. Personal service in the immediate neighbourhood of the monarch at Vienna now became their chief ambition, supplanting in importance their duty (a duty which their birth should have obliged them to undertake) towards the country for which their ancestors had lived and died. They undertook the task of governing the country in the offices conferred on them by their sovereign. With this fact, however, the fourth and most important symptom—the economic decadence of the Hungarian magnates—is most closely connected.

The legislative system of Hungary had indeed protected the property of the nobility against every political or legal danger ; but no legislature has the power to provide that the expenditure shall not exceed the receipts. The law of aviticity (which secured the possessions of the noble families (1351)), a number of other more or less calculated legislative measures, above all the fact that in Hungary persons not of noble birth could not possess landed property, protected the estates of the Hungarian magnates, whether they were ancestral or recently acquired. The continual increase of colonisation and of foreign trade added to their revenues. The deficiency of the means of communication and the decline of industry, together with the abundance and cheapness of labour and of food-stuffs, made it practically impossible for the magnates to spend their whole incomes, so long as they stayed in their own country. On Hungarian soil, like Antaeus, the nobles could not but derive fresh strength from mother earth.

Once on foreign soil this advantage ceased, and the strength derived from it was gone. In Vienna the Hungarians exchanged the simple and healthy enjoyments of their homes for the extravagances of a Court life on a high level of culture and civilization. In Court society they could not wear their ancestral costumes (which, though representing a value of thousands of florins, were often centuries old), but were compelled to adopt the dress of fashionable Europe. Their ancestral estates were unable to supply the wants of their owners who lived on foreign soil. As many, if not more, servants were required where everything had to be bought for money, whereas at home everything had been provided by the soil and had cost next to nothing. The somewhat vulgar but comparatively cheap pleasures of the table were replaced by the Court entertainments, balls, games and the like, which, though more refined and aristocratic, were far more expensive[1]. In scientific phraseology, as regarded expenditure the Hungarian aristocracy acted on the principles of capitalists with fixed revenues, whereas their incomes were entirely dependent upon the annual produce of the soil. If we add that the conditions of credit and borrowing were exceedingly severe[2], and that, owing to the peculiar economic conditions of Hungary, a single bad year was often sufficient to compel even the wealthiest landowner in the country to raise a loan, it is quite evident that residence at the Court of Vienna must have threatened the financial position of even the most eminent and the most wealthy Hungarian families.

Yet it was no easy matter, during the reign of a sovereign like Maria Teresa, for any family to avoid such a course, unless it chose to allow its ancestral fame and glory to rust within the bastions of an ancient castle. Family pride required that Hungarian magnates should take part in the entertainments and service of the Court, side by side with the Bohemian and German aristocracy. It was here only that they could acquire those administrative and military qualifications, which enabled them to serve their country and their sovereign in positions of increasing dignity. If they desired their sons to be properly brought up, their futures to be secured and due provision to be made for their daughters, they might well place them where they could be educated side by side with the sovereign's children, and

[1] An exhaustive description of these latter is to be found in the verses and letters of Baron Orczic (cp. pp. 86–7) and Barcsay, *passim*.

[2] As to what these conditions were, even 50 years later, see Count Stephen Széchenyi's *Hitel* (Credit).

where the gracious Queen took an almost exaggerated motherly interest in their welfare and herself guided them in the choice of a career[1]. The splendour, the pomp, the easy and enjoyable vanities of Court life acted as a dangerous enticement to the weaker vessels, while the undoubtedly superior culture, the numerous family and political ends and interests, that could be served by remaining at Court, exercised a similar influence on those who possessed strong wills and more serious minds.

Finally, it was imperative for the Hungarian aristocrats to arrange a *rapprochement* with their sovereign, not only in their own personal interests, but in those of their whole country as well. The nobility was still one with the nation. As the lord and monarch of several nations of this character, the Habsburg ruler would undoubtedly bestow his favours on each, in proportion to the readiness displayed by the several nobilities to serve him. Consequently no kind of service was purely personal, no methods were mean or despicable, every adroit step taken or service rendered might prove of advantage, not only to the individual, but to the nation as a whole. The age we are treating of was one in which it was extremely difficult to distinguish between the monarch and the State. Maria Teresa was everywhere a gracious mistress, to the Hungarians she was absolutely a benevolent mother, and the other aristocracies regarded the activity and advancement of the Hungarian nobility with a certain feeling of jealousy.

Besides the "common" Court at Vienna, there had been a kind of "branch" Court composed of Hungarian nobles at Pozsony since 1766, where Mary Christina, the daughter, and Prince Albert of Saxe-Teschen, the son-in-law of the Queen, resided in the royal castle. In her instructions to her daughter, Maria Teresa practically revealed her own Court policy. The greatest complaisance and indulgence, an almost motherly solicitude, are seen united to a jealous pride in her royal dignity and splendour. The Hungarian nobility were attracted to Vienna by a combination of those causes which turned the

---

[1] Notes referred to above (Mus. Germ. 4°, 460) : "(1) Im Betreff der Sitten hat die Selige Frau den ungarischen Adel nach Wienne in das Teresianum und Emanuelische Stift durch verschiedene Verheissungen gelockt."

old nobility of France, whose pride and independence were as great as those of Hungary, into the obedient dependants of Louis XIV at Versailles. In France, indeed, the King too was national, more so than the nobles themselves, but the Hungarian Court nobility failed in their endeavour (1741) to persuade their ruler to reside permanently in Hungary and to attach her to the nation. Yet they did accomplish the patriotic task of winning the sympathies of the "common" monarch for their country, though residing in a foreign capital, and despite the rivalry of the aristocrats of the neighbouring State. The enormity of the historical crime of the Hungarian aristocracy is that they ruined themselves financially in Vienna, and, by thus losing their independence, deprived their nation of one of its principal supports. But their offence is considerably lessened by the fact that, though they dwelt on foreign soil and adopted foreign manners, their chief desire was always to serve the interests of their own country.

Consequently, whether for personal or political reasons, the Hungarian aristocrats spent the greater part of their lives in Vienna, where they educated their children and married into foreign families. As, however, the practice of the Court required that they should spend part of the year on their country estates whenever they returned to Hungary, their example continually induced their compatriots to adopt the foreign style of living.

As we have seen, the Hungarian magnates began to build their palaces, gardens and pleasure resorts in the reign of King Charles III (1711–40). Naturally enough, during the reign of Maria Teresa, the building of such places increased on an enormous scale[1]. The only palace which astonished travellers

[1] According to a calculation of mine which is by no means exhaustive, 219 castles and manor-houses were built in Hungary during the reign of Maria Teresa. Of Count Louis Batthyány, the last Count Palatine of Hungary not of royal blood, Francis Galgóczi (*Batthyányi L. emlékezete*, p. 33), in bidding him farewell, speaks in the following terms : " Amid all the bustle of his life he desired to adorn his native land with superbly beautiful buildings. A magnificent spectacle is offered now by the castle of Körmend, so wonderfully built, so finely furnished and so richly ornamented by him, that everyone who sees it is overcome with admiration : it challenges comparison with any other building of the kind to be found in any foreign country whatsoever. The superb castle which he built merely to serve as a halting-place during his journey up and down the country, is an ornament to Bicske and fit to

could compare to the mansion of Eszterháza was that of Versailles[1]. The sovereigns, members of the royal family, and the
ambassadors of the great foreign Courts honoured it by visits
that were almost annual. Though not so splendid as Eszterháza
the castles of Cseklész, Királyfalva, Köpcsény, Ivánka, Nagy-
Czenk, others near Pozsony and Sopron, and those of Ozora,
Gödöllö, Szent-Antal, Keszthely, and others farther inland,
challenged comparison with the finest ones to be found in
foreign countries. These too were honoured by visits from
the sovereigns, from members of the ruling dynasty, and from
distinguished foreigners. During the summer and autumn
months they became, as it were, the suburbs of Vienna.
Clothes, servants, furniture and the like, all had to be such
as were to be found in Court circles, for the traditional hospitality and the pride of the Hungarians could not permit of
the foreign guests having to forego one tittle of their accustomed
comfort. In the interests of the good name of Hungary, the
magnates were practically compelled to adorn their residences—
often placed in the centre of a large estate, or in a spot where
labour could only be obtained at great cost—with a pomp and
luxury surpassing that in vogue among persons of equal rank
elsewhere[2].

The traditional and anecdotal history, so much in vogue in
Hungary, is particularly fond of dealing with the process of
transformation by which the older national chivalry of Hungary
adopted the culture of the Court, and of Europe in general,
and renounced Hungarian customs. Here too the older world
struggled hard against the new. The fight between national
customs and universal foreign culture was not confined to

serve as a permanent residence for any dignitary. What a beautiful house he erected
in Buda, so fine indeed that it might serve as a symbol of that town! Here too, in
Pozsony, he had a large stately summer-residence built, and, in addition, he had a
pleasure garden laid out, not so much for his own delectation as that others also might
take the air and enjoy themselves."

[1] Bernouilli, *Reisen*, vol. IX. p. 281.

[2] All accounts of the splendour of the Hungarian aristocrats agree so completely,
and that splendour is so absolutely in conformity with the general conditions, that we
cannot attribute any degree of authenticity to the observation made by the county of
Pozsony (Chanc. Arch. No. 1117 (1784)) that "Status etiam magnatum majori nunc
cum parsimonia quam antehac conditionis suae decorum tuetur."

Hungary alone. During the whole course of the eighteenth century, the invasion of French manners and culture affected Germany quite as deeply as the Court of Vienna influenced Hungary. Towards the close of the seventeenth century, England too had had to pass through a similar experience; the great Russian poets of the nineteenth century have described the course of a similar struggle in their country, where it also began with the eighteenth century; and wherever a more developed and more universal culture came in contact with an isolated national culture, we find traces of the same state of things. The only elements of this attractive foreign culture which the nations in question most readily adopted, were those which it involved no mental or moral effort to imitate, i.e. externals rather than essentials. Hence, as a natural result, such a crisis was always attended by an increased laxity of morals. In Hungary the older culture was vindicated, not merely by the authority due to its age and by its national peculiarities, but by the belief that the adoption of the newer culture necessarily involved moral decadence[1]. The gentry, brought up to respect "Kurucz" traditions (traditions of the Rákóczi War), ostentatiously wore Hungarian costumes as a protest, while their distinguishing characteristics were long forelocks (reaching sometimes to the ankle!) large pipes and—rudeness. Paul Ányos, the greatest Hungarian poet of the day, describes his detestation of the foreign customs in the following terms:

"Morality favours not perfumed handkerchiefs,
Dainty dresses and neck-kerchiefs.
Veils, large silver buttons and leopard skins
Are more in accord with Hungarian wishes[2]."

The diffusion of a foreign culture is generally attended by the political preponderance of the nation from which it originated, and is consequently all the more likely to produce a national

[1] Cf. the satirical verses written against the new fashion of keeping mistresses (*Jank. Coll.* vol. III.). The change in the whole style of living and, in particular, the economic consequences of the new customs have been characteristically described by a poem of 1764, composed, according to an authority of the eighteenth century, by Baron Ladislas Amadé. The whole is to be found in the Appendix IV. (*Speculum moderni temporis*).

[2] *A régi magyar viseletröl* (*Of the old Hungarian costumes*), dedicated to the noble youths of Nagy-Szombat (1782), p. 41.

reaction. The propagation of French culture all over Europe was preceded and facilitated by the age of Louis XIV. Previously, during the days of the Spanish hegemony, Spanish culture exercised a similar though a less influence. Even the conquests of the entirely foreign Turks were accompanied by the adoption of many elements of Turkish civilization in Eastern Europe. In Hungary the reaction was not so much against the foreign nation—for the Court culture of the eighteenth century was just as little German as it was Hungarian—as against the Viennese Court itself and its foreign politics; in fact, the anti-German tendencies in Hungary were merely a side-issue. By the adoption of the foreign culture, a large proportion of the Hungarian aristocrats became economically so entirely dependent on the Court, that they lost their former power of determined resistance in national and constitutional respects.

According to the notes, to which we have previously referred, a feature of the reign of Maria Teresa was the considerable expenditure incurred by the Hungarian magnates on journeys between Vienna and Pozsony[1]. To the best of my knowledge, no Hungarian authority accuses the Queen of consciously aiming at their financial ruin. The opinions expressed by foreign authorities are different. An extremely clear-sighted and clever traveller, whose only defect is that he is too fond of fault-finding, describes the relations between the Hungarian noblemen and the Court at Vienna in the following terms[2]:

"The proud Hungarians, who on their country estates were engaged in planning schemes of liberty, have been allured to the Court or to town. By the grant of dignities, titles, and offers of marriage, and in other ways, every opportunity has been given them of spending their money in splendour, of contracting debts, and of throwing themselves on the mercy of the sovereign when their estates have been sequestrated. Thus enticed away from their homes, the Hungarians have thought it an honour to form connections by marriage with

---

[1] "O. p. Ohnentbehrliche Depensen zwischen Wien und Pressburg." The remarks refer to the vice-regal court at Pozsony.

[2] *Briefe eines reisenden Franzosen*, vol. I. pp. 477 *seq*. These letters were, as a matter of fact, written by a Swiss of the name of Casper Risbeck.

some of the great German families, whose authority at Court and whose influence on the affairs of the whole monarchy is altogether greater than that of the Hungarians. By wedding women from Vienna they have limited their own freedom of action, and their foreign wives, by introducing more refined customs and a higher standard of comfort into their new homes, have done all in their power to bring about sequestration. The whole aristocracy of Hungary is now related to that of Vienna, and these alliances have served to propagate the so-called fine manners, which have exhausted the resources of the Hungarians and made them the slaves of the Court. There is scarcely a single prominent family in Hungary which is free from debt, and, following the example of their Viennese compeers, the Hungarian nobles take particular pride in their debts. Having thus converted the most powerful part of the Hungarian nobility into spendthrifts, debauchees, and cowards, the Court has no longer occasion to fear a revolt. The extravagance, which the Hungarians have been induced to practise, has bound them by other and stronger ties to the Court. The quest of offices is no longer a question of honour. They have been induced by the attractions of pay to sacrifice part of their freedom, in order to be able to meet the enormous increase of their expenditure. Another master-stroke—aimed at weakening the national spirit of the Hungarian nobles—has consisted in putting up their privileges for sale, in facilitating the acquirement of Hungarian estates by German families, or in directly bestowing on the latter those Hungarian properties which had devolved on the Crown[1]. The wealthiest nobility of Hungary now includes numerous German families, which serve to increase the influence of the Court in that country. The two nations are being welded into one, their manners are being assimilated, and the indifference of the Hungarians to their privileges grows

---

[1] According to the *Almanach von Ungarn* (1778), the number of Hungarian houses of magnates was 108—two being princely, the members of the others being counts (82) and barons (24). The figures relating to foreign families which had acquired property in Hungary were 18, 69 and 160 respectively (the latter including nobles of a rank inferior to that of baron). N.B. It must not be forgotten that, in Hungary, every member of a noble house (both male and female) bears the title of that house, e.g. every son of a count is a count, every daughter a countess, etc.

as the number of those participating in the same increases, while
their indifference to the fate of their country advances as her
individuality is effaced[1]."

This is the opinion of Risbeck, a foreigner. In general, the
facts adduced, though naturally exaggerated, are true enough.
But we have no right to accuse the Government, and still less
the Queen, of having consciously provoked such a state of things.
The charges here made are the same as had continually been
brought against every Court in Europe, ever since the days when
Charlemagne had endeavoured to concentrate the aristocracy
of his whole empire in one single Court. The consequences of
a policy of centralisation develop so naturally that it is quite
unnecessary even to suppose that they are consciously provoked,
and the only reason why they were particularly evident in this
case was probably due to the fact that the Viennese Court was
the sole factor in the work of centralisation. No doubt the
system followed by the Queen and other monarchs did jealously
guard and enhance the prestige of the throne, but it would be
mere slander even to hint that they deliberately employed any
such double-edged weapons.

There is a further exaggeration in Risbeck's account of the
financial embarrassments of the nobility. There were traces of
such even at the opening of Maria Teresa's reign, but it did
not become a general feature during her days[2]. It would be
an indiscretion to say more. But there can be no doubt that

[1] Similar charges are to be found in various passages of St Simon's work on the
Court of Louis XIV. Among other things, the Duke accuses the great monarch of
being only too pleased if the grand seigneurs ruined themselves by gambling, for the
help which he rendered on such occasions only served to enhance his power and
graciousness.

[2] On June 19, 1745, Count John Pálffy, the Count Palatine, wrote to Count Louis
Batthyány from Pozsony in the following terms : " The great nobles who reside here
are head over ears in debt. I myself am paying interest on 500,000 florins." Cp.
Speculum mod. temp. (in Appendix IV.) :

> "Nunc debita crescunt, deficit crumena,
> Quae fuit utcunque vivo Patre plena,
> Plures namque fiunt per diem expensae
> Quam solvere possit pagus toto mense."

In 1785 Prince Nicholas Eszterházy, in consequence of the extravagance of his son
Antal, begged for the appointment of a sequestrator, for he feared that, when the
latter succeeded to his inheritance, he would put an end to the wealth of the family.
Chanc. Arch. No. 9426 (July 26, 1785).

the Eszterházys, Pálffys, Batthyánys, Károlyis, Grassalkovicses, and members of other prominent families, were able to fill important public offices and display a large measure of pomp without looking for any pecuniary reward. Those members of eminent families who during this period (1740–80) held high offices of State, were quite capable of defraying, out of their own revenues, the expenses connected therewith. In fact, as we have seen, the Hungarian nobility supported their sovereign with voluntary grants of money for raising troops in war-time, not only in 1741, but in all the subsequent wars—for the last time actually in 1778–79.

We must not leave out of account military service either: for though it opened the way to the highest distinctions, its financial results, in consequence of the *esprit de corps* then in vogue among military officers, could not fail to encourage the contracting of debts.

In our opinion, it was not the payment attached to offices which proved the principal means of increasing the financial dependence of the magnates on the Court. The leading families of Hungary did not so much need an increase of revenue as cheap and secure conditions of credit, and they could obtain loans of the dimensions required from the Government only.

Out of the funds raised from the Jesuit properties secularised in 1773, Maria Teresa gave loans to the extent of nine million florins to magnates who had fallen into debt[1]. The debtors, for the most part, paid an annual interest of 4 °/₀. On April 24, 1781, Joseph II decreed that these debts should be repaid[2]. According to a statement issued by the Royal Chancellery, the amount placed in Hungary alone was 2,765,400 florins. Of this sum a considerable proportion was indeed in the hands of commoners[3], but the majority of it had been employed to adjust the financial affairs of the magnates. The principle that induced the Emperor to decree that the capital thus invested

[1] Report of the Venetian ambassador dated Sept. 1, 1781 (State Archives in Vienna).

[2] Chanc. Arch. No. 2922 (1781). Imperial Rescript.

[3] One of the debtors was actually a Jew (Moses Oesterreicher, of O-Buda), who had received a loan of 3000 florins. List of debtors in Chanc. Arch. No. 4474 (1781).

in loans should be recalled, was that it was undignified on the part of the State to act as the creditor of its subjects[1].

On April 30, the Hungarian Chancellor replied expressing the desire that the existing state of things should be maintained. In no case could the Hungarian nobility pay, for some families owed several millions to foreign creditors. The measure would benefit only the Viennese bankers, who would thus obtain the bills of the Hungarian gentlemen. The Chancellery, on the contrary, recommended that a further sum of several million florins should be advanced to Hungary, in order that the industry and agriculture of the country might be furthered by the aid of cheap loans. Even the Venetian ambassador was of opinion that the measure would be difficult of execution. One of the chief debtors, Prince Schwarzenberg, had indeed repaid 600,000 florins, having obtained a loan elsewhere, but the others would not find it so easy to negotiate cheap loans.

The Emperor adhered to his decision, and out of the capital used for loans (of which as much as 2,313,883 florins was still in the hands of private individuals in 1782, all but 1,673,249 florins had been recalled by the close of 1783)[2]. By that time the policy of the Emperor had found other means to assert itself, and was no longer dependent on paltry subterfuges of this kind[3].

To recapitulate, in 1780 the Hungarian aristocracy were still in full possession of their estates, and had a practical monopoly of the chief military and civil offices, and were enabled to maintain this pre-eminence not only because of their descent and of the services rendered by their ancestors, but by reason of their own superior culture and ability. If there ever were real "lords" in Hungary, it was the aristocrats of the eighteenth century who deserved that title[4].

[1] "Weil es sich für den Staat nicht schickt, aktiv Kapitalien bei seinen Unterthanen zu haben."

[2] According to the annual returns of 1784 (Chanc. Arch.). Those who returned the whole capital borrowed, included a Count Batthyány, Count Cziráky, Szirmay, Zay, etc. I would only remark that comparatively large sums were in the hands of *indigenae* (foreigners who had obtained property in Hungary).

[3] Chanc. Arch. No. 3808 (1786).

[4] The point is, of course, that the title of lord and distinctions between the different ranks of nobility were always something of an exotic in Hungary; v. *infra*.

We are, however, face to face with the first symptoms of those evils which subsequently deprived the Hungarian aristocracy of this pre-eminence. On the one hand, a certain barrier separated them from the bulk of the nation : on the other hand, the change in economic conditions had rendered them more or less dependent on the Court at Vienna. We must, however, lay stress on the fact that this tendency was merely in the germ, it had not fully developed, nor was its influence as yet very perceptible.

III. *The Gentry.*

"Happy is the noble who has 5000 *livres* a year and does not know me," was a favourite *mot* of Henry IV, the darling King of the French nobility. In 1780 there were many happy men of this description in Hungary, and these happy men composed the nucleus of the Gentry.

As we have seen, the letter of the old Hungarian law recognised no distinction between magnates and gentry. "The portion of liberty belonging to the magnates is no greater, nor that of the gentry less." It was not until the accession of the Habsburg dynasty (1526) that the barrier separating the aristocracy from the other nobles began to assume any importance. The fundamental privilege of the estates of the realm was the right to partake in the sittings and debates of the national assembly[1]. In this respect, at the time when the "Hármas Könyv" (*Tripartitum*) was composed, there was no distinction made between the members of the gentry and the magnates. The estates were summoned *viritim* by Ferdinand I to the coronation Parliament of 1563[2].

During the first century of the rule of the Austrian dynasty, the creation of hereditary earldoms and baronies, and the appointment of hereditary high sheriffs, on the Western, and particularly on the German, model gradually developed into

---

[1] Ürményi, *Jus Publ.*, ch. 11, § 2: "Censentur autem inter Status et Ordines omnes, qui jure suffragii in Comitiis Regni et jure territoriali respectu bonorum per se possessorum, gaudent."

[2] Fraknói, M., *Orsz. Emlékek.* vol. IV. p. 405, 406. (*Acta Diaetalia.*)

a custom. The first statute of the Parliament that sat after the coronation of 1608 was actually responsible for separating the gentry from the magnates, describing them as a separate order, just as it did the prelacy or the royal free boroughs. This measure put an end to the primitive system of assemblies, to which, in theory, every noble had the right to be personally summoned. From the point of view of general historical conceptions, the privileged class now became separated from the freemen. Just as the magnates were now distinguished from the gentry by their receipt of a personal summons to attend parliament, so, lower in the scale, the exemption from taxation formed the barrier of distinction and the main bulwark of the privileges of the nobility. Act VI of 1723, while maintaining the exemption from taxation of the nobility, decreed that the *armalistae*, who had received the rank of nobles without royal donation, should be bound to pay local rates[1]. There is no contradiction to this measure in Act XIX of 1751, by which the Queen granted an exemption from taxes for life to those *armalistae*, who had taken part in the last war at their own expense. It was in conformity with the general development of institutions in Europe that the gentry also should have their privileges more sharply defined than those of the general body of the nation, which, though free, possessed no power.

Yet, apart from personal participation in the debates of Parliament, there were no further political distinctions as yet between magnates and gentry. They were both alike exempt from taxation, both had serfs under them, both were entitled to exercise jurisdiction and obliged to do military service. Each could aspire and attain to high offices of State, including that of Count Palatine, and it was rather the question of title, than of rights or property, that distinguished the aristocrats from the wealthy members of the gentry[2].

However, though the difference in point of political rights

---

[1] "Armalistae—conscientiose, juxta Comitatuum ideam, pro domesticis Comitatuum necessitatibus taxabuntur."

[2] Ürményi (ch. 14, § 26) is unable to discover any other difference than that the office of "commissariatus Director" could be filled by a magnate only. Niczky directly emphasises the fact that even the office of Count Palatine was open to members of the gentry.

was trifling, the difference in the manner of exercising these rights was extremely obvious and significant. As we have seen, during the reign of Maria Teresa the magnates made the Court the centre of their activity. They were attracted thither alike by political and religious feeling, and by family interest. The wealthier members of the Hungarian gentry, on the other hand, for the most part kept aloof from the Court during this whole period, living at home and working for their counties and their house. As a consequence, while the financial position of the magnates was weakened and their independence thereby endangered, the wealth of the gentry, resting on a firmer basis, was continually increasing and their economic position constantly improving, a result which steadily increased their importance as a class in the control of the affairs of the country. In fact, as we have already had occasion to point out, owing to its colonisation and productive capacity, South-East Hungary (where the bulk of the gentry had their estates) developed much more rapidly than the North-West districts, which were owned by the magnates.

Several causes helped to differentiate the political status and ideas of the gentry from those of the magnates. Of these, undoubtedly the most important was that connected with religion. The counts and barons, for the most part, owed their promotions, and the favour shown them by the dynasty, to the services they had rendered to the cause of the Catholic Restoration; for the dynasty considered itself to be concerned in the triumph of the older religion. When, as a result of the powerful personality and persuasion of Peter Pázmány, the Hungarian magnates became Catholic[1], the enjoyment of the great Church dignities and estates bound them by an ever strengthening bond to that faith, which attached them to their sovereign and separated them from the great majority of the gentry. The predominant party among the gentry of the eighteenth century was devoted to Calvinism, but it owed its preeminence not so much to superior numbers, or to the extent of the property of its members, as to the fact that the latter represented the purest and most consistent

---

[1] In 1606 only three of the great families had remained constant to the Catholic faith.

development of all those features, which gave to their order its general and national significance.

The most important crisis in the life of the nobility of every country is the period when those conditions, which have determined its development and its part in national history, cease to exist. The existence and prosperity of the Hungarian nobility—as of other aristocracies—developed out of military service. The almost unceasing obligation to serve in the armies of the country had kept alive all those traits and characteristics which had given their privileged status to the nobility. Even in the eighteenth century no disarmament of the nobility was provided or enforced by the laws. Act VIII of 1715 (which legalised the standing army maintained by the King) at the same time contained regulations for the maintenance of a *posse comitatus* by the nobility. During the century there were many general levies of *posse comitatus* similar to that of 1741, which was raised in response to Maria Teresa's passionate appeal, and which, for the glory of its achievements, challenges comparison with any of its predecessors. But the country had ceased to be in a constant state of siege or invasion ; there had come an end to that exclusive devotion to military efficiency, which had dominated the whole life of the nobles and the whole period of the Turkish wars (1526–1718). By Act XII of 1723 evasion of the duty of serving in the *posse comitatus* was no longer to involve *Nota Infidelitatis*, i.e. loss of life and property, but merely an arbitrary punishment. All those in quest of military service could now join the standing or professional army, but the Hungarian gentry as a body devoted their energies to securing to themselves in time of peace that importance in the national life which they had formerly won by the sword in war. The King was antagonistic to the nation, or at least might easily become so ; the Court at Vienna was continually identifying itself more closely with the interests of the magnates ; and there was as yet no *bourgeoisie*, no culture, no organisation at all, outside the ranks of the nobility.

It was in the administration of the counties that the Hungarian gentry found themselves able to fulfil the new rôle assigned to them. In this connection we may mention the office of county-court judge (*táblabiró*) also, even though its inclusion involves a certain measure of anachronism. It is however the class, rather than the office, that is of importance, more especially the requirement that all holders of the office should belong to the more cultured, wealthier and more prominent gentry—a requirement just as essential in the eighteenth century as in 1847. To-day this fact must occasion a smile, more or less of ridicule; for the mere name of *táblabiró* in Hungary is now the incarnation of all that is conservative without principles, of all that is patriotic without sacrifice, or liberty-loving in spite of the oppression that was meted out to the serfs. But having come into existence and obtained their predominance, this class could not fail to render services to the nation during the period of its superiority, though later ages, in which other classes have performed the same services, have been unable to appreciate its merits. For a whole century this class exercised a powerful influence on the development of the national spirit of Hungary, and for that reason it will be necessary for us to treat of its functions in detail.

Ever since the days of the *Eupatridae* at Athens and of the patricians at Rome, the exercise of judicial functions, just as much as the bearing of arms, has been a most important duty of every aristocracy. Both military power and judicial functions have for their object the complete protection and security of property, and may lead to the acquirement of new rights. Therefore in the history of the medieval nobilities quite as much attention should be paid to the great days of assize as to the decisive battles.

In Hungary the administration of justice was not only the right, but the duty, of the nobility. King Sigismund inflicted fines on all who refused to undertake the office of county magistrate[1] (*szolgabiró, judex nobilium*). Act VII of 1478, considering this compulsion to be a kind of breach of privilege, restricted the measure to the more disorderly counties. However the royal courts, out of which, later on, the King's Bench

---

[1] *Sigismund. Decr.* VI. § 2. In 1435 the fine was 25 marks (100 ducats). In 1468 (Act IX) King Matthias Corvinus doubled the amount of the fine. The latter monarch introduced the system of trial by jury.

developed, were maintained intact and included sixteen members of the landed gentry who were skilled in legal lore[1]. The law itself proves that in this high office the chief qualification was not so much strictly legal proficiency as sober sense and experience of life. By the provisions of Act IV of 1507, anyone who refused to accept this office was sentenced to forfeit his property. And as the number of cases increased to an enormous extent in the counties, there were added to the sheriffs and the *judices nobilium*, other landed gentry, who helped in the administration of justice as "extraordinary assessors." The origin of this practice cannot, however, be definitely traced to any law. So far back as Andreas III's reign (1291), the laws mention the presence of King's men in the counties. In these we can recognise the forerunners of jurymen[2]. Act XXIV of 1613 summoned the counties to elect "extraordinary assessors." The number of the latter was not fixed, the only stipulation being that they should belong to prominent noble families. We do not know at what period these "extraordinary assessors" became "ordinary." There can be no doubt, however, that the institution took deep root. Act X of 1681, by which the King confirmed the privileges of the nobility, put this latter Act (XXIV of 1613)[3] on a level with the Decree of Andreas II, and with the *Tripartitum*, I. 9, etc. After all this we have no reason to be astonished that, at the opening of the eighteenth century, the office of *táblabiró* already existed everywhere, and that the privilege of filling these posts was reserved for the most prominent, most distinguished, and most learned members of the county nobility.

The general protraction of lawsuits was responsible for an increase of the influence of men of this stamp, skilled as they were in legal science and initiated into all kinds of business. The high sheriffs were for the most part absent. The sheriffs,

---

[1] "Ex Regnicolis Sedecim Nobiles potiores et praestantiores hujus Regni Jurisperiti : illi videlicet qui sapientia praesunt " (1459).

[2] Salamon, F., *Kisebb munkái (Minor Works)*, p. 239.

[3] The Act runs as follows : "Ut autem Justitiae administratio meliori modo possit procedere, ultra ordinarios Juratos Assessores, deligendi sunt per Comitatum et ex potioribus Nobilibus plures Assessores, qui ad Jurium administrationem juramento sint adstricti, iique Sedibus Judiciariis intersint."

county magistrates and other officials were exposed to the chances of the elections. In the sphere of county administration, where everything depended on the outcome of elections, the *táblabirák*, as holding office for life, represented the only element of stability, while at the same time the highest officials of the county were drawn from their ranks. Their sphere of activity was continually widening. During the period of the Turkish wars (1526–1718) the activity of the county gentry had been comparatively restricted, and the greater part of the work had been done by the magnates. The latter were now, for the most part, absent in Vienna, and military prowess was no longer required. The general condition of the country was unsettled, in particular the questions connected with the division and assignment of land. After the final expulsion of the Turks, the greater part of the land had returned to its former owners, but the claims of the various churches, municipalities, families, and individuals had to be investigated and the boundary-lines had to be drawn between the several properties. There were very few estates, indeed, which were not the objects of litigation. The public taxes introduced in 1715, the quartering and feeding of the standing army, all gave rise to trouble and to conflicts of interests. Here the knight's sword was of no avail to cut the knot, the labyrinthine forms prescribed by the laws and by older customs had to be followed, and, where the last offered no guidance, common sense had to solve the difficulty. In organising the Supreme Court of Appeal (*Curia*) and the King's Bench, the legislature of the eighteenth century reserved to the counties a sufficiently wide sphere of jurisdiction. According to Act XXVIII of 1715, the county courts were competent to try all criminal acts of violence, and further to deal with all cases relating to the distribution and inheritance of property situated in one and the same county, of cases of compensation, libel and calumny, of runaway servants and peasants, and of suits relating to demarcations, pledges and tithes. Act XXXV of 1729 actually extended the sphere of activity of these courts, adding to the list cases of debt (up to 12,000 florins) and cases referring to pledges of any amount whatsoever. All these cases were now to be tried by either the *judices nobilium* or the sheriff, or the county assembly (*sedria*) itself, and consequently the independence of the counties, in judicial matters, was still very considerable. There was not, indeed, any permanent county court of justice—that court sat once a month or once a quarter only; but the *judices nobilium*, the jurymen and the sheriffs were constantly sitting in judgment. The county bench (*megyei tábla*) itself—a fact dwelt upon by Ürményi—was chiefly engaged in criminal cases, civil suits being decided for the most part by the officials of the administration[1]. Other work for the counties was the fixing of prices for all articles of food and labour, and the control of the property of orphans. In contrast to the older military system, all these developments necessitated the influence of officials in the county government; in particular, it rendered paramount the landed gentry who formed the nucleus of local administration.

There was no lack of men able, as independent persons, to fulfil all these manifold duties. The various dangers, to which private property was exposed, were alone sufficient inducement to the landed gentry to study law; and those who were patriots were impelled to do so by the oft-renewed attempts to infringe, misinterpret, or invalidate the laws of the country. Considering the great lack of universities and colleges of a similar status, it would otherwise be practically impossible to explain the fact that the Hungarians were even then styled "a nation of lawyers." In a work of his, written while he was quite a young man, Count Christopher Niczky (who was afterwards the right hand of Joseph II in his attempt to overthrow the older judicial and administrative system of Hungary) considered the fact, that the nobility studied nothing but law, to be a sign of the backwardness of the nation[2]. In his opinion the cause of this state of things was the complicated nature of the law of property, which forced the nobles to study it and delayed progress in any other science. There can, however, be no doubt that this accurate and even many-sided investigation of Hungarian law

---

[1] Ürményi, *Jus Publ.* III. ch. 8, § 4. It was on the basis of these laws that the whole system of the administration of justice was explained by Nicholas Skerlecz to the Emperor in 1785 (15,241).

[2] *Staatskenntniss*, ch. 29.

was inspired not merely by private interests, but by public duty[1].

The age of national insurrections was, at the same time, one of arbitrary military despotism, and both came to an end simultaneously. Had the evolution in Hungary proceeded on the same lines as elsewhere in Europe, this age should have been followed by one of unlimited royal power. But, as we have seen, in Hungary an unlimited monarchy was out of the question, for the nation regarded its King as a foreigner, and was not inclined to sacrifice its own interests to those of the State. Consequently the King endeavoured to extend his power on the basis of his legal prerogatives. The efforts made to discover and demonstrate the legal basis of resistance to his endeavours were not merely dictated by party interests, with a view to safe-guarding the privileges of the nobility; they were in fact the germs of a great political movement.

The gentry, who lived for their families, estates and counties, were, as regards manners and customs, the upholders of the traditions of an older Hungary, consequently they were the ideal of patriotic writers[2]. In the aristocrats and high prelates they saw, not only more powerful rivals, but the ready servants and imitators of foreigners. The greater the pomp and power shown by the magnates, who basked in the sun of royal favour, the more closely did the gentry become connected with their neighbours in their own and in adjoining counties, who professed feelings and filled positions of distinction similar to their own.

---

[1] See "Grundbesitzverhältnisse in Ungarn um 1720." (A lecture of mine published in *Berlin Internationale Wochenschrift*, 1908.)

[2] Paul Ányos addresses the younger generation of the nobility in the following terms:

"You know, my friends, what feelings thrill us
When we still see among us an aged man
Whose face reminds us of the days gone by,
His whitening locks hanging loose.
If we look deep into his worthy soul,
We find no fault in his character.
Simply dressed, with cleanly neatness,
His life is temperate and truly pious.
Morality his chief aim,—not arrogance,
Resulting in sin and then in poverty."

(*A regi magyar viseletröl*, p. 41.)

The great political questions of Europe troubled them but little[1]. I believe there never has been another period in the history of Hungary when so-called "public opinion" was so indifferent to foreign powers[2]. However that may have been, tney watched every action of the high sheriff with the eyes of Argus, stopped every breach of law or statute, and checked the attempts of the bishops to extend their power and influence, as well as any excesses committed by the military in their forages for supplies. Every measure sent to them for execution by the *consilium locumtenentiale* was diligently examined by the gentry for any traces of a breach or infringement of the law, so that they might not become the unconscious instruments of carrying such into effect. They protested against any such infringements, for even the most primitive form of *State* must occasionally come into conflict with the medieval constitution; if their protests had no effect, they waited for the assembling of Parliament, where they could put forward their grievances and were at any rate able to unburden their hearts, even if they received no redress.

Such were the prominent members of the gentry, the *tábla-birák*, regarded from a political point of view. It would be incorrect to view them as State officials, as Joseph II did; for that would involve their condemnation on *a priori* grounds. They moved within narrow limits, they were familiar with the abuses of power and politics, not with their difficulties. In their administrative and judicial capacity, they were guided rather by common sense or the practices of centuries than by book-lore or by deeper conceptions, by the fundamental principles of the State or of humanity. But—and fortunately enough this remark applies to very numerous cases in Hungary—it was the man that was of importance, not science or institutions.

[1] Bessenyei, in his *Philosophus*, endeavoured to ridicule them on this account.

[2] Even in the case of Frederick the Great's attacks on Austria (1740 and later) there could be no talk of a general movement, especially if we consider the attitude of the Protestant gentry. The most popular of all foreign nations was the English (see Scypp-Lehmann, *Reise in Ungarn*, 1787); the least popular the Russian. Lehmann, Johann, *Reise von Pressburg nach Hermannstadt*, 1785: "Engländer sind in ganz Ungarn besonders willkommen. Die Ungarn haben vorzügliche Achtung gegen diese Nation."

In the first place, the *táblabiró*[1] was independent economically. The system of primitive economy was still predominant; very little was required beyond what was produced by the soil. Old Francis Bossányi may be taken as representative of the whole class. He was the grandfather of Francis Kazinczy—the regenerator of Hungarian literature—who described him not only as a real person but as a type of his class. "He lives in a thatched cottage constructed of loam[2]." He would not accept fees or presents from anybody; in fact, he lodged all those who made legal applications to him—servants, horses and all—throughout the duration of their suits. He cared but little about his property, his stud, his cattle, his sheep; he kept them for his pleasure, not for profit, and his herdsmen sent in their accounts at their leisure. His sheds were filled with corn, hay and straw, his cellar with wine, and his underground storehouses with food. In time of famine he preferred opening them to the needy, without demanding either bond or interest, to selling their contents to speculators. Winter and summer he wore clothes of the same colour. His son-in-law brought his betrothed a pair of cordovan leather boots as a wedding-gift, on his return from the Parliament of 1751. On the wedding-day he came on horse-back and took the young bride home in a coach-and-six, and in her new house the bride herself prepared the simple supper, consisting of a dish of lentils. The old man renounced his inheritance in the county of Nyitra, because his relatives, who lived there, offered less than he thought he "had a right to demand." He acted as commissary when the boundaries of the county of Máramaros were surveyed, but it was not till later, and in a moment of pecuniary embarrassment, that he spoke about the 2000 florins "fees" which he had earned but never taken[3]. "An example of the fact that there is such a thing

---

[1] This expression is here used, *anticipando*, as one generally familiar and characteristic of a particular class. It means one of the gentry marked out to be a county official alike by his wealth, family connections and intelligence. N.B. The class is collectively referred to as *táblabirák*.

[2] *Pályám Emlékezete* (*A Retrospect of my Career*), p. 4.

[3] A similar action was taken by the magistrates of the county of Pest who, between 1774 and 1778, refused to accept the increase of salary that had been allotted to them. Chanc. Arch. No. 10,874 (1785).

as mistaken goodness and careless magnanimity," remarks the writer, who in his old age also was obliged to work hard for a living, though he was the pride of a whole nation and the Nestor of its literature. However, without this carelessness and indifference in pecuniary matters, the age of the *táblabirák* is quite unintelligible. Social eminence was not due to wealth, which in a society of nobles could not give anyone a position. The only standard by which men could be judged was by their birth and by the honours each had won in the county administration.

In the county, the influence of Bossányi and his friend Gabriel Baranyi was unbounded. When the time came for the election of new officers, " Baranyi instructed the multitude to wait in dead silence for Bossányi to call out a name, and even if he made a mistake by chance, to acclaim it." " For," adds Kazinczy, " the multitude had still full confidence in their leaders, as they had never found that confidence to be abused." In that district, Bossányi was not the only man who commanded such a measure of respect. As early as 1735, at the time of Péró's rising, Count Erdödy, Bishop of Eger, wrote that the Calvinists of the district flanking the Tisza all submitted to the authority of Mr Borbély[1]. Later on, about 1750, a missionary friar declared that all the Protestants of the borders of the Tisza would become converts were they not prevented by the respect paid to one of their number[2]. In later days, the unrestricted influence of a Joseph Vay or a Louis Domokos in the same counties was known to everybody. In our opinion, the characteristic trait of the Hungarian nation is that, however suspicious and jealous of its rights, and however necessary it may consider the maintenance of its independence when dealing with foreigners, it is ever ready to obey and to follow the guidance of anyone, whom it recognises as a true patriot, in any direction likely to lead to the attainment of its ideals. The combination of these two traits explains why the Hungarian nation was able to preserve its integrity amid so many difficulties and vicissitudes. And, as we have seen, it

[1] Mus. fol. 168 m, dated Pozsony, May 9, 1735, and addressed to the Chancellor Count Louis Batthyány.
[2] Found in Krones' work (after notes by Rogács, a Jesuit of Ungvár), p. 78.

was precisely among the gentry that both these traits were most strongly in evidence. This fact accounts for the great moral influence of this order, which, however, was due not only to its wealth and extraction, but in particular to its intellectual attainments.

Judged by an absolute standard, the latter were undoubtedly none too great. Francis Kazinczy remarks of his grandfather that he was a terrible hand at swearing. Later on too, during the reign of Joseph II, very many complaints were lodged against the strong language and excesses of the *táblabirák* and county officials of the districts inhabited by the gentry, particularly of the county of Szabolcs. The purity of their domestic lives and of their morals also left much to be desired[1]. In their education at Sáros-Patak, Debreczen, or in the Jesuits' colleges, social gatherings were of far more importance than the curriculum of the teaching itself. Their refinement was strictly practical, and adapted to suit the events and changes of county life. They did not do much in the way of reading books, but they knew by heart the Bible, the *Tripartitum* (their Bible of the Law), and any other book that fell into their hands. No statistical knowledge, no physical science or aesthetic refinement was required, the only thing necessary was a ready tongue to cite paragraphs in refutation of the opposing royal lawyers of the *consilium locumtenentiale*, and occasionally, in Parliament, against the Court party, or to quote Scripture or the Fathers against the arguments of religious antagonists. Such a knowledge sufficed for the needs of the hour, and as a consequence, despite its restricted character, was the only means of obtaining honour and influence. Part of the Protestant nobility were particularly familiar with religious literature, in which they endeavoured to secure consolation and a solution of every possible problem[2]. But Protestant nobles of this type seem to have been in the minority.

"Merrie old England" is the title given to that country during the age of Elizabeth, and I believe that, since the time of Louis the Great (1342–82), the Hungarian nobles had never

---

[1] Cf. Anton Szirmay, *Pécsi István esete* (*The Case of Stephen Pécsi*), and Chanc. Arch. *passim.* There were many crimes of this kind dealt with in the courts.

[2] These latter included Kazinczy's father. Cf. *Pályám Emlékezete*, p. 13.

had so many merry days as during the reign of Maria Teresa (1740-80). A living record of this gay life is supplied by the numberless congratulatory verses (on the occasion of "name days" and *epithalamia*), for practically every gentleman's house had its own cringing "Court poet." But this poetry too betrays the coarse and sensual character of the taste of the age, and I believe the delight and pleasure occasioned by these verses, always recited and sometimes actually printed (which their authors ·hoped would secure them an immortal fame, and in which every sheriff was compared at the very least to Romulus, Árpád and Moses), to have been far less than the enjoyment of those anonymous efforts of vulgar lewdness (also still extant) which were written down in secret and passed on from hand to hand[1].

However, with the exception of scattered cases of unbridled passion or unscrupulous licence, domestic life—the true basis of every social development—was sound enough in Hungary. Whether due to the absence of a Court or to any other reason, it is the fact that there are very few countries where the disorganising influence of petticoat-rule was so little able to assert itself as in Hungary. "Proud, arrogant hearts can be won by humility only. Consequently, the prudent Hungarian mothers train their daughters to respect the men as far as possible. When they wed, their husbands learn to value them. In a word, the women of this people are very submissive. Hereby they appear to be innocent and modest, and this excellent trait of the fair sex makes them lovable and deserving of respect. This modesty of theirs, which is often exaggerated, actually prevails on them to speak but little in their husbands' presence, and even if they do venture to speak, they talk in very subdued tones. Besides, they are excellent housewives; and in this respect they fulfil their duty in an exemplary manner. They know very little about outward show or the use of cosmetics, and they trouble their husbands very little in that respect. Dresses are passed on from mother to daughter. The peasant women work hard. They dress neatly, though poorly; only their high boots do not

---

[1] Old Anton Szirmay was an enthusiastic collector of these latter. See Mus. MS. 4°, 720.

at all become their womanly limbs[1]." The same observer makes the military officers responsible for awakening a tendency to coquetry in the Hungarian women, and attributes to their influence the fact that the women acquired or allowed themselves greater liberty. But in other respects the older manners remained in force until the close of the century. The surest proof of this fact, and its natural consequence, was the strict training of children. "Nowhere have I seen children so obedient, so respectful to their parents, as those I saw in Hungary[2]."

Comparing the conditions in Hungary with those in vogue elsewhere in Europe, we must describe the gentry of the eighteenth century as knights, endowed with every virtue and cursed with every vice of the age of chivalry, except that they were not engaged in fighting. After a calm of half a century had still further lulled them to sleep, the famous insurrection of 1809 (against Napoleon) and the disastrous battle of Györ showed not only Europe, but the gentry as well, that the main foundation of their existence was a thing of the past, and that the administration of justice and the exercise of personal authority were after all but a superficial substitute for them.

In one respect, however, the *táblabiró* was not a knight, but a person able to win the sympathy even of the present age, viz. in the deep patriotism which possessed his whole life. In his naïve pride, his relations to his "noble" fatherland were at all times of the closest. Practically every act of his, every event or change in his life, reminded him of his fatherland and concentrated his attention upon it[3]. The influence exercised upon him on everyday occasions by his thoughts for his country— no mere empty phrase on his lips—is in reality an ancient trait of character reminiscent of the old days of Sparta and Rome[4].

---

[1] *Lettres sur les Hongrois*, pp. 53—55.

[2] *Freimütige Bemerkungen eines Ungars über seinen Vaterland* (1799).

[3] On this point it is sufficient to refer to the numerous congratulatory verses and other documents (Mus. Library). Among the printed ones are the verses of Orczi, Ányos and Bessenyei. Cf. the festal addresses of official personages, etc.

[4] When paying a visit to Francis Bossányi, Imre Péchy greeted the latter in the following terms: "I rejoice with all my heart to see that His Sacred Majesty God Almighty has been pleased to allow Your Honour to attain these days of rejoicing in sound health and a state of body gratifying to us all. God grant that Your Honour may live to pass many happy returns of this day in sound bodily health, together with

But we seem to see with our own eyes how the genuine expression of true feelings was doomed to turn into a meaningless phrase. The Hungarian noble of the eighteenth century was a member of the county corporation and of the "noble" country. In a narrower sphere the *county* (*comitatus spectabilis* or *tekintetes vármegye*) and, in a wider sphere, the *patria inclyta* (*fatherland* or *tekintetes Haza*)[1]—of which every county constituted a part, just as the noble was a part of the individual county—comprehended his whole life. What an advance Hungarian history had to make before Count Stephen Széchenyi dedicated a work of his to the *Majesty* of the country ("*felséges Haza*")[2]!

The county, and nothing else, was the unit and the motive-force of this older Hungary. Parliament rarely met, and it was still more rarely that the ever-present influence of the Crown favoured those ideas which interested the gentry. All that was really Hungarian, and a product of the peculiar spirit of the nation, was still to be found in the county. The moment that the military duties of the county administration— formerly its most important duty—had ceased, its administrative functions began; and, owing to the ever-increasing demands made by the State, these latter were constantly extending to fresh fields of action. In other countries, this was the age in which the growth of an army of royal officials began; in Hungary such a development was impossible, because the constitution and the national existence were still identical. Unless it desired to provoke a desperate and probably invincible resistance, the

your beloved family and relatives, for the good and to the delight of the public at large and of our *poor neglected fatherland.*" Francis Kazinczy, *Emlékiratai* (*Memoirs*), p. 17 (unpublished MS. 142 g, in Academy Libr.).

[1] This was practically the official title. When Galgóczi (*loc. cit.* pp. 35—37) had bidden farewell to the Count Palatine, Louis Batthyány, the latter took leave, first of His Majesty the Roman Emperor, Joseph II, then of his sovereign lady the Queen Maria Teresa and of their Hignesses the Princes of the House of Austria, and finally said : "I should be guilty of ingratitude were I not to bid farewell of thee, *Honourable Hungarian Fatherland* (*Tekintetes Magyar Haza*)." The expression "Fatherland" (*Haza*) was a collective one, standing for the nobility.

[2] *Spectabilis* was the title due to the official gentry (*alispán*=sheriff) ; *táblabiró* did not become general until later on. The title of the other gentry was *egregius*, *generosus*.

Felséges was the exclusive prerogative (as title) of the King.

State Government was still obliged to entrust the execution of its decrees and schemes for the most part to the county, which was the organ of the "estates." "The county is responsible for the administration of all political and judicial matters within its own territory[1]." Emphatic expression was thus always being given to the conception that the county was the country in miniature. The high sheriff and the county assembly (*congregatio*) everywhere conducted their own affairs in the same manner as the King and the national assembly (Parliament) did those of the country. Nor must we forget that this lower organism of the constitution was more perfectly developed than the higher one, and that, whereas Parliament only occasionally made its power felt, the influence of the county assembly was continuous.

This power of the county was exercised by its landed gentry in the *congregatio*[2]. "As Parliament discusses the propositions of the King, the county assembly debates the decrees which it receives. Nothing is to be followed out, or carried into effect, unless decided upon by the county assembly, either unanimously or by a majority of votes. And what the said assembly has decided upon cannot be altered without their approval[3]." The writer who thus extends the legal sphere of action of the county assembly was an adherent of the Court.

These general assemblies were summoned to meet from time to time by the high sheriff. They not only passed resolutions, but were responsible for electing the staff of county officials, who, however, had to be recruited from their own ranks. In the intervals between the several *congregationes*, these latter exercised the executive and judiciary powers. At the head of the staff was the sheriff, assisted in larger counties by a second sheriff; in addition, there were county advocates (*fiscales*) and notaries at headquarters, and magistrates and assessors in the various hundreds or subdivisions of the county. Naturally

---

[1] Ürményi, *Jus Publ.* III. ch. 5, § 3.

[2] *Es ist der grösste Fehler der Verfassung, dass alles durch General-Congregationen behandelt wurde.* Every county believed itself to be a country and its assembly to be a Parliament. Note by the Emperor Joseph II to No. 5996 (1785).

[3] Ürményi, *Jus Publ.* III. ch. 5, § 3.

enough these latter, as well as the *táblabirák*, belonged to the most prominent county families, otherwise they would have had trouble in carrying their decisions into effect—in fact that was the sole reason for their election. It would indeed have been difficult to conduct the affairs of the county without their assistance, for there was a great scarcity of county *hajdus* and hussars, who were the direct instruments of the executive power.

Even those, who at this period were adherents of the power of King and State, regarded the county as a sacred and inviolable institution. Its origin was traced to the Avar Khans of the eighth century, or at any rate to Saint Stephen[1]. "The county officials are the guardians of our internal security, the censors and judges of our morals; and in truth they provide us not only with our bread and our glory at home, but they are our protectors against foreign influences also." The only parallel to them in history is that offered by the censors at Rome, who proved the independent protectors of the old morals and laws against aggression from all quarters in much the same way. The *táblabirák* laboured at home, rising from the position of assessors, till they became acquainted with people and places, and, as they grew older, with the various cases. In most places they filled their offices not for payment but for the honour of the thing[2]. It is in these men that we get a true picture of the gentry at home.

The county offices were filled by election, and, consequently, any elected officer who desired to retain his position, was to a certain extent under obligations to those whom he controlled. The only officers who could boast of a greater measure of independence were the *táblabirák*, who were elected for life. However great we may consider the moral integrity and moral weight of the county nobility to have been, there can be no doubt that this drawback of the elective system was already noticeable[3]. The constitution not only encouraged a patriarchal

---

[1] Ürményi, *Jus Publ.* III. ch. 5, § 1.

[2] Reviczky, *Status Regni Hungariae*, close of vol. II.

[3] For these abuses cf. Chanc. Arch. for 1781. Many instances of the kind were offered by the counties of Borsod, Bereg and Fejér. The county of Zemplén in particular gave the Emperor many opportunities of showing his dissatisfaction with the conduct of its affairs. Cf. Chanc. Arch. No. 6856 (1782).

indulgence in dealing with persons of equal rank, but promoted the utmost indifference to the most important and most sacred interests in the treatment of inferiors.

At the elections themselves, personal authority and persuasion did not always carry so much weight as Kazinczy would have us believe (p. 138). More recent Hungarian writers date the commencement of canvassing and election abuses from the beginning of the nineteenth century. Then the policy pursued by the Government admitted the uneducated peasant-nobility to the council-chamber of the county, and began the intimidation and outvoting of the good old class of gentry[1]. But there can be no doubt that all these abuses had obtained a firm footing even in the eighteenth century, and were one of the causes which convinced Joseph II of the necessity of entirely overthrowing the county system. The custom of supplying electors with food and drink, and the use of violent measures, were already very general: and the Emperor Joseph himself has left us a powerfully drawn picture of an election[2].

The bad sides of the county administration were already very conspicuous. During 1782 the county of Hont condemned to death 115 gipsies (including women) suspected of cannibalism, an act which the Emperor never forgave. The sheriff of the county of Bereg, George Bessenyei, an uncle of the famous writer, oppressed the serfs with the burdens of taxation and compelled them to carry poultry, butter and other articles of food free of charge. All this was with the object of currying favour with the "administrator" Kapy[3]. It was a universal

---

[1] Horváth, Mihály, *Huszonöt év Magyarország történetéböl* (*Twenty-five Years of Hungarian History*), 1st ed. vol. I. pp. 26, 27.

[2] Chanc. Arch. No. 14,867 (1785). The Chancellor considered a reform feasible even if the elective system were maintained. The Emperor, however, thought otherwise. Honourable and clever men were by no means ready to expose themselves to the trials of an election where so much *Ungestümes* was practised. "*Oder wie sollte sich ein solcher, vollkommen ausgebildeter Mann damit abgeben den Tag vor der Congregation in den Wirtshäusern wo der Adel einkehrt herum zu gehen, und mittels Herbeischaffung von gebratenen und Cabusta* (cabbage) *dann mittels Hergebung einiger Flaschen alten Wein, Ausschmauchung einiger Pfeifen Tabak, Geduldung, ja Belobung alles Unsinns so allda geschwatzt wird, sich auf eine so widerwärtige und zugleich erniedrigende Art der Stimmen des grossen und stürmischen Haufens zu bewerben.* JOSEPH."

[3] Chanc. Arch. No. 6063 (1782).

custom to offer gifts of money to the commissioners present at installations of officials, and the money for that purpose naturally came from the pockets of the rate-paying masses[1]. We have already had occasion to refer to the negligence and even *mala fides* with which the King's decrees relating to the improvement of traffic and trade were carried out, or rather nullified. In addition, each investigation proved how carelessly or unscrupulously the county archives were used in the most important suits relating to property; and there were many instances of embezzlement in the management of public monies[2].

But the main charge—one which was continually recurring—was that the life of the common individual (i.e. of the serf) was of no value in the eyes of the gentry. As provided for by the older jurisdiction, either the manor court (which was endowed with the *jus gladii*) or the county court had the right of passing sentence of death on vassals. The above-mentioned case of the county of Hont (p. 145) acquired a regrettable notoriety, and all this took place subsequent to the royal decree dated March 30, 1778, which ordained that an appeal should be made to the King, wherever there were any doubts as to the justice of the death penalty[3]. In the county of Zala a murderer—who had stolen 300 florins from his victim—was impaled alive[4]. In the county of Bihar, in 1741, two highwaymen were put to the rack[5]. After the Government had resolved to put an end to the system of torture, the counties declared that it was impossible to maintain order without such means, particularly in the barbarian districts of the South-East; and even the Royal Chancellery recommended torture as a means of extorting confessions in exceptional cases[6].

There seemed, however, one way of making the county comply with the wishes of the central Government. The high sheriff was

---

[1] Chanc. Arch. No. 2001 (1785).

[2] *Ibid.* No. 11,517 (1784) and No. 12,010 (1785), referring to the counties of Borsod and Bereg.

[3] *Ibid.* No. 6076 (1782).

[4] Sárváry, Jakab, *A büntetésröl* (*Of Punishments*), p. 147.

[5] *Ibid.* p. 247.

[6] Krassó county archives, No. 1498 (1782). Report submitted by Chancellery No. 1538 (1782). Nevertheless, even a foreign writer says that "the policy of the counties in Hungary is vigilant, rigorous and unselfish." Lehmann, Johann, *Reise von Pressburg nach Hermannstadt*, 1785.

always appointed by the King—as was the administrator (who could easily be removed, in cases where there was no high sheriff for the moment in office). In fact, experiments were actually made without much success to employ these means of coercion. According to the instructions to high sheriffs issued in 1768 they were in fact to carry out intentions of Government[1]. Even within the limits prescribed by the constitution, the high sheriff was able to effect a good deal; to mention only one point, he nominated candidates for all offices in the county. But, as Maria Teresa had perceived, in the most important questions there were no differences between the high sheriff and the county nobility. Moreover, the high sheriff, being usually a *grand seigneur*—a magnate who did not trouble about matters of government—was merely concerned in keeping up appearances as a miniature king in the county where he held office. Nor could he even be compelled to reside constantly in its capital[2].

In 1780 the county system was still practically at its zenith, at any rate, it was the most powerful existing product of the social and political organisation of Hungary. Yet those faults which led to the later fall of the system, were already in evidence. As a deliberative, elective, and executive body with strictly class interests, the county assembly could have no higher motives. It preferred even the most insignificant interests of the privileged classes to national ones which, to all appearance, would not bring any direct advantage to the nobility. It already contained the germs of partisanship, of a system of canvassing, nepotism and corruption. It seemed as if all those factors which were reducing the ancestral system of administration to a level with barbarism—the foe of all culture and progress—had become rooted in its very being. The moment the reins of government fell into the hands of a party in whose eyes the chief consideration was the power of the State and the welfare of the people—not the interests of privileged classes and the letter of historical law—it was in the county that the new system met the most determined resistance. As regards internal politics, the reign of Joseph II is, therefore, to a great extent the age of the struggle against the counties.

[1] Chanc. Arch. No. 1783 (Nov. 21, 1768).   [2] *Ibid.* No. 13,206 (1784).

Yet, on the other hand, we must not forget that the county was the natural outcome and true product of the existing social order, and that, as a consequence, far-reaching and legitimate interests also contributed to the maintenance of a system in which they were themselves involved. Even if we admit that the leading gentry were short-sighted, biassed, corrupt and even ruthless—what other *Hungarian* element could have replaced them in the conduct of the administration? The serfs were still entirely illiterate, and their permanent settlement, so far as the greater part of the country was concerned, was of quite recent date. As for the *bourgeoisie,* their administration of the towns will be found to display the abuses of the county system without their redeeming qualities, and in addition they were poor, uneducated, and for the most part of foreign extraction. If we would be just and seek to understand the passionate devotion to the system as well as the equally vehement attacks to which it was subjected, we must admit that in the eighteenth century, before the culture and literature of Hungary had risen to any eminence, the county, as governed by the *táblabírák,* was the only practicable means of carrying on the government and administration of the country by any influence or by any officials not of foreign extraction.

IV.   *The Bourgeoisie and the Royal Free Boroughs.*

Scarcely had Maria Teresa breathed her last when a whole series of denunciations flowed in from towns all over the country —from Szeged, Kassa, Pozsony, Pest—complaining of the numerous abuses committed by the town councils and accusing them of wantonly spending, or of devoting to their own selfish purposes, the monies belonging to the citizens and, indirectly, to the State[1].

[1] Cf. the letter addressed by Janko, accountant of Szeged, to Prince Kaunitz, dated March 10, 1781 (Court Archives, Vienna). See also Hungarian National Archives, No. 1968 (1781).

It may be as well to remark that all the towns here described are royal free boroughs—to which the sovereign had granted charters of immunities and liberties in the usual medieval style, permitting them to administer justice, impose tolls and duties, and to elect their own officials. The inhabitants—at all events at first—were usually foreigners (*hospites*) and, for the most part, Germans.

Thus in the towns, as well as in the counties, the general conditions were anything but sound; in fact, we may definitely state that, at any rate during the reign of Joseph II (1780–90), the complaints against the councils of the royal free boroughs were even more numerous than those lodged against the officials and "congregations" of the counties. In the short period between 1780 and 1784, all or a considerable part of the councillors of numerous towns were either deprived of office on account of malversations or else bound over to refund from their own pockets the sums they had embezzled. The towns in question were Pozsony, Sopron, Pest, Kassa, Szakolcza, Pécs, Fehérvár, Körmöcz, Korpona, Köszeg and others[1]. Naturally there was an important and essential difference between the towns and the counties: for whereas in the former fraud or corruption were the crimes most generally in evidence, in the counties the abuses calling for redress and punishment were most frequently the arbitrary measures adopted by the officials. We can see, therefore, that in the towns there was little hope of regeneration, and it is a singular contrast to the state of things existing elsewhere that in Hungary the *bourgeois* element did nothing to encourage either order or thrift—a phenomenon of which we must proceed to investigate the causes.

In the first place, we must protest against the conception that regards municipalities in the Middle Ages as modern institutions directed by the masses. It is true that in France the *tiers état* became identified with the nation, but everywhere else—and in Hungary also—the order ruling in the towns was as much a privileged class as the nobility or the clergy. It resembled the latter, in being resolved to use the advantages of its position to the full. Moreover, the town-dwellers in Hungary —being aliens not only in language but also in nationality and in culture—were thus separated by a wide gulf from the population of the surrounding districts. To a certain extent

---

[1] In the town of Pozsony, large sums had been embezzled from the trust funds belonging to orphans (No. 6101 (1781)); in Sopron embezzlement had taken place (No. 444 (1782)); as in Körmöcz (Nos. 220, 221 (1781)): in Pécs there were cases of bribery (No. 1969 (1781)), etc. The Emperor (No. 8323 (1784)) removed the whole town council of Pest and ordered new elections to be held.

they actually bore the stamp of alien colonies, so great was the distance between them and the other inhabitants of the country. In the letters patent issued by King Bela IV to the people of Korpona in 1244, we find the declaration that the evidence of Magyars shall be of no avail against the townsmen[1]. In other towns in Upper Hungary that were mining settlements, the Magyars and Slovaks were excluded from all guild privileges[2]. Later on, after the schism in the Church had occurred, non-adherence to the Catholic faith became a similar obstacle to the acquirement of the rights of citizenship in most towns. Moreover, there was no absolute equality of rights even among inhabitants of the same town. "Those who merely possess citizens' sessions or live in the town only as μετοίκοι are excluded from all common benefits, their only concern with public affairs is that they are rate-payers and recognise the jurisdiction of the local council (*magistratus*)[3]."

In general, so far as government and administration was concerned, the same system prevailed in the towns as in the counties[4]. In the towns the magistrate or consul (the mayor) corresponded to the sheriff, and the town councillors to the *táblabirák* in the counties, being like them elected for life. The two councils to be found in every town were the smaller internal, and the larger external (common) council, similar in all respects to the "partial" and "general" assemblies of the counties. For instance, in the town of Pécs, the government

---

[1] Fejér, György, *Honi városaink* (*Our Hungarian Towns*), p. 47.

[2] E.g. at Löcse, in 1598. Cf. Hetényi, *Honi városaink*, p. 188. Schwartner (*Statistik*, 2nd ed. vol. I. p. 128) adduces many instances of the same. Similar measures were taken at Selmecz, Besztercze-Bánya, Nagy-Bánya and even to some extent at Buda too.

[3] Ürményi, *Jus Publ.* III. ch. 15, § 5. Cf. Szlemenics, *Magyar polgári törv.* (Hungarian Civil Law), I. p. 58. By citizens of royal free boroughs were meant, not all the inhabitants of the said towns, but only such of them as had been admitted to full citizenship as real members of the corporation by common consent of the council and citizens, and had taken the customary oath (burghers). The other inhabitants (*zsellér*)— for the most part artisans but not members of guilds—were subject to taxation and were compelled to give quarters to soldiers without however having the right to elect or to be elected. They could possess property, houses and gardens (city "sessions") and being freemen were under the jurisdiction of the town.

[4] *Ibid.* "Magistratus Civitatenses eodem paene rerum agendarum systemate, re-publico-politicas in gremio sui, si pauca excipiantur, quemadmodum comitatus intra jurisdictionis suae limites administrant."

of which was organised in 1780, there were ninety councillors—thirty of German, thirty of Hungarian (Magyar), and thirty of Rascian extraction. Each nationality had its own "tribune"; and no external (common) council was permitted by Government, as such might give rise to disturbances and nationalistic quarrels[1]. These corporations had both deliberative and elective functions. In the towns, however, the term of office was fixed at between one and two years, whereas in the counties new elections were as a rule only held every three years.

The chief differences existing between the two were the following: in the first place, the head of the town was not a high sheriff or other official nominated by the King, but always a chief magistrate who was an elected official[2]; in the second place, a special spokesman and representative of the external council, the *tribunus plebis* (called in the Hungarian (Magyar) towns *Fürmender = Vormund*, guardian), sat among the magistrates. These were the two features that gave the towns an apparently democratic character.

However, despite the fact that they possessed the main features of *municipia* and were not presided over by any official appointed by Government, the Hungarian towns never rivalled the counties and their elected sheriffs in resisting or repudiating the arbitrary measures of the sovereign. It is not the institution, but the spirit which it manifests, that is of importance; and, tried by such a test, the towns must be deemed to fail. They were lacking in one of the principal characteristics of democracy—viz., in ability or will to offer resistance to royal encroachments.

Further, despite the attractive title of *tribunus plebis*, there was no question of equality of rights in the towns themselves. Only members of a guild could obtain full citizenship of a town, and even the number of those entitled to the franchise on this basis was for the most part restricted[3]. The *inquilini*, as we

---

[1] Chanc. Arch. No. 1438 (1781), *Acclusa*.

[2] Confirmed by Acts XLI of 1681 and XXXVI of 1715.

[3] In Buda only three saddlers, in Komárom five barbers, in Pozsony only eight weavers, could obtain full citizenship. Cf. Hetényi, *loc. cit.* p. 189. *Inquilinus* means one who was an inhabitant of a village or town—but without political rights. He owned a house but possessed no land.

have seen, somewhat resembled the μετοίκοι of ancient Greece in not possessing any political rights and in having to bear the burdens of taxation. The journeymen were simply "exploited" by their masters, who made it practically impossible for them to become independent[1].

Like all other aristocracies, that of the towns also endeavoured to make itself hereditary. Consequently, in every town there were special tariffs of fees for admission to citizenship, according as the applicants were sons of full citizens, nobles or foreigners. The fee demanded of an *extraneus* was generally double that for the sons of citizens, and, judged by the value of money in those days, the fees for admission were by no means moderate[2]. The first and foremost point of view was that there should be no shortage in the food supply of the citizens already admitted. Naturally enough, these restrictions proved an obstacle in the way of settlement[3].

This public extortion in the towns was just as contradictory to the new principles of the Government at Vienna as was the selfishness of the landed proprietors to be met with in the counties. As the rights of citizenship constituted a kind of guarantee of subsistence, they acquired a veritable monetary value; and, as a consequence, in many places the custom obtained of selling the existing workshops and businesses at a price[4].

The *consilium locumtenentiale* ordered an investigation to be held; as early as 1780 it had decreed the annulling of monopolies and restrictions, with a view to encouraging trade and

1 The journeymen assisting the tailors in Fülek had to work from 2 a.m. till 9 p.m. The "working day" of the potters of Pozsony and Györ was from 4 a.m. till 7 p.m., that of the shoemakers of Galgócz from 3 a.m. till 9 p.m.—i.e. an average of from 15—19 hours. Even if there was a break in the work, as there naturally must have been, the strain was an enormous one. The same was the case elsewhere too, especially in Germany. Cf. Adam Smith, *Wealth of Nations* (1840), vol. III. p. 128.

2 One table from 1775 is to be found in Mus. Lat. fol. 306. Previously the fees had ranged between 13 and 26 florins : now they were reduced to 4—8 florins. The most expensive citizenship was that of Buda, Köszeg, Györ, Ujvidék, Pest, Pozsony, Sopron, Szeged, and Zágráb (Agram). It was comparatively cheap in the smaller towns.

3 E.g. in Szeged in 1775, of 21 new citizens 3 were *extranei*, in Debreczen of 109 actually only one was an *extraneus*.

4 Cf. Chanc. Arch. No. 1803 (1785).

promoting the growth of the population. It called upon the authorities, both in towns and counties, to declare whether there were any abuses of the kind still in vogue in their respective spheres of influence, and whether in their opinion such should continue to be tolerated or not.

The counties, as consumers of the goods supplied by the towns, declared generally in favour of free industry (i.e. advocated breaking down the system of guild privileges), and this view was most energetically supported by those counties in whose territories there were scarcely any towns, as Somogy, Bács, Máramaros, Bereg, Csongrád and others. The county of Liptó expressed a desire, not only to stop the abuses of monopoly, but to do away altogether with the guild system. It declared that the whole activity of the guilds consisted in eating and drinking, a practice that served only to raise the prices of the articles produced in the town. In the sphere of influence of all these county authorities, there was naturally not a trace to be found of similar abuses. The reports from the counties of Szerém, Túrócz and Borsod consisted of a frank confession that the whole question was beyond their comprehension.

Among the towns, Zólyom and Fehérvár (where guild monopolies of the kind complained of were in vogue) declared in favour of annulling them. So did most of the Alföld towns also; for, as we have seen, they were able and only too ready to make room for new settlers. On the other hand, the towns of the North-West, especially Nagy-Szombat and Pozsony, wished to uphold the privileges of the guilds and the custom of selling rights at a price.

With the counties, the main point was everywhere that free competition cheapened manufacture. But the towns, apart from the economic question, were influenced by a fear that the new system of freedom might cause injury to their old established political rights. The guild was just as much a corporation for the protection of privileged interests as was the county system for the nobles.

We see, further, that in Hungary, in most cases, the towns themselves declared in favour of free industry, a fact that clearly proves that the industrial guilds did not altogether predominate in them. As a matter of fact, in those towns which were already, or were destined to be, important on account of their population and wealth, the leaders of the citizens were nobles not commoners[1]. So general was the hegemony of the nobility all over the country that in the town of Gyöngyös, for instance, which was the property of *compossessores*, a veritable civil war broke out in 1768 because a bootmaker, who was a commoner, had been elected to the office of mayor[2].

The Government was disposed to make the town offices permanent and held for life instead of elective, and naturally enough those families, which had already filled offices themselves, endeavoured to maintain their privileged position. Hence a separate aristocracy of office (*patricii*) was gradually evolved in the towns. These *patricii* did all in their power to secure a monopoly of the *beneficia* of the town and to exploit them to their own advantage. Apart from actual cases of embezzlement, we find numerous signs of a patrician clique which regarded the *ager publicus* as its own property. The town council of Kassa imposed taxes on the town walls, which were diverted for their own benefit, and used the town forests as a means of adding to their private incomes[3]. According to the accounts of the town, between 1777 and 1779 the councillors disposed of 2493 florins' worth of town wine[4]. At Székes-Fehérvár, the council reserved the town-common for their own use, and in fact actually divided it among themselves, to the exclusion of the other citizens[5]. At Pest, the councillors were exempted from the payment of bridge tolls; and, in 1783, the members of the council of Buda endeavoured to extend the same privilege to themselves and their families[6].

The smallest number of complaints about financial abuses came undoubtedly from the towns administered under the

---

[1] In 1764, Maria Teresa ennobled the whole town council of Pest. In Debreczen we find nothing but noble judges, captains and " tribunes."

[2] Horner, *Gyöngyös város története* (*History of the town of Gyöngyös*), p. 25.

[3] Chanc. Arch. No. 2273 (1785).

[4] Cf. the denunciation of George Zeleznik, *ibid.*

[5] Chanc. Arch. No. 9331 (1785).

[6] Chanc. Arch. No. 3828 (1783)—naturally the Emperor did not consent—and cf. No. 1253 (1784).

influence of the Hungarian gentry, such as Debreczen, Szatmár-Németi and Komárom.

The abuses here revealed therefore are the same as constituted
the dark side of the county system, but their effect on the subject
classes was an entirely different one. In the counties the abuses
themselves strengthened the ties between the general body of
the nobility and the officials as a class. Their object was not
so much to further the interests of any particular family or
individual as to promote those of the whole nobility as a class.
Though probably harmful to the country at large they strengthened the county system. The only persons injured by them
were the peasants, who did not belong to any of the estates
of the realm. I know of no instance where the nobles of a
county brought any complaint against the staff of officials
elected by themselves. But the abuses of administration in the
towns were felt as personal grievances by all the citizens, who
considered themselves injured by the selfishness of individual
families or *coteries*. Consequently, as a result of its enormities,
this administrative system in the towns was unable to take deep
root, even though controlled by a privileged order of citizens.
An uninterrupted succession of complaints continued to be lodged
by citizens or elective parishes against their councils and mayors.

In their relations to their political superiors, the royal free
boroughs were absolutely wanting in independence. Though
they constituted an estate of the realm and possessed privileges,
the King was after all their lord of the manor. They were
properties belonging to the Sacred Crown[1]. Consequently, they
paid not merely taxes but a special royal tribute as well—the
first to the sovereign as king, the second to him as lord of
the manor[2]. In addition, they rendered service to the King,
just as the nobility did, by means of voluntary gifts and loans.
The mining towns were actually administered by the Chamber
of Mines, which was an imperial department of State and in no
sense Hungarian. For all these reasons, the town magistrates,

[1] "Peculia Sacrae Coronae et suae Majestatis Caesareae tanquam inclyti Regis
Hungariae." Act XXII of 1601.
[2] In 1780 the 33 royal free boroughs paid 15,413 florins under the head of *census
regius*; and the 116 towns of the Szepes district paid 18,527 florins.

however arrogant they might be in their behaviour towards their own people, cringed submissively before the superior royal power and its officials. When there was any trouble or innovation, or when complaints were lodged against a town council, a royal commissary could proceed at once, and could act with an authority quite different from that which his colleagues dared to exercise in the proud counties. The town of Pécs celebrated its enfranchisement and the opening of its career as a royal borough by bribing the royal commission deputed for the purpose of installing it in its privileges[1]. A similar charge formed one of the chief complaints lodged against the council of Kassa. As early as 1781, the Emperor Joseph deposed General Nicholas Eötvös, and fined him for malversations in the administration of affairs at Kassa, where he had been royal commissary[2].

In other countries the towns were the centres of wealth; in Hungary, during this age, they were not in the advantageous position usually secured by the possession of wealth. The circumstances already mentioned all cooperated to prevent the burghers, as such, from becoming wealthy. Anyone who acquired a fortune, either as a councillor or by trade, had comparatively little difficulty in acquiring noble rank, even if he did not possess it already[3]. The new noble, in the enjoyment of his rank and of its privileges, found that the *esprit de corps* of his new order—an influence far more powerful than the inclinations of any individuals within the order—permitted him to acquire more wealth, but demanded that he should spend it in a manner worthy of a gentleman. Even if this influence did not make itself felt on the first representative of the newly ennobled family, at all events it did upon his sons. Those who might have been Hungarian Fuggers or Medicis, at once took their places among the magnates. Such families were the Turzós,

---

[1] No. 2923 (1781).

[2] No. 4320 (1781). August 31. It may be noted that here and elsewhere it was difficult to define the limits of corruption. Customs which had been regarded as common patriarchal practices, and at least tacitly allowed under Maria Teresa, were regarded as criminal and strictly punished by the rigid Joseph.

[3] This privilege was directly conceded by Act xv of 1649.

the Henckels, both in Hungary, the Hallers in Transylvania, and others. Consequently those who remained burghers proper continued to be hampered by the shackles of the guilds, to support themselves by their daily work, and to judge all other interests and ideas by the standard of their own narrow and restricted privileges. Such examples may be found, in particular, among the *bourgeoisie* of the North-West Highlands, whom their foreign speech continuously prevented from considering themselves as an integral part of the nation. On the other hand, in the scattered towns where Hungarian (Magyar) was spoken (particularly in Debreczen and Komárom, which contained large numbers of nobles[1]), despite all isolation, there was a much stronger feeling of national unity; and it was only in these towns that there could be any talk of the development of a Hungarian *bourgeois* life on a sound basis.

The main hindrance to the rapid increase of wealth in the towns, apart from the selfishness of the nobility, was, as we have seen, the policy of the Government at Vienna. The mining towns were oppressed by the Imperial Chamber of Mines[2]. Several towns of the North-West Highlands were badly hit by the cessation or decline of the wine trade. In 1784, Pozsony ceased to be the headquarters of the Government, and suffered accordingly. Löcse lost ground altogether. A decided advance was to be observed in the South-East only, where the impediments in question were far less active than elsewhere, as the population was a new one and for the most part Hungarian (Magyar). Another grave obstacle in the way of the acquirement of wealth was the terrible amount of destruction produced by natural causes, in particular by the fires, which on several occasions ravaged Köszeg, Trencsén, Besztercze-Bánya and Körmöcz about the year 1780. As a consequence, the Hungarian towns are remarkably poor in memorials testifying to the wealth and generosity of their citizens. In the eighteenth

[1] Of all the royal free boroughs, Komárom contained the largest number of nobles. There was a constant succession of suits, for the town was not at all inclined to permit the nobles to make use of their privilege to sell their wine freely on its own territory. Chanc. Arch. *passim*, in particular No. 10,439 (1785).

[2] There was no end to the suits brought by Nagy-Bánya, Felsö-Bánya, and Besztercze-Bánya against the Imperial Chamber. See Chanc. Arch. for 1781.

century, only one famous town memorial involving any considerable expense was erected, viz. the Trinity Column at Körmöcz, which cost 60,000 florins (£6000).

In other countries the towns were the headquarters of the intellectual movements, and the eminent services rendered to the whole nation by men belonging to the *bourgeoisie* naturally reflected credit on the whole class. In Italy ever since the fifteenth century, in France and England in the sixteenth and seventeenth centuries, in Germany in the eighteenth century, the literary revivals had their leaders in men of *bourgeois* rank. In other countries the legal and medical professions, and the majority of the officials, were recruited from the *bourgeoisie*. In Hungary, too, there were eminent writers of *bourgeois* origin[1]. But the latter rose to prominence, not as burghers, but as members of the Church, or under the influence of foreign patronage. The members of the legal profession were all nobles; in fact, advocates belonging to other classes would not have possessed the energy and authority necessary to deal with the judges, who were also noble. No one not of noble rank could be elected to any office in the counties[2]. Non-nobles were also excluded from the deliberations of the boards of Government and of the high tribunals. By law, they could not even hold the office of post-master[3]. It is only in the despised office of the Treasury and in the customs service that we find men who were not nobles. Even in the ecclesiastical hierarchy, that eminently democratic corporation, non-nobles very rarely rose to high offices. The law of 1514 made it impossible for sons of peasants to be elevated to bishoprics. Even if the King had nominated them, they had legally no right to tithes. The medical profession did not hold out any particular ad-

---

[1] A list of these has been compiled by George Fejér, *loc. cit.* p. 64. Among those of the eighteenth century we find the names of Adam Kollár, Stephen Kaprinay, Louis Schedius, Gottfried Schwarz, Schwartner, J. Péczeli, Daniel Cornides, Rajnis, Kazy, Pray, M. Hell, Zvittinger, Dugonics, S. Timon, K. Koppi and Ignatius Born (of Gyulafehérvár).

[2] Act VI of 1723. In the whole period, up to the reforms of Joseph, we find only one case of a non-noble filling a county office—in the county of Verőcze. Cp. Chanc. Arch. No. 5018 (1783).

[3] Act XV of 1715.

vantages. Even about the middle of the century there were no good doctors at Pest, and invalids had to be sent to Pozsony[1]. One of the most famous professors and *savants* of the age, Nicholas Sinay, applied for the grant of nobility in Debreczen as early as 1781, which he actually received later on. Consequently, though men of wealth and intellect could force their way to the front in the royal free boroughs, they merely employed their gifts as means by which to escape from the narrow limits within which they were confined.

To the advantages given by wealth or intellect there were however exceptions, resulting from the peculiar position of individual social classes or religious denominations. For example, the wealthiest inhabitants of Pest were undoubtedly the merchants professing the Greek orthodox religion, yet their faith disqualified them even from buying houses in the town, and, for all their wealth, they could not dream of being admitted to the council[2]. Nor before the reign of Joseph could they think of aspiring to nobility, which had always been in the gift of the sovereign. They were, therefore, wealthy without being of noble rank or even burghers proper, and a similar position was held by the Armenian tenants and traders[3].

The other exception is furnished by the non-Catholics, in particular by the Lutherans. So long as Maria Teresa reigned, neither material wealth nor intellectual achievement could secure a position in politics or in society to Protestants of *bourgeois* origin. Wealthy Protestants were at most able to assert themselves in their own towns, and there, for the most part, only in the service of their respective churches. Protestants of high intellectual attainments, whose learning and abilities should have entitled them to a prominent share in the government of the country, were compelled either to content themselves with the hardly-earned subsistence of a pastor or a teacher, or forced to seek intellectual eminence abroad. On the whole,

[1] E.g. Count Joseph Eszterházy in 1747. *Post. Mem.* p. 42.
[2] Chanc. Arch. No. 5030 (1785).
[3] The wealth of these two denominations is most strikingly proved by the fact that, when an opportunity occurred in 1781 of securing land and nobility in the Bánság ("Banat"), the majority of the purchasers were recruited from their ranks.

therefore, there can be no doubt that a very considerable amount of material and intellectual capital lay idle in the country or was driven abroad, owing to religious intolerance. In Hungary, as in every other country, the mere existence of an arbitrarily repressed intellectual class was a constant menace to the prevailing order of things[1]. This class constituted the mainstay of the absolute royal power, which offered greater encouragement to it. The absolutist monarch was inclined to admit into the ruling class men eminent for intellect or wealth—two immensely important factors in the modern State, which had hitherto been suppressed in medieval Hungary.

In the royal free boroughs, therefore, there existed an element which fostered an almost self-conscious antagonism to the predominance of the Hungarian nobility. Consequently, it is only natural that, even at an early period, this *bourgeois* element should assist the attempts made to overthrow the Hungarian nobility and the constitution with it. There could indeed be no question of patriotism or attachment to national interests in the royal free boroughs and mining towns where the inhabitants were foreigners—generally Germans—in speech and civilization. In the sixteenth century, when the country was suffering from grave national disasters, the towns kept entirely aloof from the rest of the country, and did not trouble themselves very much about the fate of the common fatherland[2]. The national assemblies naturally had recourse to reprisals. As far back as the year following the loss of Buda (1541), the royal free boroughs were forbidden to acquire new property and were deprived of the estates obtained since the death of Louis II[3]. The estates left in their possession were put under the administration of the county authorities. Act LXII of 1563 made it their duty to permit nobles driven from their homes by the Turks to purchase houses within their territories. The Parliament of 1608 (one

---

[1] A warning on this point was administered by Count Niczky, who considered the admission of non-Catholics into the civil service as imperative from the point of view of the interests of the state. See the close of his work, already referred to.

[2] The notes of the deputies (M.P.'s) for Bártfa and Körmöcz, to be found in the *Magyarországi Országgyülési Emlékek* (*Hungarian Parliamentary Memoirs*) edited by Fraknói, are very instructive on this point.

[3] Act XXXIII of 1542.

of those in which the force of circumstances rendered the will of the national and noble party the decisive factor) had recourse to still more effective means to bind the royal free boroughs closer to the country. There were still numerous complaints lodged to the effect that Hungarians (Magyars) were forbidden to purchase houses or hold civic office in the royal free boroughs, in the mining towns and in those situated in Slavonia (the district now called Croatia). In consequence, it was decided that henceforward (1608) judges and councillors should be elected from among the Magyars, Germans and Czechs (i.e. Slovaks) alike, without respect to nationality or religion[1]. This measure was confirmed by Act XLIV of 1609, which inflicted a fine of 2000 florins on towns or persons guilty of transgressing it[2]. Act XL of 1613 actually calls for an exaction of such fine from Besztercze-Bánya as a guilty party.

In the sixteenth century the town element was as yet simply indifferent to the national cause, and actually antagonistic to the nobility; in the seventeenth century, when German absolutism began its work, the behaviour of the *bourgeoisie* and its submission to foreign rulers began to be a real national peril[3]. The cooperation of the Court with the towns was indeed to some extent neutralised by the fact that the new Calvinistic faith formed a close tie between the latter and the nobility; but the non-Catholic inhabitants of the towns, unless exposed to extreme persecution, did not draw away from the King, for they regarded him as their protector against the nobility. It will suffice to instance Pozsony and Sopron, and to point to the well-known fact that the Saxons in Transylvania did all in their power to put themselves under Austrian supremacy[4]. To the

[1] 1608 *ante coronat.* 13.

[2] The measure was further confirmed by five Parliaments during the seventeenth century.

[3] Act XI of 1609: "Civitatum Incolae pro majori parte ex Germanica constent Natione."

[4] A memorable record of this endeavour is to be found in the letter (1614) of the Saxons to the Emperor Matthias:—"Saxones ad suam Majestatem Caes. principesque Christianos recurrunt, se suasque civitates *gratis* offerunt *germanis*, ita tamen ut in libero religionis exercitio retineantur." This letter dates from the reign of Gabriel Bethlen (1613–29) the greatest and most just of the princes of Transylvania. See Szilágyi, Alex., *Erdélyi Országgyülesi Emlékek* (*Records of the Diets of Transylvania*), vol. VI. p. 504.

towns of the Szepes district alone is due the credit of having faithfully stood out for liberty of conscience and for national freedom. The "bloody days of Eperjes" (where, after the Tököly insurrection in 1687, the Imperial general Caraffa plundered and murdered the inhabitants) had inseparably united the lot of the Saxon burghers of the Szepes with that of the Hungarian nobles in the counties. However this case was exceptional; and, fearing that the King might overpower them with the aid of the towns, the county representatives passed a law through Parliament in 1687, making it illegal to add to the number of new boroughs, which had already been enormously increased[1]. Nevertheless, the Parliaments of 1715 and 1751 both empowered new royal free boroughs to send representatives to the national assembly. In these cases, however, and also during the fruitless and stormy Parliament of 1764–65, the county representatives persisted in upholding the privilege which gave their own votes the decisive weight in the assembly, and did not allow those of the borough representatives to be of equal value[2]. It was just in proportion as the prevailing characteristics of the towns became more foreign that the national spirit of the Hungarian constitution urged the county members to exclude those of the towns from their full civil rights and from a share in legislation. In all this we see a purely medieval feature—that of the knights attacking the towns, which we find in every other country in Europe: just as we also find another feature—that of the students attacking the *bourgeoisie*. In Hungary, the frequent and often bloody collisions between "town and gown" that followed on the transference of the university from Nagy-Szombat to Buda, were due not merely to these general causes but to a large extent to nationalistic hatred as well[3].

---

[1] Act XVII of 1687. An analogy to this may be found in England about the same time, when Charles II granted two members to the borough of Newark by royal charter, with the obvious intention of controlling its representatives. The Commons protested so vigorously that no fresh enfranchisement save by parliamentary statute was ever attempted. See Anson, *Law and Custom of the Constitution* (Oxford, 1897), vol. I. p. 335.

[2] The practice had not been uniform in medieval times, but the rule here asserted was that, while the borough representatives could speak in the assembly, they could only vote as a body and that their collective vote was counted as a single vote.

[3] At any rate a poetic lament for Stephen Király Szatmáry, a victim of one of

As a consequence, the large majority of the towns were ready instruments in the hands of the Government. Only their aid—as it were that of a *tiers état*—was not sufficient to destroy the rights of the three leading privileged orders (ecclesiastics, magnates and gentry). The towns had rather the inclination than the power to help the Government. They were extremely scattered, and were unable to secure unity of action even amongst themselves. As we have seen, the Government, while desirous of making use of them, nevertheless fought shy of developing their power to the full, out of regard for Austria and in particular for Vienna. Consequently, the towns of Hungary, isolated and even divided against themselves, hesitating between various and conflicting interests, were unable to exercise any decisive influence on the history of the country even in the eighteenth century. To the end the medieval *bourgeoisie* remained an exotic plant unable to strike deep root in Hungarian soil.

From a national point of view, Hungarians have no reason to regret this fact. In Hungary, in the eighteenth century, the maintenance of the Magyar national character was the one vital necessity ; everything else, even the material and economic development of the country (the furthering of which should have been the work of the *bourgeoisie*) with all its significance, was in comparison of but secondary importance. The town corporations based on medieval privilege, in particular those founded by Germans in other countries, did not succeed in eventually obtaining predominance. The German towns in Hungary were just as incapable of becoming an integral part of their adopted country or of furthering its development[1]. It was fortunate, therefore, that in Hungary the organism of the nation possessed other means of fulfilling the historic mission of towns—the concentration of intellect and wealth—and was thus finally able to absorb the alien town element also into the nation.

The importance of the nobility in the national life of the

these free fights, charges the *Germans* with being guilty of the young man's death. *Mus. Jank. Coll.* vol. III. p. 129.

[1] It will suffice to refer to the German colonies established in Poland, Russia and Scandinavia.

country was enhanced by the fact that they were so numerous in Hungary. In numbers, the aggregate population of the royal free boroughs was very little in excess of the nobility. In 1780, the total population of the royal free boroughs amounted to 356,000 ; in 1787 (including the nobles and priests living in them), it had risen to 402,000. It, therefore, hardly represented one-seventeenth of the aggregate population of the country, and it is specially important in this connection to remember that even the inhabitants of the towns themselves were by no means all " burgesses."

We can here make a comparison of the populations of the towns by districts, following a method similar to that employed in dealing with the counties (v. p. 32). We find that the population of the towns situated in the North-West, like that of the counties, either stagnated or decreased, whereas that of the towns situated in the reconquered districts of the South-East increased to a remarkable degree. A comparison between the relative positions of Pozsony and Budapest affords a picture of the general conditions of population. In 1780, Pozsony was the foremost of the Hungarian towns in point of population. The next in order were Debreczen, Selmecz-Bánya and Buda. These towns alone had populations of over 20,000. After them, the most populous towns were Szabadka, Szeged, Pest and Zombor, each of which possessed more than 14,000 inhabitants. By 1787, however, Debreczen was the most populous, Pozsony had fallen to the second place, while Pest, Szeged and Szabadka already exceeded 20,000.

The list given below (p. 165) shows the development of the populations of the towns by districts[1]. We see that in the North-West the population remained unchanged ; in fact, in the mining towns it actually decreased. In the South-East and in the Trans-Danubian district the population in 1847 was (roughly) double what it had been in 1780. The only exceptions are the border towns of Sopron and Köszeg. The population of the towns of the Alföld had more than doubled, even if we exclude Pest, the population of which increased almost sevenfold during the said period of 67 years. After Pest, Ujvidék showed the most

[1] See note 1 on opposite page.

rapid increase. Buda and Eger, the headquarters of the ancient civil and ecclesiastical administrations, and also important wine-growing centres, showed a comparatively small increase. The populations of the towns of the counties of Szepes, Abauj and Sáros did indeed advance in numbers ; but, with the exception of Kassa, the progress was slow. If we exclude Budapest, the increase in the aggregate population of the royal free boroughs during this whole period was barely proportionate to that of the rural districts—a phenomenon without parallel in Europe at

[1] In the nature of things, the population of the market towns increased more rapidly than that of royal free boroughs situated in the same district. Only we have no trustworthy statistics concerning the former.

Name of royal free borough			in 1780	No. of inhabitants in 1787	in 1847
Pozsony	...	...	29,138	26,898	37,255
Nagy-Szombat	...	...	7,458	7,102	7,717
Szakolcza	...	...	5,654	5,707	6,852
Körmöcz-Bánya	...	...	10,884*	5,244	5,052
Besztercze-Bánya	...	...	5,041	5,041	5,630
Selmecz-Bánya	...	...	24,403*	18,774	18,120
		Totals	82,578	68,766	80,626
Györ	...	...	11,457	12,822	17,200
Komárom	...	...	11,007	12,067	19,113
Sopron	...	...	11,484	12,113	14,987
Köszeg	...	...	4,997	4,966	6,823
Pécs...	...	...	8,435	8,922	15,318
Székes-Fehérvár	...	...	11,274	11,780	22,633
		Totals	58,654	62,670	96,074
Buda	...	...	23,943	24,873	34,893
Pest ...	...	...	16,746	22,417	109,861
Szeged	...	...	17,801	21,579	35,861
Eger (episcopal seat)	...	15,822	16,852	18,675
Debreczen	...	...	27,001	29,153	55,065
Szabadka	...	...	18,730	20,708	41,701
Ujvidék	...	...	5,604	8,998	18,896
		Totals	125,647	144,580	314,952
Kassa	...	...	5,657	7,905	13,672
Eperjes	...	...	5,671	6,000	9,948
Bártfa	...	...	3,564	3,760	4,796
Löcse	...	...	4,543	4,984	5,611
Kesmárk	...	...	3,990	4,170	4,391
	Aggregate Totals		290,304	302,835	530,070

* This total undoubtedly includes the population of the outlying villages.

this time. Unfortunately it was due, not only to the advance of agriculture, but to the decline of industry and mining. It was also a result of the peculiar conditions of Hungary, that the population of the market towns largely increased, and thus to a certain degree made up for this decline. But even this development was found to a striking degree only in the Alföld. It is here alone that we find the sudden and continuous rise of populous centres such as Hódmezövásárhely, Kecskemét or Csaba. Arad and Temesvár rose to the position of royal free boroughs before the close of Joseph's reign, for in this district the territory had not yet been fully settled, and there was still room for new creations. In the mountain districts, however, and in the Trans-Danubian district, the same places predominated alike in importance and population as a hundred years before.

The few data given below will serve to prove that in the eighteenth century the royal free boroughs did not constitute financial sources of sufficient importance to entitle them to a decisive voice in affairs of State by reason of their wealth. As there was no excise duty on articles of consumption, the direct war tax provides us with our only test[1]. As we have already mentioned, the *portae* of the royal free boroughs represented scarcely one-eleventh of the total in 1780. As the aggregate number of the inhabitants of the towns amounted to one-fifteenth that of the whole non-noble population, it follows that the inhabitants of the royal free boroughs, the centres of trade and industry, on an average paid no more taxes per head than the wretched peasants of the rural districts. I believe the case is unparalleled; and, whether it serves as a proof of the poverty or of the selfishness of the towns, it at any rate refutes any statements tending to create the impression that the towns of Hungary rendered eminent services to the country, at least from the material point of view.

[1] In 1787 the royal free boroughs of Hungary, Croatia and Slavonia paid altogether 380,315 florins to the military treasury. The largest contributors were Debreczen and Buda, the new capital: Debreczen paid 35,991 florins 32½ kreuzers, Buda 35,819 florins 20 kreuzers. Then follow Pozsony (27,553 florins), Sopron (25,142 florins) and Pest (19,287 florins). The annual contribution of Varasd, the town in Croatia which paid most, was 1876 florins: that of Zágráb was just half that amount, viz. 938 florins.

One of the peculiarities of the Hungarian constitution was that, side by side with the persons and classes possessing precisely defined rights, there were others in a species of transition. According to the laws of evolution, these latter were either the rudimentary remains of an older class or the precursors of a newer formation.

So far as the noble order is concerned, a half-way position of this kind fell to the lot of the *armalistae* (v. pp. 104, 128) and the nobles, who possessed but one session and, further, of all those nobles who did not owe allegiance to the King, but to the Church, and in particular to the Archbishop of Esztergom and the Bishop of Zágráb, or to the Count Palatine[1].

According to Act XXV of 1548, nobles with one session had to pay taxes. This measure was, by Act VI of 1595, extended to the *armalistae*, to the noble vassals of the spiritual peers and to the freedmen. Here, therefore, a distinction is made between a part of the freemen (who maintained the traditions of the past, particularly in virtue of their military service) and the privileged body of the nation. The distinction between the former and the *misera plebs contribuens*, however, is made significant by the fact that Act VI of 1723 provides that they shall contribute to the local requirements of the counties only, not to the war tax. Consequently they were still obliged to furnish a *posse comitatus*; and Act LXIII of 1741 formulated this obligation in law, and provided regulations for the carrying out of the same.

The other transition is that offered by the inhabitants of the Jász-Kún district and the "Hajdú" towns. As armed tribes or castes, which were for the most part under an obligation to do general military service, they most faithfully represented the traditions of the older Hungarian public liberty. After 1715, when war ceased to be their leading occupation, the inhabitants

---

[1] " Praeter Regni Nobiles tres adhuc Nobilium sunt sortes in Hungaria, *Palatinales* nempe, *Archiepiscopales* et Abbatiales, qui quamvis Regni Nobilibus de jure aequiparari nequeant, a Contributione tamen immunes sunt et Nobilium nomine veniunt, quin plerosque eorum praerogativas cum summo Regis et Regni derogamine sibi adrogant. Ad quid enim—illi—Palat. Archiep. et Abbat. Nobiles, quando tanta Regni nobilium copia est ut nisi D.O.M. Apostolici sui misereatur Regni, Rex vero totis occurrat viribus, exiguum post tempus tot in Hungaria Nobiles numeraturi simus quot homines." Grossing, *Jus Publ.* p. 78.

of the Jász-Kún district were also subjected to the payment of taxes. Their independence consisted mainly in the fact that they were not subordinated to any particular lord of the manor. As their supreme over-lord, indeed, the King did give them in mortgage to the Teutonic order of knights, but he permitted them to redeem themselves and to take their place among the estates of the realm. As far back as the thirteenth century, the County Palatine was the judge, who tried cases in which Cumanians were concerned, and by Act XI of 1485, as the holder of that office he received a salary of 3000 ducats. They were under the control of officials and magistrates elected by themselves, who did their best to check their unruliness. In general respects they formed a county, without serfs.

We have many evidences of the fact that the lot of the inhabitants of the Jász-Kún district was a comparatively favourable one in spite of all oppression. Not only did they pay off the mortgage of 500,000 florins in a relatively short time ; not only were they able to fulfil their military obligations by the supply of armed men and money, but as early as 1784 their local exchequer contained a considerable surplus[1]. But the most striking proof of their prosperity is the constant increase in their numbers, which enabled them continually to recruit the population of the Alföld with fresh contingents from their older settlements. The populous towns of Félegyháza and Szabadszállás are Cumanian settlements of the eighteenth century. They advanced farther South too, in the district between the Danube and the Tisza. As early as 1785, Kis-Ujszállás alone sent out 388 families; while altogether 619 families were preparing to migrate to the county of Bács. The Chancellery ordered them to settle in Moravicza and Pacsér[2]. They possessed the right of migrating at will: and in this manner they were able to counterbalance the overcrowding consequent on the denser colonisation of the land[3]. The stricter demarcation of boundaries, which they naturally conceived to

---

[1] Chanc. Arch. No. 11,732 (1785).

[2] *Ibid.* Nos. 11,506 and 12,643 (1785).

[3] The privileges of the inhabitants of the Jász-Kún district are the subject of Act XXXIV of 1715. Their rights were restored by Act XXV of 1751.

be inspired by ill-will, gave rise to considerable hatred of their superiors: and the number of complaints coming from them is only surpassed by that of the complaints lodged by the "Hajdú" towns[1].

The constitutional position of these latter was the most living memorial of the struggles against the Turk, as well as of those for liberty of conscience and the maintenance of the constitution. In the spirit of the treaty of Vienna, the Parliament of 1609 made their nobility dependent on the investigations of the Count Palatine. The number of free "Hajdú" villages, which had at first been considerably larger, decreased at the opening of the eighteenth century to six; and by Act XCV of 1715, these too were to be absorbed in the counties[2]. Naturally enough, the founders of the new order of things did not recognise the rights of those who fought for the older order. A royal *resolutio* dating from 1733 did indeed take cognizance of their privileges; but at the same time it bound them to pay taxes and to quarter soldiers. As the King was their supreme over-lord, they had to pay a special contribution in recognition of this fact; and they were put under the control of the officers of the Chamber. Besides, they were still under obligation to render military service, as before[3]. The carrying out of this obligation was incorporated in law by Act LXIII of 1741.

Consequently the "Hajdú" towns, despite all their privileges, were in the unfortunate position of being subject to all the burdens imposed on the nobility, on the royal free boroughs and on the peasants, only retaining a certain part of their self-government. This explains the fact that this district was continually one of the chief centres of discontent—alike with "captains," magistrates and Government[4]. In particular, in

[1] The "Hajdús"—Hungarian mercenaries—were the main body of Stephen Bocskay's forces during his war for the maintenance of rights and liberty of conscience (1604). After the war, he knighted some 9000 of them, and gave them several towns in the Alföld.

[2] Among the "Hajdú" towns which lost their franchise and became private property was Nagy Szalonta, the birthplace of John Arany. Hence the ancestors of this great poet, though ennobled by law, were peasants.

[3] Ürményi, *Jus Publ.* III. ch. 6, § 14.

[4] There was a "captain" acting as royal commissary in the "Hajdú" district with the same sphere of authority as the high sheriff.

1780, the "captain" George Csanády was the cause of an insurrection, as a result of which peace was never entirely restored in that quarter during the reign of Joseph[1]. The ringleaders had to be banished in order to restore order, but their followers never ceased to complain of the oppression of the "captain" and to protest the justice of their cause.

For the "Hajdú" towns, therefore, from a constitutional point of view, the eighteenth century was an unfortunate period. They were constantly being deprived of the principal and most treasured privileges attaching to the nobility. In addition, a proletariate sprang up in them, and the condition of their inhabitants daily assimilated itself to that of the peasants.

V.   The Peasants and Serfs (Jobbágy).

This whole Hungarian society—the powerful King, the splendid prelacy and aristocracy, and the numerous nobility—was supported by the work of the serfs. This fact must never be lost sight of when treating of medieval society.

The serfs themselves were a complete and organised order. Among them, too, we find an arrogant aristocracy—the owners of whole sessions and big farmers—who looked down in contempt on those cottagers and tenants possessing neither land nor cattle. Even the meanest peasant, who owned but the eighth of a session, refused to be classed with the cottager[2]; and the system of class distinctions penetrated even to the lowest grade of the social ladder. The judge, the council, the all-powerful proprietor and his officers, the priest who stood half-way between them and their lord—all afford a complete picture of medieval society in miniature.

It is a well-known fact that, after the unfortunate issue of the

---

[1] Chanc. Arch. No. 1719 (1781), referring to the inhabitants of Nánás and Böszörmény. Of these affairs the Emperor himself wrote as follows, "Die Beschwerden wider die innerliche Administration in den Haidukenstädten waren sehr dringend und wurden leider mit ziemlich starken Strafen belegt, dann auch die Kläger von Haus und Hof abgestiftet." *Verbesserungsanstalten*, p. 34.

[2] At the *conscriptio* of 1784, in the county of Bars.

peasant revolt in 1514, the yoke of the Hungarian serfs became more oppressive. Up to that date the laws had maintained the right of migration at will. It is no mere accident, but the result of absolute historical necessity that the *Tripartitum*—the codification of the rights of the Hungarian nobility—was compiled at the same time as this systematic oppréssion of the serfs began. Neither is conceivable without the other, and they unite to form the picture not of society in Hungary only but also in every medieval state. The Code of 1514—as its preface declares—came into being under the influence of the "vile peasant revolt." In it the spirit of retaliation predominates, and the two and a half centuries that passed between its incorporation and the creation of the new regulations referring to socage, improved the condition of the peasantry but little[1].

The period of the Turkish wars, while it demanded all the resources of the nobility, was unable to really alleviate the lot of the serfs. As it was there was no lack of peasant risings, for many of the peasantry thought the yoke of Turkish rule more tolerable than the united oppression of Hungarian nobles and German soldiers. But, in general, the patriotism of the Hungarian peasants was above all suspicion during this period. Is any other consideration than the idea of national unity sufficient to explain the fact that the peasants, living in the territory conquered by the Turks, at the same time paid taxes to their Hungarian lords and to the King of Hungary?

From the overthrow of the peasant revolt dates the law which relegated the Hungarian peasantry to the position occupied by villeins in other countries of Europe—that "the remembrance of this their treachery and this civil punishment make its effect felt on their descendants unto late generations, and that they may see for themselves what a terrible crime it is to rise against their masters, every succeeding age shall know that henceforward (with the exception of the loyal free boroughs and those peasants who maintained their loyalty) they shall lose their privilege of emigrating at will, as a punishment for their treachery, and shall be subject to their respective proprietors as serfs pure and simple

[1] The improved regulations were proclaimed by the *Urbarium* of Maria Teresa, 1767 (v. pp. 175, 178 and esp. pp. 191—2).

for all time[1]." As the revolt led by George Székely was, to the
best of our knowledge, exclusively a movement of the *Hungarian*
(*Magyar*) peasants, these latter (who, in our opinion, must up to
that time have occupied a more favourable position as compared
with other nationalities) would feel most acutely the blow inflicted by this law.

The right of migrating at will was restored to the serfs by the
Parliament of 1547. "Many older and more recent examples
have demonstrated the avenging wrath of God for the grave sins
of his people ; and, as it seems that nothing has for the past few
years been so damaging to the once prosperous kingdom of
Hungary as the oppression of the agricultural labourers, the
estates have decided that the right of migration at will, of which
they have been deprived in previous years, whatever may have
been the cause of such deprivation, shall be restored to them[2]."
This measure, despite all its qualifying clauses, prevented the
Hungarian peasants from becoming mere serfs without any
rights at all.

At the opening of the sixteenth century the nobility deprived
the peasantry of the last remains of their ancestral liberty. This
measure was the only means of enabling them to hold their own
against the Turks and the Germans. The opening of the
eighteenth century was the age of restoration. By this time,
however, the settling of the peasantry in a permanent home had
become imperative in the interest not only of the nobility, but of
the State. Otherwise the Church tithes, the ninth part due to the
proprietor, even the war tax and the maintenance of soldiers
would be endangered. Acts CI of 1715 and LX of 1723 took
this principle as their starting point, and thereby rendered the
right of free migration somewhat illusory.

The Parliament of 1514 had also defined the amount of burdens
to be laid on the serfs for the maintenance of their respective
proprietors. One florin in gold (ducat) was to be paid annually ;
besides, each serf had to give one day's work (in socage) a week,
one chicken a month, and two geese a year. Beyond that, every
ten peasants had to supply one fatted hog a year. Of harvest

---

[1] Act XIV of 1514 : cf. *Tripartitum*, III. 25.
[2] Act XXVI of 1547.

produce and of the vintage, one-ninth belonged to the lord of the manor or proprietor and one-tenth to the Church. Of ten bushels of corn or ten gallons of wine, therefore, only eight remained. All other burdens previously laid upon the peasantry, in addition to these, were still enforced[1]. Finally, the greater part of the whole taxes of the country also fell on their shoulders.'

The period of Turkish dominion only served to establish this state of things on a firmer basis; whereas previously the burdens imposed by the proprietors had been almost the only ones to which they were subject, the peasants now began to feel the weight of national burdens. Act VI of 1557 bound the tenants of sessions to a species of *corvée*, compelling them to work for nothing during six days every year. To keep the castles in good repair, the peasants of the neighbouring counties had to supply one cart for every four *portae* and one labourer for every *porta*, for a period of twelve days[2]. Whereas previously, even in the sixteenth century, subsidies had been quite exceptional and comparatively trifling in amount, in the seventeenth century they gradually increased, and in the eighteenth century they became a permanent institution of ever growing proportions.

The individual nobles, therefore, retained their revenues ; but in addition the country too maintained and exercised its rights over the serfs. Consequently the whole of Hungary was interested in the prevention of the total ruin of the latter class. The predominant nobility was selfish and greedy, but their own interests, as well as those of the country, made it imperative that the Hungarian peasantry should not sink beneath the loads imposed on them. Both the country (the State) and the nobles oppressed the peasant, but, so far as they could, each of them protected him against the ravages of the other.

In the period of Turkish dominion only one fresh burden was imposed on the peasants ; the Parliament of 1548 obliged them to perform two days of service (in socage) every week during the time devoted to viticulture, harvesting and haymaking[3]. In

---

[1] Act XX of 1514.

[2] Act LII of 1618. According to Act LXII of 1609, a *porta* consisted of 4 populated sessions or 12 cottagers.

[3] In consequence of the unsettled state of the country this Parliament temporarily suspended the right of free migration restored in 1547.

addition to this the fifty days of service in socage, hitherto
enforced, were exacted from them. However, in order that the
restriction of migration "should not give the lords and nobles
the power of exercising tyranny over the wretched peasants, it
has been decided that the latter shall retain their liberty and
shall not be taxed, plagued or robbed beyond the bounds of
justice, honour and equity[1]."

As a consequence the peasantry had no political rights ; the
principle here enunciated threw them absolutely on the mercy of
their superiors; and, despite all the confirmation of their liberties,
they were reduced to the condition of the French peasantry—
"peuple taillable et corvéable à merci et à miséricorde." Yet
neither their feudal superiors nor the King were able to dispose
of them and of their property at will. Consequently one
foreign traveller actually considers their position as almost
enviable in comparison with that of the other peasantries of
Europe[2].

Such was, in its main features, the material condition of the
Hungarian peasantry. Owing to their legal relations to their
feudal lords, the oppression to which they were subjected was
more serious. They were exclusively under the jurisdiction of
their lords, or of that lord on whose estate they were arrested,
and could not even appeal to the county courts. They could not
appear as witnesses against nobles[3]. Any suits they had against
men of noble rank had to be entrusted to their superiors, for, in
such cases, they could not themselves bring actions.

The first condition in itself was sufficient to make everything
else illusory. The feudal lord was at the same time the judge,
and, though at all times there were some of patriarchal tendencies,
there were also oppressors. As we have seen, the law afforded
no other guarantee than the good-will of the proprietors. It is
true that in the *corpus juris* we often meet with threats and
punishments administered to the oppressors of the poor people.

1 "Nec ultra quam justum, honestum et tolerabile est taxentur, crucientur aut
rebus suis spolientur."
2 Townson, *Travels* (1797), p. 132.
3 "Rusticana attestatio contra Personam Nobilitarem nihil valet." *Tripartitum*,
II. 27.

Only, if we read the text, we see that it deals, not with feudal lords but with robber knights and " Hajdús[1]." Thus not only did the feudal lord possess the right of punishing his serfs —extending in most cases to the *jus gladii* (right of capital punishment)—but there was no chance of appeal, since the serfs could not give evidence against feudal lords or against their bailiffs. Hence every prescribed feudal obligation defines only the minimum which the proprietor could exact from the serf, and this minimum could be extended as his pleasure or interest might require. If in later centuries the lot of the peasantry showed a comparative improvement, this result was due not so much to the wisdom or humanity of the legislators as to the generosity of the lords. The contributions of the serfs in money, in kind and in labour were regulated not so much by any act of legislation as by the contracts relating to socage (*Urbarium*[2]) concluded between the various parishes and their proprietors.

Thus the lot of the Hungarian peasantry, from a legal point of view, compared favourably with that of the serfs in other countries. In particular the terrible abuses, which elsewhere degraded the peasants to the position, not merely of mere " draught animals," but even of slaves without any families, were never universally practised in Hungary. Thus we find no trace of that immoral custom which aimed at destroying the purity of domestic life—though in other respects morals in Hungary were hardly better than they were in other countries. Furthermore, the serfs were able to found families. In Hungary, the savings of serfs, which reverted to the feudal lords not only in France but also in a part of Germany, were inherited by their children without any deduction in favour of their feudal superiors. Without justifiable cause neither serfs nor their families could be ejected from their sessions by their lords.

The poverty of the Hungarian serfs offered a crying contrast to the pomp of the magnates and the easy life of the gentry.

---

[1] Act II of 1608 (*p. coron.*).

[2] The *Urbarium* was a regulation of the rights and duties of serfs in their dealings with their proprietors. It was beneficial to the former and was published by Maria Teresa in 1767, without the cooperation of Parliament (v. *infra*, pp. 191—2).

Many abuses were committed, in consequence of which the tyrannical behaviour of the Hungarian nobility became proverbial. However, when Maria Teresa decreed that these feudal matters should be regulated in the Austrian Hereditary Provinces —after a similar process had been initiated in Hungary—Borié, the councillor who had always been the bitterest enemy of the Hungarian nobility, exclaimed, "The state of things is more terrible here than in Hungary[1]!"

As we have seen, the Hungarian Parliament always considered as one of its prerogatives the power to regulate by law the lot of the peasants, and refused to leave it to the mercy or to the practice of individual lords or counties. Act CI of 1715 entrusted the county officials with the protection of the serfs against their lords, in particular as concerned migration. Act XVIII of 1723 bound the landed proprietors to respect the rules relating to socage, but placed the right of control in the hands of the county officials. It is quite natural, therefore, that Act XXXV of 1729 should declare that the county courts should deal with the grievances of socmen. The same Parliament also admitted the evidence of serfs against noblemen—though with important restrictions.

Hungarian society did nothing more towards the liberation of serfs in this period. We must not, however, be unjust in our criticism of its action, for its whole existence depended upon the institution of socage. So long as the obligation of the maintenance of a *posse comitatus* was in force and constituted a vital condition of the existence of the State, the nobility, as a caste of warriors, was entitled, from a political point of view, to claim to be supported by the agricultural and labouring class. The raising of a *posse comitatus* in 1741 contributed in no small measure to increase the political importance of the nobility. It is no wonder, therefore, that the Parliaments now renounced any attempts at further alleviation of the lot of the serf (*jobbágy*).

Despite all its humanity and love of liberty, the French culture which was again beginning to extend its influence, and which found many adherents and imitators in Hungary during the reign of Maria Teresa, did not succeed in evoking any particular

[1] Hock, *Der österr. Staatsrath*, p. 68.

interest in the lot of the serfs. The French poets and philosophers preached love and respect for an abstract " people," industrious, sober and restrained, they did not speak, in direct terms, of any concrete people ; and admiration for an idealised abstraction was not at all incompatible with a continued oppression of the concrete original. Both in manners and in outward appearance the latter undoubtedly resembled the ideal " people " just as little as the majority of medieval knights resembled the heroes of romance.

When any of the Hungarian nobles tuned his lyre, he was quite sure to sing a hymn of praise on the rustics. Baron Orczi, who as a good landlord must have been acquainted with the peasants' character and condition, addressed these poor yokels in the following lines[1] :

" Ye, whom envious Arrogance undeservedly
    Has condemned to a mean lot, who know not Glory—
    A worthy parish counting many worthy souls—
    Whom Wisdom treasures, and courtly Nobility disdains,
    Poor rustic folk, a truce to your vexation.
    Come, listen while I prove your worthiness."

*   *   *   *   *   *   *   *   *

" Meek Innocence is dwelling in your midst,
    'Tis but the wealthy whom Sin rules over—
    As simple as your rustic attire,
    Or even more simple is your talk, your speech ;
    Your life is pure and sweet in innocence,
    Your pleasures unmixed with any evil thoughts."

Let us turn now to Bessenyei, who was also under the influence of French culture, and, in addition, a courtier seeking to win favour with the Government. We find that, while he preached esteem for the peasants, he repeatedly urged that severe treatment was the only means of keeping them in check[2].

" Thou vicious noble-man, who squanderest the inheritance of thy fathers, knowest thou of how much more value is a poor man than thou, the poor man who bears the burdens of his king,

[1] *Két nagyságos elme*, vol. I. pp. 22—29. For a characterisation of Lawrence Orczi, see John Arany's *Prose Essays* (*Prózai dolgozatok*), p. 287, where the great poet shows how little either Orczi or Barcsay thought of a liberation of the serfs.

[2] *A Holmi*, p. 112, *sub tit. Köznép* (*The Masses*).

his country, his lord, his judge and his priest?" Here we have the influence of the French moralists. Not even Rousseau could have expressed himself with more force.

"Of old in certain countries, when a peasant had committed an offence and was condemned to suffer punishment, the justices had him summoned before them and began to shout at him, cursing and swearing: 'thrash him, beat the base villain!' Where the law prescribed thirty stripes of the rod, the furious judges in a torrent of passion cried for fifty, sixty, a hundred." Here we have the gentleman sympathising with the oppressed. Then follows the reasoning of the Hungarian noble: "It is imperative however that the peasantry be kept under control by strict laws and corporal punishment, for, if they once rise and are able to move from their places, they carry out ravages more violent and terrible than those of the fiercest beasts of prey or of the Hyrcanian tiger. They can be managed best of all by inspiring fear and by small acts of benevolence—though too much of the latter will only spoil them. Think of the army of peasant crusaders who served under King Ladislas (1514)." Finally the writer commended the lot of the peasantry to the favour of the fair sex.

Such are the views of the Hungarian writers and poets, who were well acquainted with the ideas of equality propagated by the new French poetry and philosophy. Ákos Barcsay—probably the most thoroughly French of them all—wrote as follows to a learned Hungarian lady of the aristocracy:

"I remember how, when the *Urbarium*[1] was published,
As we danced in thy house we wept over the fall of our country[2]."

Similar views are expressed by a Hungarian statistician and politician[3]. In his opinion the burdens imposed on the serfs in Hungary were by no means excessive. This was proved best of all by the fact that not only was emigration unknown, but that there was actually a considerable number of settlers continually coming into the country. The leading classes in the State, therefore, may be said to have endeavoured to alleviate the

[1] See p. 175, note, and pp. 191—2.
[2] *Két nagyságos elme*, vol. II. p. 232.
[3] Reviczky, *Status Regni Hungariae*, Part I.

hard lot of the serfs, from a personal and individual point of view, by a good treatment of a patriarchal character. But their condition was considered so natural and necessary that the nobles either did not think at all of a radical and thorough reform of it, or believed that such reform would jeopardise the very foundations of national life.

There can be no doubt that the peasants themselves did not take so favourable a view of their condition. Most of the official documents entered after 1766 (when the idea of a reform of the *Urbarium* took a definite shape) contain the complaints and wishes of the peasantry. They saw a promise of a better future and endeavoured to take advantage of the more favourable auspices. The few popular songs that have come down to us undoubtedly offer a more faithful picture of the mind of the serfs than do the idylls of the Court and noble poets. The oppressed people, who felt only the burdens of society, compared its effects to the havoc wrought by the elements. Very rarely, I believe, was any song sung with greater earnestness than must have accompanied the following lines:

> "Save us, Lord Jesus, from all kinds of evil,
> From county authorities, fisc, hamster and Tartar[1]."

All this might be endured somehow, but the ravages of the German soldiers were worse than the *contributio*, the socage or the compulsory furnishing of relays (*praejunctura*). The song above cited closes as follows:

> "And you might add—'and from the German soldiers,
> Themselves, their horses and their generals.'"

Another song deals with the matter more in detail[2]:

> "Tommy in our house, our backs stripemarked,
> Shouts 'Bring wine, you villain Jack.'
> He cut up my goat and washed it down with wine,
> And carved off the heads of my fowls:
> He cut the throat of my calf too,
> And made havoc of my farm-yard."

[1] Univ. Libr. MS. misc.
[2] *Mus. Jank. Coll.* vol. VIII. p. 9.

There is another song which enumerates all conceivable
species of tyranny[1]:

> "The unhappy lot of the peasant is beyond compare,
> For his wretchedness exceeds the volume of the ocean:
> No peace is his; he must be ready day and night,
> And on his feet.
>> Early in the morning
>> The bailiff comes for him,
>> Summoning him to work
>> Pickaxe in hand,
>> If he fail to respond
>> On the rack is he laid[2]."

The difference between the actual state of things and the
poetic conception of the peasants' condition is illustrated by
a comparison between the above truly piteous lament and a
poem, contained in the same collection, in which a gentleman
speaks of the peasant as living in the bosom of nature, enjoying
the luxury of the verdant grass and the warbling of the birds.

As everywhere else in Europe, in Hungary too the maintenance of a medieval society was purchased at the price of
excessive and intolerant oppression. Only we can find no
instance in history of its having been possible to insure the
safety of historic treasures—nationality, culture, progress—
without making this sacrifice. Whether we take the slave-
hordes of the mines and the *latifundia* in ancient Greece or

---

[1] *Dubinszky versei* (*Poems of D.*), Mus. Lat. MS. 8°, 96.

[2] The other important stanzas of this poem—the author of which, despite its
popular tone, seems to have possessed literary attainments—are the following:

> "He labours all the day,
> Toiling without reward,
> Receiving no word of thanks;
> Tithes without number must he pay;
> And if he offend,
> To prison he goes,
> Where neither meat nor drink is his share."

> "The magistrate distrains for taxes, the parson for fees,
> The Jew and innkeeper for unpaid drinks,—
> Everything is seized, then comes the eviction,
> Scarcely his shirt is left him.

> My parched throat must water cool,
> My empty stomach barley bread fill:
> With dried curds and buckwheat dumplings
> Must I be satisfied."

Rome, or the proletariates of the capitals of modern civilised States, we find the same state of things everywhere ;—it is only by the labour and subjection of the masses that the select and intellectual minority is enabled to further the advance of society. A natural result of this advance is that the blessings of culture are extended in ever-increasing measure to the lower grades of society, whose influence is consequently and continually widened. The life of the British workman to-day has become better and easier than that of a peer three hundred years ago, and it is only upon some broad foundation such as this that the pyramid of the intellectual and moral culture of humanity can be raised to a higher level. So long as we admit the truth of this axiom, we must confine our efforts to mitigating the existing contrasts so far as possible, and must not aim at entirely eliminating them.

Starting from this point of view, we must ask whether the serfs could, unaided, have defended the intellectual treasures of the country, in particular liberty of conscience and national independence? Our answer must be decidedly in the negative. In the matter of religious convictions the laws permitted the free practice of recognised religions " in so far as they did not injure the rights of the landed proprietors[1]." Before the close of the seventeenth century the majority of these proprietors had been reconverted to the Catholic faith ; and, led not so much by the letter of the law as by the intentions of the Government and their own religious zeal, they had used their power to reconvert their dependants. Naturally enough, violence was required in many cases. But, whereas in the towns and among the gentry resistance was offered, the religious history of the peasantry is characterised only by an implicit submission to the will of the more powerful. Some cases of sturdy passive resistance show the energy of the Protestant faith, but were not sufficient to modify the success of the Catholic Church. There was very little more trouble in reconverting the serfs to Catholicism than there had been, two hundred years before, in converting them to Protestantism. Individual cases of emigration occurring after the middle of

---

[1] "Salvo jure dominorum terrestrium," Act xxv of 1681. A variant of the principle "cujus regio, ejus religio."

the eighteenth century can scarcely be taken as exceptions. We have no desire to draw any other conclusion from this fact than that the differences between the various systems of religion had not taken hold of the comparatively illiterate vassals, who took no interest at all in nice distinctions of doctrine[1]. The methods adopted by the Counter-Reformation of the eighteenth century were very similar to those employed by Louis XIV in his conversion of the Huguenots, except that there were no "Camisards" in Hungary[2].

To decide the second question—as to the maintenance of nationality—is more difficult. Despite all the theories of historical materialism, the despised and over-wearied Hungarian peasant showed himself the truest patriot of all. For a short time after the Peasant Revolt of 1514 he seemed (not unnaturally) to incline more towards the Turks than towards his oppressors. Yet, directly he became acquainted with the Ottoman, he turned back again to the Hungarian noble as his protector. All his feeling revolted against oppressors from without, and especially against the Austrians. In the wars for liberty of religion waged against Austria the peasant bore the foremost part. In the first, under Stephen Bocskay (1604–6), the Court party saw merely a revolt of peasants[3]. In 1671, after the nobles had been crushed by the execution of their leaders and the confiscation of their goods, the peasant arose and fought for liberty. From the end of the seventeenth century dates the song:

> "For father and mother I shed my blood,
> For my fair betrothed bride will I be slain,
> For my Magyar nation to-day will I die!"

[1] In his *A Holmi*, Bessenyei gives several illustrations of the *superstitions* in vogue among the common people. They persecuted not only witches but male devils too. "In Hungary not long ago a man of the name of Rósa was burned for a male devil. The sentence ran somewhat as follows : ' Rósa, who for twenty years was a captain in the service of Pluto, subverted all things both human and divine and *sold the Hungarian clouds to the Turks*, shall be burned at the stake.'"

[2] Ranke (*Geschichte der Päpste*, vol. II. p. 23) quotes a letter of Lázár Schwendi to the Prince of Orange : "En Ungarie tout est confusion et misère. Ils sont de la plupart Hugenots, mais avec une extrême ignorance du peuple." The letter is undated, but it must have been written between 1565 and 1575.

[3] Pelthi, Gorgely, *Rövid Magyar Krónika* (*Short Hungarian Chronicle*), p. 161.

It was a revolt of peasants, directed alike against priests, nobles and Germans, which brought Rákóczi into Hungary and gave him his first support in 1703. In proportion as the nobles gathered round him, Rákóczi, who, with all his feeling for the serf (*jobbágy*), did not care to play the part of a second Dózsa, forgot more and more those who had supported him at the beginning of the war. The pathetic songs of this period breathe the pride and the jealousy of the people against those who had not borne the burden, but who took the whole reward:

"It was the horse of the poor man, not of the lord, that went to Vienna."

This feeling explains why the peasant declined in importance, and played a mere secondary part after 1711, though he remained Magyar to the very marrow, and preserved his inveterate hatred against Germans. But, in the eighteenth century, the peasant, like the noble, turned his energies towards economy.

It cannot be maintained that any single political act or undertaking of the eighteenth century excited real enthusiasm among the peasants. There is reason to believe that the greatest national achievement of the century—the raising of troops to defend the honour of the Queen in 1741—stirred no emotions among the peasants, even among those who by speech were Hungarian (Magyar). Otherwise there would have been no need for the plaint of the women-folk in the following song :

For the Queen.
"Every county is making preparations
—The flower of the country—
For they cannot but submit[1]."

Military life, so finely sung of by Valentine Balassa the hero and the poet of the Turkish wars in the sixteenth century, must have lost much of its ancient splendour when we find verses like these :

"They will soon carry me off to fight the Prussians,
But to no comfortable quarters."

And the girl too complains :

"Wert thou a "Hajdú," I'd love thee:
But a soldier thou art, I cannot love thee.
Cut-throat is the name that becomes thee,
The gallows the fate thou deservest[2]."

[1] *Mus. Jank. Coll.* vol. VIII. p. 13. [2] *Ibid.* p. 99.

The serfs bore their yoke, but its iron entered into their souls. For the Hungarian (Magyar) peasants there was some consolation in the fact that this yoke had been imposed on them by members of their own race; for the others, even this poor consolation did not exist. But, although the general reader must experience pain when looking back on those years of oppression, the historian must ask whether the same end—the performance of services required for the maintenance of society—could have been attained by other means more in harmony with the social conceptions of to-day. Naturally enough we are not dealing here with the abuses and arbitrary conduct of individuals, which must at all times be condemned and cannot be condemned severely enough : we are concerned with the legal development and with the system of labour and taxation.

Let us examine the nature and proportions of the burdens entailed by socage. We have not space to give a complete picture of the whole country, but must confine ourselves to a few characteristic details.

At Erdöszada, in the county of Szatmár, the revenue of the proprietor was as follows: each house paid one florin[1]. The value of the service in socage was 498 florins 10 kreuzers; it consisted of 822 days of labour with oxen, and 1295 days of manual labour. Every kitchen had to supply one calf, of the value of 51 kreuzers—representing in the aggregate a sum of 12 florins. The value of the weaving was 4 florins 12 kreuzers. The serfs had to cut wood—14 cords representing as many florins. The payment in cash and the labour that could be redeemed in money, therefore, represented an aggregate value of 655 florins.

To this must be added the ninth part (nonage) of the crops (payment in kind). The chief product was buckwheat; of this 206 bushels (v. Appendix I.) were due to the lord of the manor, which, at the average value of 34 kreuzers, represented a sum of 116 florins 44 kreuzers[2]. The amounts of other products due to the lord were : of wheat, 67 bushels = 67 florins ; of oats, 20 bushels = 10 florins (1 bushel = 30 kreuzers); of tobacco,

---

[1] In the village there were 13⅜ sessions and 127 houses. For details, cf. Chanc. Arch. No. 4072 (1782).

[2] The old florin = 60 kreuzers or denaries. Appendix I.

7 centals = 9 florins 48 kreuzers (1 cental = 1·24 florins); of wine, 4 gallons (v. Appendix I.) = 14 florins (1 gallon = 3·30 florins). Finally, lambs had to be supplied to the value of 3 florins, as well as honey and wax at a similar value. The aggregate value of a ninth part of the crops was therefore about 225 florins.

There was also another indirect tax—the right of keeping a public-house—which the proprietor exercised the whole year round in places where no wine was grown, and from St Michael's Day to St George's Day only in places where wine was grown[1]. In the public-house 157 gallons of wine were consumed, the profit of the lord of the manor being 30 kreuzers (half a florin) on every gallon. Besides, 31 gallons of spirits were consumed, representing a profit of 163 florins 48 kreuzers, and 27 gallons of mead yielding a profit of 40 florins 52 kreuzers. The total indirect revenue was, therefore, 283 florins; and the aggregate revenue yielded by the 13⅞ sessions about 1150 florins. The rent thus paid for each session to the feudal lord was more than 80 florins, that yielded by each house on the average 9 florins. If we take the value of the ninth part as the basis of our calculation, we find that the aggregate income of the serfs from the produce of their land was only 2000 florins. This fact, however, is in itself sufficient to prove that great indulgence had to be exercised in the exaction of the ninth part (nonage).

The contract concluded between the inhabitants of Türje and the monastery, their feudal superior, gives us a clear picture of all the existing conditions[2]. According to it, the serfs were entitled to clear forest land; the assarts (thwaites) thus obtained became their property, and could be sold by them. But if the owner of such thwaites left the place, the lord of the manor could redeem the same at the rate of 4 florins an acre. It was the duty of the serfs to carry the mails of the lord of the manor in turn. Migration was permitted, anyone notifying his intention of migrating had to pay 4 florins, those giving no reason for their departure had to pay 12 florins, and the property of those who left without giving notice was forfeit to their lord.

In 1744 the parish undertook to pay the schoolmaster's

[1] Cf. the regulations of the *Urbarium* introduced by Maria Teresa. Chanc. Arch. No. 5481 (1785).

salary, redeeming thereby one day's service in socage. Formerly the socman who drove oxen had worked for 18 days, the socman who did manual labour for 14 days.

Ever since 1766 the serfs belonging to the village had been given a preference over strangers as regards "pannage[1]". In this case the lord received tithes as well: the latter had formerly been paid in money. The *arenda* (redemption of tithes) had previously been 2 florins 50 kreuzers for each house; now the tithes were again to be paid in kind.

For the conditions prevailing in newly planted villages, we may take as illustration the contract concluded in 1724 between the Magyari family and the parish of Gyönk[2]. Every serf, whether he possessed cattle or not, had to work three days a month. Cottagers paid 50 kreuzers a head in lieu of work. In addition, every peasant had to supply two capons a year, while the duty of following the lord in hunting was regulated by universal custom. Besides the ninth part (nonage) of the produce, certain fees had to be paid to the proprietor for each draught ox and draught horse.

Those who migrated from the district might sell their vineyards, but were not allowed to destroy either buildings or tillage. The right of keeping public-houses and butchers' shops belonged to the village. Hunting, however, was prohibited under pain of a fine of 4 florins. The newly-planted vineyard was to be exempt from the payment of dues for a period of seven years. The village magistrate was to pay the *arenda* in cash, at Michaelmas and on St George's Day. Finally, the meadow-land was to be distributed among the serfs in the same way as the other landed estate.

As a result of the enormous difficulties attendant on the supply of service in socage and of the payment of the nonages and tithes in kind, the larger and wealthier villages gradually redeemed all these payments[3]. In this period there was scarcely

---

[1] As provided for by the regulations in the *Urbarium* of MariaTeresa (ch. 11. § 7). " Pannage " is the *glandinatio* or right to feed swine on acorns in the forest.

[2] Chanc. Arch. No. 8285 (1785), county of Tolna.

[3] From this period date the contract between the town of Lippa and the Chamber for a fresh period of 25 years (Chanc. Arch. No. 2641 (1783)) and that between the town of Mezötfúr and the Kállay family (4300 florins a year, Chanc. Arch. No. 15,023 (1785)).

a single market town of importance in Hungary which did not pay a part at least of its obligations in money. As a rule, it was an integral part of the contracts relating to socage to determine the form of government of the villages in question, viz. the amount of influence to be exercised by the proprietors on the election of the village magistrates.

According to the contract[1] made with its lord, the town of Léva was to give a ninth part (nonage) of those products (which had been fixed as suitable for the purpose by the Parliament of 1481[2]) and in addition of maize too. The latter product, however, was not subject to the payment of a tithe.

The *magistratus* (council) was to be elected by the parish. Should the former act against the interests of the parish, they were to be deposed by the proprietor, who was to issue a writ for a new election. In cases of legal disputes, as they depended often on the verdict of ignorant agricultural labourers and artisans, no distraints could be issued without the consent of the court baron. More important cases were to be brought before the latter. Punishment inflicted should not be pecuniary but corporal, for fines "generally enervate the *misera plebs contribuens*[3]."

The greatest trouble was everywhere caused by the question as to whether thwaites and newly cultivated land should be exempt from or liable to the payment of charges; another cause of trouble was that the proprietors were in the habit of appropriating unoccupied lands, though they continued to make the same demands on the parish as before. Let us examine one or two cases of grievances of this kind, which were continually appearing all over the country. The complaints made by the parish of Rákos (county of Sopron, under the bishop of Györ) were as follows[4]:—1. The village public-house, burned down in 1770, had been rebuilt and appropriated by the proprietor 2. Their right of cutting wood had been restricted, though the forest belonged to them, not to the bishop. 3. The bishop had

[1] Chanc. Arch. No. 6404 (1785).
[2] 1481, Acts I and X.
[3] This point too was included in the *Urbarium* issued by Maria Teresa (ch. VIII. § 3).
[4] Chanc. Arch. No. 8354 (1785).

seized the night-watchmen's hut. 4. The bishop kept 400 sheep, which did considerable damage to their pasture-land, forests and crops. They preferred to keep no sheep themselves rather than put up with the present state of things. 5. They prayed that the unoccupied vineyards, seized by the bishop, should be distributed among them. 6. The wine tithes were being exacted from them by another standard of measure than that of Pozsony. 7. They had not the prescribed amount of landed property, and begged for compensation from the unoccupied plots. 8. The scribe asked 30 kreuzers for the bill of complaint. 9. They desired themselves to redeem the meadow-land mortgaged to the inhabitants of Ruszt and redeemed by the bishop. 10. Finally, they asked for a distribution of the fittings of the houses left unoccupied.

Far graver are the charges brought by the village of Hirip[1] in the county of Szatmár. According to its plea, the inhabitants were compelled to do continuous service in socage for five to six weeks in the summer, and were consequently obliged to neglect their own farms. The thwaites, which they had already sown, had been seized by the bailiff. The latter had indeed given other land in exchange, but it was of a far inferior quality. They had been deprived of the right of cutting wood.

Numerous complaints were lodged by parishes in the county of Vas, in particular by those situated on the estates of the Batthyánys. During the year 1784 the serfs of the manor of Németujvár actually rose in revolt. Baron Ladislas Prónay, a member of the *consilium locumtenentiale*, was deputed by the Emperor Joseph to investigate the causes and provide a remedy for these disorders. The chief points of his report[2] on the complaints of the serfs were as follows:—1. At Nagy-Medves, the lord of the manor had given the vassals lands of inferior quality to those they had formerly possessed. 2. They preferred to give up their vineyards altogether rather than pay taxes on the same as exacted by the *jus montanum* at present in force[3].

---

[1] Chanc. Arch. No. 9610 (1783).

[2] Chanc. Arch. No. 4065 (1785).

[3] Acts XXXI of 1655 and XCVII of 1715 forbade the lord of the manor to exact any dues in addition to tithes.

3. They were compelled to supply oats on the basis of the *jus montanum*. 4. They were forced to carry cartloads a long distance—three days' journey. 5. The remissness in the collection of tithes had caused them considerable loss[1]. 6. *The lord of the manor was retailing excellent wine,* thereby damaging the trade of the village public-house. 7. Any man who came late to his work was punished by having to give three days' service in socage. 8. The survey hitherto in force was faulty, and must be replaced by a new one. 9. The several tenements and cottagers were required to do their service in socage twice over. 10. Finally, a page of the contract relating to socage had been torn out by the *judex nobilium*.

The royal commissary considered these complaints and demands as unjustified. Yet the same were to be heard continually, with every sort of variation, from one end of the country to the other. With a view to obtaining redress or a compliance with their demands, the villages sent delegates (mandatories) every year to Vienna, where they lived at the expense of those who sent them, and caused numerous villages to fall deeply into debt[2]. At last the Chancellery endeavoured to remedy matters by having "unqualified mandatories" of the kind removed from Vienna by force, the excuse being that such proceedings resulted in the "enervation" of the poor ratepayers. By their promises, most agents of the kind succeeded in prevailing on those who sent them to make considerable sacrifices. The peasants residing in Croatia and Slavonia, having on one occasion assembled at the Zágráb Fair, addressed a petition to the Emperor complaining of all their troubles. They would like to enter His Majesty's presence, but the county authorities would only imprison them on the first attempt. They had to support everything and everybody, but they looked in vain for justice from the counties. If they could only have a legal protector dependent solely on the grace of His Majesty, they would gladly pay him 1000 florins by adding two to three kreuzers to every

---

[1] By Act xxx of 1569—confirmed by Act xi of 1715—the corn had to be subjected to the levying of tithes before St Stephen's Day (20 August) to avoid injuring the poor people.

[2] Chanc. Arch. Nos. 1402 and 1666 (1781).

florin of taxes[1]. The conviction that the serfs were burdened by unjust exactions in dealing with their superiors, and that what they considered justice could be obtained from the sovereign alone, was continually gaining ground. It is easy to imagine the power this conviction must have exercised upon simple minds. The moment any obligation hitherto imposed on the peasantry ceased to be regarded by them as justifiable, the very foundations of their whole system of service were shaken. It will suffice to cite one instance of the enormous influence such ideas and the men who preached them obtained over the Magyar peasantry. In 1782 some person, in the name of the parish of Czegléd, submitted to the Emperor a petition drawn up *in German*[2].

We have perhaps treated of these matters beyond the scope of our subject and the space at our disposal. However, these data, which throw light on the pretensions and desires of the peasantry of various parts of the country and cover practically the whole sphere of their political life, prove clearly enough that their lot in Hungary cannot have been a particularly hard one. Since trouble could be originated, and even disturbances come, from such causes as those that inspired the good folk of Rákos and Medves, there must already have been a recognition of the fundamental principles which underlie the rights of property and persons. Not only did the new settlers, whose numbers were increasing from year to year, and who naturally had to be granted comparatively important favours, themselves participate in a large number of advantages; their example and their prosperity helped to raise the level of the peasants in general. In the eighteenth century the Hungarian serfs were no longer "thralls" (*Leibeigene*); they were rather tenants in fee simple, who were fully informed as to their rights and duties by precise contracts. There are even instances of artisans voluntarily becoming serfs[3]. As the primitive financial conditions of the country prevented the services due from being paid in money, the serfs were forced into a kind of patriarchal dependence on their lords

---

[1] Chanc. Arch. No. 8508 (1783).

[2] Chanc. Arch. No. 4945 (1783). Czegléd was, and is, a characteristically Magyar town.

[3] Chanc. Arch. No. 8629 (1783). We have an instance of an inhabitant of Gálszécs doing so in 1671.

which was liable to many abuses. They were subject to the infliction of stripes and to confinement in the stocks; though neither of these are extraordinary in the days of Maria Teresa and Joseph, when flogging was in vogue all over the monarchy.

As we have seen, the continual progress of civilization began to improve the lot of peasants in Hungary. We have seen that Parliament also took an interest in their welfare up to a certain point. None the less, in treating of the history of the Hungarian serfs, we must lay stress on the regrettable fact that they looked for the alleviation of their lot in the eighteenth century, all over the country, not to Parliament or the nobility, but to the favour of the monarch.

The starting-point of this evolution was the celebrated *Urbarium* (Statute relating to socage) issued by Maria Teresa. When, on Sept. 14, 1764, Parliament rejected the proposal for a redemption of the obligation to furnish a *posse comitatus*, the Queen for the first time called upon the estates to consider the condition of the *misera plebs contribuens* in order to alleviate their condition and to quiet the conscience of her Majesty[1]. But Parliament did nothing, for any radical change would have been opposed to the views even of the most cultured. Such a scheme for the redress and regulation of the various grievances and abuses, as the Queen had now drawn up, was conceivable as the product of many years' work of mechanical routine in the Chancelleries; it could not result from the rapid, noisy, and hasty deliberations of an eighteenth-century Parliament. Consequently, the Queen regarded it as a duty of conscience to relieve the burdens of the people herself, taking advantage of her prerogative to act without the assistance of Parliament.

It was the duty of the sovereign to provide for the maintenance of the basis of contribution, and it is by this principle that Hungarian publicists[2] have defended the prerogative of the monarch to regulate the conditions of socage. The Hun-

---

[1] Horváth, M., p. 366.

[2] Ürményi, *Jus Publ.* III. ch. 4, § 41: "Ex eodem denique Principio (quod Regia Maj. conservationi fundi contributionalis intenta esse debeat) fluit etiam Urbarialis regulatio, quid videlicet Rusticus domino terrestri pro terra et beneficiis in dominio possessis tam in pecunia quam et in operis praestandum habeat."

garian Parliaments have at all times exercised this right of government, and, although it was a cardinal privilege of the Hungarian nobles that they had the right of disposing of their possessions, the addition of the word "just" imposed certain restrictions. As early as 1756, a statute relating to socage was issued for Slavonia; 'hat for Hungary proper and Croatia followed in 1767; while that for the regulation of socage in the "Banat" dates from 1780 (the year of incorporation)[1]. For the carrying out of this improvement, the chief credit is due to the Court councillor, Brunsvick. We must lay stress on the fact that the regulation of the conditions of socage was carried out in Hungary long before such a measure was taken in Moravia, Bohemia and Silesia, where—according to the Council of State of Vienna—the abuses were much greater than in Hungary. The Queen devoted all her energies to the performance of this extremely difficult task. "For the sake of a few magnates and nobles," she wrote to Count Nicholas Pálffy, the Lord Chief Justice, "I do not intend to risk eternal damnation." With the Queen the chief consideration was sympathy with the people's lot, but there can be no doubt that her councillors were only too glad of the favourable opportunity to shake the very foundations of the Hungarian constitution—in a peaceful manner and under the guise of humanity[2].

The regulations issued in 1767 were by no means radical in character. At bottom, its most important points differed but little from the regulations actually in force in most parts of the country. In only one point were those regulations significant in respect of principle. Hitherto, owing to the force of circumstances and to the power exercised by the stronger party, the burdens the law had imposed on the serfs were set down as the minimum which could be exacted from them—a course that opened the way to endless oppression. The

[1] Szlemenics, Paul, *Magyar törvények tört. irata*, p. 195. For previous history of the "Banat," v. pp. 49, 58.

[2] A long extract of the regulations of Maria Teresa will be found in M. Horváth's history (vol. VIII. pp. 384—8). The full text is given by Nicolai (*Reisen*, vol. VI. supplement), and copious extracts are to be found in Townson's book, and a complete discussion would therefore be superfluous here.

decided tendency of the decree issued by Maria Teresa was to convert this minimum into a maximum. Any change in the future (renewal of contracts, etc.) was permissible only if more favourable to the peasants than the former state of things had been. Further, the all-powerful county authorities were, according to the terms of this decree, replaced by special commissaries endowed with power to decide in all cases relating to the *Urbarium*. The serfs were once more brought into direct contact with the supreme authority of the State. It is one of the undying merits of the great Queen that in this manner, without deranging the existing order, she held out hopes of a better future to the plebs, and all this on the basis of historical right, with every precaution to avoid injury to any interests. At last the peasants knew who was really concerned in their welfare. In some places exaggerated hopes resulted in deeds of violence, and, though such cases were comparatively rare and were everywhere without result, the lowest grades of society were affected by the consciousness that the Hungarian nobility, who had hitherto been the oppressors of the people, were now held in check by the more powerful arm of an exalted benefactor. This effect of the measure, and its reaction on Vienna, explains a good deal. Austrian politicians at once drew general conclusions, believing that they had at last found a means of alienating the masses from the standard of the nobility and from the national cause.

The nobility themselves looked upon the change in this light. They had been deprived, not merely of revenue, but of political importance. As Barcsay's above-quoted verse says,

"I remember how, when the *Urbarium* was published,
As we danced in thy house we wept over the fall of our country."

Even a writer whose attachment to the Court is above suspicion—the man responsible for the projects for the Parliament of 1764—considered it a perfectly unjustifiable proceeding to ignore the former state of things except in so far as it was favourable to the serfs[1]. The same writer enumerates a number of instances of actual loss resulting from the measure. In the

[1] *Urbarium*, Art. 27 ; cf. p. 176.

Alföld large villages had rented several farms, paying an *arenda* for the same. According to the new principles, the *arenda* could not be increased, though the value of land was constantly rising. The regulations forbade the nobles to recover the said farms with a view to colonising them.

As in every other field, in that of the reform of the condition of the peasantry too, the Government of Maria Teresa acted as a mediator between the older system and that of the modern State. It endeavoured to do as much good as it could, on the basis of the older institutions, and with the aid of the adherents of the older *régime*.

In the question of the condition of serfs, too, Joseph II took up a more decided position than his mother had done. For a great part of his life he was concerned with their fate, and when, on his death-bed, he was forced to renounce the results of his enormous activity, what he had done for the peasantry still remained as one of his surest claims to fame. The first institution which he sought to destroy, was that which was the clearest evidence of the half-thraldom of the peasants, viz. service in socage. Perceiving that it would be a difficult matter to realise his plan everywhere at once, he at first decreed that such service could be redeemed for money on the Crown estates[1]. The question was so important that not only the person deputed to report on the matter, but every councillor of the Chancellery gave individual expression to his views[2]. For our purpose, the opinion and the arguments of Count Charles Zichy (later Lord Chief Justice) are the most important of all.

He held that the redemption of service in socage for money was to be recommended in places where gold circulated among the labourers and where agricultural products were consumed. In such places, the greater facilities for marketing and transporting produce gave the peasants an opportunity of acquiring money and of employing their labour to a proper purpose. As yet the conditions in Hungary were not of such a character. There were few consumers, there was no industry, and consequently agricultural products and labour could not command a fair price. Even trade was practically confined to the districts

[1] Chanc. Arch. No. 9341 (1783).   [2] Neuhold, K., Court Councillor.

flanking the rivers, so that even the carrying of goods could not be regarded as a general source of revenue. Where could the peasants of many districts find the money required for redemption?

If this was the case, the change would be injurious to the interests of the Treasury, of the peasants (who could not even cultivate their lands properly), and of the consumers as a whole. There were indeed districts in Hungary, more fortunate than the rest, where the necessary conditions were at hand. Where possible, the serfs might redeem their services, but only in certain districts. The rule could not be made general.

An official of high rank, one of whose principal tasks was to study the conditions of the country with a view to a solution of the problem, reported of the North-West counties—where, as is well known, most ready money was to be found—that even there the scheme was only practicable in certain districts[1].

In Hungary, in economic respects, the products of the soil were still of paramount importance. Money was not yet the principal regulator of economic life. The existence of a noble *posse comitatus* proves this fact just as clearly as does the payment of obligations by tithes, nonages and service in socage. Every disturbance of the regular course of development, however sublime the ideas to be attained by the upheaval, produced an economic crisis alike among nobles and vassals. Without the arbitrary despotism of the landlords, even a settled population would have been an impossibility[2]. We must not forget that we have to deal, not with North American settlers, but with half-nomad Ruthenians, Wallachians and Servians, and with the shepherd population of the Alföld.

Politically, the most important fact is that—according to the convictions of the Court and of the Viennese Government, rather than that of the interested parties—the Hungarian nobility and constitution was the incarnation of despotism, while the central Government was the champion of liberty.

---

[1] Balassa, Francis: cf. Chanc. Arch. No. 8824 (1784).

[2] Cf. the petition of the county of Szabolcs against the conscription (Chanc. Arch. No. 16,246 (1785)).

CHAPTER III.

NATIONALITY.

IN the history of Hungarian literature and public life, of all the traditional views that find universal acceptance, scarcely any is more prominent than the opinion that the eighteenth century was the age of the decline of nationality in Hungary. It is contended that the national spirit was lulled to sleep both by the good and evil results of the policy of Maria Teresa, and only awakened by the vigorous efforts which Joseph made to force the German language and influence upon Hungary. We meet with this conviction alike in Francis Toldy, in Michael Horváth, and in Tanárky. By accepting the truth of this tradition, the Hungarians of the nineteenth century, with their high ambitions for the improvement of their whole intellectual existence, practically passed a sentence of condemnation on the preceding age. In order to do it justice, we must distinguish two points of view as touching the question of nationality. The first is what we may call the statistical part of the question, viz. the proportion of the increase or decrease of the Hungarian (Magyar) element as compared with those of other tongues. The second—which can be answered by history alone—is the amount of energy that the idea of nationality was able to inspire in those who were properly Hungarian (Magyar) in character. The first marks the extent of the movement, the second its intensity.

Despite the universal conviction above-mentioned, the facts show that, during the whole time between the occupation of the country by the Magyars and the age of Széchenyi, there was no period when more was done towards consolidating the Hungarian nationality than during the eighteenth century, branded as it has been with the stigma of stagnation and lethargy. This surprising result is revealed to us, not by an investigation of the important and clamorous political movements, but by a careful observation of that silent, almost imperceptible, process of colonisation which entirely changed the ethnological map of a large part of the country. In the same way, even the transformation of continents and oceans has been due, not so much to the activity of volcanic forces, as to the action of the tiniest organisms.

In dealing with the problem of the new settlers and of colonisation, our essay must deal not so much with those districts in which the Hungarian or other races developed undisturbed from time immemorial, as with those in which there was a constant struggle for the possession of the soil. For a knowledge of the conditions of life, the places where transitions and struggles occurred are the most instructive for study.

The great plain of the Lowlands (Alföld), which we are so fond of regarding as the favourite home of the Hungarian (Magyar), had on several occasions to be reconquered by that nation. After the ravages of the Tartars (1241), the Cumanians chose that spot to wedge themselves into the body of the nation. In point of religion, culture and language, they were a foreign people. For a whole century, they continued to weaken and harass the nation, but, after their conversion, they constituted its mainstay alike in war and in peace. Scarcely had the Cumanians become absorbed by Magyardom, when their common nationality was exposed to a still graver danger. It was again the Alföld that suffered most from the yoke of that Turkish dominion, which has left almost indelible traces in that part of the country. By its conquest, the Sultans cut off Transylvania from the rest of Hungary. Hungarians (Magyars) were to be found in the larger villages only, and in the northern regions. So far back as the battle of Mohács (1526), they began to be pressed out by the Serbs (Rascians)[1], who followed in the tracks of the Turkish armies and pressed northwards in ever-increasing

---

[1] They came from Ipek, in old Servia, called Rascia. It is the country near Novibazar. They were and are called Rascians, but they resent the name as an invective.

numbers[1]. In the territory occupied by the Turks, with the exception of the largest open spots which offered protection to individuals only, not to a nation, the Hungarian element was nowhere safe. In the days of Matthias Corvinus, hundreds of populous villages and townships flourished in places of which even the names have now been almost forgotten. The Hungarians, who had been nursed in liberty, were obliged to choose between the uncertain refuge afforded by large townships or the excitements of a "Hajdú" life. We must lay stress on the fact that the pre-eminent centres of the older culture—Budapest, Székes-Fejérvár, Esztergom, Pécs, Szeged, Temesvár, Kalocsa— were the towns that suffered most. Town-life did not harmonise with Turkish institutions, and villages alone were tolerated. However large and populous Kecskemét, Vásárhely and even Debreczen might be, since their populations consisted for the most part of agricultural labourers and cattle-breeders, they had the greatest difficulty in supplying the culture and civilization of regular towns. It was in this part of the country that the work of the ages of Louis the Great and of Matthias was destroyed, and the fact, that it was here that only market towns, and not towns endowed with corporate rights, survived, is still making its influence felt. In the southern Marches the population was almost exterminated, and ever since 1526 the area of the waste districts had continually been extending towards the interior of the country. The only places that offered refuge to the Hungarians were Transylvania on the one side, and the northern Marches on the other. Only the heroic deeds of the Zrinyis and Dobós, and the organised power of the Princes of Transylvania and of the Hungarian nobles, saved the Magyars, as a whole nation, from a fate similar to that of the Serbs, Bulgarians or Wallachians. A people may be transformed, won over or transplanted—but the only way of dealing with an aristocracy is to exterminate it. In the greater Alföld the aristocracy, both spiritual and temporal, had either been really exterminated or had degenerated. They were replaced by the Spahis, whose foot-

---

[1] Marsilius, *Danubius*, p. 25: "Thraces in Hungariam confluxisse, postquam Hungari majorem Hungariae partem deseruerunt, occupantibus Turcis Temesvar et Budam."

steps were dogged by Rascian Serbs and Wallachians, the latter of whom were continually at war with the relics of the former Hungarian population[1]. A new migration had begun, and for a period of two hundred years the proportion of Hungarians (Magyars) in the Alföld continuously declined, as compared with that of the other races.

It must suffice to cite a few instances in order to show the distribution of population. In 1602, the inhabitants of Kalocsa were for the most part Turks and Rascians[2]. Even as late as 1712, this town contained altogether 100 houses. The conditions were similar all over the diocese[3]. According to official returns of 1692, after the expulsion of the Turks, the total population of the counties of Baranya, Tolna and Somogy—including the town of Pécs—numbered only 3221 souls, of which number the said town claimed 1652[4]. Such was the fate of the district where Louis the Great (1367) had established the headquarters of Hungarian learning. Where large communities were preserved, the result was the extinction of numerous villages that had formerly been populous. Lady Montague, the celebrated English traveller who viewed Hungary in 1717, declared the country to be almost as thinly populated as when contemporary travellers described it in the twelfth century. Between Buda and Györ there was scarcely a trace of any civilization. Almost the whole country was covered with forests as far as Eszék, and Hungary

---

[1] Of the town of Tolna, the English traveller, Brown, 1673, remarks that the Hungarian and Rascian inhabitants were at daggers drawn. German ed. p. 117.

[2] Istvanfi, *Hist.* vol. XXXIII. p. 791 (pub. 1622).

[3] Katona, *Hist. Metr. Archiepiscopatus Colocensis*, vol. II. p. 154.

[4] Supplement to the famous system of government of Kollonics (Acad. MS. Fol. 26):

Pécs ...	...	1652 inhabitants.
Dombovár	...	278 ,,
Kaposvár	...	120 ,,
Simontornya	...	278 ,,
Szekszárd	...	290 ,,
Tolna ...	...	160 ,,
Siklós ...	...	300 ,,

Every year they paid a "census" of 2639 florins and 160 florins in kind. I may remark that, to my knowledge, this is the first example of precise data referring to a census in Hungary.

was the Elysium of game and birds[1]. The terms used were
practically the same as those employed by the first discoverers
of North America and Canada, but the eyes of those who gazed
on this other destitute country were saddened by beholding
the ruins of an ancient civilization[2]. After the Turks had left
the country, official records show that only a few Greeks and
Jews remained in the Alföld[3].

The idea of repeopling the country arose simultaneously
with the recovery of the Alföld from Turkish hands. The
important point for investigators of the conditions of nationality
is to see how this repopulation was carried out. According
to the scheme of Kollonics, both Hungarians and foreigners
were to be planted in the country. The towns, however,
should be inhabited by Germans only. The German settlers
should enjoy exemption from taxation for five years, the
Hungarians for three years only. The sole result of the
Turkish overthrow, therefore, would be to replace an Ottoman
by a German hegemony. Far more radical were the proposals
of an over-zealous German writer of 1687—the first apostle
of the *Verwirkungstheorie*—for the repopulation of Hungary[4].
As in that country, he said, not the least important cause of
the frequent rebellions was the villainous robber-people that
had established itself all over the kingdom, the remedy proposed by publicists was that the greater part of this rebelliously
inclined population should be driven out of the country to other
lands, and that their property should be occupied by loyal
nationalities—a proceeding which would weaken the power of
such rebellious inhabitants as were left behind. Such a measure,
he contended, was justified by the right of conquest. One of
the favourite devices of the ancient kings of Assyria and Egypt
is here recommended as a means of securing the territory recovered from the Turks.

---

[1] According to the *Erdebeschreibung* of Häckhel (4°, Ulm, 1740) in Buda on a single
day 80,600 pigeons were offered for sale.

[2] Cf. *Letters of Lady Montague* (Letter XXIII. On Buda).

[3] Kollonics, *Einrichtungswerk*, Acad. MS.

[4] Flämitzer, Joh. Nic., *Der in böhmischen Hosen ausgekleidete ungarische Libertiner*
(Würzburg, 1688), p. 113.

The Court of Vienna did actually start to work energetically on these lines. As early as 1690 fresh gangs of Rascian Serbs began to settle in the southern districts of the country, while every year fresh contingents of Germans swarmed into Buda and other towns. The Magyars, who hurried from distant parts to re-occupy the Alföld, were confined to a stretch of country round which these two nationalities were gradually closing.

In point of nationality, the greatest service rendered by the Rákóczi revolution was that it put an end to this process. It is true that in many places a war of extermination was carried on between the Rascian Serbs and the Magyars. But the military superiority of the " Kurucz " soldiers was maintained for several years, and put an end to the immigration from the two quarters above-mentioned[1]. Hence, the immigration that took place after the Peace of Szatmár (1711) was effected under totally different auspices.

I. *The Servian (Rascian) Settlers in the Alföld.*

The future of Hungary may be said to have depended on the issue of the struggle between three different tendencies, the respective interests of three distinct races, each of which endeavoured to obtain possession of the Alföld. The manner in which this struggle was conducted clearly demonstrates the peculiar character and vitality of each of the three—the Magyars, Rascian Serbs and Germans.

In the Alföld, the most dangerous adversary of the Hungarians was undoubtedly the Serb element. Their brethren who had remained subjects of the Ottoman Empire formed a kind of rearguard for the protection of the Serb immigrants who, under the leadership of such men as Brankovics or Csernovics, had for over two centuries been migrating into Hungary. Leopold endowed them with such extensive political and religious privileges that, for all he cared, they might have formed a State of their

---

[1] " Kurucz " was the popular name of the insurgents after 1672, and is derived from *cruciatus,* crusader. The peasant army in 1514 was raised by a papal bull for a crusade against the Turks, but turned against the nobles. In the same way the later peasant insurrections against the Austrians took the same name. It is still used to denote the anti-Austrian party.

own within the territory of the Hungarian Crown—an opportunity which the Hungarian Protestants had never been permitted to enjoy. The extreme antagonism existing between the two races and their faiths was at all times a guarantee that the Vienna Government could rely on the savage and ruthless courage of the Serbs. As a rule, the Emperor was the ally of the Czar, the head of their Church—a fact that further enhanced their political value. Finally, they seem to have been well equipped, both economically and physically, for the struggle for life. They were cattle-breeders, and at this period this seemed to be the only occupation suitable for the Alföld. The enterprising spirit of their traders was conspicuous. They were already acclimatised. The settlements planted by George Brankovics so far back as the days of the Hunyadis, are still to be found in the very heart of the country; and under the aegis of the Crescent they had advanced further inland. Though foreign and hateful in the eyes of the Hungarians, the Serb people did not turn their ambitions and endeavours towards the Viennese Court, despite all the favours extended to them. It is true, indeed, that during the eighteenth century they were always to be relied upon for assistance against the Turks, but, whenever any opportunity offered, they showed a prepossession in favour of the Russians and the Czar.

In 1702, Dositheus, Patriarch of Jerusalem, wrote to Peter the Great, that the Emperor Leopold was persecuting the Christians far more ruthlessly than even Diocletian and Maximian had done[1]. He spoke in the name of the Christians of the Greek Oriental Church. Two years later, on Nov. 25, 1704, a Servian named Bosics went in person to Moscow to complain of the Austrian intrigues. In the name of the Servians living in Hungary he begged the Czar to make them his subjects, for they were very numerous and at all times ready to fight against the Turks. Now the Hungarians, who had risen in revolt, were summoning them to take arms against the Emperor[2]; but the allies of the former were the French and Swedes—the Czar's foes—and, in unanimous agreement with their brethren of the

[1] Brückner, Alex., *Peter der Grosse*, p. 456.
[2] v. Manifesto of Francis Rákóczi, Aug. 9, 1703.

same faith who were subjects of the Ottoman Empire and of
Venice, they had determined to concentrate their hopes in the
Czar. Should these hopes be frustrated, they would all perish[1].
Their future ideals had impressed this people far more deeply
than their present situation, which they owed entirely to the
favour of the Emperor at Vienna.

Consequently, in Vienna too they had to be considered as
possible enemies; and the necessary preparations for meeting
such an eventuality had to be made. In 1691 their waywode,
George Brankovics, was cast into prison, but even in his captivity
this prominent Serb appealed to the Czar to intervene in his
behalf[2]. After the "Banat" had been occupied, a stop was put
in that part of the country to the constant migrations of the
nomad Serb goat-herds, which jeopardised the security of property. They were compelled to do regular military service, and
an attempt was made to force them to settle in permanent
homes. As a result, large numbers of them fled to Russia,
and they emigrated in even greater numbers after the Péró
insurrection of 1735 had made their position a still more
onerous one[3]. They could be of service to the Vienna Government, but it would have been dangerous to give them the
predominance.

A still more important point was that their civilization was
on the lowest possible level. It has already been observed that,
in the eyes of a few short-sighted individuals, this circumstance
was actually a merit[4]. But, in the struggle for existence, they
must undoubtedly have become agricultural labourers, had

---

[1] *Loc. cit.* p. 457. In 1710 Bogdan Popovics was at Moscow on a similar mission.
During the Turkish War of 1711, 19,000 Rascian Serbs desired to unite with the
Russians.

[2] "Regesták Külföldi Levéltárakból" contributed by H. Marczali to the *Történelmi
Tár* of 1881.

[3] This was a peasant insurrection—named after its chief leader Péró (Peter)
Szegedinecz. He was a Serb, but contrived to secure the support of Magyar peasants
too, who imagined they were fighting for Rákóczi. The fact that this is the first occasion
when we hear of Russian intervention in Hungary, is well worth mentioning. At the
time the insurrection broke out the Imperial troops were engaged against the French
and Spaniards. Hence, in a letter dated Kassa, May 19, 1735, Baron Fischer advised
the Chancellor, Count L. Batthyány, to induce the troops of the Russian ally, which
were then concentrated on the frontier, to march against the insurgents.

[4] E.g. Baron Kämpfer.

they desired to maintain themselves in the midst of a denser population. Consequently in their case too the vital question that has always controlled the destiny of nomad peoples was still unanswered—viz. whether they could succeed in finding a sufficiently large territory to ensure their existence, despite their want of civilization. In this case, the competition of Hungarian and German settlers prevented them from obtaining the required territory, and, as they were unable to compete with them, they either emigrated or were reduced to poverty. Yet the Serbs, as a people, are vigorous and impassioned and capable of zealous attachment to their nation and their faith. The greater part of the "Banat," the southern half of Bács county, several districts of the county of Baranya and most of the frontier regions remained still in their hands. But, however important these districts may be, their possession is a mere trifle in comparison with the prospect that seemed so near to realisation at the opening of the eighteenth century, viz. the monopolisation of the Alföld by the Rascian Serbs. "Never were there more Servian-speaking inhabitants among them than at that period," says Ladislas Szalay in his history of the rising of Rákóczi[1]. It will suffice to mention the fact that, during the Rákóczi wars, Servian troops appeared not only before Szeged and Arad, but at Nagy-Várad, Debreczen[2], Kecskemét[3] and Eger, and in the Balaton district[4], in order to understand the important changes that have taken place in that territory—changes which we may hope will be of a permanent character, and which are indeed still in progress.

II. *The German Settlers in the Alföld.*

However, it was the settlement of German colonists that best realised the intentions of Kollonics. They alone were capable

---

[1] *Magyarország története (History of Hungary)*, vol. VI. p. 4.

[2] Szücs, J., *Debreczen város története (History of the Town of D.)*, vol. III. pp. 701—6. Cf. Szalay, L., *Hist. of Hung.* vol. VI. pp. 95—100.

[3] Hornyik, J., *Kecskemét város története (History of the Town of K.)*, vol. IV. In 1704 the Serbs destroyed the greater part of the town and massacred the inhabitants.

[4] In the county of Somogy, too, the vicinity of the township of Attala was inhabited by Serbs, as is proved by a letter written by Gorup, provost of Györ, in 1661.

of fulfilling all expectations, both in promoting civilization and in safeguarding the political and military interests. In this part of the country the struggles carried on were not only political but religious in character, and the Catholic Church—which never ceased to regard the Serbs as enemies—was able to secure the alliance of these German settlers. So soon as the Turks had passed out of Hungary, German settlers following on the heels of the Imperial army, flooded Buda, Pest and the environs of the chief towns. They advanced far into the heart of the country and when the "Banat" fell into the hands of the Emperor, a considerable portion of it was reserved for them. If the inhabitants of the scattered mining towns and Saxon settlements had maintained their isolation for so long under the rule of Hungarian kings, and still considered themselves as belonging to the German nation, what might not be expected from a uniform and systematic process of colonisation carried out in almost depopulated territory, under the powerful aegis of the German Imperial army?

All the means at the disposal of the State were employed both by Leopold and by his sons for the benefit of these German immigrants[1]. Ever since the days of Sully, every European Government had known that its principal source of power lay in the amount of its population—the *aerarium vivum*, as curialistic writers persisted in calling it even down to 1782[2]. In Hungary the Government was also the largest—in fact, almost the exclusive—landowner in the new territory; and it desired to improve the condition of its neglected estates by the aid of foreign labour. The policy of settling Serbs in Hungary formed but the first measure of that superb political crusade to which Prince Eugène has given his name, which considered Constantinople itself as the ultimate object of the victorious Imperial armies; and at the same time planted Catholic German colonists in Hungary, promising there an even greater future to the champions of a centralised Imperial monarchy. The

---

[1] We have an official report for the year 1781 showing the monies expended on immigrants between 1719 and 1780. The total exceeded 4,000,000 florins.

[2] Chanc. Arch. 4742 (July 29, 1782): "Aerarium vivum, quod in contribuente plebe consistit." The work of Tzdenczy.

German settlers, therefore, were the apostles of civilization, nationality and religion—as the politicians of Vienna conceived these principles. Imperial agents actually traversed the Holy Roman Empire, promising land, tools, cattle and exemption from taxation to all persons ready to migrate into Hungary[1]. The country indeed had a bad hygienic reputation—the Germans called it "the cemetery of Europe"—but this fact was due solely to the excess of good fare. All the more tempting was the picture given of its fertility. In Hungary the vines produced gold—not in the figurative but in the literal sense. Rye, if sown for three years in succession, turned into wheat, so enormous was the productive power of the soil[2]! When we find reports of this kind occurring in scientific works, it is easy to imagine the effect which these wondrous promises had upon the poor proletariate of the countryside and towns of Southern Germany.

For the immigrants were almost without exception natives of these southern and south-western districts. This fact was due not only to religious motives—for the Franconian, Bavarian and Swabian districts were almost the only Catholic ones—there were weighty political reasons as well. In Northern Germany, the electorates of Brandenburg, Saxony and Hanover had already developed into powerful States of considerable extent. Their rulers felt the need of an increase of population, and, far from encouraging an exodus of their human capital, were actually inviting foreign immigrants to settle in their dominions. Frederick William I, the King who did most towards colonising Prussia, was the contemporary of Charles VI; the Huguenots were just immigrating into Hanover; and Saxony, regarding Poland in much the same light as Austria did Hungary, was sending her surplus population in that direction. The fact that there were comparatively few Bavarians among the new settlers is also explained by the territorial extent of that electorate. The majority of the emigrants from the Empire were subjects of the counts and knights of the Empire, of Imperial free cities,

---

[1] Many contracts relating to cases of this kind dating from the time of Charles VI, are to be found in the Archives of the Chancellery and of the Royal Chamber.

[2] Häckhel, *Erdbeschreibung*, p. 3851.

and in particular (as is only natural) of Princes of the Church Owing to the limited territory belonging to the various feudal lords, oppression was more widespread in these cases and the feeling of unity least in evidence. On the other hand, the petty feudal lords gained more from the support of the Emperor than from their own insignificant estates, consequently they either threw no obstacles in the way of the emigrants, or at most claimed some pecuniary compensation. It is no mere accident that the Swabian district—the one split up into most petty lordships—gave its name to this whole new and vast migration to the East.

We have no reason to question the patriotism and national feeling or, at any rate, the loyalty of an Austrian, a Saxon or a Brandenburger, nor to deny that, in large townships like Nuremberg, Augsburg or Frankfort, a certain particularism replaced such feelings. But how could their feudal sovereigns have been regarded by the subjects of a Count Leiningen, of a Baron Sickingen, of the numberless petty knights or cities, or of a monastery supplying $1\frac{1}{3}$ soldiers to the Imperial army? Such immigrants, though destined as the apostles of German nationality, had possessed no opportunity of realising what was meant by a "fatherland" or a "nation" at home.

Apart from national and religious interests, the immigration of these settlers was particularly important from a civilizing point of view, for Hungary had now become a colony. In all parts of the country where the Royal Chamber or Church had property, Swabian or other new villages were built on the deserted plots. It was not only to the Alföld, to the Bakony district and the Trans-Danubian regions that the German swarms were admitted; they penetrated as far as the distant counties of Zemplén, Szabolcs and Bihar[1], and there too forced themselves upon the Hungarians, who had hitherto passed an isolated existence. An almost unbroken chain of German villages extended over the length and breadth of the country[2],

[1] E.g. Rátka in Zemplén county, in 1754, Trautsonfalva *ibid.*, Rakamaz in Szabolcs, St Job in Bihar county, in 1765. Cf. Chanc. Arch. No. 1785.

[2] I have been able to find over 800 *new* instances of German settlements occurring between 1711 and 1780.

and, being better farmers, their steady perseverance enabled the Germans to win land even from the Hungarians.

All this was only one half of the work of colonisation. As a civilized people, the Germans after all preferred the towns. Under the influence of the new settlers, and of the stimulus provided by the maintenance of a large army and the existence of a class of wealthy landowners, the country began to recover itself and to offer a golden future to industry. Even before this date, as has several times been remarked, the German element predominated in the towns[1]; now it was given access to the heart of the country, and to the market towns as well. In 1740 Buda was a purely German city, while most of the inhabitants of Pest were of German extraction[2]. At Pécs, Fehérvár, Szeged, Arad, the bulk of the population was German. At Szabadka, Ujvidék and Temesvár, Germans shared the municipal government with Rascians. Pétervárad was almost exclusively a German town, as was the inner part (city) of Szigetvár[3]. Wherever master craftsmen were wanted, Germans were to be found. At Kecskemét, we find a German school in 1782[4]. Somorja was inhabited by German Lutherans[5], who petitioned for a separate church; at Léva, too, there was a German congregation, which petitioned for a pastor and a schoolmaster in their own tongue[6]. German was the official language employed by the fishermen of Tolna, by the guilds of Szekszárd, by the millers of Esztergom, by the shoemakers' and masons' guilds of Léva and the Catholic parish of Sárospatak[7]. At Békés-Gyula, we find German tailors; and Német-Gyula (German Gyula) still constitutes a separate ward[8]. Even in

---

[1] Bél, Mátyás, *Notit. Hung. nov.* vol. I. p. 647: "Universis de Liberis Regiisque urbibus adfirmamus: Tantum eas et opibus valere et cultu, quantum Germanicarum coloniarum admiserunt."

[2] *Ibid.* vol. III.

[3] Count Teleki, *Reisen*, p. 209.

[4] The schoolmaster was John Buzás, who expounded the French letter of Dulaurier written to the Pope Pius VI, which was translated into German by the Abbot Rautenstrauch.

[5] Chanc. Arch. No. 6363 (1783).

[6] *Ibid.* No. 3713 (1783).

[7] *Ibid.* No. 5832.

[8] *Ibid.* No. 561 (1781).

the little township of Pakrácz, in Slavonia, all the guilds were German[1]. Hundreds of instances of the kind could be cited, but it must suffice to mention the fact that, of the numerous bills and receipts made out by artisans to be found among the rolls of 1780–85—with the exception of those coming from Debreczen and Szatmár-Németi—there are scarcely any which are not in German[2]. The postal officials, the customs officers, the staffs of the offices of the salt *régie*, of the Royal Chamber and of the Crown estate offices, were all Germans. All the way from Buda viâ Szeged to Szeben, all the innkeepers were Germans[3].

From the moment they entered the country, an important distinction appears between the two classes of immigrants—agricultural and urban. Those who were peasants did their duty and worked satisfactorily. Of the artisans and, in general, of the town inhabitants (he is dealing with Pest) Mátyás Bél speaks as follows[4]:—"To the Serbs (Rascians) living in the town were added the Germans, who had been invited to come. A struggle was made against them, but not always with success. Not only did an excessive love of wandering induce many to pass on after a few months' sojourn ; even those who remained did not all thrive to the same extent. Among the newcomers the conviction prevailed that, as the barbarians had been driven off the fertile soil, it was possible to live in Hungary without work and without 'sweat of the brow.' All they had to do, so they believed, was to divide the spoil[5]; they were far too indolent to be the founders of a new colony." A German traveller warned visitors to Hungary to be on their guard against the unscrupulousness of the German innkeepers[6]. According to a Swiss traveller, the German colonists emigrating to Hungary were the scum and refuse of the Bavarian, Swabian, Frank and Rhine districts. On their arrival, they at once spent the little

---

[1] Chanc. Arch. No. 6203 (1783).
[2] Several from Temesvár and Becskerek are in Servian.
[3] Lehmann, *Reisen*, p. 64.
[4] *Notit. Hung. nov.* vol. III. p. 88.
[5] " Ad Porsennae bona diripienda, se venisse rati " (Livius). Mátyás Bél had a liking for classical quotations.
[6] Lehmann, *Seypp.* pp. 64, 65.

money they had brought with them in drink; and as the Government did not take proper care of them, they died of grief or of diseases contracted, not from the climate, but from their debauchery[1]. Finally, as for the so-called "intellect" of the country, i.e. the civil servants, who were for the most part Austrians or Czechs, the same Swiss traveller declared that they did not possess a vestige of patriotism, that they knew nothing, and were entirely lacking in goodwill and ambition. Their characteristic peculiarities were arrogance, selfishness, ruthlessness and a certain swagger[2].

The Roman legions had not been merely conquerors, by their settlement they laid the foundations of culture wherever they carried their victorious banners. Now too a Roman Emperor was ruling, and the victories of Prince Eugène promised not only conquests but the fulfilment of an important civilizing mission. Let us now see the manner in which the Imperial army went about its task. Hitherto, in order to avoid the charge of partiality, we have refrained from quoting the opinions of Hungarians (Magyars) on the immigrants. Bél was a Slovak, but he was certainly more in sympathy with the Germans than with the Hungarians, and was an out-and-out Imperialist. Lehmann was a patriotic German, and Risbeck went so far as almost to give the Germans the superiority over the French; consequently their evidence is of sufficient weight. For a testimony to the character of the Imperial Austrian army it must suffice to cite a book which was the cause of a public scandal in the Hungarian Parliament, and which recommended the extermination or banishment of the Hungarians (Magyars) as the only means of putting an end to their criminal defiance of the Imperial power. The author of this work, *Der in böhmischen Hosen ausgekleidete ungarische Libertiner*, must be looked upon as an absolutely trustworthy witness when he gives evidence against the German soldiery. His testimony is as follows: The terrible despotism practised in Hungary ought after all to be checked, all the more so "because with their oppression, bullying, in-

---

[1] *Briefe eines reisenden Franzosen*, vol. I. p. 463: "Das liederlichste Gesindel aus Bayern, Schwaben, Franken und den Rheinländern."

[2] *Ibid.* vol. I. p. 450.

satiable thirst for plunder and inhuman ravages, the German soldiers are so unbridled, that many volumes would be required to relate all their deeds of violence and their acts of inhuman cruelty. The Turks treat the people far better than they do[1]." We must repeat: these are not the words of some ranting "Kurucz," but of Johann Nicol. Flämitzer, an Austrian subject and a former captain in the Imperial army, who is loud in his denunciation of the *perduellische perfidia* of the Hungarian estates.

The colonists were to pay taxes, the officials to send in reports; the soldiers were probably strong enough to put down any Hungarian attempts at separation. There could, however, be no talk of the establishment of German nationality in Hungary. That part of the colonists, possessed of the most moral weight and economic importance, was German in speech only, and did not long remain faithful even to that custom. The presence in the country of the other Germans only served to add fresh fuel to the flames of Germanophobia.

III.   *The Magyar Settlers in the Alföld.*

The Rascian and German settlements were of importance, not only from a national, but also from a political and constitutional point of view. They were organised by the Government at Vienna with the open or covert purpose of eventually using them as levers for overthrowing the Hungarian constitution. In both cases we are dealing with genuine colonisation, the settlers were not in search of a new home, but were intended to transform their adopted country in the interests of older national ambitions. The Germans had their eyes on Vienna, the Rascian Serbs on Moscow.

---

[1] Flämitzer, *loc. cit.* p. 116. The title of the book contains the following denunciations: "Mit was für perduellischer Perfidia die Stände und Unterthanen des Königreichs gegen die höchst gerecht und befugsame Verordnungnen Ihro Kayserl. Mayestät die Waffen geführet, dadurch nicht allein ipso facto aller gehabten Privilegien und Freiheiten *verwürcket*, sondern auch denen von Gott gesegneten Siegreichen Waffen allerhöchstgedachter Kaiserl. M. sich selbst tanquam jure belli subactos zu Erbeignen Unterthanen pflichtig gemacht haben."

After the expulsion of the Turks we can trace the beginnings of an immigration of a different character, which also populated the Alföld, but was not subordinated to any political tendencies—the sole purpose being the cultivation of the soil. The settlement of Slovaks in the Hungarian Alföld was the work of the landed proprietors. They saw that their estates were depopulated ; they desired to enhance their productive capacity; and for that purpose imported the hard-working, unpretentious and submissive inhabitants of the Western Carpathians.

Of the Hungarian serfs it was said that they were "litigious companions," since they clung so firmly to their rights[1]. If the settlement of Magyars was likely to promote litigation, that of Germans was likely to be expensive; and the extensive privileges offered them in the "Banat" constituted a tempting precedent. The Slovaks, on the other hand, who received land in the Alföld (which they regarded as a kind of earthly Paradise) in place of the poor, barren soil they possessed, would without doubt be just as submissive as in their old northern home. In many cases the change of habitation did not even involve allegiance to a new lord[2]. Most of the Slovaks were Lutherans, and those of that denomination were settled only on the land of the more tolerant lords or of such as professed the same faith. The ecclesiastical lords and the bigots invited only Catholic Slovaks to settle on their estates.

Of the Lutheran Slovak settlements, the most important were those in the county of Békés. Here the Harrucker family (barons) played practically the same part as Lord Baltimore in Maryland or William Penn in the country to which he gave his name; they accepted settlers of every nationality and denomination, but planted them in separate places[3]. Csaba, which was founded in 1715, was the principal colony—a kind of Slovak Boston. So early as 1722, it began to send out groups of settlers who repeopled Szarvas, in conjunction with the people of Aszód. At the same period Mezöberény too was repeopled

---

[1] " Id certum est colonos Slavos fructuosiores heris esse solitos quam Hungaros, si adtendas operarum assiduitatem."

[2] Bél, Mátyás, *Notit. Hung. nov.* vol. IV. p. 32.

[3] See the chapter on " Economic Conditions."

—these are facts which in themselves prove the extraordinary increase of the population and the advance of their prosperity[1].

"A blessed soil is that possessed by Baron Hérók! What troubles distress his serfs? They do not even know what vassalage is, and are unacquainted with penury[2]." A particular cause of envy was the way in which benefices and royal prerogatives were redeemed on this estate. A common settlement of these colonists of the county of Békés was Nyíregyháza (1754), the old "Hajdú" privileges of which had been invalidated by Act LXVII of 1638. Later on, fresh colonists were sent to this district as well as to Csaba and Szarvas, from the mother country, i.e. the Highlands. From the headquarters in the regions watered by the Körös they made their way into the counties of Szatmár, Arad and Csanád.

It is a characteristic fact that the customs of the Slovak villages beyond the Tisza were modified to fit in with those of the large Hungarian townships. In the mountain districts, not even the largest free borough possessed as big a population as several villages did in this part of the country. The people who had been accustomed to live in thinly-populated parishes now began to vie with the Hungarians in this respect too, so decisive an influence did the unchanging formation of the land and the uniform manner of cultivation exercise on the destiny of the towns and villages.

A second main group of Slovak settlements covered the district between the Danube and the Tisza. In many places the Northern Slavs met their Southern brothers. From Aszód to Kis-Körös (1715) and to Keczel (1734), in the whole county of Pest, with the exception of the large market towns, the Slavs constituted the bulk of the population. With the Germans, who also swarmed to these parts, they could not get on very well; they agreed much better with the Hungarians. They extended to the county of Bács as well, and constituted the bulk of the population of Bács-Ujfalu, Kernyaja, Kula and Doroszló. In this district, whose chief coloniser was the Archbishop of Kalocsa,

[1] Thessedik, *Landmann*, p. 94.
[2] *Ibid.* p. 101. This is the only Hungarian quotation to be found in the German text of this book.

there were numerous Catholic settlements. But colonies of this kind were not formed by the landed proprietors only. Industrious natives of the barren Highlands came uninvited to the Alföld, where they performed the bulk of the field labour[1]; and these itinerant labourers generally left one or two permanent settlers behind on the fertile soil[2]. According to Baron Ladislas Prónay, the northern parts of the counties of Gömör and Nográd furnished large numbers of emigrants of this character[3].

From the point of view of Hungarian nationality, the settlement of the Slovaks in the Alföld was an extremely felicitous measure. It everywhere proved an obstacle in the way of German and Rascian expansion, and nowhere did it hinder—on the contrary, as we have seen, it actually aided—the advance of Magyardom. To the Hungarians alone did these Slovak settlers show an inclination to accommodate themselves. Even their extraordinary love of wandering, which has been used as a reproach against them, was rather beneficial than otherwise— it served to preserve large territories from being inundated with Rascian (Serb) settlers. Of less importance were the Slovak settlements in the Trans-Danubian district. But the inhabitants of the Highlands did get across to the counties of Fehér, Esztergom and Komárom, whither the landed proprietors imported Slovak settlers to mingle with the Germans.

Simultaneously with the conquest of the country by the Turks, several Croatian colonies were established in Hungary. They played practically the same part on the western confines of the country as the (Rascian) Serbs in the South and the Wallachians in the East. Only, as a result of their professing the Roman Catholic faith, they never constituted so distinct an

---

[1] Cf. Baron Lawrence Orczi's *Address to Ákos Barcsay—of Agricultural Labour* (*Mezei foglalatosságról*):
"Here am I encamped with strapping Slovaks,
Two hundred harvesters of Kis-Hont county."

[2] Korabinszky, *Geogr. Lexikon* (of Szabadka): "Zudem kommen alle Jahre aus Mähren, auch aus dem Liptauer, Árvaer, und Thuróczer Komitate viele Leute beiderley Geschlechtes in die Feldarbeit hieher, von welchen immer einige, die keine Lust haben in ihr Vaterland zurück zu kehren, hier sesshaft werden."

[3] Arch. *Cons. locumten.* No. 44,855 (1787); Chanc. Arch. No. 15,926 (1785).

element, and were in a comparatively short time absorbed by the Hungarians or other older settlers. We find them not only in the counties of Somogy and Zala (where they were afterwards regarded as Croatised Magyars who had returned to Hungary) but in the counties of Vas, Sopron and even Pozsony. In the latter county, the Croatian village of Senquitz is particularly famous as having been the birthplace of Gabriel Kolinovics and Martin George Kovacsics, two celebrated historians of the eighteenth century. We find Croats settled in many places where there are no longer any traces of them to-day. At Rohoncz there was a Croatian shoemakers' guild in existence so late as 1780[1]. In general, this Croatian migration to Hungary was a result of the misfortunes of the Croatian magnates, whom the advance of the Turks drove back to their estates in Hungary. This settlement also was a work of the landed proprietors, and was not effected under the guidance of Government.

Taking all these settlements together, we can form a complete picture of the nationalistic conditions in Hungary, and particularly of those of the Magyar, whose situation was the most important question for the Hungarian State. We believe that to compare the position of Magyardom in the eighteenth century, both in regard to its numbers and power, with that of the same race in the nineteenth is to offer a most convincing proof of the vitality and power of absorption which it possesses. There may be persons who prefer to review with proud self-consciousness the ages of Louis the Great and Matthias Corvinus, when the political predominance of the Magyars could not even be questioned. Yet strength is probably better proved and developed by struggles than by undisturbed possession, and in the eighteenth century—a fact on which we must lay stress before proceeding—the struggle was carried on by Hungarian (Magyar) society without the aid, and often in direct defiance, of the Government and the State.

The expulsion of the Turks eventually produced almost no change in the ethnological conditions of Hungary, so that they can be described in very few words. In the North-West the Slovaks

[1] Chanc. Arch. No. 6069 (1780).

were continually absorbing the German populations of the towns ;
semi-nomad Wallachs and Ruthenes dwelt in the mountains of
the North-East and East, or wandered to the plains beyond ;
to the South, the Serbs formed a fringe that gradually narrowed
as it approached northwards ; to the South-West were scattered
groups of Croats; and in the counties lying due West the Germans
coalesced with their kinsmen of the Austrian Provinces[1].

A glance at the map will show that the lesser and the greater
Alföld, as far as the Maros and the Francis Canal respectively,
as well as the greater part of the hilly district beyond the
Danube, is mostly, or rather almost exclusively, peopled by
Magyars. This has always been the general aspect of this part
of the country as a whole. But a little more than a century ago
there was a considerably larger sprinkling of foreign elements
in the districts occupied by the Hungarians, and it became
even questionable whether the great Alföld would retain its
Magyar character. Besides, the region inhabited by Hungarians
did not yet by any means possess the political and economic
predominance which it enjoys to-day. The change was not
effected at once, but was due entirely to the exertions of the
Hungarians of the eighteenth century. For a Hungarian it is
a stirring task to describe this process and the means by which
it was accomplished, though the complexity of the factors involved makes the undertaking a difficult one.

Naturally enough, we are unable to determine accurately
the number of inhabitants who spoke Hungarian, or their exact

---

[1] A letter of Sir Robert Murray Keith, British Ambassador at Vienna, dated from
Temesvár, Nov. 29, 1790, illustrates the state of the "Banat." "This Banat is one of
the most fruitful countries of Europe, wherever industry is in any shape exerted. A
large three years' old ox can be bought here, in time of peace, for less than a pound
sterling; a lamb for sixpence, and a load of hay, as much as four oxen can draw, for
three and sixpence.

"One very strange thing is remarked by every traveller through the Banat. The
villages are large, though distant, and we meet, by turns, Wallachian, German,
Sclavonian, and French, nay even Italian villages; the inhabitants of which have
different languages, religions, manners, features and modes of government ; having no
other intercourse with each other than that of mere necessity, and *never intermarrying*.
A dash of the Gipsy nation and a sprinkling of Jews are met with everywhere, and the
whole furnishes a grotesque and singular variety. The French are mostly from
Lorraine, sober and industrious people, the Germans from Swabia, strong and active ;
and I was pleased to find that both nations thrive and grow rich."

proportion to the other nationalities. Neither the official censuses nor the diocesan returns had any regard for such questions ; in fact the language predominating in the several parishes was not included in the returns of the various dioceses until the second decade of the nineteenth century[1]. Even with the aid of the most perfect apparatus of archives, registers and rolls, it is impossible to arrive at any result, for each several official document deals with individuals, families or classes only. The more or less perfect absorption of the settlers by the Hungarians in the eighteenth century was a very slow process, it was not the work of the organised power of a central Government, but of the moral predominance of a national Church and of a nobility established on a medieval basis. This fact alone can account for the peaceful and gradual process of Magyarisation, which is as old as the history of Hungary and which was accomplished before the introduction of the system of universal schooling—now so essential a factor in the transformation of the whole course of popular life.

We must approach the object of our investigations by the circuitous method of quoting particular instances to establish general conclusions.

In the county of Pest, in the heart of the country, towards the middle of the eighteenth century, there were undoubtedly more foreigners than Hungarians[2]. Kis-Körös, the birthplace of the great national poet Alexander Petöfi, was still entirely Slovak in character and was in fact not peopled at all until 1715[3]. At Szent-Endre there were as yet scarcely any Hungarians at all, and on the Island of Csepel there was only one purely Hungarian parish.

In the county of Szabolcs we find the large Slovak township of Nyiregyháza and the German Rakamaz, in fact there were still nine Ruthenian and three Wallachian parishes there in 1787.

---

[1] For the first time in the diocese of Esztergom, in 1819.

[2] In the *Notitia* of Mátyás Bél 147 parishes or townships are mentioned as having existed in the county. Of these, the two capital towns were non-Magyar—the contrary being true of Czegléd, Kecskemét and Nagy-Körös. The bulk of the population of Vácz too was non-Magyar. Kalocsa was only beginning to become Magyar in character. Of the other townships (parishes) only 55 were purely Magyar, 16 had mixed populations, the rest (73) were non-Magyar.

[3] Bél, Mátyás, *loc. cit.* p. 587.

In the county of Somogy, where, as we have seen, the
Rascians had penetrated, the latter have disappeared altogether,
though so late as 1787 they still occupied 19 parishes, while
46 were in the hands of Croatians and 15 of Germans. Here
too one-fourth of the inhabited places belonged to non-
Magyars[1]. In addition, there were the larger townships, where,
as we have seen, numerous foreign settlers were entered as
"Hungarians." In 1781 the council of the town of Szeged was
almost entirely composed of Rascians and Germans; so early
as 1767 Count Niczky declared that the majority of its
members professed the Greek Orthodox faith[2]. Of the larger
townships in the county of Békés, only Békés, Orosháza and
Öcsöd were purely Hungarian. In the others, the predominating
element was Slovak. In addition, there were large numbers of the
Rascians and the Wallachians in the county, so that the Emperor
Joseph believed this district to belong for the most part to
the Greek Orthodox Church[3]. Of the county of Gömör, where
the Hungarians had to compete with prolific Slavs, its learned
chronicler writes that the former had recently begun to increase
considerably in numbers[4].

Of the Győr district, which included the counties of Győr,
Sopron, Mosony, Komárom, Esztergom, Veszprém and Vas (of
the population of which counties at least one-third was at this
time Magyar), in his official instructions the Emperor Joseph
wrote as follows: "Among the inhabitants there are a few
Hungarians, though the most of them are Croats and there
are large numbers of Germans[5]." All these transformations (to
which we might add instances from every other county in
Hungary) left a deep impression on the public consciousness
in their respective districts. Everywhere we find memorials of
the foreign nationality, even where its language has become
entirely extinct.

---

[1] According to the census, 82 out of 322.

[2] *Staatskenntniss*, § 11.

[3] Chanc. Arch. No. 6737 (1783): "im Békéser Komitat meistens Griechen."

[4] Bartholomeides, *Not. Com. Göm.* p. 236. This is contrary to the general
opinion that the Hungarian nationality lost ground in this county.

[5] *Verbesserungsanstalten*, p. 43: "Die Inwohner bestehen aus einigen Ungarn,
die mehresten aber aus einer Gattung von Kroaten und sehr viel Deutschen."

The data above given will be sufficient to convince every-body that in the greater part of Hungary, a much larger proportion of the population speak Magyar to-day than a hundred years ago.

But let us suppose—as is by no means the case—that the proportions of the various nationalities had remained unchanged everywhere. Even then, the Hungarians would have constituted a relatively much smaller part of the population than they do to-day. For, with the consistency of a law of nature, as it were, the population of the Magyar counties increased far more rapidly than that of the others. The new lands were for the most part situated in Magyar districts, while those settled by people of other tongues were less capable of development. Hence the latter were obliged to send their surplus population to the Alföld and to the Hungarian towns, where sooner or later it became Magyarised.

We have already shown (pp. 32, 33) that the population of eleven predominantly Hungarian counties, which numbered 1,537,969 souls in 1787, had risen to 2,844,819 in 1847, whereas the increase was much smaller in the same number of counties whose character was mixed or pure Slovak. But even in the regions formerly occupied by the Turks, the difference between the increase of population of the Hungarian and non-Hungarian counties was considerable. For example, between 1787 and 1847, there was an increase of barely one-fifth among the popu-lation of the three so-called "Slavonian counties," which rank among the most fertile parts of the whole country. During the same period the three counties of Croatia showed an increase of population of a bare third[1].

In general, taking the population of the ten municipalities which were almost purely Hungarian in nationality, we find

[1]

Slavonian Counties.			Croatian Counties.		
	1787	1847		1787	1847
Veröcze ...	119,685	137,072	Zágráb ...	208,568	286,733
Pozsega ...	68,070	73,129	Varasd ...	91,451	131,898
Szerém ...	81,271	106,927	Körös ...	68,907	71,636
	269,026	317,128		368,926	490,267

that, during the sixty years taken as the basis of comparison, it increased by 75 %, whereas that of the whole country increased by 50 % only. If, therefore, the Hungarian element —apart from any results of Magyarisation—increased more rapidly than the others, it is perfectly evident that, towards the close of the eighteenth century, it constituted a much smaller proportion of the population than it did later on.

But what interests us here is not so much the change that took place between the age of Joseph II and 1847 as that which immediately preceded his accession. It is his reign that marks the commencement of a new era in the history of the nationalistic question. Before his days, the proportion and position of the various nationalities had depended on the moral, material and intellectual importance of their members. During his reign and in the period following it, the improved administrative system gave the Government constant opportunities for altering the numerical proportions of the different nationalities. The imposition of an official language and of a universal system of education were the chief means of carrying out the idea of nationalising and of Germanising the country ; the policy was very clear and a literature was developed to establish its aims. But all this was not and could not be the task of the whole of Hungarian society in our period. Such a policy of nationalising the country in the Magyar—not in the German— sense was not and could not be attempted in the eighteenth century by the Hungarian society as a whole. Here, as else- where, the nobles could control policy, but it was religious and not political differences that formed the starting-point of such nationalising aims. Here then, we can observe in their origin, at a time when they were quite unaffected by foreign ideas, those influences which eventually Magyarised the greater part of the Alföld and, in the face of enormous difficulties, laid the final foundations of Magyar supremacy in Hungary.

The Hungarians (Magyars) seemed to be conscious of the importance and difficulty of this task awaiting them. During the first year of Joseph II's reign, Abraham Barcsay wrote in the following terms :

"The neighbours of the Garam, Vág, Morva and Danube,
Endless streams of famishing Swabians,
Pour into the lands of Cumania—but in vain,
For Providence will preserve the Magyars' tongue[1]."

The first point of importance is that the Hungarians hastened to re-occupy their old homes simultaneously with the immigrating foreign colonists, or in many cases actually anticipated them. In the northern parts of the Alföld, the descendants of the former inhabitants crept back almost imperceptibly, as did the new Hungarian settlers from the neighbouring counties. Immediately after the Peace of Karlovicz (1699), Vésztö was re-occupied; in 1717 Gyoma was peopled, in 1719 Szent András. In other places, e.g. Eger and Pécs, the Magyars were reinforced by those Turkish inhabitants who had been left behind and had been converted to Christianity. In the first half of the eighteenth century, Félegyháza and Szabad-Szállás were occupied by the Jazygians and Cumanians who later on, during the reign of Joseph II, also sent out numerous prolific offshoots into the county of Bács[2]. After the return of the church dignitaries, Hungarians also helped in the work of raising Vácz, Esztergom and Kalocsa from their ashes. In places where even under Turkish dominion the Hungarian inhabitants had remained—e.g. the large parishes of Kecskemét, Nagy-Körös, Czegléd, Szentes and Vásárhely—there was nothing to prevent expansion, the occupation of the farms previously uninhabited, and a more extensive cultivation of the soil. It is largely because of the vitality of these settlers, and owing to their facility in adapting themselves to their surroundings, that the traces of two centuries of ravages disappeared so rapidly, and that in point of nationality the Alföld regained its normal aspect. The Alföld soon looked for all the world as if the Magyar nation had never had to bear the yoke of Turkish and German slavery.

The natural increase of this Magyar population during the eighteenth century must have been particularly large, even without including the new settlements and the absorption of

---

[1] *Költeményes Holmi*, vol. II. p. 106: "Ujólag való ébresztés a versírásra."
[2] Chanc. Arch. Nos. 11,506 and 12,643 (1785).

foreign elements which took place. Not only was there an
end of the Turkish dominion but also of the Oriental plague,
which may rank as the chief of its horrors. In 1711 there
had been enormous ravages of this disease, and, after the new
Turkish war began in 1739, there was a reappearance of it. As
the Crescent advanced, its path was marked afresh by the
presence of this mighty ally of barbarism, and the plague
terrified the Parliament of 1741 as much as it did that of 1712[1].
In some of the more distant regions of the country—in the
counties of Máramaros and Bereg—it appeared sporadically
so late as 1743[2]. But after that date it threw no obstacles
in the way of the increase of the Hungarian population, and
its disappearance was a clear proof of the fact that Hungary
had returned to civilization. We must not forget that it was
owing to their geographical position that the districts inhabited
by Hungarians suffered most from its ravages.

After the expulsion of the Turks the Hungarians were
threatened by a still greater danger. It was the Magyars belonging to the Reformed Church who had held their ground
under Turkish dominion, and there can be no doubt that,
together with the Calvinists of the North-East counties and
Transylvania, they constituted the greater part of the Hun-
garian-speaking population. More than one leader of the
Catholic restoration, though seemingly ready *propter bonum pacis*
to tolerate the presence of the Protestant faith in the country, in
reality would not have felt much compunction in banishing it.
How easy, indeed, how natural it seemed to follow the example
of France, which, a generation previously, had banished the
Huguenots!

The correspondence between the Prussian Court and their
ambassador in Vienna proves that the former did not consider

---

[1] In the years 1738-40, 8697 people died of the pest in Debreczen (Szücs, *Debreczen
város története*, vol. III. p. 773). At the time this town could not have contained
more than 25,000 inhabitants—according to the *Erdbeschreibung* of Häckhel its
population was on a level with that of Ulm. Consequently one-third of the inhabitants
perished. By way of comparison, we may mention the fact that, in 1831, the great
epidemic of cholera carried off 2152 of the inhabitants of the same town—i.e. one-
twentieth of the population.

[2] Cf. the letter of Count Alexander Károlyi to the Chancellor, Count Louis
Batthyány, dated Szegvár, 14 Feb. 1743.

such measures impossible. Many of the Protestants would have emigrated, had not their wealth mostly consisted of real estate, which they would have had great difficulty in selling on the spot[1]. When informed of the measures taken by the commission sitting at Pest, the Prussian King expressed his conviction that there was a desire to deprive the Hungarian Protestants entirely of their liberty of conscience. " If for that reason they should desire to migrate and to seek a home in some other land, I should be delighted to welcome them in my country[2]." The emigration of the Huguenots benefited Prussia more than any other country and, ten years later, the Protestants banished from Salzburg also took refuge there. A large number of individuals left Hungary also to enlist in the Prussian army, but the banishment or emigration of Protestants from this country never became general.

When, in 1725, the Prussian ambassador appealed to the Archbishop-Primate Imre Eszterházy on behalf of a Protestant clergyman who was a victim of persecution[3], the high-minded prelate expressed the conviction that the two denominations ought to be able, as common citizens of Europe, to live together in brotherly unity[4]. If the head of the Roman Catholic Church in Hungary was so deeply sensible of the solidarity of the common intellectual foundations, how much more must he have been inspired by the consciousness of a common national feeling. This danger very soon became a thing of the past. In turning against Protestantism, the Catholic clergy injured the interests of Hungarian nationality, for they attacked one of the important and vital elements of Magyardom, viz. the Calvinist nobles and burghers. But in their eyes the chief point

[1] Letter of the ambassador Graeve to Frederick William I, dated Vienna, 7 Feb. 1720 : " Viele wünschten das *flebile migrandi beneficium* zu ergreifen."

[2] The Prussian Ministry to the ambassador in Vienna, dated Berlin, May 20, 1721 : ''Ohne Zweifel ist es dahin angesehen die armen Leute umb ihre ganze Gewissensfreiheit zu bringen. Sollten dieselben sich dann eher aus Ungarn retiriren und sich anderwärtz etabliren wollen, so werden wir Ihnen dazu gerne die Permission in unseren Landen verstatten." Ilgen, Cnyphausen. In the Berlin Archives.

[3] Stephen Gyöngyösi, " predicator" at Kassa.

[4] Christian Brand, legate in Vienna, to the King of Prussia, dated Vienna, 26 Sept. 1725 : " Unterdessen, bis es Gott würde ändern wollen, müsste man wie *communes Europae cives* zusammen brüderlich leben."

of view was the religious, not the national one. Yet, wherever they had to deal with a foreign language and nationality as well as with a foreign religion, they used their influence largely for the purpose not only of religious conversion but of Magyarisation.

The identity of the interests of Catholicism with those of the Hungarian nationality is particularly shown in its dealings with the Rascians (Serbs). Here too, as among Oriental peoples generally, even to-day, religious feeling formed the firmest basis of an absolutely distinct national life. Where powerful historical traditions have not yet created a dynasty, a nobility, or a *bourgeoisie*, the hierarchy is the chief corporate body for organising and uniting the various elements. In the days of the Árpád and Angevin Kings, the confines of the Hungarian bishoprics coincided not only with those of the kingdom of Hungary, but with those of Western civilization. Protestantism never bore any fruit among the Southern Slavs, and these conditions continued unchanged at a later date. The Ottoman Conquest was aimed not so much against Christianity at large as against the Romish religion ; submission to the Turk was easy for the subjects of the Oriental Patriarch, never for those of the Pope. After the Turks had been driven out, the straggling groups of Greek Orientals left behind could not offer any effectual resistance to the Hungarian Catholic prelacy, whose predominance was assured by the weapons of religious conversion and of military power. It was in their distinctive faith that the Serbs (Rascians) and the Wallachians found the chief palladium of their nationality. To strip them of their nationality was, therefore, the best means of prevailing on them to abandon their ancestral faith. The power enjoyed by the prelates in the re-occupied territory—as feudal lords, as representatives of the central authority, and as heads of the Church—weighed heavily on those new settlers who were possessed of a strange religion and a foreign speech. At Kalocsa, Gabriel Patachics, the Archbishop, forbade the use of the Rascian language under pain of twelve stripes or a fine of twelve florins[1]. Similar means —though the application elsewhere was less drastic—were used in the other districts of the dioceses of Kalocsa and of Pécs to

[1] Katona, Stephen, *Hist. Metr. Coloc. Eccl.* vol. I. p. 72.

propagate the Catholic faith, and to strengthen the cause of Hungarian nationality. The Sokácz and Bunyevácz tribes were, and are still, alienated from their Servian kinsmen by religious differences[1], and though they preserved their languages, the Catholic Church succeeded in winning them over to the side of the Hungarians. The fact that even this primitive method of Magyarisation met with scarcely any resistance is explained by the want of organisation of the tribes in question and by the low level of their civilization. On the other hand, the work of Magyarisation was of merely secondary importance in the eyes of the bishops; indeed, had it been otherwise they would certainly have attained more important results.

This criticism is not meant as a reproach, for the spirit of Hungarian society in the eighteenth century naturally looked upon an extensive addition to the ranks of the Magyars as an object that was in itself undesirable. However broad the basis on which it stands, the main characteristic of an aristocratic society must always be exclusiveness; and the extension of rights and privileges bears at all times the appearance of curtailing these rights. The use of the Magyar language was so distinctive and characteristic of the Hungarian prelates and nobles that it must have seemed a sacrifice and renunciation of an exclusive right to extend it to the *misera plebs contribuens*. The history of every age shows that all those measures, which aim at the numerical increase of a nationality, are used alternately as the tools of democracy or absolutism. The intense feeling that imbued the Hungarian nobles as members of the "fatherland" was in direct opposition to the modern current of thought, the object of which is solely to further the spread of the Magyar tongue. The appearance on the scene of the language as a factor in the creation and maintenance of the State, was a change due entirely to the age of Stephen Széchenyi. It had to be preceded by the development of a literary culture and by its recognition as a national treasure. It was in the language that "the greatest Magyar" looked for the safety of his nation and

---

[1] Both tribes are Serbs, but Catholics by faith: the Bunyevácz tribe came from Herzegovina, the Sokácz tribe from Old Bosnia.

a guarantee of its future prosperity. He is indeed related to have said that even parricides should be pardoned if they spoke Hungarian, so small were the numbers of that nation. The eighteenth century was not familiar with any complaint of this kind. The nation consisted then of the privileged estates and orders, not of the millions, the masses, though it was particularly fortunate that the number of Magyars among the latter in Hungary amounted to several millions. That the greater part of this nobility was also actually Magyar becomes clear the moment we investigate its relative position in the various counties.

The greatest proportion of nobles was to be found in those Magyar-speaking counties which had escaped the Turkish conquest. Of the population of the county of Komárom one-eighth, of that of Veszprém county two-fifteenths, of that of Györ county one-ninth, of that of the county of Szatmár one-eighth, of that of Szabolcs county one-ninth, and of that of the county of Borsod nearly one-sixth, enjoyed the privileges of the nobility. In 1847, in the counties of Szabolcs, Szatmár, Borsod and Pozsony alone, there were 119,000 nobles[1].

On the other hand, in the county of Mosony every 160th, in that of Zólyom every 43rd, and in that of Szepes only every 50th man was a noble. These districts were not affected by the Turkish conquest, their nobility only was Hungarian (Magyar), and not the whole population.

In the territory formerly occupied by the Turks, in the counties of Baranya and Torontál, the proportion of nobles was 1 in 80, in Arad and Tolna counties 1 in 40, and in the counties of Temes and Krassó only 1 in 160.

Of the non-Magyar counties, those of Turócz and Máramaros were the only ones containing any considerable proportion of nobles. In the little county of Turócz—the Hungarian Rutlandshire—4800 nobles were to be found in 1847[2]. In the county of Máramaros, at the same date, the number of nobles

---

[1] In the county of Pozsony the decisive factor was the island of Csallóköz (Schirtt), a great part of the inhabitants of which were nobles.

[2] Mátyás Bél traces the large number of nobles in the county of Turócz back to Béla IV, *Notit. Hung. nov.* vol. II. p. 304.

was 26,300. I believe that in both these cases the phenomenon was due not so much to general as to local causes, e.g. the endowment of whole villages with the rights of nobility[1].

The connection of these rights with the Hungarian language becomes still more evident if we compare the conditions in Croatia (which also resisted the inroads of the Turks) with those prevailing in the Hungarian counties which had struggled against the foe with similar results. In the latter, as we have seen, 10—15 % of the population were nobles. In the county of Varasd, on the other hand, the proportion was only 3 %; even in the county of Zágráb (where the populous district of Turmezö was a significant factor) it was only 7 %; and conditions similar to those prevailing in Hungary proper were confined to the county of Körös, in which 11 % of the population belonged to the privileged class.

The nobility was bound to be everywhere the principal champion of the idea of Hungarian nationality. In whatever part of the country they settled, the nobles were members, not only of the Hungarian " fatherland " and of the Corporation of the Sacred Crown, but of the Hungarian nation too.

In the present stage of their development, the nations of Europe each represent a unit of culture, which endeavours to assert itself within the bounds of a separate State. Besides language, various historic forces serve as the basis of this apparent uniformity. The French nation owes its position as a distinct factor in the history of Europe to its government, the Spanish nation to its religion, and the Italian and German nations to common historical traditions and a common literature. The Hungarian national feeling—if traced back to its origins— was not merely the proud self-consciousness of a ruling tribe, which looked upon the rest of the inhabitants of the country as its subjects by conquest, but at the same time a peculiar characteristic of the upper classes by which they distinguished

---

[1] I have taken the data for the comparison of figures from the work of Elek Fényes already quoted on several occasions. They refer, therefore, to the year 1847. Considering the comparatively rapid increase of population of the Hungarian districts and the conservative character of the nobility, it goes without saying that, in 1780, the nobility represented a still larger proportion of the population of the districts inhabited by Hungarians.

themselves from the people of foreign speech, from their serfs, and from the cottagers[1]. In the realm of nature atrophied organs often serve to throw light on important phases of an earlier stage of development: similarly, in the uniform national spirit of a country, we may still detect undercurrents which betray the original existence of a caste-system.

Even when the serfs, among whom they lived, were all foreigners by speech, the nobles and their families constituted a separate Hungarian colony. Mátyás Bél was familiar with the conditions in the counties inhabited by Slovaks, and his acquaintance with them was derived from close personal intercourse. In speaking of the said counties he always treats of the nobles as Hungarian and as ethnologically distinct from the plebeians[2]. Of the nobles of the county of Turócz, he says that they did credit to their ancestors and loved to make a display of Hungarian luxury. The nobles of the county of Liptó, since they could not learn Hungarian at home, went to the Alföld to do so[3]. In the county of Nógrád, the whole nobility was of pure Hungarian blood; and no obsequies were complete without a Hungarian funeral oration[4]. In the county of Bars the common people were nearly all Slovaks, but the notabilities were Hungarians[5]. The writer speaks in similar terms of the nobles of the counties of Nyitra and Hont, saying that they clung fast to their ancestral tongue. In treating of the county of Zólyom—and here only—he mentions it as a peculiar and commendable feature that the nobles did not disdain the language and customs of their serfs[6]—though even here the neglect of the pure ancestral tongue did not become by any means general. In Croatia, too, the Hungarian language was

---

[1] Cf. the appeal of the county of Hont against the introduction of the German tongue, Chanc. Arch. No. 9730 (1784): "Lingua distinguit populum a plebe."

[2] *Notit. Hung. nov.* vol. II. p. 304. So also in Szepes.

[3] *Ibid.* vol. II. p. 549.

[4] "Nobilitas profecto omnis Hungarici est sanguinis.—Sacer orator carmen patrium recitat." *Ibid.* vol. III. pp. 26—28.

[5] *Ibid.* vol. III. p. 170.

[6] *Ibid.* vol. II. p. 401: "Immo, non paucos in nobilitate videas, linguam et mores Slavorum suos sibi fecisse; quod adeo nihil habet vitii ut mereatur etiam commendationem."

pretty generally spoken by the nobles. Of the nobles of the county of Varasd, Count Domokos Teleki remarks that they did not speak Hungarian well[1].

The foreign inhabitants of the towns were Hungarians in point of dress, if not in speech. As we know, this was true not only of the Germano-Slovak districts, but of Croatia too[2]. Anyone who by virtue of the class to which he belonged was a member of the Hungarian State, displayed this fact by those emblems which elsewhere serve as the symbols of common origin and culture. This phenomenon was to be observed even in the lower grades of society. A quick-sighted traveller was struck by the fact that the Swabians in the counties of Temes and Bács wore Hungarian costumes, whereas German clothes were still in vogue in the counties of Baranya, Tolna and Somogy[3]. The former were free settlers who had acquired property belonging to the Chamber; the latter were the serfs of individual feudal lords. From a literary point of view it is an interesting fact that during this very period the first Hungarian newspaper (*Magyar Hirmondó*) recommended the wearing of Hungarian costumes as a distinctive national token.

The identity of the Hungarian nobility with the national idea was not caused merely by the force of habit, nor by a purely mechanical attachment to what was ancient. When the Government endeavoured to substitute the German for the neutral Latin tongue as the official medium, the counties all protested with equal vehemence against this attempt to infringe the rights of the Hungarian language, and those most energetic in their protests included populations of non-Magyars, who were thus the foremost champions, not only of the idea of a national State, but of Magyardom.

To give examples, the county of Trencsén thought the best method of rising to the level of the other peoples of Europe was *not* by propagating the German language but by urging

---

[1] *Reisen durch Ungarn*, pp. 219—222.

[2] *Ibid.* p. 222: "Die allgemeine Kleidertracht der Kroaten ist die Ungrische, auch das Frauenzimmer ist in Gala ungrisch gekleidet, gewöhnlich aber teutsch. Die Bürger, die Kroaten sind, kleiden sich ungrisch."

[3] *Ibid.* p. 206.

the Hungarians to cultivate their national speech. Magyar should henceforward be the official tongue of the authorities as it had hitherto been of the Parliaments[1]. As there was no such thing in the world as a pure national State, it was more fitting that the serfs should follow their masters than *vice versa*. No real patriot could fail to demand that the Hungarian language should be made the official medium.

The county of Árva declared that, even if the King ordained the use of German by the other authorities, it could not avail itself thereof[2]. It thought it only fair that in the Hungarian kingdom the prevailing language should be Hungarian, to which even the foreign peoples living in its borders were gradually becoming accustomed[3]. The county of Szepes considered that those who did not know Hungarian would have no difficulty in learning it[4]. The county of Zágráb, though it preferred the use of Latin, thought it a great dishonour for the nation (naturally enough, it refers to the Hungarian nation only) that its language should be threatened with extinction[5]. Yet we must not imagine that the threatened danger alone aroused the Hungarian nobles and made them realise the treasure which they possessed in their national language and customs. The age of Maria Teresa has been regarded as pre-eminently one of Germanisation. This may be true in political respects, but it is not so in point of language and culture. The history of Hungary is a record of an almost unbroken struggle between the older Magyardom and foreign—particularly German—influences. The latter attracted individuals by its higher level of culture; but the bulk of the nobility was never taken unawares by the dangers which continually threatened not merely their political but their national independence. In the course of the eighteenth century the attack assumed a more menacing guise than ever before, partly owing to the advance made all over Europe by the absolute

[1] Chanc. Arch. No. 7541 (1784): "Laudabili exemplo non aliud deducitur, quam ut Ungari quoque gentium Europæarum non ignobilis pars ad magis magisque excolendum Nationale Idioma incitentur—ita in Dicasteria quoque invehatur."

[2] *Ibid.* No. 8141 (1784).   [3] *Ibid.* No. 7809 (July 9, 1784).

[4] *Ibid.* No. 9065 (July 19, 1784). Szepes had only just been acquired from Poland, 1769.

[5] *Ibid.* No. 10,305 (Aug. 25, 1784) : "Summa gentis ignominia."

and centralising system of government, partly as a result of the winning personality of the Queen herself. Yet this age is as rich in signs and deeds of conscious and unconscious resistance as any period of past or present Hungarian history. This feature of the age is not confined to the actions of individuals, it is, in fact, most striking in cases where the whole nation, or a considerable part of it, is concerned.

Individual members of the aristocracy abandoned the ancestral customs and even the language, but the nobility, as a body, remained Hungarian in feeling and threw its whole political weight into the defence of Hungarian nationality. To be just—were the Hungarian aristocrats more German than the Germans, Swedes and Russians of the same period were French? In fact, we may compare the Germanophile attitude of these Hungarian aristocrats with the Anglomania so much in vogue among the French nobles of the period just preceding the Revolution.

Without exaggeration we may say that during the period preceding the reign of Joseph II, the authority and strength of the Hungarian national idea depended exclusively on the authority and weight possessed by the Hungarian nobility. The peculiar character of the age is due to the circumstance that the principal supports of modern national life—literature and education—were already making their influence felt, while the more ancient pillars of Hungarian nationality—the nobility and the prelacy—were yet as strong and unshaken as ever.

The requirements of the day were greater and, instead of the energy of individuals or classes, the whole strength of nations was summoned to the fray. All credit is due to the ruling classes in Hungary for the fact that from its very beginning they were not wholly opposed to the transformation. The first apostles of the literary and scientific Renaissance were nobles and prelates. Their influence on foreigners and on the foreign inhabitants of the country was due not only to their position as the owners of wealth, as the holders of political and military power, as possessors of the patriarchal privileges of landlords and as justices of the peace, but as the sole representatives in

Hungary of everything that makes a nation worthy of its name and of a place as a member of the human family[1].

This unassuming power not only maintained Magyardom intact ; it actually extended its limits, almost without conscious design, in days when the modern means for spreading national feeling were still unknown and when their employment was a thing of the future.

" Peragit tranquilla potestas, quae violenta nequit."

Anyone belonging to the ruling class, even if of foreign extraction, had to profess himself a Magyar.   Towards the end of the eighteenth century scarcely any difference was made in Parliament between the *indigena* living in the country and the *nativus*[2].   This unassuming influence worked irresistibly, subjecting to itself and absorbing all other elements, where its path was not obstructed by some other organisation of like tendencies. The peoples living on the confines of the country were saved from absorption by the intervening distance, for, in default of schools, there was no one to teach them Hungarian.   In other places—particularly in the case of the Ruthenes and Wallachs— an extremely low level of civilization, and above all a nomadic mode of life, proved greater obstacles to Magyarisation· than did national and religious differences.   The Rascians (Serbs) dwelling in the interior of the country were also in some places strengthened or induced by their religion to maintain an independent existence, and even those Slovaks professing the Lutheran faith offered considerable resistance[3].

Those nationalities, however, living in the centre of Hungary, among Hungarians, and controlled by Hungarian proprietors and priests, very soon became Hungarians of their own accord. Similar causes induced the inhabitants of the huge territories

---

[1] An interesting memorial of the Hungarian hegemony is preserved in the MS. department of the National Museum.   On the occasion of the marriage of a relative of his, a young schoolboy toasted the newly-wedded couple in three languages—Latin, Hungarian and Slovak.   In a solemn dialogue the bridegroom assured his bride that, though she was a Slovak, he would not love or honour her the less.

[2] Among the deputations sent to the Parliament of 1790 those representing five counties were of foreign extraction and bore foreign names.

[3] *Manch-Hermaeon,* p. 383.

conquered by Rome to learn her language. It was not that they were compelled to do so, but because it was the only course open to anyone who would obtain privileges, culture, and opportunities of self-help[1]. In Hungary it was not the language but the privileged society that constituted the nation, yet the word Hungarian (Magyar) meant in Hungary practically what *civis Romanus* had meant centuries before in the Empire.

The process of the Magyarisation of the various towns and settlements was carried out imperceptibly; only the results—astonishing even to contemporaries—are tangible. The Germans who had come into the country were the first to undergo this change. These men, who had no *patria*, who in their old homes had been familiar only with the burdens imposed on them by their prince and their country, were attracted like so many atoms by the idea of national unity and national feeling in Hungary. Their dialect was replaced by a national language, their village by a fatherland, and their tyrant by a nation. As early as the second generation they protested against being looked upon as Swabians or as Germans[2]; and it became their one desire to receive the same consideration as native Hungarians[3]. Besides the Germans, the Slovaks too were quite ready to become absorbed in the Hungarian nationality. It was observed long ago that, when the Hungarian and another nationality dwell side by side, the disappearance of one or other people results; but that, when the German nationality dwells side by side with another, there is no such tendency to coalition[4]. In the preceding age many Hungarian districts had in this manner been lost to the Hungarians[5]. But we may safely say that, since the days of Maria Teresa, such a co-existence has generally ended in the triumph of the Hungarian element.

[1] v. on this point Lord Cromer, *Ancient and Modern Imperialism*, pp. 99—100, 104.

[2] Address of the county of Zemplén to Prince Kaunitz (June 22, 1784, Vienna State Archives) : "Ipsi advenae et exterae coloniae brevi tempore in Hungaros transformantur, quorum jam filii, si non Hungari compellentur, indignantur." Chanc. Arch. No. 7591 (1784).

[3] Address of the county of Heves. Chanc. Arch. No. 7592 (June 26, 1784).

[4] Bél, Mátyás, *Notit. Hung. nov.* vol. III. p. 27 (treating of the county of Pest).

[5] Count Domokos Teleki instances the environs of Kassa (*Reisen*, p. 41).

Another fact worth mentioning is that it was quite the fashion for families of foreign speech to adopt Hungarian names even in the eighteenth century. In his diary Michael Cserei has recorded several instances[1]. From a strictly numerical point of view, therefore, there can be no doubt that the Hungarian element advanced considerably, probably in a larger measure than it has ever done since. All the more remarkable is it that contemporaries and later writers have alike reproached the Hungarians of this age with listlessness and with a lack of enthusiasm for those ideas for which their ancestors had shed their blood. Those who came forward as the champions and apostles of a new and happier future—Bessenyei, Orczi, Ányos —all wept tears of sorrow over the fall of the nation, which was deserting the path trodden by their forefathers.

For the guidance of our judgment as to the advance or decadence of a nation, the sentence pronounced by that nation itself—in its literature and public life—is far more important than anything else. More instructive for our purpose than a legion of statistical data is an investigation of the ideals after which it strives, the obstacles which it avoids and the dangers which it fears.

In revealing us his thoughts in the conversation with his own soul, his *daemon*, George Bessenyei (1747–1811) began by saying that the Hungarian nation had but little affection for its language. The latter was an orphan child without mother or father[2]. The Latin language predominated everywhere, in comparison with it the Hungarian speech was a mere slave. "So long as the laws of the land are in Latin, and that tongue is used by lawyers and judges, the Hungarian nation will learn neither its own nor any foreign language." The universal speech of the Middle Ages still weighed heavily on national thought in Hungary, and it is against the tyranny of this tongue that the writer complains, not against the weakness or want of patriotism of his contemporaries.

[1] *Journal of Acad. Arch.* No. 9; Antal Szirmay, *Hist. Secreta*, p. 221, quotes another instance—the family of Hidegkövy (formerly Kaltenstein) of Sátoralja-Ujhely (from which the famous Louis Kossuth was descended on the mother's side).

[2] *Holmi. Második Beszéd*, p. 155.

No one was a more enthusiastic champion of the cause of Hungarian literature and the Hungarian language than was Baron Lawrence Orczi. Yet, however bitter the satire with which he lashed his age, the chief object of his recrimination was not the neglect of the national tongue and the cultivation of a foreign idiom, but the prevalence of foreign hyper-refined customs. It was to timidity rather than to lack of scholarship that he attributed the backwardness of Hungarian literature[1].

The only writer, who gave expression in words of keen bitterness to his grief at the disappearance of the Hungarian tongue as well as of the old customs, was Paul Ányos. He could not conceal his fears that, "under the specious pretext of giving a finish to the literary edifice, the Hungarian fatherland would be deprived of its independence and the nation would lose its nationality[2]." But, when he turns from the corrupters of the older manners to address his song to those who still held the ancient Hungarian costumes in esteem, we cannot find any reference to any such decline of the Hungarian tongue.

What we hear in all this is rather the voice of encouragement urging the Magyars to attain a new and higher level, than one of reproach accusing the contemporaries of being responsible for the fall of the Magyar language from its former place of honour. These scattered traces of decadence are counterbalanced by a legion of facts, which show Hungarian national feeling to have been constantly advancing and increasing.

No want of erudition, of political vitality, or of patriotism caused the depression in the literature of this period. One writer in 1741 avers that the playful muse of poetry is despised by the proud and manly Magyar: and in fact the literature of that period shows not one work of the first rank[3]. Nevertheless, the great problem of refining the language, without de-

---

[1] Cf. " Barkócz iprimáshoz való ajánlasa prózában " (*Költeményes Holmi*, vol. I. p. 12). Orczi on several occasions expresses his conviction that the backwardness of the nation was not due to a lack of feeling, e.g. :

" But grant a Barkóczi to the poor Magyars,
This good but unpolished nation,
That they no longer be the butt of other peoples' ridicule."

[2] *Gondolatok a magyar viseletröl* (*Thoughts on Hungarian costumes*), p. 117.

[3] *Lettres sur les Hongrois* (1741).

stroying its primeval originality, had already occupied attention. Ten years later, John Ribinyi, teacher at the Lutheran School at Sopron, would not praise the vernacular too loudly because he feared to excite the envy of neighbouring nations. Applying the categories of a professor of the humanities, he found that the Hungarian language was capable of expressing alike common and lofty thoughts—and all intermediate sentiments—that it was able to express love or hate, mirth or mourning, wrath, hope or fear. "I confess Italian is pleasant, French beautiful, German earnest. But all these qualities are so united in Magyar, that it is difficult to say in which its superiority consists[1]." He shrinks indeed from placing it in the same plane with Greek or Latin, but yet blames those who neglect the tongue of Hungary for that of Rome.

Our first king (St Stephen) did not give his laws in Latin to damage the national language. At that time that language was used all over Europe, and without it the Magyars could have had no intercourse with other nations. The others did not know Magyar, nor the Magyars any foreign (living) language. "But I freely confess that they did not cultivate their own idiom so as to make it quite polished, finished and copious: in that field we and our children have enough to do. If we do not rival one another in this work we sin against the fatherland, against the Magyar name, against ourselves, and against our ancestors. Our fathers, for all their highmindedness, could not perform this task, occupied as they always were with wars and other sorrows; we, whose life is more peaceful and who have more opportunity to cultivate letters, must use all our strength to enrich and to refine our language. Such a cultivation will be of profit to us. In the Parliament, and in the County Assemblies, we must speak Magyar, and it is shameful if we cannot clothe fine thoughts in fine language. But of more weight than utility is duty: we must follow the model of the classical nations, and of the modern French, English, Italian and German literatures."

It is perhaps characteristic of the eighteenth century that the highminded orator needs for the fulfilment of all this—a Maecenas.

Enthusiasm and learning there was in plenty; but there was

---

[1] *Oratio de cultura linguae Hungaricae*, Sopronii, 1751.

a very deep-rooted cause why Hungarian literature could not develop in that age. Ribinyi shows this further on, when he commends the study of Magyar authors. "But, you will ask me, who are the Hungarian writers, the study of whose books I so much recommend? How much I should like to satisfy your desire and my wish on that point. Everyone who cares in the smallest degree for our country, knows that there are such, but I am not permitted to tell you them now, and, even if I were, it would not be right." He dared not quote a Protestant writer for fear of drawing down the Censor and the Government upon him, and his religious convictions did not allow him to quote a Catholic writer. How can one speak then of a national literature, so long as the first question considered is the religion of the writer? So long as this confessionalism retained so firm a hold on men's minds, the unification of the nation by a common culture and by common ideals necessarily remained a pious wish.

Scarcely anyone to-day would agree with Francis Toldy, who selected the year 1772 as the starting-point of a new era in Hungarian literature[1]. It is indeed extremely difficult to draw the line between the age of Gyöngyösi and that of Bessenyei. In Transylvania this change was practically imperceptible, for there purely Hungarian writers and translators were always to be found. In Hungary proper the most suitable mediator between the older Magyar school of poetry, which was entirely national in character, and the new "French" school of taste was Baron Lawrence Orczi. From 1772 an advance is indeed perceptible when the members of the noble Hungarian Guard at Vienna began to unite under the influence of Bessenyei, but this advance owes yet more to the decline of confessionalism so characteristic of this decade. In 1780 this regeneration actually attracted the attention of contemporaries, and the county assembly of Máramaros protested that it was strange that the Emperor Joseph II should wish to introduce the German

[1] The year in which George Bessenyei (1747–1811) published his first tragedy *Agis*. Bessenyei was the head of a brilliant literary clique in Maria Teresa's noble Hungarian Guard, which was usually stationed at Vienna. Though he wrote in Magyar he represented the "French" or cosmopolitan school whose source of information was usually Voltaire. Stephen Gyöngyösi (1625–1704) was an earlier poet who championed the "Magyar" school—based on popular folklore, tradition, and history.

language just when such efforts were being made to improve the Hungarian vernacular[1].

In 1781 the *Magyar Hirmondó* stated that Magyardom was making rapid strides. "The Hungarian tongue is developing perceptibly. Probably during no single period has so much been done—and with such praiseworthy assiduity—to further these two ends as is being done to-day[2]." George Bessenyei, Orczi, and Paul Ányos alike laid stress on the fact that the new Hungarian literature was only just beginning. They were delighted to live in an age in which it had again become honourable and fashionable to write in Hungarian.

The scholars, who compared the prosperity of the nation under Maria Teresa to that which it had attained centuries before under Louis the Great and Matthias Corvinus, considered the main factors of culture to be far more firmly established now than then. Now measures were being taken to provide not only for the culture of the Court and for the erection of Academies, but for the education of the people also[3]. The common intellectual treasures had been rendered accessible to every class of the nation, and men saw in this fact the chief pledge for the future of the country. Literature and the school, the successor and transformer of the older Hungary, were already coming to the front.

Foreigners have always been impressed by the devoted attachment of Hungarians to their nation and their fatherland—even when carried to excess. Observers remarked that certain of the Hungarian aristocrats preferred the favour of Vienna and the Court to attachment to their country. But these nobles were always kept separate from the others. The same writer, who has given us the most lively description of the manner in which the Hungarian aristocracy came under the influence of the Court, has devoted pages to telling us how much more earnest, moral and

[1] Chanc. Arch. No. 8915 (July 28, 1784) : "Hoc praesertim seculo peculiari zelo eruditi excolere et polire adlaborant."

[2] 1781, p. 240.

[3] Reviczky, *Status Regni Ung.* IV.: "Ornamenta, Francisc. Nagy, *Panegyricus ob confirmatas in Hungaricis ditionibus literas*, 1780, Jun. 20, Augustissima rem publicam literariam integram, toto diffusam Regno et quasi ingentem quendam spiritum per grandis corporis alicujus venas meantem complectitur."

patriotic were the Hungarian aristocrats than their Austrian contemporaries[1].

According to another traveller, the Hungarians were remarkably attached to their tongue, so that a stranger addressing them in it was sure of being welcomed as a friend. He found their patriotism, ardent ambition, endurance and patience worthy of the highest praise. The failings, which he discovered in them, were the results rather of a want of culture than of over-refinement. And this traveller journeyed through Hungary on several occasions between 1780 and 1785, without finding any traces of decadence anywhere[2].

We must not understand these panegyrics in the sense that the Hungarian nation, living in peace and undisturbed, and enjoying constitutional liberty, was looking forward to a splendid future during the last years of Maria Teresa. The present day is so void of ideals, so entirely swayed by the difficulties of the moment, and so inexorable does the eternal law of gradual evolution seem even to the greatest optimists, that it is almost impossible to comprehend that happy, naïve belief in the advent of a better age which was so characteristic of the late eighteenth century all over Europe—that implicit following of the new gospel of Rousseau and his school, which ushered in Utopian dreams of a united humanity, of the common brotherhood of individuals and peoples. In Hungary too this school made its influence felt. But society was still based on privilege, and it was rooted in that past from which, like every genuine Renascence, it was obliged to draw its ideals. The tenets of the *contrat social* fixed a deep gulf between the course of historical development and the future. In Hungary national

---

[1] *Briefe eines reisenden Franzosen*, Letter 29. By way of illustration he relates that of 24 readers in the Imperial Library of Vienna 2—3 were studying classic authors, one the *Memoirs of Sully*, and the others were perusing novels, poems or illustrated works. "Ich sah verschiedene Male einige Ungarn am Tische, die mit ihrer Lektüre alle Deutschen beschämten die zugegen waren. Die liessen sich ihre seltensten vaterländischen Geschichtschreiber geben, und man sah in ihrer Miene, dass sie ihrer Verstand mit der Lektüre nähren, und ihr Herz zugleich wärmten. Sollte nicht die Regierungsverfassung etwas beitragen, dass die Hungarn mehr Vaterlandsliebe haben, und mehr auf die Geschichte ihres Vaterlandes achten als die Österreicher" pp. 401, 402.

[2] Scypp-Lehmann, *Reise in Ungarn*, pp. 32—40.

feeling was so strong that even the new current of thought was able to assert itself only by entering its service.

Anyone who has carefully watched the development of the national spirit in Hungary will not be surprised even by the fact that, in this age of constant progress and advance, the only phenomenon observed was the departure from the traditions of the past which threatened the nation with entire effacement. Of the poems handed down to us there is in particular one which expresses patriotic grief and despair in vigorous terms hardly paralleled by any other product of Hungarian literature—which is, unfortunately, only too rich in efforts of the kind[1]. But this was only a temporary outbreak of exasperation at the bad turn the Parliament of 1764 had taken. The better part, and indeed the bulk, of the nation, though they loved to muse upon the past and looked back with sighs of regret on the glorious days of yore, never allowed themselves for one moment to forget the present or the future.

[1] We can quote only the most important stanzas of the long poem (*Mus. Jank. Coll.*):

> 4 " No longer what he was of yore
>   The Magyar bears an iron yoke:
>   No more has he a fatherland;
>   His King a perjurer.
> 5 In days gone by, a glorious fame
>   For prowess was his meed;
>   The mighty nation was on its guard
>   And all its deeds were crowned with praise.
> 8 What was of old, is now no more;
>   The Germans have overthrown all.
> 10 So the glory of the Magyars,
>   Their liberty and honour,
>   Trampled down by the usurper,
>   Are leaning by a gaping grave.
> 11 The councillors of our King
>   Despoil us of our wealth:
>   Poor the wit and damned the soul
>   That dwells within them, with all their malice.
> 12 The prosperity of our fatherland
>   The happiness of our Magyar race
>   They will do nought to further,
>   But rather endeavour to destroy.
> 14 If the Magyar dare defend his laws,
>   He draws the King's hatred upon him,
>   And is punished,...etc."

The frequent intercourse with foreigners and foreign countries made it impossible to escape French influence altogether. But, where we have the poet himself before us, we see that he is not inspired by the Utopian dreams of the eighteenth century but goes in search of happiness, both for his country and himself, along the paths trodden out by his ancestors. Nobody gives us a better picture of the hopes and expectations of the nobility and Magyardom, and of the light in which they regarded their present condition, than Baron Lawrence Orczi. Often his verses are cumbrous, full of scientific terms and abstruse allusions, but his words have the force of directness in the poem we are about to quote. After reviewing the condition of the peoples of Europe and looking in vain for the presence of liberty, he stops to consider the Hungarians:

"Render praise to the Father of Nations
For making thee citizen of such a land."

Only the conditions of property are not yet on a proper footing:

"Pray God to diminish the causes of litigation,
And to stop the mouths of the sons of Verböczy (i.e. pettifogging lawyers)."

Against every other evil a remedy can be found by an appeal to the King:

"Now is the time ripe to appear before the throne;
Prostrate thyself at our good sovereign's feet:
The peasant no longer complains of his lot;
Thou too beg new laws to bring thee peace.
She (i.e. Maria Teresa) shall bid the Church's servants not be miserly,
And stifle the foolish arrogance of great lords,
Rouse to life the ancient prowess of the nobles,
And stir to action the sluggard peasantry."

The following stanza proves that the speaker is no despiser of society, but a noble patriot who desires to purge his country and his order of abuses:

"Let priests pretend sanctity at the altar,
Great lords attend on the royal Court,
The gentry do sentry duty on the frontier,
The peasants store the grain in the barns.

M. H.

> Let the burghers ply the trade of the country,
> Bringing work and plenty into the land;
> They too must dispense with lazy revels,
> And the weekly feasts and orgies[1]."

The separation of the orders, and the performance by each of its strict duties, was the chief requirement. Foreign crimes, luxury, godlessness and lechery, should be shunned. By such means the Hungarians had preserved their independence, and by such means they would be able to thrive henceforward too, for:

> "Happy is the man born in Magyarland,
> Who possesses a freehold as his portion,
> —Good soil with fat fields adjoining,
> Ten ploughs and a hundred cows in his farmyard."

The kingly power, however, was the surest guarantee of the liberty of the nobility:

> "Many are the nations that admire this realm;
> Amazed they scan its peculiar form;
> And praise the condescension of the King,
> Who deigns at times to embrace his vassals.
> Thy nation boasts of splendid laws,
> Which enhance the pomp of the estates;
> The King puts himself on a level with his vassals;
> Often they go together before the courts."

What that was not theirs in the present could Hungarians expect in the future?

> "Thou payest no taxes, hast no soldiers quartered on thee;
> Thy carts are not ransacked at the toll-bridges;
> Thy horse is not held up at toll-gates,
> Nor do the customs officers bar thy way."

> "Thou livest at thy ease on the rich produce
> Of the soil thou hast sown by the grace of thy King;
> Thou must not grudge to give of thy golden sheaves,
> Thou canst safely give alms of the firstfruits of thy estate."

Yet this poem was after all the "swan's strain," the dying utterance of that old Hungarian nation which was one with the nobility. It was written in 1772—"in the baths in Buda below St Gellért's Mount"—the year in which Poland, a country that

---

[1] *Futó Gondolat a szabadságról* (*Thoughts on Liberty*), "A magyarok" (The Hungarians), pp. 55, 56.

had had a historic evolution so similar in many respects, and had striven after similar ideals, became the prey of her three powerful neighbours. For Hungary these were halcyon days; no one could foresee that before long the nobility and the nation alike would be engaged in a life-and-death struggle with the Crown.

The ideal States in the eyes of the educated society of the seventeenth century were the noble republics of Venice and Holland. Oft-quoted sentences of Montesquieu, Voltaire and other French writers prove that they, while detesting the arbitrary power of kings, and considering the people still incapable of self-government, regarded the aristocratic kingship of Hungary as a masterpiece of constitutional government[1]. Who would have dreamed of its speedy downfall?

Side by side with the nobility, the predominant class which had a great past and a great future, and possessed power and responsibility, stood the other chief constituent of the Hungarian nation, the Magyar-speaking serfs.

The foregoing chapters have proved that the condition of these serfs was incomparably better than that of the French serfs at the time of the Revolution. Not only were their burdens comparatively slight, and their subsistence assured, but, by this time, greater opportunities were also open to them.

We have no record of any political utterances of this class, we can merely quote the verdict of those who have dealt with them from this point of view. Of the opinions expressed on this point that of Joseph II himself is particularly significant. The Emperor did not mention any other nationality of Hungary without upbraiding it, but he was always full of praise for the Hungarians (Magyars), whom he placed on a level with the Germans, an action that was very significant in his case.

---

[1] E.g. *Esprit des lois*, L. VIII. ch. 9: "On a vu la maison d'Autriche travailler sans relâche à opprimer la noblesse hongroise. Elle cherchait chez ses peuples l'argent qui n'y était pas et ne voyait pas des hommes, qui y étaient. Lorsque tant de princes partageaient entre eux ses états, toutes les pièces de sa monarchie, immobiles et sans action, tombaient pour ainsi dire les unes sur les autres; il n'y avait de vie que dans cette noblesse qui s'indigna, oublia tout pour combattre, et crut qu'il était de sa gloire de périr et de pardonner."

Naturally enough, on every occasion he deals with the common people only—in particular with the serfs.

Of the commissaries appointed by the Emperor, Paul Almási took particular care to draw his attention to the intellectual life of the serfs. He was the same man who had shown the clearest insight into the economic needs of Hungary. So far do these two apparently contradictory factors coincide in their results. According to Almási the neglect of their dress did not justify anyone in drawing conclusions as to the intellectual capacities of the people. They were not so backward as their clothes led one to suppose. Indifference to external appearance was a national peculiarity. In general the peasants were sober-minded and endowed with plenty of common sense, and, with the exception of the herdsmen who lived all the year round in the fields, they were moral too. Those professing the Calvinist faith were all able to read and write, though among the other denominations there was still a great deficiency in this respect[1]. The Government would not have much need to interfere, for, because of constant reading, the people were able to think for themselves. All that was required was to direct their inclinations aright[2].

Another contemporary writer in like manner takes the difference existing between the herdsmen and the agricultural labourers as his starting-point in judging the Hungarian national character. His views at the same time express the conviction of the better educated part of the Hungarian aristocracy. "The Hungarians of the Alföld may be divided into two groups. The one is composed of the people living together in the villages. The principal trait of their character is a noble pride, and it must be a difficult task indeed which their sense of honour does not compel them to finish. They love a simple life, and are so attached to their fertile country that very few of them ever lose sight of the soil on which they live and die. This

---

[1] "Der Bauer hat überhaupt Realität, Menschenverstand und im Allgemeinen geredet, bis auf die das ganze Jahr hindurch aufs Feld wohnenden Hirten, auch Sitten." Report to be found in Archives of *consilium locumtenentiale* (No. 33,688 (1787)).

[2] "Die Bauern sind mehr als man es glaubt zur Lectüre aufgelegt, besonders die protestantischen Ortschaften." *Ibid.*

nobleness of heart is very little present among the rough inhabitants of the outlying farms and the herdsmen, who constitute
the second group. Their savagery and unbridled licence leads
them to commit thefts and other crimes[1]."

It is our firm conviction that this division into two distinct
groups is perfectly justified, for the distinction was due to deep-
seated historical causes. The sons of the *puszta* (the Hungarian
plain or prairie), who did not appear until later on as the
heroes of novels and poems, were a direct contrast to the peaceful agricultural inhabitants of the large market boroughs of the
Alföld. Both were alike Hungarian and it would be a mistake to
believe that the *csikós* (Hungary's "cowboy") or the *betyár*
(her "highwayman") preserved the Magyar type better than
the farmers. But the geographical conditions and the historical
development both helped a civilized and a semi-barbarous class
to dwell together for so long. In fact the period of Turkish
dominion actually witnessed a certain amount of retrogression
in this respect. The historical importance of the eighteenth
century for the Hungarian nation, in our opinion, consists chiefly
in the fact that the Alföld, which at the opening of the period
was pasture land, became the scene of a profitable agriculture
at its close. This economic transformation profoundly affected
the character of those Hungarians permanently settled on the
Alföld, who were occupied with the cultivation of the soil and
were thoroughly organised in their relations to parish, Church
and State. Their character developed to a far greater degree
than that of the herdsmen whose whole existence was bound
up in the solitary life of the plains, the transformation of which
through the progress of civilization was only a question of time.
The large agricultural centres of the Alföld marked the advance
and expansion, not merely of civilization, but of Magyardom.

Thus, we see that the Hungarian serfs were making distinct
economic and educational progress as well as increasing in
numbers, while at the same time the nobles were still maintaining their economic and political privileges. Was there not,
then, sufficient ground for the belief that these two chief elements

[1] Count Domokos Teleki, *loc. cit.* p. 129.

of the Hungarian nation must eventually grapple with one another in an irreconcilable conflict of interests, of which the only result could be the final overthrow of the nation?

The official documents of the eighteenth century offer the best answer to this question. The large Hungarian parishes (townships) throve and progressed, not in spite of their proprietors, but under their protecting wings. The moment they observed that their serfs were becoming rich, the Károlyis and Koháris gradually emancipated them, and the burden of service thus changed into a comparatively easy pecuniary obligation. In the area of Kecskemét and Nagy-Körös, Baja and Nyiregyháza there was no allodial land. The estates of the proprietors situated in the "Banat" and in the county of Bács were offered to the poorer people as places of settlement. A sensible conflict of interests was possible only where no contracts could be concluded between the feudal lords and the people, as at Czegléd, which belonged to the *piae fundationes*, and at Makó, which belonged to the Bishop of Csanád[1]. Among the Cumanians and the "Hajdús" there were many cases of oppression; whole townships were deprived of liberty and converted into serfs. But the resistance here shown must not be considered as savouring of an attack upon the nobility at large—the people themselves desired to preserve the nobility; it was directed against individual lords and more especially against officials. The Hungarian peasant was dubbed "litigious," and there was, indeed, no lack of suits relating to the *Urbarium* in Hungarian districts. But an examination of the documents over a series of years, shows the number of complaints lodged in places inhabited by Hungarians to be strikingly small, in comparison with the number of suits brought in districts where people of foreign speech lived.

On the whole, therefore, we may safely say that, in 1780, the unity of the Hungarian nation was not threatened by any social danger.

---

[1] See Chapter II. sec. 5, "The Peasants and Serfs."

CHAPTER IV.

THE CHURCH.

AT the opening of the modern age, the Reformation and the Catholic reaction were permeating and transforming the older social order all over Europe. The struggle between the different social and political orders was accompanied by a conflict between the old faith and the new. The antagonism between the two was deeply rooted in the innermost recesses of men's minds; but nowhere and at no time did this antagonism appear without coming into direct contact and connection with the political and external elements of national life.

This connection is everywhere in evidence; it is probably nowhere so clear and so striking as in Hungary. Half a century after its introduction, the Protestant faith was predominant in Hungary, and its advance was furthered both by the party which leaned to the Turks and by that which looked to the Germans for support. The King himself (Maximilian II) seems for a time to have hesitated[1]. The Prelacy was the only social order to maintain the older faith, and after 1576 it engaged in the struggle apparently without any prospect of victory, merely because its very existence was bound up with Catholicism. Even among the prelates we meet with cases of hesitation and actually of conversion to Protestantism, though in general, after the accession of Rudolf II, their intellectual capacities and political position had given them the lead in the Counter-Reformation movement. Their enormous wealth and their

---

[1] Cf. "Regesták a magyar történethez" (*Történ. Tár*, July, 1878). He showed marked hesitation at the Parliament of 1563.

abuse of their power alike helped to spread the new teaching, which aimed its bitterest attacks against them[1]. In order to recover the lost ground the representatives of the old religion had to display the same merits and services as had originally given a privileged position to their early missionaries and teachers.

For several centuries the distinction between the two conflicting religions which had the greatest political importance and the deepest consequences was that the Catholics clung to the dynasty, which remained true to the old faith. Since the Protestants considered that this alliance imperilled their political and religious liberty, the latter party looked rather to the Turks for support. They were just as little desirous of Osmanising Hungary as the Catholics were of Germanising it, and their situation is after all best explained by their relations to the Emperor and the Sultan. Consequently (though the statement may seem open to question), while a large part of the nation professed the Protestant faith, and by its energetic opposition saved the constitution and, perhaps, the nationality of Hungary, none the less the influence of the Catholic Church harmonized more with the historic development of the nation. The most glorious traditions of her past called upon Hungary to fight against the infidels, for she had won her place in the history of the world by such struggles in the past. Everywhere else, indeed, it was natural and almost necessary that the interests of the weaker Protestantism should be identified with those of Islam, the foe of Christianity; but in Hungary the alliance with the Turks at a time of constitutional and religious struggle involved a denial of the nation's past and future. It is this fact that accounts for the tragic fate of men like Bocskay and Gabriel Bethlen, who were the leaders not only of their party but of their nation: they could achieve victories, excite enthusiasm and command devotion, but they were never able to revive the whole energy of the national spirit.

Much as we may attribute to the eloquence and powerful personality of Peter Pázmány, and to the moral and intellectual

---

[1] *Tubero de Temporibus suis Comment.*, Schwandtner, vol. II. p. 176.

influence of the Jesuit schools and writings, and though external influences were admittedly not without their effect, the fact that Catholicism regained lost ground so rapidly and effectually was due in the first place to its national tendency. Attention has often been called to the fact that, in the Protestant literature of Hungary, general European movements occupy much the largest share of consideration, whereas her Catholic literature rests on an absolutely national basis. In all other countries the Protestant religion organised a national church, but in Hungary this object was attained by the universal Catholic faith, in the person of Peter Pázmány. The great national importance of this powerful man consisted in the fact that he created a genuinely national church. Surrounded as he was, on the one hand, by a German Catholic King and by Ultramontane influences, on the other by patriots who were Protestants though Turkophiles, he succeeded, almost independently of either, in laying the foundations of an institution which renewed the traditions of the patriotic age of the Hunyadis. Hungary began to become Catholic again, without however becoming German, and was able to retain her old privileged position even in her dealings with the Pope. Moreover, the full force of the national spirit was once more brought into play against the Turks. The guiding idea of the *Zrinyiász* (1646), the greatest epic of the age, was that the breach with the older faith had rivetted the Turkish yoke on Hungary, and that only complete religious reunion could break it from her neck.

In 1670 a part of the aristocracy fixed their hopes on France and sought aid from her against the dynasty. The blood of Peter Zrinyi, Frangepán and Nádasdy, shed to no purpose (1671), not only set up a barrier between the King and the aristocracy, but, for the first time since the existence of Hungary, served as a pretext for the King to substitute his arbitrary power for the constitution as sole deciding factor. The unfortunate result was that even the Catholic Estates displayed considerable indifference towards the Turkish war, which began to be waged with complete success in the last decade of the century. None the less, it was their energetic conduct which prevented Leopold from resorting a second time to the weapons of terrorism. For a time, under Francis Rákóczi (1703–11), all denominations seemed to join hands for the defence of the country's rights. "Concordia religionum animata libertate."

It is fine and inspiring to picture to oneself the golden age of religious concord and mutual toleration, the outlines of which must have been before the mental eyes of those who took part in the assembly at Szécsény (1705). But as a matter of fact, despite the zealous and well-tried attachment of Rákóczi himself to the Roman faith, he led a movement which was quite as much Protestant as constitutional or national. It was a union of all those factors which had separately endeavoured to liberate Hungary from the power of the Emperor in previous times. But notwithstanding the fact that the head of the movement and many of its leaders belonged to the Catholic Church, it was the Calvinists from the vale of the Tisza who formed its mainstay. Rákóczi himself wrote, "nine-tenths of my army were Calvinists[1]." It was the latter who laid down their arms at Majtény, while the Catholic magnates nearly all went into banishment. The Catholic French, who received Rákóczi and his followers, now replaced the Turks, who had received Protestant exiles in the past.

The bulk of the Catholic Estates in Parliament remained loyal even during the Rákóczi rebellion—the prelates almost to a man. This fact gave them their predominance after the reconciliation at Szatmár (1711), when the future prosperity of the country depended on the final adjustment of the relations between King and nation. As we have seen, the prelates on the Hungarian side almost exclusively dictated the new conditions. Their leading idea was that Hungary should be made entirely Catholic again, and become the chosen country of the Blessed Virgin[2].

[1] In *A Kalapos Király* (*The Hatted King*—i.e. Joseph II, so called because he was never crowned) Paul Ányos contrasts the Rákóczi rising with previous ones :
"With the golden banner of liberty in their hands
These men sought their faith to the hurt of their country.
And though their last leader was a truer man,
His rebel followers despoiled churches :
For that God permitted not his army
To be the liberator of their country."

[2] The following passage from the records of the Parliament of 1708 is of supreme

Wherever else the two religions stood in opposition to each other, the immediate result was social disruption as well. But in this case, the ecclesiastical orders obtained privileges within the realm as the aristocratic orders had done before. In the Holy Roman Empire, to the very last, the equality of the two religious faiths was maintained with the strictest consistency—in fact with an almost hair-splitting exactness. In France the distinct separation of the two—if not absolute equality—was permitted. In Hungary too, the Evangelical Estates appeared in Parliament as a separate body up to 1681. Here also, at least on the Protestant side, the prevailing idea was that the two parties must decide in conjunction, by mutual agreement, on all national—and particularly on all religious—affairs. The example of the German Imperial Diet was continually before their eyes. As in that country the guarantees of the Swedes and France gave the Peace of Westphalia its peculiar significance, the Protestants in Hungary endeavoured to give their Treaties of Vienna (1606) and Linz (1645) the importance of international treaties. When we consider how this radical disruption of national unity rent asunder Germany, whose only formidable enemy was France, we can easily conceive what must have become of Hungary as a result of the struggle between the Emperor and the Turks. The Rákóczi rising proves that, during days of grave crisis, the fatherland was yet after all the supreme consideration in Hungary. The expulsion of the Turks, however, had given to the Catholic party assurance not only of peace abroad but of victory at home, and in this direction Rákóczi's rising produced but little alteration.

It was after the downfall of the conspiracy of the great Catholic Hungarian magnates (1670) that King Leopold I vowed, after a pilgrimage to Maria-Zell, that he would make Hungary a truly apostolic country and extirpate heresy from the land[1]. This was the origin of the famous phrase, *Regnum Marianum*, and the project coincided with the epoch at which

---

importance : " Siquidem sola Romana Catholica fides in hocce Apostolico Regno *haereditaria* est, Augustana vero et Helvetica Confessio contra severissimas Regni hujus Leges et prohibitiones, sub armorum strepitu, propter bonum pacis *tolerata*."

[1] Report of Pufendorf, the Swedish Ambassador.

the first effective blows were aimed at Magyardom and constitutional liberty. The Parliaments of 1681 and 1687, confining the free exercise of the Protestant religions (Lutheran or Calvinist) to certain stipulated places in eleven counties, virtually put an end to religious equality in the districts adjoining Austria. Henceforth it was practically impossible for the reformed religion to recover the territory it had lost, and to compensate itself elsewhere for what the Catholic Church had taken from it. After the Peace of Szatmár, when the power of the dynasty seemed at its zenith, when the Turks had been crushed, when Prussia—so often the ally of dissidents in Hungary—was still a second-rate Power, the conception of the *Regnum Marianum* became one of the main ideas of public policy.

The chief aim, alike of Jesuits and of Catholic prelates, was naturally the abolition of heresy and the restoration of the older Catholic unity. None the less, though their denominational zeal brought so much trouble upon Hungary, they were able to use a great national idea as the basis and foundation of religious union.

In the opinion of these propagandists, at any rate, the situation of Hungary offered very many points of resemblance to that of Spain after the expulsion of the Moors. In both countries, it was only after struggles lasting centuries that the nation succeeded in recovering her lost provinces. The national victory was the triumph of the Cross; the political struggle had assumed the sanctity of a crusade. This union of patriotic and religious conceptions gave the national spirit of Spain that impulse, which enabled it not only to exercise a hegemony in Europe, but to transform and develop the whole of Catholicism in accordance with its ideas of morals and culture. Now, when Spain, France and Poland—the three older defenders of the Catholic faith— had either fallen or were on the downward path, all the greater were the hopes fixed upon Hungary, where the hierarchy was celebrating triumphs unknown since the days of the Thirty Years' War. Did it not open the way to the conversion of the whole of Eastern Europe, and to the restoration of the former Hungarian *archiregnum*, whose King had been the standard-bearer of the Church? The examples offered by the *illustres Godos* in Spain, like those of St Stephen and the other canonised Kings in Hungary, formed the starting-point alike of religious and of national development.

After she had overpowered her enemies from without, Spain had endeavoured to rid her soil of those traitors to the Cross who had remained in the country; and in Hungary there were many people who looked on Protestantism as a sort of relic of Turkish dominion. They regarded it as the cause which prevented the only religion that dispensed the means of grace from reigning supreme and alone in the lands of St Stephen. Moreover, it was of political consequence that this foreign religion divided the once united Hungarian nation just as completely as the presence of a foreign element had divided the people of Spain[1].

As the expression of an idea that was alike religious and national, the conception of a *Regnum Marianum* seems even to us to have been in a measure justified. But though the analogy to Spain, a country that never faltered in its religion, is striking, several remarkable differences prove that the idea of a universal religion was after all not so firmly established in Hungary, as in the empire of the Catholic Kings. In the first place that district of Hungary which, from a national point of view, was most purely Hungarian, remained true to the most radical doctrines of the Reformation. In Spain, the nobles could boast of pure Gothic descent, just as much as they could of their unwavering devotion to their religion, but in Hungary the pure Hungarian districts were the headquarters of Calvinism[2]. In Spain, it was at the head of the whole nation that the King overthrew the Moorish empire and obliterated the last trace of the Mussulman religion; in Hungary, the King led a victorious army chiefly composed of foreigners, who raged as furiously against patriots

---

[1] Máriafi, *Igaz Magyar* (*True Hungarian*), vol. I. p. 90: "It follows as a matter of course that Lutherans, Calvinists, Unitarians, members of the Greek Oriental Church, and even those papists who do not show any extraordinary devotion and zeal towards the Blessed Virgin Mary, *are not true Hungarians*."

[2] Yet Stephen Máriafi (v. *supra*) protests against their speaking of their faith as "Hungarian religion." *Ibid.* vol. I. p. 13, note: "But with what countenance do the Calvinists presume to call their religion 'Hungarian religion, Hungarian faith,' which religion is the deadly foe of the genuine old Hungarian faith professed by the real old Hungarians for over five hundred years."

as they did against the Turks. There was no organic link connecting the Spanish nobles with the Jews or the Moors, but in Hungary Protestants and Catholics alike were the sons of an oppressed and forlorn country, and members of the same order struggling for the retention of its privileges. In short, whereas in Spain every element of foreign and domestic politics contributed towards maintaining the unity of religion, elements of extreme importance cooperated to prevent any such restoration in Hungary.

I.

Up till 1790, the political status of the Protestant religion was defined by Act XXX of 1715. This provided for the confirmation of the already mentioned Acts of 1681 and 1687, which had formerly determined the rights of the Protestants but had been liable to all kinds of different interpretations. The Parliament could no longer serve as the forum for the investigation of complaints—had it continued to do so, the Protestants themselves would have been the first to suffer; the supreme conduct and control of religious affairs was made a royal prerogative. In the Act itself we have the actual declaration of the King's discretionary power; Acts XXV and XXVI of 1681 and XXI of 1687 were left in force only for the time being[1]. Complaints were to be investigated by royal commissaries, while such Protestants as had grievances could appeal to the Throne for redress, not in a body, but as individual suitors only. In former days, at the assemblies of Szécsény and Ónod (1705–7), the constitution of Poland, with its wild ideas of liberty, had been taken as the ideal, and subsequently the Catholic party were able to allude to the example offered by that neighbouring republic, which had excluded dissenters from its Parliament in 1719. This fact shows what fate must have overtaken the Protestants in Hungary, had they not been protected by the royal power. Without doubt the precedent offered by Poland influenced the action of the religious committee of the Parliament (which sat at Pest and

[1] " S. Majestas *adhuc* censuit *conservandos.* "

Pozsony in 1720 and 1721) in exaggerating the antagonism that existed between the two denominations. The Parliaments of 1723 and 1741 concerned themselves but little with the Protestant question: and in 1731 the King regulated the status of the Protestant Church by a decree of the *consilium locum-tenentiale*[1]. This decree too was provided with a clause to the effect that it was to be in force until further measures were taken. According to the said decree, the Protestants were no longer to possess full civil rights. They were excluded from the public offices by the legal form of oath administered, which demanded that they should honour the Blessed Virgin and the saints. The restrictions imposed on the schools and the severe punishment of apostasy from Catholicism made the spread of their faith impossible. However, the two Protestant Churches remained in existence as religious corporations possessed of inferior rights, though they had to struggle now, not for predominance, but for very existence. Hungary, whose chief dignities had been held by Protestants in the seventeenth century, merely tolerated them in the eighteenth, excluding them from that share in the government formerly theirs by right, and seeming to give them up as an easy prey to the Catholic Church.

We should like to adduce another historical analogy. The Catholic party looked upon Hungary as a new Spain, in which the extirpation of foreign foes was to be combined with an abolition of religious disunion; and the measures taken by the Court and the predominant party greatly resembled the policy of the French Government towards the Huguenots, from the days of Richelieu to the revocation of the Edict of Nantes. The seizure of La Rochelle rendered the Huguenots incapable of further political resistance, just as the overthrow of the Rákóczi rising and the expulsion of the Turks did the Protestants of Hungary; and subsequently for a time each dissenting religious party was allowed to indulge in its religious worship unhindered, though without any political guarantees. Another point of resemblance is the fact that, though each of these two

---

[1] *Carolina Resolutio*, published in the author's *Enchiridion Fontium Historiae Hungarorum*, pp. 706—8.

dynasties commenced its struggle against the dissenters in the interests of a centralising policy, both Bourbon and Habsburg were compelled to rely on the alliance of Protestant States abroad. It was by means of the alliance with England, Holland and Prussia, that the Emperors were enabled to overcome the Turks, Tököli, and Rákóczi. But the same alliance prevented the Catholic Church for the moment from reaping the entire fruits of her triumph. There might be persecution, usurpation of rights and oppression, but so long as Prince Eugène's advice prevailed, all these were limited by the possibility of a revolution and of external interference.

The accession of Maria Teresa (1740) heralded the opening of a new epoch, in so far as the Monarchy now entered into a life-and-death struggle with Protestant Prussia, her former ally[1]. Before this date policy had dictated toleration in dealing with men who professed the same faith as the allies; now politicians must have seen danger in the ties of religion that existed between the Protestant subjects of the Monarchy and her most formidable antagonist. In the days of Charles III, the part played by Protestants like the Rádais or Jeszenáks had been a most distinguished one. Now the Court kept the Protestant nobles at a distance, actuated by suspicions, not merely of their faith, but of their political feelings. The change was immediately perceptible. In the days of Charles III legal forms were strictly adhered to, and in not a few cases those, who displayed an attitude of bitter and ruthless hostility towards the Protestants, forfeited the good graces of the monarch[2]. Those Protestants, who appealed to the sovereign in the interests of their schools,

[1] Here too the parallel with France is a striking one. Louis XIV revoked the Edict of Nantes in 1685, when his chief foe was, not the House of Habsburg, but Holland and William of Orange, his former allies.

[2] The case of Althan—a cardinal, Bishop of Vácz, who protested against the Carolina Resolutio, because it granted the Evangelicals certain rights, and was deprived of the enjoyment of temporalia, though he was a near relative of the King's favourite—does not stand alone. The King's anger fell on Count Joseph Eszterházy too, who protested most loudly against administering the oath to Protestants at the Parliament of 1729. He was stripped of all his military and civil dignities. In the following year, when he was restored to office, he attributed this fact to the protection of the Blessed Virgin Mary—as did his biographer. Kolinovics, Post. Mem. Jos. Est. pp. 79 and 220.

rarely met with a rebuff[1]. In the Trans-Tiszan counties scarcely any attempt had been made to put an end to the predominance of the Calvinist elements. Now, however, the State itself conducted the religious propaganda on behalf of Catholicism.

In the counties, the only case, in which the taking of the oath was not required was when no Catholic *magistratus* was to be obtained at all. In Szepes, in 1742, Gregory Stansich Horváth could not be given the office of *táblabiró*[2]. Special royal instructions, issued to the *föispán* of the county of Szabolcs, forbade the nomination of Calvinists for high offices. As a consequence the county nobility took energetic steps to counteract this measure, inviting the flower of the Calvinist aristocracy of Transylvania to the new elections. If he nominated Catholics only, the High Sheriff was convinced that they would "vote for the weakest to secure their own predominance[3]." A report of these events in Szabolcs, which fell into the hands of Frederick the Great, compared the persecution to that of Diocletian[4]. Hence the idea of emigration again began to make headway; and on April 19, 1743, the Government had to issue an energetic decree forbidding it.

After the conclusion of the war in 1748, the religious reaction increased still further in intensity. In the county of Hont, an endeavour was made to deprive the Protestants of sixteen churches at once in 1749. In his book, which appeared in 1750, Martin Biró, Bishop of Veszprém, promised a veritable war of extermination[5]. The principle guiding the action of the *consilium locumtenentiale* was that Protestants had no right at all

---

[1] v. Molnár, Aladár, *Közoktatás története* (*History of Education*), pp. 454—7. The school of Sárospatak in 1724 and 1733.

[2] *Intoleranz*, p. 186.

[3] Cf. the letter of Count Alexander Károlyi, High Sheriff of the county of Szabolcs, to Count Louis Batthyány Chancellor of the Court, dated May 29, 1743: "There is a lack of Papists suitable for the office of sheriff (*alispán*). And the special instructions issued to me by your Excellency forbid me to nominate Calvinists for high offices of the kind." The instructions issued to High Sheriffs on Nov. 21, 1768, likewise make it the duty of the latter to support the true faith—"fides orthodoxa secundetur" (Chanc. Arch.).

[4] In the Royal Archives in Berlin, "Extract Schreiben aus Ungarn," May 7, 1743.

[5] The famous *Enchiridion de fide*, published at Györ (1750).

M. H.

to chapels of ease (*filiale*). For, however extreme the intolerance might be, it was believed that the persecution would not begin in real earnest until, as a result of the conclusion of peace, more soldiers came into the country[1]. Yet there had already been terrible cases of persecution, reminding us of the worst side of the Inquisition ; such, for instance, as the warning offered in 1727 in the county of Trencsén. A Lutheran peasant on his deathbed was visited by a Catholic priest. By accident or design, the dying man let the sacred wafer fall from his mouth. The county officials decided that his body should be exhumed and burned, and the ashes scattered to the winds. Though his daughters and son-in-law swore that they had no part in his offence, they were fined 50 florins. The King confirmed the sentence, but, as a religious prince, added that no priest should in future ever visit a dying man of whose faith he was not sure.

As a set-off to the general system of oppression, the nobility, who could not brook compulsion, seemed to be about to appeal to the last resource—an armed revolution. Even cautious statesmen, like the Prussian ambassadors in Vienna, thought such a course neither impossible nor hopeless[2]. The Queen herself, when after protracted negotiations she finally agreed to receive the monster deputation of Protestants, expressed her conviction that several Hungarian towns, in particular Debreczen, were not to be trusted.

We must not imagine that the statements of the Bishop of Veszprém or of a few hot-blooded nobles and commoners are without significance. It is true that they are exaggerations, for there can be no doubt that the majority of men professing the same faith did not express such decided views, or were actually of a different opinion. However, it is only in times of peace that the predominance belongs to those parties whose aims are openly professed. In troubled times, those who endeavour to attain something beyond their avowed objects always get the

[1] Report of the Prussian ambassadors Podewils and Graeve, dated Vienna, July 4, 1749. In Berlin.

[2] Podewils and Graeve to Frederick the Great, Vienna, Aug. 9, 1749; "Mit Gewalt und Verfolgung wird der Clerus in Hungarn nichts richten, dem schwierigen Soldaten können sie wenig trauen, die Prątestanten sind des Landes besser kundig, und können Ihnen allenfalls 300,000 (sic !) Mann entgegensetzen."

upper hand. Peace means the victory of the moderate parties, disturbances are attended by the triumph of extremists, and in those days there was a prospect of a struggle, and neither side was lacking in warlike catchwords[1].

Their intimate relations with foreign States of the same faith, which was one of the most important motives for the molestation of the Protestants, was at the same time a considerable obstacle in the way of their absolute subjection. Ignatius Bajtay, at this time engaged in compiling Hungarian history for the instruction of the Crown-Prince Joseph (afterwards Emperor Joseph II), sorrowfully remarks that the Protestants living in the country were protected not merely by the Acts of 1608, but by the influence of England, Holland and Prussia[2]. However, he was of opinion that there was nothing in the world which the sovereign could not attain by rational action, by a cautious policy and a due opportunism[3].

Hungary was saved from the horrors of a religious war at home not only by the intervention of foreign powers, energetic enough in the case of Frederick II, and resulting in the solemn protest of the Pope against Bishop Biró's book[4]; her salvation was due much more to the internal conditions of the country. After all, the Government set political aims before ecclesiastical, and it could scarcely have got on without the support of the Protestants in the Parliament which it was forced to summon. There could be no doubt that the persecution of the latter, even if successfully and quickly accomplished, would render the monarchy for a long time incapable of playing any part in foreign politics. France was a living example of the danger involved by such measures, for the revocation of the Edict of

---

[1] In the counties of Csongrád and Heves an insurrection did actually break out in 1753, but the nobles took no part in it, and it was strictly confined to the serfs.

[2] Acad. Archives, *History of the Hung. Kingdom.* 8vo.

[3] *Ibid.* Fessler (vol. x. p. 320) remarks that "das letzte macchiavellistische Prinzip hätte der echte Priester Gottes nicht niederschreiben sollen."

[4] The Protestants asked the Prussian King's support. Knowing that direct interference could only do harm, he took another way. He wrote to the Bishop of Breslau, Count Schaffgotsch, that the persecution of Protestants in Hungary might force him to do the same with his Catholic subjects. The Bishop wrote in this sense to the Pope, who censured Biró's book (1751).

Nantes had done her enormous damage, whereas the refugees had proved a considerable gain to the lands of the Hohenzollerns. Consequently, the only means to which recourse could be had were those recommended by Bajtay, and of these there was no lack[1]!

The complaints of Protestant parishes and individuals against the oppression to which they were subjected were innumerable. A joint appeal by all the sufferers was not permitted ; the Queen referred the several complainants to the *consilium locumtenentiale*; while anyone who communicated with the ambassadors of foreign powers was simply hanged[2].

We must remark that all these grievances were, for the most part, inflicted only upon villages and towns. The nobles were allowed liberty of worship, and their conversion to the predominant faith merely involved an improvement in their political and material status. In the case of the ruling class, the measure of persecution was not in excess of that pressure which opposing parties exercise openly against one another in the parliamentary State of to-day. In our period, participation in the government of the State was made dependent upon holding certain religious convictions, as it is to-day upon holding certain political principles. To be just, we cannot see any other difference between the party-life of the twentieth and that of the eighteenth century. On the other hand, the peasants came under quite different laws ; their masters could drive them away, chastise them, or convert them by force ; and, in the case of each law securing to the Protestants liberty of conscience, since 1681 there had been added the saving clause " salvo jure dominorum terrestrium."

This purely political oppression was not influenced even by the alliance made between the Bourbons and Habsburgs in 1756. Yet this was the last of the renewed attempts made by the united forces of the Catholic States to overpower the Protestant countries which had grown to greatness during the struggle for hegemony between the Catholic Powers. On the other hand, a close connection between the Protestant nobles of Hungary and the great Protestant Alliance was out of the question, for

---

[1] Royal Resolution, Aug. 30, 1753 (Chanc. Arch.).
[2] Report of Podewils and Graeve, June 4, 1749.

Frederick II was not only the enemy of the kingdom and of the monarch, he was above all bent upon overthrowing the privileges of the nobility[1].

II.

According to the declarations of the Protestants themselves, the persecution consisted of the following points:

Though numerous laws declared for liberty of worship, apostates from the Catholic faith were persecuted and punished by imprisonment[2]. The petition submitted to Maria Teresa in 1774, emphasised the fact that proceedings of this kind were being taken not only against commoners but also against nobles[3]. Missionaries were punished, and they were not allowed to convert even Jews to their faith.

The children of mixed marriages (even in cases where a *reversalis* had been given) were brought up as Catholics, and were actually torn away from their parents[4]. Mixed marriages could be celebrated by Catholic priests only, who forced the Protestant party to the marriage to give a *reversalis*, or even invented one[5]. Evangelical orphans were taken away from their guardians and brought up in the Catholic faith. We find frequent instances of such measures being taken, not only in Hungarian towns[6], but even in the case of a distinguished magnate family in Transylvania, where Calvinism never ceased to be the predominant element[7].

The most famous case was that of Agnes Bánffy.

Count Denis Bánffy was one of the most cultivated, but also one of the most dissipated and prodigal magnates in Transylvania.

---

[1] Circular issued by the *consilium locumtenentiale* in 1757.

[2] An apostate of this kind was actually beaten until he recanted. Report of Graeve, dated Vienna, Aug. 13, 1749.

[3] *Brevis et sincera deductio status religionis evangelicorum—divae olim—Mariae Theresiae exhibita* (1790), p. 34. In the case of a *reversalis* the father bound himself to renounce his right to educate the children in his religion. As instances the cases of Francis Szemere and Borbala Szakadási are cited.

[4] Instances of this were Rettegi, burgess of Nagybánya, and Ötvös.

[5] Cf. the case of Imre Sándor in the county of Vas.

[6] At Kecskemét, Nagy-Bánya, Gyöngyös, Györ, etc.

[7] Chanc. Arch. 1782.

In 1746 he married Agnes Barcsay, daughter of the rich Baron Gregory Barcsay. Though they had three children, the husband sought amusement elsewhere and dissipated the whole fortune. In 1755 he turned Catholic and his wife allowed him to educate her two boys in his faith, though the law of Transylvania did not compel her to do so. His mother-in-law prevented his becoming bankrupt by taking over his land and by paying his debts which represented a much higher amount. After her death he signed a contract with his wife in which she gave him an alimony. In return he renounced all paternal rights over their only daughter and declared he would never try to convert her to Catholicism. All these contracts were confirmed by the Queen.

So the child was brought up in the Calvinist faith and to avoid all danger, her mother betrothed her at the age of nine to Count Samuel Teleki, afterwards Chancellor. The wedding was to take place when she was sixteen. In all these agreements, as subsequent to the contract, the consent of the father was not wanted. But the Count saw in his daughter only a means to win the Queen's favour. He decided to carry off his daughter by force, and won the consent of Maria Teresa to his design. The agent charged with the execution of the scheme was Bishop Baron Bajtay.

The Countess was with her daughter on her estate, when, on July 16, 1767, Hussars seized the castle. Their commander, Count Bethlen, produced Bajtay's letter and asked the mother to surrender her child. The bishop wrote that he would take charge of her till Her Majesty should give further orders. Teleki demanded to see the Queen's signature, the Countess declared that, if she saw it, she herself would take her daughter to Vienna. Bethlen sent his Hussars. The Countess took her daughter in a room, into which the soldiers shot until the door was forced. A lieutenant snatched the child out of the arms of her mother, and rode away without taking leave. The Queen sent her own waiting woman to nurse the little Agnes, who was carried to Vienna[1]. The Countess followed her, was received by

---

[1] Her mother was able to send her only these lines : " Do not forget your poor mother, your fiancé and your faith, and take care of your linen." All these details are taken from the Archives of the Bánffy family, formerly in Remete and now in Bonczida.

the Queen, but could not see her daughter. Maria Teresa declared to her father that she would never restore Agnes, but would convert her by fair means only. On January 25, 1768, Agnes made her confession in the Court chapel before their Majesties and the young Archdukes. She was married afterwards to Count John Eszterházy.

Such inhumanity showed what power fanaticism had over even the best of mothers and wives. Such things were even possible in Transylvania, where according to the fundamental law, the Diploma of Leopold I, Protestantism could claim the same rights as the Catholic faith.

It is no wonder that in Transylvania too the equality of religions came to naught. The Diet had the right to nominate as candidates for each office three members each of the Lutheran, Calvinist, Unitarian and Catholic confessions. The King always chose a Catholic, even if he received the least votes. So the Government became Catholic. In the towns it was decreed that half of the magistrates should be "of the religion of the prince." In the Lutheran Saxon cities foreigners of dubious antecedents and apostates obtained possession of offices and disturbed all order[1].

In defiance of the laws the Protestant guilds were compelled to take part in ceremonial processions and masses. At Szatmár-Németi, where the shoemakers' guild resisted, there would have been severe reprisals, but for Joseph II's accession. Protestant magistrates and officials too were sworn in according to the rubrics of the Catholic Church[2]. In law-suits the judges were required to take an oath at variance with the Evangelical faith[3].

Their churches and schools were taken away on account of the errors of pastors or others[4]—some of them actually because

---

[1] These renegades or apostates were called Mamelukes.

[2] Michael Mikos, a magistrate at Pozsony professing the Evangelical faith, died suddenly from apoplexy when refusing to take the oath except in the name of God simply. Such is the tale told by Kolinovics (*Post. Mem.* 72) in defence of the older form of oath.

[3] *In rē* Széki and Hellenbach.

[4] E.g. that of Nagy-Szaláncz in Abauj, that of Füle in Veszprém, and that of Foktü in Pest county. Between 1712 and 1744, in Hungary 73 churches were taken away from the Protestants, between 1744 and 1781 no fewer than 191. Cf. *Intoleranz des Kath. Klerus gegen die ungarischen Protestanten* (1792), pp. 211—215. The

the members of the congregation had repaired them without giving notice of such intention in advance[1]. Large townships like Györ, Pápa, Léva, Tata and Veszprém, were persecuted as soon as they had ceased to be frontier fortresses[2]. Even German settlers were deprived of their churches[3]. Where there were no priests, only Levites, the latter were all driven away, so that the people were left without religious teaching and consolation. The repairing of buildings was not permitted. In the county of Trencsén sick people were compelled to call in a Catholic priest. Protestant felons, who were condemned to death, could only receive the last words of consolation from a Catholic priest[4]. From the private chapels of the Protestant nobles, not merely the neighbours but even the local inhabitants were excluded[5]. Moreover the Catholic proprietors abused their rights in dealing with their Evangelical serfs. They took away their churches[6]. They did not permit the place of a deceased pastor to be taken by a fresh one. They stripped the pastors of the land and tithes that served for their subsistence, and forced them to pay tithes. It was no rare event for them to expel the whole population of Protestant villages[7].

In defiance of the laws, the Catholic priests demanded fees of

petition of the Protestants stated the number of churches taken from them since 1681 to have been 650.

[1] E.g. at Csoknya (in Somogy county) and at Csepel.

[2] Act XXIII of 1681 was interpreted to mean that liberty of worship was permitted —besides the places specified in the Act—in the frontier fortresses only. And these towns had ceased to bear that character.

[3] At Mórágy in Tolna, Zánka in Veszprém, Kis-Körös and Bugyi in Pest county.

[4] A case for the Crown was brought against the town of Karczag for neglecting to comply with this requirement.

[5] At Legyesbénye a case for the Crown was brought against a certain Bessenyei for having hung a bell on a willow-tree in his courtyard to summon his servants and having prayed there on Sunday with his retainers. Cf. Szirmay, *Hist. Secr.* p. 41. We read further that "Integrae et vastae possessiones expulsis antiquis Hungaris incolis Helveticae confessioni addictis, advenis Slavis Catholicis attribuebat."

[6] Count Joseph Eszterházy not only endeavoured to drive the Calvinists away from Pápa; at Tarján, Szendi, Báj, and Köruye, he either converted or expelled such serfs as belonged to the Reformed Church. In other places the least he did was to take away their churches. *Ibid.* pp. 228—251.

[7] The same was the case at Foktü in Pest, Erdöd in Szatmár, Tisza-Örs in Heves, and Egyek in Szabolcs county. *Ibid.*

the Protestants also, and did not permit any christenings or burials until such had been paid. At Izsa, in the county of Komárom, the fee demanded for the burial of an adult was 12 florins, that for the interment of a child 1 florin 15 kreuzers[1]. At Ungvár, as not being one of the *articularis* places, the parish priest refused to allow the interment of the *táblabiró* Mokcsai, in mid-summer, until the sum of 100 ducats had been paid[2] him by way of burial fee (*stola*). Unless they gave a *reversalis* that they would bring up their children in the Catholic faith, Protestants were often prevented for years from getting married. In lawsuits relating to marriages, the Catholic consistory decided according to the principles of the Catholic religion[3]. In fact one case, that of a Protestant couple, was actually referred to the *Pope*, after passing through the various preliminary forums[4].

The Protestant superintendents could not exercise their right of superintendence by visitations; in fact they were obliged to subject themselves to the visitations of the Catholic bishops. They could not introduce books into the country unhindered. The *consilium locumtenentiale* had all the Heidelberg Catechisms seized; and Barkóczi, while still Bishop of Eger, had the Hungarian Bible burned in public.

Of Protestant schools, those of Beszterczebánya, Selmecz, Szatmár and Czegléd were degraded to the status of secondary schools; while those of Léva, Györ, Pápa and Tata were taken away from them. In the Danube districts there were no more Reformed colleges (of university status). The nobles were obliged to send their sons, at great expense, to distant parts.

People do not generally like to suffer martyrdom unless they possess ardent faith, and the combined pressure of State and Church produced many conversions, principally among the aristocracy. Francis Batthyány was a stout Protestant, a supporter of Gabriel Bethlen, Prince of Transylvania (1613–29), but he could not resist the temptation of being made a Count. He was the tutor of

---

[1] *Sincera Deductio*, p. 45.   [2] Szirmay, *loc. cit.*
[3] *Res* Clara Margitay.
[4] *Res* Bene and Schneider. The Pope passed sentence on April 9, 1775. Cf. *Intoleranz*, p. 167. Formerly the King had decided in cases relating to marriages, e.g. in 1724, in the case of George Radvánszky.

the two Zrinyi boys, Nicholas and Peter, and saw that they were educated by Jesuits, so that this great house was lost for Protestantism. Others became converts, seeking places and titles like one branch of the Teleki family, or hoping to have their debts paid like Count Denis Bánffy. Of the scholars and writers the learned Daniel Tersztyánszky, who wrote a part of the excellent *Ratio Educationis* adopted by Maria Teresa for all the schools of the kingdom, was also a convert. So was George Bessenyei. But to the credit of the nation, be it said, these were exceptions, and the bulk of the gentry could not be won over either by force or by corruption.

These then were the various abuses experienced in religious, ecclesiastical and school matters. They were mostly in vogue in the districts flanking the Danube and in the Highlands, where the Catholic faith was making the greatest inroads upon the Protestant preserves. The same districts were the chief domain of the magnates and prelates. The grievances were due not to Government but to the landed proprietors, and the organisation of the State merely served to allow their excesses to go unpunished. Against the King—the head of the State as such—few complaints were lodged. The noble society, which was inspired by the ideas of Pázmány and Eszterházy, endeavoured to restore the exclusive rights of the older faith, and the elastic privileges of the landed proprietors served as a sufficiently plausible basis for their actions. But, as a large part of the nobility and of the privileged order belonged to another church organisation and followed other doctrines, the advance of the Catholic party brought with it at the same time a political struggle. The State was still to such an extent subject to the influence of the social order, that it became a tool in the hands of the hierarchy, now in the ascendant and growing in power, because of the organisation of its vested interests, and of its strong internal motive-force. The list of political grievances offers the best proof of the measure in which the State favoured the endeavours of the Catholics. Hitherto the conflict of interests had been more particularly that of nobles against non-nobles; in the eighteenth century the ruling class was divided against itself, and split up into two antagonistic factions.

The chief point, on which everything turned, was the *juramentum decretale*, the oath that could be taken by Catholics only—the only means of opening the way to government offices. The fact that, since the Parliament of 1729, it was made a more universal requirement every year—without the countenance of laws, in fact in defiance of them—proves better than everything else the growing social power of Catholicism. It is true that, in accordance with the provisions of the law, Protestants were nominated to act at the elections of the Palatine when it was certain that they would not be elected but no Protestant ever obtained any high office that was dependent upon appointment by the King. In the counties also, they began to be excluded from all offices—even from that of *táblabíró*. Protestants who had already been elected were deposed, unless they took the oath as prescribed by the Catholics[1]. They were deeply exasperated by the fact that foreigners—in every respect their inferiors—should obtain the highest posts in their counties[2]. Their sons were not admitted to the *curia* to practise law; even advocates were none too ready to receive them as apprentices. Without official position and authority they were unable to defend the members of their Church. Such lack of competition was detrimental to the interests of the country. What was the object of studying when the mere fact of being a Catholic was sufficient to ensure a man a comfortable berth[3]? In such case the most talented man might be without employment. Even in the case of artisans, the important point was not the religion they professed but the skill they possessed; how much more requisite was such a condition in the management of the affairs of State—even were it not prescribed by the laws of the country[4].

[1] Cf. the case of Imre Pécsy in *Bihar*.

[2] *Sincera Deductio*, p. 53.

[3] This fact is admitted even by Count Niczky (*Staatskenntniss*, ch. 29).

[4] *Sincera Deductio*, p. 54: "Si artifices non secundum religionem sed secundum artem et utilitatem quam procurare possunt dijudicantur et applicantur; quaeri merito posset, num non circa applicationem Patriae Civium ad publica officia et honores etiam tunc, cum nullae adessent Leges quae hoc praeciperent longe magis virtus et capacitas quam Religio attendi deberet? Siquidem felicitas Regnorum plurimum ab eorum directione et habilitate dependet, qui in publicis officiis constituti sunt."—Fine principles; only both Protestants and Catholics have never emphasised

When a committee was actually appointed to investigate the complaints of the Evangelicals, the chief influences in it were those of the Bishop's men and of the Catholic county gentry. Most of the counties did not even take the trouble to communicate the decrees of the *consilium locumtenentiale* relating to religious matters to the Protestants, who in consequence did not know what they had to do. In other cases the clergy appeared as plaintiff, witness and judge in one person; so that it was impossible for non-Catholics to obtain justice or legal redress[1].

In several royal free boroughs—Buda, Pest, Székesfehérvár—no non-Catholic could obtain citizenship, in fact in these places even Protestant nobles were not permitted to buy houses. At Székesfehérvár Protestants were actually not tolerated even as inhabitants. At Nagy-Bánya they were not admitted to any guild or to the *magistratus* (town council)[2].

All this, naturally enough, could not take place without the approval of the head of the State, who had the right of regulating religious affairs by virtue of what was practically a personal prerogative. But however deep and profound we may conceive the religious feeling of Maria Teresa to have been, however many instances we may find in her history of her having preferred religious aims even to political interests, there can be no doubt that, so far as Hungary is concerned, she herself and her Government were guided by the endeavours of the ruling party of Hungarian society; in this direction neither Queen nor State ever took the initiative or pointed the way. In the opposition to her system of government in Hungary the Catholic extremists were no less concerned than were the oppressed Protestants[3].

them except where they were the oppressed party. Even England did not emancipate the Catholics until 1829.

[1] These "inquisitions" and the abuses attendant on them are treated in detail by "Egy bécsi embernek levele valamely Római szent birodalomban lakozó magyar baratjához" (The letter of an inhabitant of Vienna to a Hungarian friend of his dwelling in the Holy Roman Empire), 1783. In the National Museum.

[2] Of the 2450 inhabitants of Nagy-Bánya, in 1780, 1369 were Catholics, and 1081 (nearly half) non-Catholics.

[3] The most violent declaration of this opposition, the *Vexatio dat intellectum*, attacked the Government of Vienna, as indifferent, almost entirely from a religious point of view. It was written by Canon Richwaldsky, an intimate of the Primate, the same man to whom Baron Lawrence Orczi addressed one of his odes.

It will now be needful to make ourselves familiar with the Catholic party, with its organisation and with that latent power which was its chief motive force. Support it did indeed receive from without; but—and this was an essential condition of the results it attained—it contained within itself the chief source of its strength.

III.

Up to the close of the seventeenth century, the Catholic religion had predominated in those districts of Hungary only where the government of the Habsburg had obtained full recognition. Notwithstanding repeated attempts to reconquer them, the Catholics had lost all hold on Transylvania and on the North-East counties. In the Alföld the Turks did not hinder the spread of Protestantism, while they persecuted the Catholic Church[1]. At Szeged the Franciscans were unable to perform their religious duties except at the risk of their lives, in secret, often hiding in the fens. There and in the county of Bács, however, all attempts to extirpate this faith proved abortive. But in the more northerly districts scarcely a single Catholic parish remained. The dioceses of Csanád, Kalocsa-Bács, Nagyvárad and Pécs, if not nominally, were in actual fact very near to being included among the "partes infidelium." The Roman Church had to take refuge beyond the Danube; its situation is finely symbolised by the legend of the holy chapel of Andocs. A Calvinist in search of shelter in some sacred place bound his oxen to the altar with his profane hands. The sacred building was lifted up and carried bodily by the powers of Heaven to Andocs beyond the Danube. Here it has stood ever since, for so many years without foundations[2].

Where Catholicism was maintained by the successful activity of Pázmány and his followers, practically a fresh start had to be made with the work of converting and teaching. In the second half of the seventeenth century the care of souls was entrusted in

---

[1] Katona, *Hist. Metr. Coloc. Eccl.* vol. I. p. 73.

[2] Kazy, *Hist.* vol. v. p. 40. The Jesuit writes as follows : " Mira sunt, nescio an etiam vera, quae de aede vulgo jactantur."

most places not to secular clergy but to Franciscan friars[1]. In the southern districts of the Alföld, this activity of the friars lasted until the reign of Joseph II. As late as 1782 the Franciscans were doing parish priests' work in the county of Bács and the "Banat." It was in that year that the first election of a priest took place in Zombor[2].

In the thinly-populated "Banat" the Church had to display practically the same activity as had won for it a hold on Europe in the Middle Ages, and has secured it an eminent place for all time in the history of civilization. The priest was teacher, doctor, magistrate, all in one. The sublimest feelings of religious zeal had to be brought into play, for there were no worldly treasures to be gained, only souls to be won. The State and social order just firmly established by the Peace of Szatmár (1711) handed this district entirely over to the Roman Catholic faith as its intellectual possession. Here the non-Catholics did not compete with Catholicism; maybe they could not compete, for the Protestant mission had up till then produced but scanty results.

The prelates of the famous old Church centres had returned from exile. But a fresh start had to be made with the ecclesiastical organisation of the Alföld just as with its cultural development. In the diocese of the Archbishop of Kalocsa, in 1718, there were only 15 parishes in existence; between that date and 1780, 60 new ones were created. At first the aggregate income of the Archbishop amounted to no more than 2500 florins[3]. There was no chapter fund at all. When, in 1734, Gabriel Patachics took over the archbishopric, many of the churches were rather hovels than places suited for divine worship. On the altars there were no images of saints, no ecclesiastical vestments at all, and consequently there was scarcely any vestige of manifest Christianity[4]. The children were tempted to attend school by presents offered by the archbishops—a proceeding similar to that adopted by the founders of the first monastic schools[5]. So great was the lack of suitable candidates for holy

---

[1] Ed. Brown, *Travels*, p. 167 (of the environs of Galgócz).

[2] *Magyar Hirmondó*, 1782, p. 142.

[3] Katona, *Hist. Metr. Coloc. Eccl.* vol. II. p. 154.

[4] *Ibid*. vol. II. p. 208 : "ut vix vestigium apertae Christianitatis superesse videretur."

[5] Cf. the *Magyar* letter of the Archbishop Count Imre Csáky dated 1731. *Ibid.*

orders that in the diocese of Veszprém men were actually ordained who had been hardly two or three years in a seminary[1]. The seminarists in the diocese of Eger had to engage to accept the care of a parish, even before they had completed their studies, in case their superiors required them to do so. The first schematisms and histories testifying to the new development of Church life in this district show that the bulk of the priests working in the dioceses of Kalocsa, Csanád, Eger, and Várad were not natives of their respective dioceses at all, but immigrants from the Trans-Danubian regions or from the Highlands.

In the counties formerly occupied by the Turks, where there was scarcely any other foe to contend with except the havoc and destruction that had been wrought, and where the life not merely of the Catholic Church but of Western Christianity had become entirely extinct, the chief rôle among the champions of the Church was still played by the Franciscans. The inferior character of their education and refinement was in itself enough to render them more fitted to deal with the people, who were absolutely unenlightened, than were the members of the richer and more refined orders. As a consequence of the great demand, their numbers continually grew in dimensions[2]. In the territories inhabited by serfs the same order of monks was everywhere in the van and used the methods which had won over the vacillating savage masses to the cause of the Church as early as the thirteenth century. In other places, however, the struggle was a harder one. The Church had to make headway, not against unbelief and barbarism, but against the Protestant faith, Protestant culture, and against the gentry and *bourgeoisie* who had adopted both. It was here that the *triarii*—the Jesuit order—appeared on the scene. They turned its own weapons—the

---

[1] Molnár, Aladár, *Közoktatás története* (*History of Education*), p. 290.

[2] According to the *conscriptio* of 1770, in the diocese of Esztergom there were 885 Franciscans, 156 Capuchins, 68 Minorites; in that of Kalocsa, 101 Franciscans; in that of Eger, 551 Franciscans, 22 Capuchins, 193 Minorites; in that of Veszprém, 180 Franciscans; in that of Pécs, 223, in that of Györ, 211, in that of Nyitra, 146, in that of Csanád, 83 Franciscans, etc. Chanc. Arch. No. 5274 (1781.) At that time there were altogether 5419 Franciscans, 355 Capuchins and 312 Minorites in the country. According to Szirmay, "Mendicorum et mendicantium monachorum turba infinita."

pulpit, the professorial chair, the power of the press—against Protestantism. Just as the temporal nobility were bound to the Protestants, politically, by the interests involved in secularisation, by their political, moral and scientific doctrines the Jesuits were enabled to win over the Catholic aristocracy to their side and to enlist them in the service of the Church. To gauge the importance of the part they played, the chief point is not to compute the number of colleges and missions they controlled or the amount of their wealth—all this was merely a symbol and a result of their influence—but to realise the fact that they educated practically the whole of the aristocracy and prelacy of Hungary, determined the aims and ideals of the younger generation and influenced the young men destined to fill high offices, and this task they performed with all the grandeur of saints devoting their whole lives to the accomplishment of one single object, by the adroitness peculiar to their order and by lavishing on their pupils the affection of foster-fathers[1].

Like the Catholics in France in the days of Henry IV, those in Hungary regarded the Jesuits for some time as a foreign element of disunion. They were looked on not merely as the persecutors of a strange religion, and as none too particular in the choice of the means they employed, but at the same time as spies and agents of foreigners—in France of the Spaniards, in Hungary of the Germans. The Diets of Szécsény and Ónod (1705–7) condemned their political and educational activity just as the assemblies of Korpona and Beszterczebánya had done in the seventeenth century.

The character of the hopes and expectations which the promoters of Catholicism based upon Hungary is best proved by the fact that in this country the Jesuits, the champions of the universal dominion of the Church, became zealous apostles of patriotic feeling and of an independent national constitution. After the Peace of Szatmár (1711), the national party, which had obtained the upper hand and was imbued with hierarchical ideas, had better opportunities for religious propaganda than had the State, which could not consider religion alone but was obliged to

---

[1] Krones, *Jesuitenorden in Ungarn.*

take into account other conditions vital to its existence. Even the enemies of the order admitted that the Jesuits constituted one of the mainstays of the constitution as defined by Verböczy[1]. Nothing affords a clearer proof of this alliance between the patriotic and religious ideas than the fact that the Jesuits laid the foundations of the new national history of the country. Katona, Pray, Kaprinay, Hevenesy, priests belonging to the Society of Jesus, are entitled to as eminent a place among the creators of Hungarian historical science as are the students of the congregations of St Germain and St Maur among those who did so much to found a critical system as a basis for universal history. Yet even at a later time the bulk of the nation held aloof from them. The Primate Barkóczi took the college of Eger out of their hands and entrusted it to the care of Piarists; Baron Orczi considered their views and methods of teaching antiquated. But their scholarship and organisation made them able to control education to such an extent that, even after the disbanding of their order in 1773, former members of the order continued to fill professorial chairs.

The origins and results of these scientific endeavours were invigorated alike by national and religious feeling and closely interwoven with the ideas which inspired the other religious and political struggles of this period. This Jesuit school of history endeavoured to prove that the prosperity and ruin of the Hungarian people depended upon their faithfulness or hostility to their Church; as the prophets in the Bible had done with the chosen people. So soon as Hungary had been converted and had joined the ranks of Christian States, her first King and saint dedicated her to the Blessed Virgin. The most glorious period in the history of the nation had been that of the two centuries of crusades against heathens and heretics. The schism and paganism that ensued had been accompanied by the distresses of the age of Kún László (Ladislas IV) (1272–92); the spread of the Reformation had been accompanied by the Turkish conquest. Consequently anyone who at that moment, when the grace of God had set the country free, refused to pay homage to those who had commanded the respect of St Stephen, St Ladislas,

[1] *Manch-Hermaeon*, p. 294.

Louis the Great and Matthias Corvinus, were guilty not only of sinning against the true faith, but of denying and trampling upon the most glorious traditions of the Hungarian nation[1].

In the political struggle against the Protestants, the same homage and respect for national tradition was the motto of both parties. For the assurance of their future and the gratification of their noble ambitions and desires the Catholic youth looked to those traditions in which above all they recognised the mystical power of their religion. Consequently the intimate alliance between the national Catholic aristocracy and the Jesuitical system was brought about by the most intimate feelings and interests; and this fact really moulded the intellectual character of the Hungarian society of the eighteenth century.

The object of the ecclesiastical policy of the day being the establishment of the *Regnum Marianum*, the whole attention of the youth was directed towards realising this ideal from the moment the work of schooling began. The *Sodalitas Mariana* included among its members almost the whole of the aristocracy and of the chief dignitaries in the kingdom[2]. Living faith was rewarded by numerous miracles, for the holy and wonder-working images of Kis-Czell, Mária-Pócs, Mária-Schnee and Dömölk enhanced the enthusiasm of believers and increased their attachment to the Church and their teachers. The objects of this reverence themselves did their best to increase the antipathy towards those members of Hungarian society whose religious convictions took a different course. One of the principal headquarters of the *sodalitas Sacri Dei parae rosarii* was actually established at Dömölk—in the county of Vas—a centre of the non-Catholic nobles of the Trans-Danubian district[3]. The

---

[1] This is the general drift of the work, in three volumes, entitled *Igaz Magyar* (*The true Hungarian*). Of its author, Leo Szeicz, a friar of the Brotherhood of Mary of Eger, Francis Kazinczy (*Magyarországi utak*, p. 25) writes as follows: "In my conception of him I was mightily deceived. Reading his writings, I had thought him to be a spiteful man, of uncertain thoughts and unacquainted with many things: now, however, I have learned that he is a well-read man, who has written much, is possessed of untiring industry and is particularly well acquainted with Hungarian history."

[2] Fessler, *loc. cit.* vol. x. pp. 347—8.

[3] Cf. *Post. Mem. Jos. Eszterházy*, p. 234. Not only did the Lord Chief Justice himself join the society, but his example was followed by many of the king's councillors

members of this society were not only unanimous in their actions against the Protestants; in every question, of whatever nature, they could rely implicitly on each other's support, whether in the county, in the law-courts or at Court[1].

The accession of a queen bearing the same name was considered an auspicious omen for the *Regnum Marianum*[2]. When, in 1741, Maria Teresa arrived in Pozsony to open Parliament, the burgomaster delivered a speech in which the expression *Regnum Marianum* was frequently repeated[3]. The Catholic writings of the period continually recurred to it. It seemed unjust that those who did not worship the Blessed Virgin and the saints should be tolerated in this sacred country, and it was to this Marianising tendency in particular that the aggressive character of Catholicism was due.

The implicit confidence in the immediate aid of God and the saints began again to make its effect felt in the spiritual conciousness of men. On the body of a Hungarian officer (serving in a Hungarian regiment), who fell during the war against the Prussians in 1778, was found a prayer containing an appeal to the Virgin Mary, to the Archangel Michael, to the other angels, and in particular to Saint Clare, to protect him and give the victory to the army fighting for God's laws[4]. No attempt was made to disguise this new tendency of the faith, which suggested that the saints could actually be compelled, by outward ceremonies and prayers, to offer protection and to secure victory. On the occasion of a public service held at the outbreak of the war in 1778, the preacher put the question—"What must we do to secure the aid of Heaven?" The answer was ready to hand. "We must pray, fast and sorrow, for by universal prayer and fasting we can, so to say, wage war against God and practically

(K.C.) and nobles. In Korabinszky's work we read the following passage about this society: "1744, wurde hier eine adeliche Gesellschaft zur schnelleren Ausbreitung der Katolischen Religion gestiffet. Die Mitglieder erhielten dabey einen Stern den Sie an der Brust trugen, und zahlten dafür 6. flor."

[1] *Manch-Hermaeon*, p. 291.

[2] Majláth, Count J., *Neuere Geschichte der Magyaren*, vol. I. p. 40.

[3] Kolinovics, *Nova Periodus*, p. 164. In the speech the ancestors of Maria Teresa were referred to as "Mariani pugiles."

[4] Nicolai, *Reisen*, vol. V. p. 65. The prayer itself is given as a supplement, XIII. 4, p. 25.

force Him to aid our armies[1]. If we pray with one consent, we constitute an army fighting against God and use force to prevent His resisting[2]." "Our inward enemy is sin. But the inhabitants of the town had expelled and eradicated that from their hearts, on the occasion of the *Portiuncula* indulgence[3]."

Such statements and doctrines—for the priest of Magyar-Óvár is by no means an isolated example—naturally prove only that religion had penetrated to the lowest grades of society. The zealous educated Catholics themselves did not regard these things, or even the foundation of churches and schools, as the surest proofs of the progress of religion. The real feeling of these men is finely expressed by the words of Baron Gabriel Patachics, Archbishop of Kalocsa: "There is but little profit in raising the cathedral of Kalocsa from its two-hundred-year-old ruins, unless the living temples of God are converted into worthy mansions of the divine spirit and unless upright ministers water the seeds. God demands to be worshipped in spirit and in truth; the inward respect for Him should be shown by outward deeds as well, though he alone can see into the depths of the heart[4]."

It was to the great benefit of the Hungarian Catholic Church and the whole national culture, that the traditions of Peter Pázmány were still paramount among the Hungarian prelates during the days of Maria Teresa. These prelates not only built churches and founded schools; a great number of them lived lives of real religious devotion. The survival of religious piety is proved above all by the fact that even the most violent denunciations uttered by the Protestants charged the Catholic prelates with fanaticism and persecution, and not with such crimes as are most frequent among a wealthy, influential and powerful clergy. If we examine the history of the various dioceses, we shall find that

---

[1] *Rede bey Gelegenheit des öffentlichen Gebetes wegen angefangenen Krieges.* Gehalten 9 August, 1778, in Ung. Altenburg (Magyar-Óvár) von Joseph Stamf, Pfarrherrn. "Wir müssen Gott so zu sagen bekriegen und unsere Kriegsvölker zu helfen gleichsam zwingen."

[2] "Wenn wir einhellig anfangen zu beten, machen wir gleichsam ein Kriegsheer wider Gott zusammen und thun ihm Gewalt an, dass er uns nicht widerstehe." *Ibid.*

[3] "Die Inwohner haben die Sünd bey Gelegenheit des ausnehmenden Ablasses Portiunkula aus dem Innersten ihres Herzens verjaget und vertilget." *Ibid.*

[4] Katona, *Hist. Metr. Coloc. Eccl.* vol. II. p. 272.

those bishops, who could not claim to have rendered services in spreading religious and moral as well as doctrinal teaching, were rather the exception than the rule. The Church was still passing through a period of trial, but her foes still admitted that inwardly as well as outwardly she was duly equipped for the struggle before her, which continually trained and increased her energies.

IV.

It was a natural consequence of the social and intellectual conditions of the country that the pre-eminence of the prelates was due not merely to their personal qualities or rank. In a constitution like that of Hungary, every right and privilege, just as well as every burden, took its origin primarily from the soil. The position which the Catholic Church occupied in the cultural and national history was measured by her importance and influence in the conduct of the political affairs of that nation.

Despite the immense changes produced by the Reformation, no constitutional parliament ever attacked the position of the hierarchy as an estate of the realm, nor threatened the landed estates by virtue of which the dignitaries of the Church claimed a place among the grandees of the country. Much had been taken from them—temporal peers had seized almost all the estates of some dioceses in the Alföld—but these were not regarded as having been forfeited for all time[1]. The Bishops of Csanád, Várad and Eger were just as important magnates in the Hungary of the seventeenth century as ever before. In Transylvania Gabriel Bethlen failed to secularise the bishops and to reduce them to the level of superintendents; and it was a necessary consequence of historic development that the Catholic Church should obtain the lion's share of the rewards for that victory over the Turks and the Protestants which her ideas and her followers alike had helped to produce.

[1] According to Count Christopher Niczky (*Staatskenntniss*, ch. 8) the bulk of the landed estates was still in the hands of the clergy, and, if they were to recover all the property that had once been theirs, very few magnate families would be left with their estates untouched.

In point of revenue, the heads of the Church could vie with the wealthiest magnates. The net income of the Archbishop of Esztergom was estimated at 360,000 florins (£36,000), that of the Bishop of Eger at 80,000, that of the Bishop of Nagy-Várad at 70,000, those of the Bishops of Vácz, Veszprém and Kalocsa at 50,000 each, those of the Bishops of Nyitra and Györ at 40,000 each, that of the Bishop of Pécs at 30,000, that of the Bishop of Zágráb at 20,000 and, finally, that of the Bishop of Csanád at 9000 florins[1]. The greater part of these revenues was devoted to church and school purposes, at any rate in the eighteenth century. When we consider that it was during this period that almost all the cathedrals, chapter-houses and school buildings were erected, that money had to be spent besides on hospitals and for the payment of teachers, and that it was universally admitted that the lot of serfs was best on the estates belonging to the clergy, we shall have no difficulty in recognising the fact that offices endowed with such enormous revenues were in those days no mere sinecures, but rather properly paid posts for the due advancement of the intellectual welfare of the nation. Wealthy magnates, such as Count Joseph Batthyány, Bishop of Kalocsa, afterwards Archbishop of Esztergom and Primate of the Hungarian Church in the reign of Joseph II, and Count Charles Eszterházy, Bishop of Eger, devoted a large part of their private income, as well as their Church revenues, to educational and religious purposes[2].

The ecclesiastical order, as such, was regarded as the first of the estates of the realm in law[3]. On festive occasions, the spokesmen of the estates in Parliament were always churchmen —in the upper house, the prelates, in the lower house, the representatives of the chapters.

Among the churchmen the authority of the Primate was paramount. This prelate not only reflected the central power

---

[1] Chanc. Arch. 10,112 (1784). So far as the bishoprics of Kalocsa, Györ and Nyitra are concerned, the figures here given practically coincide with the data given by the *Politisches Journal* of 1783 (p. 1165), a fact that establishes its trustworthiness as regards the other bishoprics.

[2] Fessler, *loc. cit.* vol. x. p. 310.

[3] Act I of 1608. Cf. Ürményi, *Jus Publ.* § 11.

of the Church in general, of which he was the representative[1];
his dignity at the same time vindicated the autonomy of the
national Church. In ecclesiastical and spiritual affairs he was
the "vicar" of the reigning Apostolic King, for the King, as a
layman, "cannot exercise in person all the privileges of his office[2]."
His dependants were exempted from the payment of customs
and excise duties[3]. Appeals from his court-baron went, not to
the county court, but to the King's Bench. Also he had nobles
of his own dependent upon him, particularly in the island of
Csalló-Köz, and he could make grants in fee, though only "ad
sexum masculinum[4]." His nobles, like those of the King, were
exempted from the payment of the *harminczad* (customs duties).
He too appointed two presiding judges of the King's Bench,
whose salaries were paid by the country[5]. The Primate could
not be president of the upper house; but he had the seat nearest
to the president, on his right, had the privilege of voting first
among the peers, and of opening the rescripts sent by the King
to Parliament with the names of the candidates whom the monarch
nominated for election as Count Palatine. It was he who put the
crown on the King's head. His power of pronouncing sentence
on the bishops was recognised by Parliament[6]; and publicists
taught that no change could be made in the conditions of the
Church without his consent[7].

The privileges of the other prelates, in particular of the
bishops of Kalocsa and Eger, were significant enough, though
far less extensive than those of the Primate. With the exception
of those of Csanád and Erdély, the bishops still had the right of
appointing their own chapters even so late as 1766[8]. The personal authority of the prelates, who were also initiated into
public affairs, was enhanced alike by their distinguished family
connections, by their merits, and by their culture. When
Joseph II succeeded to the throne, Joseph Batthyány, son of
the Count Palatine Louis Batthyány, was Primate—the same

---

[1] "Legatus natus."
[2] Memorandum of the Primate (March 7, 1714), State Archives, Vienna.
[3] Ürményi, *Jus Publ.* § 13, point 12.   [4] Niczky, *Staatskenntniss.*
[5] Chanc. Arch. 15,237 (1785).   [6] Act XVI of 1560.
[7] Niczky, *loc. cit.* ch. 8.   [8] *Ibid.*

man who had devoted the greater part of his private income too to Church purposes when Bishop of Kalocsa. A writer who has recorded the *chronique scandaleuse* of the whole Catholic prelacy has nothing worse to say of him than that he was inordinately proud of his skill at chess, though only a moderate player[1]. It is true that he "loved pretty faces," but this fact was not thrown in his teeth until later on by ultra-clericals. The archbishopric of Kalocsa was filled by Baron Adam Patachics, the scion of an ancient Croatian family who, when Bishop of Nagy-Várad, had maintained the college there out of his private fortune and had accommodated the seminarists in his own palace[2]. He had also built the bishop's residence at Kalocsa, and organised the extensive and well-furnished library of that city[3]. He was not only a patron, for he had obtained such a reputation by his scholarship that his Latin style had been compared to that of Bembo[4]. The third and best-remembered member of the Hungarian episcopal triumvirate was Count Charles Eszterházy, Bishop of Eger, brother of the Chancellor-in-Chief, Francis Eszterházy. His is the memory of a prelate devoted soul and body to the interests of his Church, and also of a magnate who was a faithful guardian of the interests alike of his country and of his order, whose purity of character and strength of will secured him a far greater authority than his high birth and distinguished office had ever done. Even the Protestants, whom he ruthlessly persecuted, could not help respecting him[5]. As yet then, there was no lack at all of men to take over the apostolic succession.

The sphere of authority of the Hungarian prelates was increased to a considerable extent by the fact that they enjoyed the right of holding visitations of the Protestants. It was in

[1] Gorani, Joseph, *Mémoires secrètes et critiques des cours, des gouvernements et des mœurs d'Italie*, vol. II. p. 208.
[2] Fessler, *loc. cit.* p. 315.
[3] Majláth, *Neuere Geschichte der Magyaren*, vol. I. p. 45.
[4] *Ibid.*
[5] He addressed Francis Kazinczy in the following terms: "You see, my dear sir, I wear the black cloth, because it is my duty to do so, and I desire to do my duty" (*Magyarországi utak*, p. 23). Fessler, who saw him at work in 1777, describes him as an exemplary bishop, an indefatigable apostle, a severe ruler of his clergy, but at the same time a paragon of piety.

reality this right that secured their Church recognition as the predominant religion. As the outward expression of this right of theirs and of their dignity, the bishops' visitations were carried out with the greatest pomp and splendour. The bells pealed, and the minister and the officials awaited the arrival of the distinguished guest at some distance from the entrance to each village. The authorities competed with one another in the magnificence of their reception; young nobles, both Protestant and Catholic, rode out to meet the bishop and accompanied him on horseback to the next parish. If his journey took the bishop to more than one county, a hundred horsemen would often await his arrival on the confines of each one[1].

The bishops not only possessed large incomes, estates and a sphere of authority in the Church, but even the secular government could not afford to dispense with their discernment. They played a part both in the national parliaments and in the county life as well. In 1756, besides the Archbishop of Esztergom, who stood at the head not only of his own county but of Szepes too; the Archbishop of Kalocsa was High Sheriff (*föispán*) in the county of Bács; the Bishop of Eger in Heves and Külsö (Outer) Szolnok; the Bishop of Nyitra in Nyitra county; the Bishops of Györ, Veszprém and Csanád also in their respective counties; and the Bishop of Pécs in the counties of Tolna and Baranya. In Croatia, too, the Bishop of Bosnia was at the same time High Sheriff in the county of Pozsega[2].

Bishops had a direct part even in the supreme control of the affairs of the country. In the Chancellery there was always at least one ecclesiastical councillor, in the *consilium locumtenentiale* at least two, in the King's Bench at least three. The majority of the other chief officials were bound to them alike by religious and private interests. The work of all governments, even when strictly adhering to the requirements of the laws, must more or less bear the stamp of the personal convictions of their members; in this case, the whole spirit of government was permeated by hierarchical interests. In the official documents the non-Catholics

---

[1] *Von dem Zustande der Protestanten in Ungarn*, von H. L. Lehmann von Detershagen (Bern, 1789), "Von der Visitation der Bischöfe," p. 49.
[2] *Calendarium Jaurinense* for 1756.

were spoken of as heretics and infidels. The Government considered it to be its business to further even the unimportant outward expression of religious feeling. At the approach of a season of fasting, for instance, the provincial government of Temesvár itself provided for a supply of fish in order to prevent there being any lack of it in the town[1].

Among the canons and abbots there were many who followed the example of the prelates. They vied with their bishops in creating charitable foundations. George Gyöngyösi, Canon of Várad, gave a sum of 25,000 florins, his house and a chapel for the maintenance of impoverished nobles, as well as a sum of 27,000 florins, a farm and a vineyard for the establishment of alms-houses. As for himself, he lived the simplest of lives, had no silver plate, only tin, only three changes of bed-linen, the same number of table-cloths, and six wine-glasses. Among the canons there were numerous foreigners—complaints as to which fact are made as early as 1741. None the less, these latter could scarcely compete with the others, for they lacked all interest in the welfare of the people as well as the sentiment of patriotism—that chief moving force among the Hungarian prelates of the day.

One of the chief concerns, not only of the Government but of the prelates of the eighteenth century, was to give a proper training to a large number of priests, and thus to enable them to undertake the work of teaching the people. As we have seen, the requirements at first could not be excessive; the territory was large, the labourers few, and priests were sent to villages after an insufficient training. As a consequence, the educational level of these priests—unless they happened to be scions of distinguished families—was not much above that of their flocks. According to George Bessenyei, the clergy were half gentlemen, half peasants[2]. In one poem of Baron Lawrence Orczi, a Catholic magnate of conservative convictions speaks to his chaplain in a tone usually employed with servants only, from which circumstance we may conclude that the lot of the lower

---

[1] Pesty, Fr., "Miveltségi allapotok Temesváron a XVIII században" (Cultural conditions in Temesvár in the XVIII cent.) in the *Századok* for 1877, No. 1.

[2] *Holmi*, p. 207.

grade .of clergy was by no means an enviable one. According to Szirmay, the country parsons, who were trained in the Jesuit seminaries, displayed the greatest possible want of education. This result was produced intentionally by that order, which feared that its pupils might surpass it in scholarship and culture[1]. If, notwithstanding, the Hungarian clergy enjoyed greater respect than did the English clergy towards the close of the seventeenth century, in the view of Macaulay, the reason was that the organisation of his Church rendered the Catholic clergyman more independent and venerable than his Protestant colleague. However, there was no lack of cultivated, enlightened and tolerant men even among the lower clergy, and Francis Kazinczy compared the parish priest of Torna to the famous Savoyard vicar of Rousseau. In any case, apart from their deficient education, the lower Catholic clergy had to distinguish themselves by the exercise of one of the highest virtues—that of resignation. It was only since 1733 that the King had compelled the bishops to give a due part of their revenues for the *congrua* of their clergy. But this *congrua* was fixed at only 150 florins (£15). When, in 1785, they prepared a list of their complaints and desires, the annual sums they asked for were only 120 florins for clothing and furniture, 140 florins for food, 48 florins for drink and 130 florins for payment of servants[2]. Their intellectual needs were, comparatively speaking, still more trifling, for they were satisfied by a sum of 10 florins for paper, ink and postage[3].

The powerful character of the Catholic religious impulse in Hungary is proved by the fact that it was able, even in the eighteenth century, to establish an offshoot so famous and so productive of results as was the order of Piarists[4]. Like all

---

[1] *Fragm. Hist. Secr.* p. 222 : "Exmissi pro parochis pagensibus rudissimi, sponte per Jesuvitas ita efformati, ne religionem eorum doctrina aut cultis moribus superemineant."

[2] Chanc. Arch. No. 13,464 (1785).

[3] In a petition, dated 1790, dealing with a similar subject (*Gravamina cleri Hungarici, Buda in jun.*), the estimate for paper was only 3 florins: but *books*, to the value of 3 florins, appeared as an extra item.

[4] The first settlement of Piarists in Hungary was, indeed, in 1660, but their real importance dates from 1715, when Parliament accepted them as an acknowledged order.

vigorous and successful movements in the Catholic world subsequent to the Reformation, this one also started from Spain
and became firmly established and settled in Italy in the
vicinity of the Papal Court. In a country divided against
itself, such as Hungary was in those days, the Piarists could
be sure of making progress and obtaining recognition, especially
because, by virtue of their rules, their chief task was not so
much outward conversion, *propagatio fidei*, as an inward mission
and, above all, education. The Jesuits too were engaged in
teaching, but their work in this field was after all merely a
means for effecting conversions and for increasing the power of
their order and of the Church. They endeavoured above all
to get themselves entrusted with the education and spiritual
guidance of the children of eminent and powerful families ;
and their rulers, with a view to attaining their ecclesio-political
objects, permitted the members of the order—though severe
in mortifying their own flesh—to exercise leniency, both in
school and in the confessional, towards the moral deficiencies
of their adherents. The Jesuits were the children of war, and
had to adapt themselves to the exclusive claims and morals of
the noble society, if they desired to acquire ascendancy over
it[1]. While the Jesuits were the aristocrats of the ecclesiastical
organisation, the Piarists could be described as its democratic
element; in fact their founder—St Joseph of Calasanz—actually
devoted his whole energy to teaching the children of the poorest
and most neglected classes. Even the Catholics declared that
the Jesuits, though eminent scholars, were too fond of mixing
themselves up in politics—a charge which could not be brought
against the new order[2]. The members of the order were poor

[1] It was a rule of the Jesuit order, indeed, that the same care should be lavished
on rich and poor alike ; but one of their principal writers (Sachini) instructed the
teachers, particularly in inflicting punishments, to consider that those, who were now
weak and insignificant, might in a short time become men of wealth, position and power,
on whose favour they would then depend. Cf. Molnár, Aladár, *Közoktatás története*
(*History of Education in Hungary*), p. 139, note.

[2] Szirmay, *Fragm. Hist. Secr.* p. 8 : " Erat quidem, quoad perfectionem omnis
generis scientiarum societas haec excellens, sed quia aularum regiarum turbis contra
institutum religionis se immiscuit et vel in sola Hungaria intolerantia sua et evangelicorum persecutione tot mala paravit, ut nobilissimum Regnum factionibus suis paene

and took no part in politics, and it seemed fitted to supersede
the Jesuits, sooner or later, as an educational institute. The
Piarists won the regard of all those who desired the young men
of the country to have a cloister education, but who were unwilling that they should be imbued with the Jesuitical system
of subservience and attachment to forms. Their patrons were
not only numerous, but their influence was also considerable.
Before long the Piarists were able to establish colleges and
secondary schools (Gymnasia, classical schools) in the most important towns in the country—Pest, Debreczen, Szeged, Kalocsa.
As a proof of their final triumph over the Jesuits we may take
the fact that Maria Teresa entrusted them with the management
of the re-established and richly-furnished noble academy at Vácz
in 1767[1]. That the conflict between them and the Jesuits was
not merely an unconscious one, but at times extremely bitter, is
proved by the observations of Andrew Dugonics, an eminent
Piarist[2]. The contrast between the two orders was considered to
consist above all in the fact that, while the education offered by
the Jesuits was ecclesiastical, that of the Piarists was secular in
character, since the part played in it by theology was a secondary
one[3]. In our opinion, it consisted rather in the fact that in
the organisation of the Jesuits, everything was equipped for
attack; and brilliant results—at least outwardly brilliant ones—
were indispensable to provide for the firm establishment of their
position. The system of the Piarists, on the other hand, did not
demand such a one-sided concentration of forces; they could not
indeed attain such pre-eminent results, but, at the same time, as
a consequence of their moderate and humane tendencies, they
did not provoke the antagonism of so many powerful and legitimate interests and ideas.

From a national point of view, apart from a knowledge of

---

everteret et his artibus maximas divitias comparavit, non potuit hos fructus facere ad
quorum finem instituta fuit."

[1] Krones (*loc. cit.* p. 98) points out that, in his history, which is in other respects
so accurate and exhaustive, Katona does not mention this fact.

[2] MS. in National Museum. Among other things, Dugonics expresses the highest
satisfaction at the dissolution of the Jesuit order (1773).

[3] *Merkur für Ungarn*, 1787, p. 12. Martin George Kovachich on the development
of education in Hungary.

her internal power, the greatest significance must be attached to the struggle of the Church against the Protestants. Even in a bare outline of the movements of the age under discussion, we must not overlook the fact that Hungarian Catholic society not only endeavoured to re-absorb that part of society which had drifted away but also tried to win over the members of the Greek Oriental Church, who constituted a distinct group in Hungary, not only ecclesiastically but as a unit of nationality and culture as well. We have already shown how the Catholic prelacy used their political and feudal power to absorb the Rascians[1]. In the field of conversion, still more weighty interests came into play, not only religious ones but those of the State and of culture. Every conversion of Serb or Wallach meant a proportionate diminution of the influence of foreign Powers—particularly of Russia—in the country[2]. From their own priests, who were on the lowest rung of the educational ladder of culture and steeped in all the sins attendant on poverty, the Government could scarcely hope for the education of the people, could hardly expect them to reclaim their flocks from nomadism and robbery to a regular and peaceful mode of life. The result of all these endeavours was the creation of the union and the organisation of the Greek *Catholic* bishoprics and parishes. In Croatia, at Körös, at Várad, and in Transylvania, such bishoprics were established; while about the same time (1771) the Greek Catholic see of Munkács was made independent of the diocese of Eger[3].

The success of the union was most complete in districts where only the masses were of another faith, without any ruling class to influence them, viz. among the Ruthenes. The results were far less significant in the case of the Serbs and Wallachs,

---

[1] v. *supra*, ch. III. pp. 224—5.

[2] That this danger was no secret even to Maria Teresa is proved by her declaration of Oct. 21, 1762: "So important is the cause of the Russians in Hungary, that the gravest consequences are to be feared. That nation is of an intriguing and deceptive nature; and if it can count on support from without, very serious troubles may result. In one country, there cannot be two rulers or patrons." Cf. the author's "II József elsö terjeszkedési tervei" (Joseph II's first schemes of expansion) in the *Századok*, 1880, No. III.

[3] Krones, *loc. cit.* p. 89.

who were organised and united by the regular hierarchy and by the universally respected Greek orthodox monks. The causes producing the resistance, like those responsible for the conversion, were not purely religious ones, but—probably to a still greater degree—of a nationalistic character—indeed the natural result of the inferior culture of these peoples. An insurrection broke out in 1755, which extended over a particularly large area, and the number of insurgents who rose against the military and religious oppression in Croatia was estimated at 30,000[1].

Even contemporaries echo the complaint that the hierarchy contented itself with outward conversion, and did not attempt to exercise any considerable influence on the education or civilisation of the new converts. The Catholic Church did not seek to transform the orthodox Greek priests into excellent teachers of their people. These semi-savages were indeed remarkably attached to their Greek pastors, and might have been transformed by their influence into good citizens. Instead of making this attempt, the leaders of the Catholic Church confined their efforts to occasionally bribing an ambitious or avaricious Greek prelate to become a convert to the prevailing Roman faith. The people, whom intriguers of this kind enticed to imitate them, merely changed their name, and became Catholic instead of Greek barbarians—that was all the result achieved.

A certain traveller has compared these Greek priests, in point of education, to the Frankish priests of the days of Charlemagne. Most of them could not read or write, and were unable to count up to ten. One of them—reputed a great scholar—told the traveller that the Trojan war was waged against Troy by the Greek and Roman Emperors, the King of France and the seven German Electors[2]. From official documents, we gather that they maintained themselves principally by trading in cattle, and theft was also of frequent occurrence among them[3]. Among their prelates such crimes were in vogue as generally originate from the intercourse of a more cultured ruling class with intractable masses of dependants.

---

[1] Royal Archives, Berlin.   [2] *Briefe eines Franzosen*, vol. 1. p. 458.
[3] *Ibid.* p. 459. For the conditions of culture on the military frontiers, cf. Schlözer, *Staatsanzeigen* (1782), vol. I. pp. 360—5.

A single fact will suffice to prove how primitive was the
state of the social culture of these races, even of those of them
who belonged to the united Church. In the first schematism of
the newly established Greek Catholic bishopric of Nagy-Várad,
scarcely one of the priests of that diocese was entered with a
surname—all had given their Christian names only[1].

But there can be no doubt that nothing hindered the
Magyarisation and civilisation of Eastern Hungary so much
as the conflict between the Catholic Church and Protestantism.
Only individual Catholic missionaries could communicate with
the Wallachs and Rascians living in that part of the country;
intercourse *en masse* was out of the question. On the other
hand, the Protestant inhabitants and proprietors were prevented
from becoming the educators of these poor backward and
neglected peoples both by their higher education and by their
exclusiveness. The fact that the Catholic prelates appeared to
the masses merely in the guise of unwelcome missionaries and the
Protestant nobles only as feudal superiors, very soon convinced
the Wallachs and Ruthenes that there was only one appeal
against this double oppression. It was for this reason that all
those, whose social position did not bind them to the Hungarian
nobility, were driven into the arms of the Court of Vienna.

V.

If we consider the combination of all these forces—the
external power and wealth and the inward zeal of the Catholic
prelates, the scholarship and skill of the Jesuits and, finally,
the intimate connection of the religious ideas of the Catholic
Church with the power of the State—it appears absolutely
marvellous that Protestantism, divided into two sects, without
a central organisation and deprived of all intercourse with
foreign countries, should have been able to hold its own in
spite of so many losses. It was not a question of dogmas
or morality, for, to judge by the impulse that possessed and
furthered the advance of the Roman Church in the days of

[1] Calendar of the Nagy-Várad bishopric for 1765. (In the National Museum.)

Pázmány, Hungary ought to have been entirely converted before the close of the seventeenth century.

The history of religious doctrines proves that, however deeply their essence may be rooted in individual consciences, their organisation and development has at all times been closely inter-connected with political and social life. The decadence of Catholicism in Hungary coincided with the Turkish conquest and with the weakening of the royal power. Its regeneration aided and prepared the way for the triumph of the national idea and for the increase in the power of the King. In Hungary, as in almost every other country in Europe, it was the religion professed by the spiritual and temporal aristocracy grouped round the Court, and this fact was due, not to its dogmas, but to its historical development.

In the sixteenth century the Lutheran part of the Hungarian nobility was still probably equal to the Calvinistic part, both in point of numbers and importance. During the seventeenth century the Evangelical (or Lutheran) confession lost ground considerably among the Hungarians, and became confined almost exclusively to the districts inhabited by Germans and Slovaks. On the other hand, the Calvinistic or Reformed faith, though losing ground, still maintained its hold on the bulk of the Hungarian gentry. We can hardly explain this peculiar phenomenon except by investigating the political and social conditions of the countries of Europe in which these two denominations predominated.

It is a striking fact that, in the principal countries professing the Lutheran faith, the power of the prince or monarch was either strongly developed or was continually on the increase. Side by side with the princes—particularly in North Germany and Denmark—we find not so much Parliamentary Estates but rather an aristocracy of office, in addition to a number of imperial and royal towns prominent for their industry and activity.

A characteristic point in connection with the spread of Calvinism, politically, is that it was the faith of republics, of knights, and of burgesses. It started from the patrician republics of Geneva and Bern in Switzerland. In France it was taken up, *par excellence*, by the gentry and by the *bourgeoisie* of the South-West. Its expansion in Scotland was one of the chief means employed by the insurgent nobles for the overthrow of the royal power. In Holland, the Reformation was established by a federation of the large commercial towns in opposition to the Spanish Netherlands, which were ruled over by a Catholic King and an aristocracy.

We are not writing a treatise on politics but a history, and although the influence of the political ideas of the eighteenth and nineteenth centuries has obliterated the close connection between politics and the Church, the fact that the Genevan Reformation never gained ground in monarchical states, or at any rate never held its own in them, seems to deserve some attention. Its vitality seems to have depended upon the co-existence of a more liberal constitutional system. This was undoubtedly a result of the external organisation of this Church. For it was only natural that a man who helped to administer the most important affairs of his Church, and refused to tolerate the overlordship of a hierarchy, should deny the right of the secular power to control political or religious interests without asking his opinion or in defiance of his wishes. In the seventeenth century, for national and constitutional reasons, Hungary considered her interests to be at variance with those of the dynasty and of Government. Her opposition received outward expression in the fact that the Hungarian gentry—the guardians of the national and constitutional spirit—remained Calvinists. For the same reasons the Hungarian *bourgeoisie* of Debreczen, Kecskemét and Komárom became Calvinists and remained loyal to their faith. Here the faith professed and the framework of its Church organisation formed an integral and a complementary part of the common national and constitutional feeling.

It is to this fact that we must look for the essential cause of the survival of the Reformation in Hungary. Ever since the modern State-conception had existed, the main traditio of Catholicism had been the waging of warfare against the heathens: that of Calvinism was the struggle, dating from almost equally ancient times, for the constitution as well as the more recent battles for faith and nation. The wealth of Hungarian history consists in the fact that both Churches could alike boast of glorious records of noble struggles for great ideas, and that the great men in both camps added renown, not only to their own party, but to the whole Hungarian nation.

As compared with Calvinism, the Lutheran confession, whose government was in the hands of its ministers and teachers and of the princes, had not the same organising influence on the Hungarian gentry. In addition, there was no possibility of denying its German origin. It found a home in Hungary in places where there was a more cultivated *bourgeoisie* of German speech to receive it. Their intellectual and commercial intercourse with Lutheranism at its headquarters in Germany was so vigorous that this fact in itself was sufficient to prevent the development among them of a special national culture.

The Calvinists also discovered that visits to foreign universities were indispensable if they were to maintain their religion. For the Reformation was in all places a regeneration and transformation, not merely of faith, but of science and education also. Young Calvinists of high attainments were sent to Heidelberg, to the colleges of Switzerland and Holland, and even to the universities of England, at first by the great Calvinist princes of Transylvania, later on by the institutes which those rulers had founded. They were no mere boys when they left home, but were thoroughly acquainted with the state of their native country and with her peculiar conditions, before they fell under the influence of the higher and more liberal culture of more fortunate foreign lands. They brought home the treasures of learning, but did not leave behind in exchange, what was far dearer to them, their national feeling.

These were the two sides of the Calvinistic world in Hungary. Its chief strength lay in the gentry and *bourgeoisie* of pure Hungarian speech and sentiment, whose political and religious convictions as well as their interests made them cling to the present and still more to the past, and look with suspicion and apprehension on any change that the future might hold in store. On the other hand, their constant intercourse with foreign theology and learning, which formed the cultural basis of their existence forced Calvinism to become familiar with the latest intellectual tendencies of Europe. It was only from the arsenal of the universities of Protestant Europe that the Calvinists could acquire the intellectual weapons required to attack the Jesuits, though their chief weapons of defence against the power of the Court and of Catholic society were to be found in the constitutional and social privileges and the purely national feeling—that is in Hungary itself.

Every institution, particularly the school organisation, of the Calvinistic Church in Hungary, was a result of this twofold spirit. In the eighteenth century, when the sphere of activity of the Protestant teachers was being continually restricted, the only means of keeping the denomination together was to unite cosmopolitan influences with national ones.

In the colleges, particularly in those of Debreczen and Patak, these two opposite tendencies met ;—the professor and scholar, who had travelled abroad and had to a certain extent mastered European literature, met the country squire, who went to the college not so much for any special study as by virtue of his social rank. The professors and clergy themselves often founded whole miniature dynasties ; for the pursuit of scholarship and of study in foreign countries became practically hereditary in certain families. The young students, destined from the very first to take orders or to occupy a chair, were known in the colleges as *togati* (scholars) and thus distinguished from the sons of the gentry, *publici* (commoners)[1]. It was not so much a similarity of religion as an identity of social organisation that caused these colleges and the bustling life within them to resemble the English institutions of the same name. In both cases, it was a principal object, not only to further the aims of the faith and the Church, but also to enable the sons of the gentry to acquire a certain general social culture. Even at school there was no equality between the sons of a poor minister, teacher or *civis* and the heirs of proud county gentlemen. The chief business of the former consisted of study, while the latter were mostly concerned with sport. Very exceptional was the case of

---

[1] Count D. Teleki, *Reisen*, p. 30: "*Publici*, adelichen Jünglinge, die nicht Theologie studieren."

Samuel Szilágyi de Piskárkos, scholar and later superintendent, himself the son of a professor at Debreczen, who "was just as superior to all his fellows as a horseman, swordsman, dancer and skater as in scholarship[1]." At the same time all pupils were subjected to the same methods of physical training and to the same devotional exercises; and this fact alone explains how it was possible to keep so large a number of young men in perfect morality and chastity.

The autobiography of Francis Kazinczy (1759–1831) gives us a beautiful picture of the student life at Patak in his day. The young noble, seeking not for the erudition of the schools but for knowledge to enable him to make his way in life, got very little guidance on this subject from his professors, who were quite out of his reach[2]. He was initiated into the elements of science by an older student, and this instruction prepared the way for an ideal friendship of the greatest possible value. It is true that the student-teacher (*togatus*) himself as a rule possessed but a limited amount of knowledge, and that not every *publicus* was a Kazinczy, eager to work and to read of his own accord. But, though the considerable liberty allowed the individual students must have resulted in a great lack of refinement, there could be no talk of depravity; for any young man who had been led into bad ways was very easily reformed by a single word from a professor.

"Yet, with all thy faults, Patak, what youths thou didst even then beget! The advance of a pupil depends rather on his own industry than on that of his teacher; for at Patak there is a library of 20,000 volumes: the books may be taken by students to their rooms, and a steady worker may light his candle from that of his fellow." Happy was the man who had studied there! Such was the pride of the whilom student of Patak in the place which at the time supplied the greater half of the Reformed Protestants of Hungary with teachers, ministers and temporal leaders.

Still more flattering, though probably not quite so sincere, is the judgment passed by another student of Patak, George

---

[1] Kazinczy, Francis, in *Tudományos Gyüjtemény*, vol. VIII. pp. 93—109.
[2] *Pályám Emlékezete*, pp. 18—30. Kazinczy was at Patak from 1769–1776.

Bessenyei (1747–1811), on this home of the Muses[1]: "In point of morality, you should visit the Reformed schools of Patak and Debreczen in Hungary, where you will see wonders. You will scarcely believe me when I tell you that, though having been among them from my eighth year, I never in my life saw or even heard of any immorality there[2]." "Taking the teachers of Patak and Debreczen into consideration from the point of view of moral education, the Protestants will find them to be invaluable men, whose merits in this respect they will never be able to reward or sufficiently to appreciate[3]." But he was not at all reconciled to their dress or fashions, though "it would not do to interfere with their dress or their manners[4]." Though their purity of life was of inestimable value, "they might admit a change in their method of teaching. Thus classical authors have to be recited without ceasing; but other authors and studies are entirely ignored[5]."

Despite all other deviations, this purely formal teaching kept the Protestant schools on a level with those of the Jesuits. If the Catholics in general complained that the Protestants received a wider and better education than their sons, the cause was not so much in the schools themselves. It consisted rather in the greater measure of liberty allowed among the Protestants which, though it permitted the existence of many foibles, at least did not suppress talent. On the other hand, ever since the beginning of the eighteenth century, in particular as a result of the exertions of Mátyás Bél, the Lutheran system of education had been giving an ever-increasing scope to exact sciences.

The relations between the teachers and the nobles who maintained the religious and educational institutions was very rarely such as to be particularly beneficial to the latter. At Debreczen, it is true, the town, as patron, watched over its college with the most jealous scrupulousness, but the number of

---

[1] When he wrote these lines, though he had probably already become a convert to Catholicism, Bessenyei was the agent of the Evangelical confession at Vienna.

[2] *Holmi*, p. 97. (*Belsö Nevelés*.)

[3] *Ibid.* p. 99.

[4] For a description and illustrations of the dress worn by the Debreczen students, cf. Stephen Szücs, *Hist. of the Town of Debreczen*, vol. III. p. 926.

[5] *Holmi*, p. 102.

nobles who imitated the generosity of their ancestors, declined in proportion as imminent dangers increased the need for their support. General Nicholas Beleznay was the principal patron of the Calvinist colleges during the reign of Maria Teresa[1]. But we only have to read how one of the leading families of gentry in Nagy-Várad behaved to poor Joseph Keresztesi to understand that the champions of learning and the zealous teachers of the people had not yet obtained that recognition, which is one of the surest signs of the advance of education[2]. Here too there was a constant struggle between the episcopalian and presbyterian schools, and the greater the need of secular support felt by the Church, the greater was the dependence of the clergy on the secular superiors of the ecclesiastical districts and parishes. A particularly degrading practice was the system observed with regard to pastors. The appointment of a pastor to a parish was never considered definitive, and the parish could renew the charge from year to year if desired. The same practice was in vogue in the case of teachers, even at Debreczen and Patak[3]. Matthias Ráth (one of the most zealous and learned of the Lutheran teachers and the publisher of the first Hungarian journal) writes that, if in Hungary the Protestant schools were before long closed and the pastors compelled to steal, like the Greek "popes," such a state of things would be due entirely to the indifference and selfishness of the wealthy and distinguished members of his church[4]. Even now there were to be found among the pastors men who ought to be not in pulpits but in prisons.

It was over the fate of these schools that the most serious struggle raged between Catholicism and the two Protestant Churches. The serfs were unable to resist the Catholics unaided; and, so long as the constitution remained in force, that was the only point where the vital interests of the ruling class could be

[1] Kazinczy, Francis, *Pályám Emlékezete*, p. 21.
[2] *Journal* of Joseph Keresztesi: " Krónika Magyarország polgári és egyházi Közé-letéröl. A Tisza család elleni panasz " (pp. 55 and 101).
[3] According to the *Magyar Hirmondó* of 1782, the system of "retaining" pastors was just beginning to go out of fashion. But in his *Journal*, Keresztesi mentions it as still thriving in 1787 (p. 151).
[4] Schlözer, *Staatsanzeigen*, 1788.

assailed.   After they had reached full manhood the whilom
students protected their old schools, not so much for their
services to scholarship and the Church, as because they were
the outposts of Magyardom and of the noble order[1].   The
Primate Barkóczi was said to have elaborated a scheme for the
forfeiture of all non-Catholic schools[2], but the influence of the
curators and of the whole Protestant nobility was strong enough
to prevent this scheme being carried out.   The Protestant
schools received a certain amount of pecuniary aid from abroad,
particularly from England, and they also possessed powerful
advocates at Court in the persons of Nicholas Beleznay and of
other Protestant officers of high rank.   However this matter
did not particularly affect the nobles, whose quarrel with the
Catholics was rather of a political nature ; for they had been
deprived of their share in the government of the country, and it
was this that they aimed at recovering.

Among the Protestant writers and *savants,* on the other hand,
whose whole material and intellectual existence was bound up
in the schools, we meet with a far keener sense of oppression.
Here, again, the Lutherans showed the greatest bitterness, for
they suffered the most, and they were not bound to the country
by so many ties as the members of the Reformed Church.   The
Calvinists also waited anxiously for the dawning of a better day.
In distant Holland at Trajectum (i.e. Utrecht), in 1779, Joseph
Keresztesi joined with the Hungarian youths who were studying
there, in the following prayer: "Make the foes of Thy Hungarian
Israel to be their well-wishers, and grant them at last relief and
peace, gather up their tears, lend Thy ears to their groans and
deliver them.   Prevail upon the powers that be to pity and to
have mercy on us, and turn the thoughts of our gracious Queen
and her councillors to good intent[3]."

Regarding the hierarchy and aristocracy as the mainstays of
her power, Maria Teresa believed she was yielding alike to the

---

[1] Kazinczy and his brother were the first students at Patak who knew *German.*
In their college days, German was unknown to Joseph Vay, to Ladislas and Menyhért
Lónyai. *Pályám Emlékezete,* p. 16.

[2] Lehmann, *Zustand der Protestanten,* p. 81.

[3] *Krónika,* p. 15.

convictions of her heart and the interests of the State when she permitted the Catholic society in Hungary to act as they pleased against their Protestant fellows. In the past, common national dangers had always found Catholics and Protestants joining forces in Parliament. Now, to prevent such an eventuality, the Court party in Vienna, guided by purely political motives, may have conceived the idea of invoking the aid of the oppressed and injured non-Catholics—as they had that of the Greek Orientals in the past—in order to overthrow Hungarian independence[1]. The pamphlets and books written in 1790 by Lutherans show that, in their ranks at any rate, this idea had every prospect of success.

VI.

With all their religious and political dissensions, the Catholics and the Calvinists were after all sons of one and the same country. After the first conversions, due to force or to interest, there could be no doubt that any violent assault on the Calvinist confession would involve considerable danger to the whole nation. Then, again, the identity of their social position, the freedom of the mode of life among the nobles, their meeting in county and national assemblies, all helped to produce a constant intercourse between the two parts of the nation thus sundered by religious differences. Even in Maria Teresa's reign, when the power and influence of the hierarchy was at its zenith, several facts prove that the gulf separating the members of the two churches was bridged over by many ideas and characteristics common to both.

In the first place, it was of great importance that both possessed a sense of a common culture and the desire to derive it from its original sources. When Antal Bajtay, a Piarist, prepared a scheme of study for the use of a young Baron Andrássy in 1747, he did not forget the Protestant writers[2]. Fessler

[1] Maximae Status pro Regno Hungariae per Franz Grossing. Mus. Lat. MS. fol. 471. For negotiations of Leopold I with the Serbs (Rascians), v. *supra*, pp. 201—4, *infra*, pp. 318—9.

[2] His letter is to be found in the Academy Archives, Oct. 57. Bajtay was afterwards tutor to Joseph II and Catholic Bishop of Transylvania (v. p. 262).

related that his acquaintance with a Lutheran gentleman named
Podmaniczky had had the greatest influence on his intellectual
development. The latter lived at Aszód, half-an-hour's distance
from his monastery at Besnyö, and on many occasions visited
the cloister where he was a welcome guest. " He was always
fond of amusing himself with the younger inmates of the
monastery and took an interest in their work. Once he entered
my cell too, and, when he asked me how I spent my time, I
answered ' In reading and studying.' He brought me the
liberal works of Fleury and Muratori, strongly advising me to
study them[1]." The Jesuit Stephen Katona was quite astonished
to learn that his works were appreciated even by many who were
not Catholics[2]: and the Archbishop of Kalocsa praised Horányi
for writing favourably of the Protestants[3].

On the occasion of festivities, name-days, re-elections of
officers, installations of officials and so forth, the nobility met
without respect of religion. When the name-day of General
Beleznay was celebrated, not only was Baron Lawrence Orczi
present, but Christopher Niczky too. When Count Charles
Pálffy was installed at Patak in 1779, the professors and pupils
of the Calvinist school greeted the new High Sheriff and the
Bishop of Eger, who installed him, in laudatory verses. The
latter, the great apostle of Catholicism, sent for the younger
brother of Francis Kazinczy, who was then at the school, and
spoke to him.

The cause of humanity also served to unite the members of
the two churches. On the occasion of a famine, the Prince-
Primate himself, Joseph Batthyány, provided for his Calvinist
serfs just as well as he did for the others[4].

So far as the sentiments of the Protestants are concerned,
Leo Szeicz himself, the author of the *Igaz Magyar*, declared that
he " never experienced any such rude intolerance " among them.
" On the contrary, when I kept company with Calvinists in the

---

[1] Cf. article by Louis Abafi on "Ignatius Aurelias Fessler" in the *Szdzadok*, 1878,
vol. VII. p. 622.
[2] Chanc. Arch. No. 2036 (1784).
[3] *Igaz Magyar*, vol. I. p. 149.
[4] National Museum MS. m. No. 569. (Panegyric verse by a Reforméd schoolmaster.)

Trans-Tisza district, they not only did not treat me rudely, but received me with particular kindness, and on fast-days had a fish-diet prepared for me ; indeed they actually joined me in my fasting, only that besides the fish, they ate chicken as well[1]. Religious topics are very rarely touched on." To the examinations in the school of Sárospatak the Jesuits of the neighbourhood were usually invited, though they were the inexorable foes of this said school[2].

The religious feelings that caused the conflict between the two churches were so saturated with political motives, that there was scarcely any further ground for hatred, when the latter ceased to exist, i.e. directly the offices were thrown open again to the Protestants. It was indeed just at this very period (1781) that both churches, in fact all churches alike, were subjected to attack by a common enemy.

It was, without any doubt, the spread of Freemasonry which did most to close the period of religious strife. The Emperor Francis I—husband of Maria Teresa—was initiated into the order of Freemasons in England in 1731, and continued ever after to be its patron and protector. A bull of the Pope, denouncing the order, was not even published in Hungary. Maria Teresa indeed did all she could to counteract its influence but without effect. Not only the greater part of the magnates, of the learned and literary class, and the most educated of the gentry favoured Freemasonry and the impulse which it gave to thought and reform, but many Roman Catholic priests, including both bishops and canons, were quite enthusiastic over it as well[3].

The irreligion and indifferentism that had been making ever-increasing strides since the opening of the eighteenth century above all jeopardised the interests of the Roman Church, though its mere existence was a menace to every positive faith. So early as 1767 the Hungarian *consilium locumtenentiale* issued an edict for the prevention of the spread of this tendency. The instructions issued to the high sheriffs on November 21, 1768, ordained

---

[1] *Igaz Magyar* (The True Hungarian), vol. I. pp. 150, 151.

[2] Molnár, Aladár, *Közoktatás története* (*History of Education in Hungary*), vol. I. p. 422.

[3] For the influence of Freemasonry on the revival of national ideas, see the author's book, *The Parliament of 1790-1* (in Hungarian).

that atheists and indifferentists should be punished. The most zealous champions of the Roman hierarchy were quite ready to tolerate the non-Catholics until they could be weeded out without danger[1]: but they could make no truce with the free-thinkers[2].

Even during this period there was no cessation of the religious quarrels of the Hungarians. For a time the Reformed Church had to fight against the greatest dangers, and was only saved because it was deeply rooted in the social and political conditions of the country. On his accession Joseph II, who was quite impartial in religious respects, attempted to use the Protestants, then struggling to recover their political equality, as a weapon against bishops and nobles. In the face of this danger the mutual anger of the churches diminished in violence, for they preferred to join forces against the common enemy of their nationality.

The religious dissensions, which might have been fatal to Magyardom at the opening of the eighteenth century, were no longer dangerous, but merely disagreeable, by 1780. Despite the differences of doctrines and forms, so strong was the social power and union of the nobles that they were able to commence the work of bridging over even the widest gaps separating the two churches. In point of culture there was no antagonism, for both churches regarded humanism as their educational ideal and favoured the study and imitation of the classics. The Catholics however, under Jesuit influence, in every field of intellectual life preferred what was older, while the Protestants, partly as a result of the spirit of their religion, partly of their intimate connection with other parts of Europe, were ready to adopt more liberal forms, both in politics and literature.

[1] *Igaz Magyar* (The True Hungarian), vol. III. p. 51.
[2] *Ibid.* vol. III. and Preface, p. 11.

CHAPTER V.

THE ROYAL POWER AND THE GOVERNMENT OF THE STATE.

THE presence of a King at the helm of State was demanded both by the hierarchy and the aristocracy of medieval States. His person, sanctified by the solemn rites of coronation, formed a link between the otherwise secular State and the Kingdom of God. The King was the defender of the faith, and the nation, which was rewarded for his good deeds, atoned also for his sins. As the first knight among his people, he was the most worthy to represent the same in dealings with the sovereigns of the other peoples of Christianity; he led the nobles to battle, his conquests enhanced the glory of his people, and for any reverses he might suffer the country had to pay in blood and land.

However, the King was not merely the leader of the privileged classes; he was the head of the whole country and had to provide for the welfare, not of certain orders, but of his whole people. It was in this spirit that the first King of the Hungarians, with due regard alike for Scripture and political interests, appointed for himself the work he had to do[1]. The King governed his kingdom by divine ordinance, *antiquos ac modernos imitantes Augustos*, and decreed that his people should live an honest life, to be regulated not merely by divine laws

---

[1] *Instructions of Saint Stephen to his Son*, ch. x.: "Non solum parentelae et cognacioni, vel principibus et ducibus, sive vicinis et incolis sis propitius, verum etiam extraneis."

but by those of the secular State as well[1].   Besides maintaining
and increasing his own dignity, the respect due to the Church, the
deference due to the prelates, besides upholding his own honour
as governor and knight, he had to provide for the well-being of
the nation as a whole.   It was for this reason that God had
given him his power.   The monarchy—in conjunction with the
Church—proved the chief agent in the progress of civilization,
but in Hungary the whole historic life of the nation was concentrated in its kings to a degree hardly to be paralleled in any
other country.   For, with the Hungarians, the king was not
merely the anointed of God and the foremost knight; he was, by
virtue of the ancient military organisation, above all the leader
of the whole nation, of the freemen.

In the Middle Ages, Holy Scripture and the traditions of
the Roman Empire fixed the ideal conception of kingship.
According to this theory the King, as the direct representative
of God and the trustee of the authority of the people, was
empowered to take any action which he considered favourable
to the interests of the country.   That the royal power was not
always guided purely by regard for the interests of the nation
was proved by history, whether sacred or profane; and every
page of medieval history is in itself a proof of the difficulty of
limiting a king's authority when it was in opposition to the
special interests and demands of the privileged orders.   For
the creation of a State, for enabling it to stand high in the
ranks of Christian powers, for protecting it against both Emperor
and Pope, and for extending its frontiers—for all this, credit is
due to the Hungarian Kings of the House of Árpád.   In the
succeeding age, kings of foreign extraction made the name of
Hungary famous and glorious all over Europe; and finally,
Matthias Corvinus Hunyadi pursued ideals not only of power
and glory but of culture, and met with a success almost
unparalleled in his age.   Yet the resistance of the Parliaments
of Estates to the kingly power is as old as the history of
Hungary.   If it was on divine and human right that the King
based the exercise and increase of his power, equally momentous

---

[1] See *Corpus Juris*, Introduction to the laws of St Stephen.

reasons justified the privileged orders, and indeed the whole nation, in their reaction or resistance to any abuse of that power[1].

Who can determine which side, in the constantly recurring constitutional struggles, was more decidedly justified by written law, and by the results of former struggles and victories? This is not indeed the question of most interest to the historian. For him the question of prime importance is, whether, in the various phases of development, it was the kingly or the opposing powers which followed the course most advantageous to the nation as a whole? For just as one uniform constitution for all the various peoples of the earth is an impossibility, no constitution could or indeed ever did remain the same in all the various stages of evolution of a particular nation.

I.

Since the beginning of the thirteenth century the idea of the Hungarian State has been represented by the Crown[2]. This holy Crown, so called since 1264, was first the King's property, but afterwards—independently of his person—the symbol of the jurisdictional power of the State. " It is not the holy Crown which crowns ; it is the will of the people," declared the Parliament of 1440.

A primitive people must of necessity connect the idea of settled government and of State with a person. Who can deny that even to-day, King and State are one in the eyes of the masses, and that only persons in a more advanced stage of evolution than they are capable of distinguishing between the two?

It was due to the primitive character of the nation at this early period that the State itself possessed an insignificant and one-sided organisation. The medieval State had scarcely any

---

[1] *Austeritas Austriaca*—a MS. dating from the close of the seventeenth century (Academy Archives, 100, 4°) : " Justum est odium quod imperat ultima necessitas, sanctum quod praescribit virtus, licitum quod conservatio libertatis exposcit, Divinum quod pro Lege et grege exarescit."

[2] Letter of Pope Honorius III, 12 Dec., 1222: "Nihil contra regem vel coronam ipsius audeat attentare."

functions at all beyond the waging of war and the administration of justice, and these were the very functions that made the nobility an element in the formation of the State.   But all they did was done by command of the King and in his name; and the various classes and orders—otherwise without any point of contact—were thus held together by the authority of the King and by the sacred authority ascribed to the Crown.   It is in the reconciliation or, where necessary, in the subordination of the special interests of these classes to higher and more general interests, that the history of the development of States consists. This has been the case both in ancient Hellas and Rome, and among the peoples of more recent times.

Strong kings, such as St Stephen and St Ladislas in particular, Béla, Kálmán, the Angevins and Matthias, made the State a power in foreign politics as well.   At home opposition to their power was extremely rare or, at any rate, unsuccessful, and all the organisations in the country—military, judicial, educational, and even ecclesiastical—looked to them as their fountain-head.

On the other hand, all the kings who were personally weak, helped to give victory both to foreign foes and to the elements of disturbance in the country itself.   The history of the Jagello dynasty (1490–1526) is the best proof that Hungary could not regard the King's power as a conception apart from the State, even at the dawn of the modern age.

Up to the days of Matthias it was the King's power that organised the State—with due regard, indeed, for the other classes, but at all times chiefly with the view of promoting its own authority.   It was not until the period of the Jagellos that the Hungarian Parliament of Estates had the chance of creating a polity according to its own ideas.   The headless trunk endeavoured to escape paralysis, and the record of its endeavour is contained in the *Tripartitum* of Verböczy (1514). Every letter of that Code speaks of the recognition and firm establishment of the nobility as a privileged class; yet the work of protecting and securing the interests of the country as a whole was left exclusively to the King.   Without him the State was still unable to fulfil the tasks before it, a fact emphasized just as decidedly in the *Tripartitum* as in the Roman law[1]. Notwithstanding all this, the Parliaments were compelled to decide without the King.

The disaster at Mohács (1526) proved that their first attempt was a failure, and that the kingly power alone was able to guide the existing forces towards one object. Liberated from the common yoke, the magnates and the gentry turned against one another, and meanwhile the Reformation engaged the whole attention of the only other order—that of the Church—which possessed any certain consciousness of its duties to the State. The men of the sixteenth century ascribed the Turkish conquest of Hungary to the non-existence of a kingly power, just as the men of the eighteenth century ascribed the disaster of Poland to the diminution in the power of her kings. Before the final dissolution, at the Parliament held at Grodno in 1791, the Polish nation made a desperate effort to strengthen the kingly power, and thus to support the tottering State; and, in like manner, only a few months before the catastrophe of Mohács, the Hungarian Parliament endowed the kingship with a veritable dictatorial power for the defence of the State[2]. "All the lords, prelates, barons and inhabitants of the country, at this present general Parliament, held on St George's Day, have unanimously decided to appeal to His Royal Majesty begging His Majesty to deign to make full use of his authority and power, and, after due deliberation, to do and execute all measures concerned with the government of the country, and to take all measures necessary to the proper acquirement, increase and expenditure of His Majesty's revenues, as well as to the defence, liberty and other requirements of the kingdom."

---

[1] *Tripartitum*, II. 3. § 2: "Posteaquam ad fidem Catholicam sunt conversi et regem sponte sibi ipsis elegerunt, tam *condendae* legis, quam etiam cujuslibet *possessionariae collationis*, atque omnis *juridiciariae potestatis* facultas, in jurisdictionem sacrae Regni hujus Coronae, qua cuncti Reges Hungariae coronari solent, et subsequenter Principem ac Regem nostrum legitime constitutum simul cum Imperio et Regimine translata est." We see the influence of the Roman law in the fact that, on the analogy of the Roman people renouncing their prerogatives in favour of the *princeps*, the Hungarian *communitas*, which had formerly ruled in theory, transferred the *majestas* to the crowned king.

[2] Parliament of 1526. Articulus I.: "Rex authoritate sua regia utatur."

It would be a difficult matter to find any other declaration of a Parliament in the history of the nations of Europe which placed the whole power so absolutely in the hands of the King as was done by this particular Act, or in fact by the whole legislation, of 1526. All the causes contributing to the creation of absolute monarchies everywhere in Europe were here at work. The nation possessed a consciousness of its deficiencies, and saw that its organisation could be perfected only by a ruler possessed of unlimited power; none the less in Hungary—just as in Poland —this power was unable to assert itself.

Is it possible for a nation in due course of time to recover that of which it has been deprived in a moment of misfortune? There can be no doubt that the conditions at work made this extremely difficult for the Hungarians for a considerable time. For everywhere else an absolute kingship meant merely the downfall of the constitution; in Hungary it involved the nation too in its downfall.

It is due to the Habsburgs that, as a result of the Turkish conquests, the fate of the nation was not, in point of public law, similar to that of Poland after her dismemberment. Hungary, too, was split up into three parts: the West, which was Habsburg, the Alföld, which was Turkish, Transylvania, which was auto-nomous. But the King of Hungary remained the *de facto* lord of the first of these and was recognised by Christendom as the *de iure* ruler of the other two, and so the historic continuity of the realm was never lost. Moreover, the fruits of the remarkable perseverance of the Habsburgs in never, even under the most trying circumstances, resigning their title to the country—with all its vast pretensions on neighbouring kingdoms—were in the end enjoyed by Hungary herself.

We have already explained the causes that made it impossible for this dynasty—since it was an alien one despite all its merits— to organise the forces of Magyardom on the lines of absolutism as native dynasties were doing in the States of Western Europe. This endeavour was of necessity as old as the dynasty itself for even the Hungarians of earlier days had recognised that a dictatorship was necessary in times of danger, and that a nation could only be welded together by an absolute king. Now they had to choose between two alternatives—either to accept an organisation conforming not to national but to foreign ideas and interests, or to maintain the older institutions already recognised as inadequate to satisfy the new needs but at all events thoroughly national in character.

The history of this great tragedy occupies two hundred years of the annals of Hungary. Each new phase of it, whether produced by external events in Europe or by domestic conditions, involved complications. The age of Joseph II brought the catastrophe, and the subsequent reconciliation was the work of those great men of the nineteenth century who began the reconstruction of modern Hungary on the foundations of political, dynastic and national ideas, which a common civilization had created.

So powerful was the influence of Western ideas that the royal power was able, by slow degrees but with an ever-increasing measure of success, to bring under its control the various elements of national life in Hungary. This extension of the sphere and authority of the State depended on foreign aid and ideas. The direct result was that any attempt made by the head of the State to reform or to create institutions was looked upon as a foreign innovation. In short, whenever the King endeavoured to create, to reform or to rule, all his endeavours or institutions remained foreign in the eyes of the nation. The modern State—that hundred-armed Briareus—appeared to the Hungarians clothed with all the terrors of a detested foreign institution, and its every triumph seemed to threaten final annihilation not only to the ancestral institutions but to the nation itself.

The various stages of this struggle were marked by specific laws, which must be interpreted as so many compromises between the King and the Parliament, and as reflecting their comparative positions at each period. An examination of these laws reveals how the kingship became stereotyped in its efforts to create a modern State, and how a peculiar and unique compromise enabled the main privileges of a medieval society to exist side by side with the prerogatives of a modern sovereign.

II.

Let us examine, first of all, the position of the King as dignitary, as the head of society. By virtue of Act I of 1687 the kingly dignity became hereditary in the male branch of the Habsburg house—and this privilege was also extended to the female branch by Acts I and II of 1723. This break with the tradition of elective kingship brought Hungary a step nearer to the great monarchies of Western Europe. Previously in political though not in historical respects she had resembled the Holy Roman Empire and the Republic of Poland. The establishment of the principle that the kingly dignity should in future be hereditary was declared by the respective Acts to be a mark of gratitude for the great benefits whereby the Habsburgs had bound the Hungarian nation for all time to their house—Leopold I by the expulsion of the Turks, Charles III by the expansion of the kingdom and the restoration of domestic peace. It was a natural result of the triumph of the Catholic Church that only princes professing the Roman faith should be allowed to accede to the throne[1].

According to numerous Acts of Parliament, the royal Court should have resided for part of every year in Hungary. In 1780, magnificent palaces awaited the coming of the King at Pozsony and Buda. In the palace itself the sovereign was surrounded by the highest dignitaries of the country; in his own house the King was the head of the aristocracy. Besides the bannerets, the chief offices at Court were filled by the royal equerries, the principal gentleman-ushers and chamberlains[2].

---

[1] Act III of 1723: "Descendentes eorundem legitimos Romano-Catholicos successores utriusque sexus."

[2] Act VI of 1765 included the captain of the Hungarian noble bodyguard among the bannerets. Ürményi, *Jus Publ.* II. 4. § 17 : "Officia Palatii Regii sustinent ita dicti Barones Regni, Palatinus quippe Regni Hungariae Judex Curiae, Tavernicorum item magistri Curiae etc." The dignity of *tárnokmester* (Treasurer) offers a characteristic illustration of the manner in which Court offices developed into national ones. He was the "master" of the King's *tavernici* (treasurer)—just as the "masters" of the horses, of the wardens of the butteries and grooms of the King's posset, were also Court officials. However, as the administration of the royal free boroughs was entrusted to his care, his power extended beyond his sphere of authority as a Court official, and his office became a national one.

These appeared in public on the occasion of great festivities only, such as at coronations and upon St Stephen's Day. The Court Chancellor was another official who was always in attendance on the sovereign, whose office was now filled by a temporal peer. Maria Teresa entrusted the security of her person to the noble bodyguard, which included young men from every county in Hungary and its dependencies. It was the great Queen, too, who founded the Order of St Stephen, to serve as a fresh link between the sovereign and the spiritual and temporal peers of the country. It was she again who, to give more forcible expression to her authority in ecclesiastical matters, once more attached the title of "Apostolic" to the kingship in 1758[1].

As for the actual sphere of royal authority, the Hungarian publicists accepted the principle of universal law established by Hugo Grotius (of which Martini had been an eminent apostle in Vienna), that the King, as the wielder of the civil power, had the right of governing the State, i.e. of so directing the actions of his subjects as to secure what appeared to his judgment to be the common safety and interests of all[2]. For the practical application of this theory, the King was invested with the following legal prerogatives : every spiritual and temporal subject of the kingdom was bound to his person by the tie of fealty—a fealty which recognized the fact that the King was the head of the State, and that his subjects refused to accept the supremacy of any other over-lords[3].

The Estates of the legislature shared the rights of the King to some extent, but the laws were promulgated in his name, not in that of the nation. The fundamental laws of Hungary determined those cases in which the King might take measures on his own initiative, and those in which he was obliged to secure the consent of the Estates.

The most important of the King's personal prerogatives was

---

[1] The breve of Pope Clement XIII (Rome, Aug. 19, 1758) gives this title to the King of Hungary.

[2] Ürményi, *Jus Publ.* II. 7. § 1 : "Imperium contineatur jure gubernandi civitatem, hoc est actiones omnium subditorum ad communem securitatem pro arbitrio dirigendi."

[3] *Tripartitum*, I. 12.

the *jus patronatus* (advowson)[1], which enabled him as "apostolic" King to appoint to vacant benefices in the Church (bishoprics, abbacies, provostships), reserving to the Apostolic See only the right of confirming the bishops-designate. The King also appointed the canons of chapters, with the exception of those attached to the two archbishoprics. However, when vacancies (*sedis vacantia*) occurred, these benefices were inherited by the King, not through the *jus patronatus*, but by virtue of his right, as King of Hungary, over all ecclesiastical and secular property. On the other hand, as patron, he possessed the right of sequestration as against prelates negligent of their estates and of their churches[2].

By virtue of the same prerogative, the King exercised the supreme control over education and pious endowments. In this manner the title of the medieval kingship is indissolubly connected with one of the most important prerogatives of the modern State[3]. By Act LXX of 1723, the Estates brought the whole system of public education, "with regard to method, form and means," under the control of the sovereign. Some older laws (which ordained that the revenues of unoccupied churches should be devoted to the foundation of parishes, seminaries and schools) were held to contravene this fundamental prerogative, and were accordingly ruled out as invalid[4].

In the Catholic Church the King possessed the executive power as the successor of St Stephen, in the more modern churches as their temporal head. According to Act XXX of 1715 and to various decrees, issued in 1731, 1745 and 1749, the position of the Protestants as Estates of the realm and, consequently, their right to legal existence in the country, was made

---

[1] Ürményi, *loc. cit.* § 7: "Inter ea quae directe et absolute Regiae Maj. exercenda delata sunt, primum locum sibi non immerito vindicat Jus Patronatus." Niczky (*loc. cit.* vol. III. p. 4) also treats this prerogative first.

[2] Act LXXI of 1723.

[3] Act LXXIV of 1715, the fundamental law on this question, runs as follows: "The right of control and of examination of the accounts of all kinds of seminaries, and colleges, whether established for the training of clergy or of secular youths, by whomsoever founded in or outside the Kingdom, His Majesty, by virtue of his apostolic office and supreme authority, reserves to Himself, to be exercised whenever He may deem necessary."

[4] E.g. Act XII of 1550.

dependent upon the will of the sovereign. Questions of dispute between the two churches were settled by the King to the best of his judgment, by royal resolution. During these arbitrations every kind of question arose—from insignificant ones relating to particular churches and schools to one which contemplated the total expulsion of the Protestants. This prerogative was not indeed based on law, but it was ratified by the tacit consent of the country[1].

The sovereign had the right of deciding matrimonial disputes between Protestants, though only in accordance with the principles of their faith; and without his consent Protestants could not build new churches or found new schools. The King also prosecuted apostates through the public prosecutor.

Without doubt, these royal prerogatives in church affairs denoted in themselves a considerable advance towards absolutism. By his exercise of them over the Catholics, the King was in possession of the advowson of the estates of one of the richest churches in the world. He included in his *clientèle* both nobles, burgesses, and all those gifted persons who were rising to eminence or trying to secure recognition in the fields of literature and science. In the establishment of an absolute monarchy in Spain, much help is said to have been given to her Catholic kings by their position as grand masters of the great orders of military monks, and by the control they obtained over the patronage of benefices. Ever since the days of St Stephen the kings of Hungary had enjoyed the same power, to a much more considerable degree.

But, in political respects, the latter must have obtained still greater importance from the fact that the Parliaments left the settlement of the whole religious question and the regulation of the status of the Protestants entirely to their decision. Though Charles III and Maria Teresa exercised this prerogative in accordance with the wishes of the ruling class of Hungary, it would have been a very powerful weapon in the hands of any sovereign who desired to turn it against the existing society.

Important from a historical point of view too is the fact that Adam Kollár (the first who directed a scientific attack on the

[1] Ürményi, *Jus Publ.* VII. 23.

whole aristocratic and ecclesiastical system of Hungary) took as
his starting-point the advowson of the sovereign.   The King of
Hungary possessed the plenipotentiary power of legislating in
church matters[1]; and there was no one above him in the administration of the temporal estates of the Church[2].   He had the
unlimited right of presenting to these benefices.   He had never
renounced his right of employing churchmen, or of using the
income from their estates, in the service of the State.   Even now
ecclesiastics were obliged to redeem themselves from military
service by a money payment.   Now the ecclesiastical order was
at the same time the first Estate of the realm ; if, then, their
privileges and Estates depended on the favour of the King, what
could the other Estates do against him ?   It sounds like a
prophecy when Kollár, in the preface to his work on the question,
calls the attention of the crown prince Joseph—just then beginning to take an active part in the government of the country
—to the great advantages which the kingly power derived from
the exercise of its prerogatives in church affairs[3].   It was this
power that placed within the range of possibility the overthrow
of the time-worn constitution so proudly maintained by the noble
society of Hungary.

In temporal affairs, likewise, the fundamental laws of Hungary
gave to the King a wide sphere of authority with which the
parliamentary Estates could not properly interfere.   His first
prerogative was the right of ennobling persons (*jus nobilitandi*)[4].
The society of nobles entrusted its head with the work of
co-optatio.   Whether this prerogative was exercised by the King
by conferring lands or merely a title on the individual, the man
thus honoured became a member of the ruling class.   Not
merely the grant of nobility, but all other distinctions and
privileges depended upon the King's will and decision.   It was
he who created barons and counts.   " By virtue of his mere

[1] Kollár, Adam, *De originibus et usu perpetuo potest. legisl. circa sacra apostoli-
corum Regum Ungariae.*   (Vienna, 1764.)

[2] *Ibid.* p. 59.

[3] *Hist. Dipl. de Jure Patronatus* (Dedication): " Nihil igitur mirum, opusculum
hoc, eximia ista benevolentia abs te tueri."

[4] Ürményi, *Jus Publ.* VIII. § 2: "Principem locum vindicat jus nobilitandi."   We
find a resemblance in English public law, where the King is considered as the source
of all honour.

authority[1]" he granted exemptions from taxes and customs duties, issued licences for markets and toll-houses, and gave charters to guilds. Act IV of 1741 considered these prerogatives as so absolutely the exclusive right of the King that it excluded even the co-regent (Maria Teresa's consort, the Grand Duke Francis, afterwards Emperor) from the exercise of the same[2].

The sphere of jurisdiction was regarded by the King as his particularly exclusive prerogative. Cases of *lèse-majesté* were tried by the King himself[3]. The crime of breach of fealty and *lèse-majesté* was the only one for which the offender was liable to the loss of his nobility; and hence, as the King himself had granted it to the holder, he alone could deprive him of it. Only the Royal Chancellery could issue orders for a new trial (*cum gratia*); it alone could annul or mitigate sentences or suspend their execution, in each case by the issue of special writs. The King's Bench passed sentence in the name of the King; only sentences that had received the royal seal could be executed. The King had the supreme control over all other courts of justice. During the Turkish wars the ideas of feudal law were continually gaining ground. In the end all property that belonged to the noble class was actually considered as subject to royal usufruct. A prosperous family was merely, as it were, the manager of its estate. On the extinction of a family or after a breach of fealty, the estate in question devolved on the King—who was regarded as the natural inheritor of all noble property.

The interpretation of laws, whose meaning was ambiguous, was undertaken by the King[4], a fact of particular importance in a country in which the laws of St Stephen and of Kálmán were still in force in 1780, though nearly eight centuries old.

This judicial power subjected the nobility to the King almost as much as the *jus patronatus* did the clergy. Above their heads hung a sword; for the threat of suits for *lèse-majesté* menaced the future of entire families of kinsmen with annihilation.

---

[1] *Tripartitum*, II. 9: "Privilegium ex mera principis auctoritate procedit, etc."

[2] § 5. As a curiosity, we may mention the fact that the *Tripartitum* is misquoted in this paragraph.

[3] "Causae vero cognitio et revisio ex quo directe ad solam Regiam Majestatem pertineret, permanebit penes ejusdem benignum arbitrium." Act VII, 1715.

[4] Niczky, *Staatskenntniss*, vol. V. p. 1. (A writer with Royalist tendencies.)

The appointment of the members of the supreme courts of justice was an exclusive prerogative of the King[1]. This extensive and, for the most part, discretionary power meant a great deal in a litigious country like Hungary, where there was scarcely any legal title that could not be called in question.

The publicist of the Court-party maintained this prerogative and the Government at Vienna accepted his view. But Act I, 1687 (coronation-oath), says expressly that the King shall preserve the laws, " prout super eorum intellectu et usu Regio et communi Statuum consensu diaetaliter conventum fuerit."

Probably nothing proves the extent to which the administration of justice predominated in Hungarian public law better than the generally accepted conception that the King's right to appoint magistracies was derived from his *jurisdictional* power. For the magistracies (to employ the Latin sense of the word) assisted in executing the laws, and were consequently also involved in the work of judicature[2]. Of all the State offices and dignities the only exceptions to the rule of appointment by the King were those of the Count Palatine and the two Keepers of the Sacred Crown, who were selected by Parliament from candidates designated by the King. In a similar way the county assemblies appointed to the various county offices, by selecting candidates designated by the High Sheriffs.

The right of granting pardons was a prerogative of the King —so much so indeed that Act X of 1485 actually extended it to the Palatine also. In Hungary, as in all other states, this right was a recognition of the King's " Majestas[3]." The King alone could save a man from *infamia*, from civil death : and he alone could remove the stain of bastardy by legitimation[4].

An obvious consequence of the spirit of feudal law was that the King was the natural guardian of the orphans of nobles and

[1] The Archbishops of Esztergom and Kalocsa, the Count Palatine and the Lord Chief Justice too appointed judges to sit in the King's Bench.

[2] Ürményi, *Jus Publ.* VII. 10: " Ab suprema judiciaria potestate denique profluit jus Majestaticum Regum nostrorum circa constitutionem Magistratuum."

[3] Act XL of 1715 (at the end): " Gratiarum dispensatione soli Regiae Majestati propria, penes supremam ejusdem auctoritatem intaminate semper permanente."

[4] According to the *Tripartitum* (1. 108), however, neither the Pope nor the King could legitimate a bastard against the wishes of the legitimate children or heirs.

it was he who transferred this office to others. Consequently he had the supreme control over the care of orphans, and over the conduct of guardians and trustees[1].

As for the coining of money, though a memorandum or proposals on the subject were occasionally submitted to Parliament, the right itself was always considered a royal prerogative ; and after the Hungarian currency had reached the level of the German one—in respect both of value and fineness of coins— there was no opportunity or indeed necessity for discussing this question further. The *lucrum camerae*, the tax accruing from the coinage of money, had ceased, and the interest on the national debt (which roughly corresponds to this *lucrum* in modern states) was as yet an unknown quantity. None the less the control of the mint and the maintenance of a standard of currency, whose good or bad character was a decisive factor in the price of wares, and consequently of great importance to industry and trade, gave the King a considerable hold over the *bourgeoisie*.

These prerogatives—that of advowson, which subordinated the clergy, that of jurisdiction, which restrained the nobles, and that of coinage, which impressed the *bourgeoisie*—are factors of essential importance even in the life of a modern state. In the eighteenth century in Hungary they served to give the King the control over the fortunes of individual classes rather than of the whole country. For example, the King was the patron of the large bishoprics and abbacies, but the smaller endowments were the private property of the Catholic and Protestant nobles, who controlled and managed them and who but rarely felt that there was a higher power above them in the State. The offices of the nobles, and, owing to his jurisdictional power, their wealth, families and even their lives came indeed under the control, or might be at the mercy, of the King ; but, on the other hand, the nobles themselves exercised almost as extensive a control over their own serfs and over the inhabitants of the counties. Again, though the control of coinage and the mint belonged to the King, it meant very little in a country in which a system of primitive economy prevailed, and where, even when ready money was to be found, Dutch gold pieces circulated far more readily

---

[1] § 15, Act LXVIII of 1715.

than did the imperial ones[1]. All these different powers—which formed part of the King's prerogative—affected as yet only those classes of people whose social rank brought them into immediate contact with the sovereign. The lower classes—or rather the masses—were still governed almost exclusively by the nobles; the parish priests, the peasants and the burgesses were familiar, as yet, only with bishops, feudal lords, and civic magistrates; they were quite unacquainted with the direct power of the King, which regulated and defined the acts of their official superiors.

The guidance of the destinies of the whole nation—and thus a control over the masses as well as over the governing class —fell to the King by virtue of his absolute right to decide questions of peace and war. The older Parliaments had indeed sought to bring this privilege under their control, but the Acts (I and II) of 1723 had bound Hungary almost indissolubly to Austria. After that date the King's supreme control over peace and war consisted chiefly in the fact that he had now the power to summon the nobles to arms in case of necessity[2]. When the interests of either of the two parties (i.e. Austria or Hungary) were at stake, the close tie existing between the two countries prevented the interests of either being separated from those of its ally[3]. In addition to the control over peace and war, the contracting of alliances and the appointment of ambassadors were considered as exclusive prerogatives of the King[4]. His control over foreign policy also included the right to protect and to administer the marches, to build new fortresses, and to recruit soldiers and to quarter them on individuals in Hungary. It was in this fashion that the authority of the State (i.e. the central or royal government) first came into direct contact with the serfs.

---

[1] Such appears to be the fact from most legacies of which I have examined the details.

[2] By Acts XVIII of 1715 and VI of 1723. This is the so-called *particularis insurrectio*. The consent of Parliament was required for the *generalis insurrectio*.

[3] Ürményi, *Jus Publ.* VIII. 24.

[4] Poland is the best proof of how the conduct of foreign affairs, by virtue of its very essence, is, even in strictly constitutional States, a prerogative of the head of the State. Poland was a republic, not a kingship, but its envoys were commissioned by the King, not by the republic. Hungary had by law the right to send a special ambassador to all the negotiations with the Turks. But this law was not fulfilled till 1790, when King Leopold II granted it in the negotiations at Sistova.

The opportunity for intercourse was hardly a favourable one, and it originated the dislike of the masses in Hungary for everything connected with the State.

Even Parliament in Hungary was subordinated to royal prerogatives, though the King had to act in conjunction with it, in respect of all other laws or regulations. The King summoned Parliament, fixed the days of its meeting, and determined the subjects for its discussion ; and his sanction was needed to give the force of law to the bills or resolutions of Parliament. The different individuals, who attended Parliament, possessed the *salvus conductus*, i.e. the privilege of immunity on account of their speeches and actions in the chambers. Yet, as in 1729, the King (Charles III) showed that he could punish them for their opposition there by depriving them of their offices, and in the same year he sent a royal writ to the county of Trencsén forbidding it again to return Bartakovics—the leader of the opposition—as a member.

The actual authority enjoyed by the King in Hungary in the eighteenth century strikes us as corresponding very little to the ideas Montesquieu entertained of it. The King did not possess the whole executive power, of which indeed each landed proprietor was an independent trustee. On the other hand, in the sphere of legislation as in jurisdiction, the royal influence was considerable and often decisive. This anomaly is all the more surprising because, as we have seen, the philosophers, who preached aristocratic liberty, showed a particular liking for the political and social system of Hungary. This fact proves in itself what every page of Hungarian history proclaims, namely, that the development of the Hungarian kingship was not guided exclusively by Hungarian ideas, and that foreign interference necessarily involved a national resistance which deeply influenced its character.

All these royal prerogatives were exercised by the King as the head either of the whole State or of large social classes. But this fact and these powers do not in themselves fully express the political position of the King in eighteenth century Hungary. To obtain a faithful picture of it we must discover the actual amount of authority enjoyed by the King of Hungary on

Hungarian soil, not by virtue of Acts of Parliament or of recognised royal prerogatives, but as the head of organisations and corporations quite independent of the State.

The King of Hungary had liberated the country from the Turkish yoke by the aid, not only of Hungarians, but of foreigners also. It was as a living memorial of this fact that large numbers of foreign soldiers—thirty to forty thousand even in times of peace—were garrisoned in Hungarian fortresses. Their military chief was the King of Hungary, who put them under the control, not of Hungarian authorities, but of foreigners. After 1741 Hungarian regiments were created in quick succession, but they were subordinated, not to Parliament, but, like all others, to the council of war, or, in other words, to the King.

The lands won from the Turks appeared to Hungarians as recovered territory—to the Viennese as conquered soil. Part of them had indeed to be restored to their former proprietors; other estates had to be yielded up to Hungarians who had rendered eminent services to their sovereign and the country. But it was not until the days of Maria Teresa that the older counties—to the south of the Maros and Drave—began gradually to be stirred into life again. Until 1780, the "Banat" was under the control of the war council and the Imperial Chamber, and even after that date the "military frontiers" continued under their control. The revenues, customs duties, jurisdiction and the whole political life of these districts were entirely removed from the control of Parliament.

These territories were occupied by former Turkish subjects, who had left their previous homes for reasons of religion or nationality. In 1690 the King, acting on his own initiative, welcomed them to the country and gave them territory on which to settle. The letters patent issued by Leopold I on August 21, 1691, put the Serbs (Rascians, who belonged to the Orthodox Greek Church) under the direction of their own patriarch, and acknowledged their right to freedom of worship; but it did not allow the Hungarian authorities to control them. The Serbs (Rascians) lived in the lands of the Sacred Crown, and possessed an entirely independent organisation and religion. In foreign and civil wars alike they served not Hungary but the Emperor.

History is compelled to take cognizance of the probably unparalleled case of these Rascians, who were organised as a separate religious and political unit, and who lived for a century on Hungarian soil before they had any connection with the Hungarian Parliament. In fact, until 1779, when Maria Teresa abolished the separate Illyrian administration and brought the affairs of the Rascians under the control of the Hungarian Chancellery, there was no link whatever between them and Hungary beyond the identity of the monarch.

As regards the Jews, their residence in Hungary depended upon the favour of the sovereign, and they paid a "toleration tax" for the privilege. Up to 1771, the amount paid under this head was only 33,000 florins, but at this time it was suddenly increased to 100,000 florins.

The connection between the older settlers and the towns inhabited by foreign-speaking people—in particular the mining towns—and the country as a whole, was practically nothing more than a "personal union." The mines were also crown property, but the King did not entrust their management to the Hungarian Chancellery. Even the salt-mines were only subordinated to it by Act XIV of 1741, but the other mines were subjected to the imperial mining-chamber and to the mint. To the latter bodies were subordinated the *comes camerae* of Lower Hungary, who resided at Körmöcz, the overseers of mines of Szomolnok and the inspectors of mines of Nagy-Bánya. All these interests and estates were, therefore, crown property and not subject to the control of Parliament.

In fact, with the exception of the war taxes, all revenues derived from salt, mines, customs, crown and treasury estates were regarded as the private property of the sovereign and as entirely outside the control of Parliament. Those managed by the Hungarian Royal Chamber (*Kamara*) alone amounted in 1780 to 5,755,988 florins; salt alone yielded 3,489,957 florins, i.e. *nearly as much as the whole amount of the taxes voted by Parliament*[1]. The annual income, derived from the gold, silver and copper mines under Viennese management, was estimated at 4 to 5 million florins. Consequently the sum voted by Parliament

[1] See Supplement (*Tabelle*).

represented scarcely one-third of the aggregate income of the King. Just one-third of the revenues of the Chamber—1,900,000 florins—was paid every year into the common imperial exchequer in Vienna, as *quota* for the Court[1].

Another institution controlled by the King was the postal service, which was entirely under the direction of the Crown. It was organised by the sovereign, in whose service it was used, and, throughout the whole monarchy, its administration was in the hands of the family of Prince Paar, in which the dignity of Postmaster-General was hereditary. By Act CXIV of 1723, the whole postal system was put directly under the control of the sovereign, though he had to consult the Postmaster-General with respect to its regulation.

The King of Hungary, therefore, was not merely endowed with legal power ; in the capacity of landed proprietor he had unlimited possession of a large part of the country. In pecuniary matters the Hungarian Parliament contributed but little to his resources. In the most important affairs of State, in questions of peace or war, in military matters, and in all the principal questions of finance, the King could act independently of Parliament without even committing any breach of the law.

Some of the chief spheres of parliamentary activity were, therefore, beyond the reach of Hungarian legislatures. They had not to vote sums for the payment either of the soldiers quartered in the country, or of the highest officials. In political respects, too, the Hungarian legislatures lacked the chief element of vitality and the great reason for existence of every parliamentary assembly, namely, the dependence of the executive on the power of the majority and its leaders. Just as in the old-fashioned legislatures, in Hungary also a considerable contrast necessarily developed between the actual power and the justifiable pretensions of the Parliaments. The opposition consisted not of one party, but of the whole assembly, no single individual of which felt any sense of responsibility. The Parliaments opposed everything since they could not renounce their pretensions, for it was by them alone that the traditions of a great past could still be united with the dreams of a better future.

[1] Cf. Report in Chamber Arch. No. 398 (May 12, 1784).

III.

Nothing favoured the increase of royal power all over Europe so much as the union of constitutionalism and absolutism in the same person, i.e. the fact that the sovereign in question often ruled over one land as a constitutional king, and over others as an absolute monarch. The fact that the first *Princeps*, Octavianus Augustus, was at the same time the absolute master of Egypt, was of importance even in the foundation of the Roman Empire. In a similar manner the medieval Emperors endeavoured to rule Germany by converting their Italian possessions into private domains—especially the Hohenstaufen, who sought to effect this with Sicily. Later on, the Habsburgs were only able to retain the German imperial crown because they had large family possessions quite independent of the Estates of the Empire. The rapid advance of the French kingship began with Philip Augustus, who conquered Normandy (1204), which became, not a feudatory province but the direct domain of the King and his family. It is superfluous to explain that the King of Spain got the upper hand of his once defiant Cortes, both in Castile and Arragon, by acquiring the gold mines of Peru and the revenues of Flanders.

We have already seen how large a part of Hungary itself was under the direct authority of the King. But, besides Hungary, the common rule of the Habsburgs extended over numerous other countries with diets and a national independent existence. Only, for a century after the disaster at Mohács (1526), the revenue and power derived from the sovereign's private domains were not enough to keep in check such important constitutional kingdoms as Hungary and Bohemia. In fact, early in the seventeenth century, the constitutional and religious parties in the various countries used the conflicts between the head of the ruling dynasty, King Rudolf, and his heir the Archduke Matthias, in order to gain a decisive victory. By the Treaty of Vienna (1606), the various countries belonging to the Habsburgs entered into a close connection with one another. They no longer formed a group of states subject to the monarch, but a union for the protection of their religious and constitutional privileges. A species of Protestant confederation consisting of the Parliamentary Estates of Hungary, Bohemia, Silesia and Austria, rendered it practically impossible for a Catholic prince to reign so long as it existed. But, at the same time, the Catholic Church rallied, and the Archduke Ferdinand headed a counter-movement in the Alpine districts.

By the conquest of Bohemia (1620–1) Ferdinand II, now the head of the imperial house, obtained the private domain necessary to strengthen his internal authority. This kingdom, confiscated for the benefit of the Catholicised and loyal magnates and of the clergy, henceforward constituted a trustworthy reserve. Ever since their decisive success in Bohemia the Viennese statesmen had considered it to be merely a question of time when they would be able to enforce upon Hungary the ideas which had annihilated independence elsewhere. Yet during the seventeenth century there arose a series of obstacles in the way of realising this project; first, the Thirty Years' War, then the important Turkish and French campaigns, and, above all, the indomitable patriotism of the Hungarian nobles, who recognised no difference between Catholic and Protestant when the existence of their country was at stake. But in the meantime the Hereditary Provinces were being constantly drawn together by a common religious, political and economic system, and no one of these Provinces made any further attempt to escape from the influence of Vienna after the failure of the conspiracy of Tattenbach in 1671. This union did injure important interests, but it was able to appeal to others of equal importance. Besides the common dynasty, the bonds that united the Empire were the common memories of great military campaigns, the common faith, the common language, and lastly the improvement in economic conditions under Maria Teresa. The Bohemian nobles, who alone could boast of separate traditions, were won over to the idea of the Habsburg "Empire[1]" by their faith and by their attachment to the Court.

[1] See note on opposite page.

This "Empire[1]," for the establishment of which the Habsburgs had laboured with such unflagging energy and such continued success, ever since the days of Ferdinand II, was not exclusively based on absolute kingship. The elements which permeated its very essence were on the one hand the aristocracy, on the other the Catholic faith. This aristocracy was not only one of birth but one of office; some of its members owed their rank to their high positions in the army or civil service. Bohemians or Germans predominated in its ranks, though it was recruited from every country in Catholic Europe. The only factor in opposition to the King was the system of Parliamentary Estates, and a conflict between their special interests and those of the monarch was necessarily doubtful in character and issue. With the supporters of the old parliamentary constitution in Hungary the Protestants, and every true son of the nation, fought shoulder to shoulder against the foundation of this united "Empire," which would make all the Habsburg dominions distinctly Catholic in tendency, and all the foreign nationalities distinctly German. In every walk of public life in Hungary the monarchy was preparing the way for those ideas and forces which had triumphed in the Hereditary Provinces. On the other hand, the interests assailed by the supporters and auxiliary forces of the monarch began to resist not merely their immediate enemies but absolutism itself. For (previous to Joseph's accession in 1780) the doctrine and the idea of a Habsburg "Empire" might be said to attack all social privileges, all religious interests, and all national feelings which conflicted with it in any way. What man in Hungary was not assailed in one or other of his cherished convictions, or did not belong to one or other of the groups and interests thus assailed?

Of the various aims of the Viennese politicians thus outlined, that of vanquishing Protestantism was the most successful in Hungary, for in this task they were aided by the majority

---

[1] The use of the word "Empire" here is not intended to denote the power of the Habsburgs, in their capacity as elected Holy Roman Emperors and titular rulers of Germany. It is employed in the modern and non-technical sense as expressing a coalition of different races and political entities under a uniform system and a single head.

dominant in Hungarian society.   But when the time for reaping
the fruits of victory was at hand, that victory was found to
involve merely the triumph of a few individuals, and not of a
whole system.   In the days of Frederick the Great, the tolerant
ruler of Prussia, it had become impossible to govern Austria or
Hungary solely on ecclesiastical or denominational lines.   None
the less the system—thus rendered impossible of final achievement—had been steadily pursued for a century and a half, and
had produced the result that no Protestant in Hungary could
or did expect much substantial benefit to come out of Vienna.

Much less complete than the Catholic victory over Protestantism in Hungary was the triumph of the King's authority
over the Estates in Parliament.   The *jus resistendi* (the famous
right of rebelling against the King with impunity) had been
abolished in 1687; the hereditary succession to the throne had
been assured in that year and in 1723; the ordinary taxes, the
recruits and military supplies, the charges for transport and
quarterage had been voted by Parliament.   During the closing
years of her reign Maria Teresa had found it possible—by an
evasion of the laws indeed—to rule for fifteen years without
calling a Parliament, to dispense with a Palatine, and to rule
through a lieutenant-governor; in no case had any resistance
been offered.   More than this, it had been possible to regulate
the financial obligations of the serfs against the wishes of the
nobles, to compel the prelates to pay taxes for the upkeep
of the frontier-fortresses, and to determine, and even to decrease,
the number of begging friars and of feast-days; it had even
been possible to alter the whole system of national education
with success and without any disturbance of importance.   None
the less, in the most essential points the older society had
managed to maintain its existence.   If their serfs did pay war-
taxes, the nobles were exempt from all burdens, for, as they put
it themselves, their " shoulders " were " virgin."   The comparative
ease with which the nobles and the clergy were induced to
consent to a diminution of their authority as against that
of the King, was due to the fact that in the age of Maria
Teresa the idea of a State was as yet indistinguishable from the
hierarchy and aristocracy.   The orders could show compliance to

an ally, and they did not consider the sovereign as their enemy. Further, though there was no Parliament nor Count Palatine, the county—i.e. the executive power—still remained the intact and undisputed domain of the old system of administration.

As regards the destruction of national feeling, scarcely any perceptible headway had been made. Not only members of Parliament and of the county assemblies, but those attached to the Royal Chancellery and to the *consilium locumtenentiale*—in fact all who were by birth Hungarians—never forgot their native country even when confronted with the royal power. Numerous laws had been successfully modified, but one fact remained at all times valid, namely, that Hungary—being an independent State —could not be governed in the same manner as the Hereditary Provinces of Austria. So strong was this feeling, nay even so omnipotent, that it was sooner or later bound to override any and all other considerations, and to destroy or to modify the influence of foreign institutions opposed to national tendencies. Thus, though the sovereign's Court had proved an excellent means of welding the various elements in the Habsburg "Empire" into one, we find that the Hungarian nobles attended it at Vienna only to further the interests of their own country and nation, despite all the enchantments of the Great Queen. What great things Maria Teresa expected from the Hungarian noble bodyguard! The latter did indeed serve to spread culture, but it made its character primarily Hungarian (see p. 18). An important political object in the organisation of the national education had been the spread of the German language. The organisation was preserved, but it served above all to further the development of the Hungarian language and literature. On this inspired soil patriotism was the prophet, and those profane people who met him were forced, in the image of the legend, to converse and prophesy in company with him.

This national feeling actually permeated both the Catholic Church, elsewhere so cosmopolitan in character, and the equally universal "caste" spirit of the nobility as well. All conquests won by the former were made not only for the faith but for the nation too ; and all that the latter succeeded in preserving was a national gain. Though much was done in the age of Maria

Teresa to encourage and prepare the way for a centralisation of the monarchy, it was very rarely that measures were taken which in any way injured Hungarian national feeling. Any act of the sovereign who had established a Hungarian bodyguard, founded the Order of St Stephen, built palaces at Buda and Pozsony, annexed the "Banat," Fiume, and the towns of Szepes to Hungary, abolished the independent Rascian administration, and declared and shown herself on all occasions to be a good Hungarian—any act of hers might have been condoned. No Hungarian could have protested against the impersonation of the unity of the "Empire" by such a figure. Hungary, which at the beginning of the century, with cries of *eb ura fakó* ("Hands off, Austria!"), had desired to break away from the King and to form an aristocratic republic like that of Poland, was now distinctly monarchical in feeling. She desired no Polish liberty, but looked to the sovereign for all good:

> "I would say—and you must comprehend me—
> If you would live a happier life,
> Pray zealously and speedily to the King of Heaven
> To send this world good sovereigns[1]."

So we can understand—however unfamiliar the tone may be to us—the desire of Révay, that the Empire of the double-headed eagle should spread far eastwards[2]; and we can comprehend the lines of John Gyöngyösi of Transylvania, who wrote:

> "May the eagle take under his wing what now is the Turk's[3]";

we find nothing strange in the fervent hymn of Baron Lawrence Orczi:

> "Now is the beginning of a golden age,
> Emperors have become the fathers of their dominions.
> Kings are the mates of good citizens,
> And great lords consort with poor peasants[4]";

---

[1] Baron Lawrence Orczi, *A szabadságról* (*On Liberty*), p. 9.
[2] Révay, *Elegies.*
[3] *Magyar Hirmondó*, 1784, p. 97. Sent from Zilah.
[4] This verse, as its contents prove, was written in 1774. "Jövendölés, ha nem hibás" (A Prophecy, unless mistaken), *Költeményes Holmi* (*Poetical Fly-leaves*), vol. II. p. 177.

and we understand the words written by Orczi in memory of Maria Teresa:

> "Thy power never over-rode the laws ;
> In thy days the rich did not oppress the poor :
> When justice fell heavily on a citizen,
> Thy grace did mitigate his punishment[1]."

IV.

Let us now see what were the instruments which the sovereign had to hand, when he wished to execute his commands.

The most important feature of the European state-organisation of the new era now opening, consisted in large bodies of officials. The kingship had, in quick succession, deprived the Estates of the conduct of military and financial matters, of jurisdiction, and of the whole sphere of internal government, and it endeavoured, with the whole weight of a uniform administration, to call forth the undivided energies of the countries under its rule. Hence it developed and created important institutions which, though the executive organs of its will, possessed independent traditions of their own and co-operated as separate factors in the work of organising the state. The Parliaments of Estates had either ceased to exist, or been reduced to mere formalities: the control over jurisdiction and military affairs— exercised by the Estates—was now unable to compete with that of the sovereign. The prelacy, the nobility and the members of the third Estate (the towns), formerly the rivals or opponents of the royal power, had become its ardent supporters, since it was now national in character. They looked forward to satisfying their personal ambitions in the sovereign's service, which they considered also as offering a suitable sphere in which to pursue their religious and national ambitions. Consequently it was only natural that these main motive-forces of the state-machinery should still betray traces of their origin in many points. They served the King—not *ad personam*, but as the representa-

---

[1] "Más ugyanezen Felség emlekezetére" (Another poem in commemoration of the same Sovereign), *Költeményes Holmi*, vol. II. p. 237.

tive of the state-principle. As corporations endowed with special rights, even though they could not resist the will of the head of the State, they at any rate felt entitled to warn the sovereign not to trespass against divine or human law, nor to jeopardise the interests of the country. In brief, the overwhelming power of the Estates was a thing of the past, and the new system of representation was not as yet able to control the actions of the governing power. The counterpoise, without which no civilized government can exist, was furnished by the instruments of the Crown itself—by those large corporations (*dicasteria*) to which the Crown had delegated the work of government. In the history of the world the French Parlement may rank as the most famous corporation of this kind ; its officials were erected into a separate social class (the *noblesse de la robe*), by the privileges and immunities which they acquired, by the judicial courts which they established, and by the services which they thereby rendered to the King. The astonishing development in France of both King and Parlement is due to the fact that jurisdiction was the cornerstone in the edifice of that monarchy. Another remarkable corporation of the same type, which helped to build up a monarchy, was the Spanish Inquisition, which was the expression of the common religious sentiments of both King and nation. A third may be found in the Dutch Republic—a country eminently commercial and financial in character—where the Grand Pensionaries exercised powers which were, in many cases, superior even to those of the Stadtholder.

In Hungary the boards or departments of government, which were the counterpart of these corporations, mostly owed their development to the age of Charles III (1711–40). The country had to be reorganised after the expulsion of the Turks, but the laws provided that the new institutions—while modern in essence—should be in form, at any rate, a continuation from older conditions. Older institutions—which served a similar purpose—were used as the models for the new ones—for the Chancellery, for the Chamber, for the *Curia* (the Supreme Court of Justice), and even for the *consilium locumtenentiale*. As compared with the older organisations the importance of the new ones increased in proportion as the authority of the new absolute and centralised monarchy exceeded that of the old medieval kingship. The power of the first was based on continuity and on the results of a national evolution, whereas the power of the King in the Middle Ages had always practically been incidental and personal[1].

It is important to note that all these institutions were alike royal and Hungarian, and it was an essential part of the constitution of the country that they should all be maintained. The fact that they were at once the instruments of the royal power and the pillars of the constitutional system may be explained as follows :—the crowned King had indeed the power of executing the laws, but it had been a natural result of the system that this power should be exercised through the nobles, who were the members of the " Sacred Crown," and who therefore constituted the large *dicasteria*. As the personal influence of the monarch on the affairs of the country was as yet far more extensive than the activity shown by the other authorities in the State, who were more particularly concerned with questions of detail, the most important of these great corporations was naturally the King's Chancellery.

The Royal Court Chancellery (*expeditio*, i.e. " despatch office ") was the direct organ of communication between the person of the sovereign and the country, as its very name shows. It issued all letters patent dealing with privileges or pardons, of which the conferring or granting was an exclusive prerogative of the King; it despatched all rescripts which gave instructions to public authorities in political or jurisdictional matters. It was at all times in direct attendance on the sovereign, and its office was generally located at Vienna, though during the sessions of Parliament it moved to Pozsony. The King governed directly through his Chancellery only, indirectly through all other institutions. It was presided over by a Chancellor—since 1766 Count Francis Eszterházy had filled the office, while Count Charles Pálffy was deputy Chancellor. Of the councillors

---

[1] In this sketch of the state of Hungary in 1780 it is my object to portray the older Hungary as still existing in the institutions which Joseph II afterwards endeavoured to overthrow; it is not therefore necessary to treat in detail of those institutions which he left intact as being the instruments of the royal power.

attached to the Chancellery, .three were magnates, the rest (eleven altogether in 1780) had been chosen from the gentry. According to the King's instructions the duty of this office was "to thwart any attempt to impair the royal power and dignity, and rather to provide for the safeguarding of all the rights, privileges, prerogatives and exclusive powers of the King, to execute the royal commands and to maintain the laws and whole system of the country." Here we get an insight into the whole spirit of the Chancellery, which, as a *collegium* or corporation, was merely the King's "despatch office." According to the instructions issued to it, it had to summon a full session when treating of any matters relating to the royal dignity, and, where necessary, to submit special reports for the King's own decision. All proposals were drafted by the Chancellery, but, whatever the opinion it might offer (and, so long as Count Francis Eszterházy was Chancellor, these opinions were always Hungarian in spirit), there stood this saving clause at the end of every one of them: "*salvo caeteroquin altissimo arbitrio et suprema dispositione Caesareo-Regia.*" Hence the ultimate decision was always left to the discretion of the sovereign. On the other hand, it was at all times the duty of the Chancellery to explain the legal aspect of every royal rescript, to state if the royal command was at variance with the existing law, to quote the articles which were infringed, and to point to the evil consequences that might ensue from such infringement. Hence it was not merely a "despatch office," but a council as well—in fact the only Hungarian council that was directly attached to the King's person. In short, the Chancellery was a kind of irresponsible ministry, only it possessed a much more extensive scope of activity than, for instance, that of the modern Hungarian Minister in attendance on the sovereign.

The King had a very large personal *clientèle* in Hungary, and, consequently, the authority and influence of the Chancellor and the councillors in the Chancellery extended all over the country. In general, the affairs relating to letters patent and personal matters were allotted to the first department of the Chancellery. The second issued instructions to the authorities to execute royal decrees and laws, which naturally extended to all factors of political life. It was through the medium of the Chancellery that the government of the whole country—the *consilium locumtenentiale*—came into direct connection with the King. On the other hand, it was the Hungarian Chancellery which was the medium of intercourse between the Hungarian authorities and those of Vienna (in particular the council of war), the Imperial and Royal Chambers, the Imperial and Royal State-Chancelleries, and the Chancellery of the Bohemian and Austrian Provinces. Through the medium of the State Chancellery it arranged for the establishment of a kind of consular service in foreign countries.

As the royal power was now engaged in re-organising the government of the country, the Chancellery had—in addition to its previous duties—the special task of supervising the practical execution of those decrees which furthered good government. Wherever it noticed any defect in this respect it at once reported the case to the sovereign, accompanying it with proposals for remedying the evil. "Our service for the advancement of public welfare shall be furthered without regard for any other considerations."

The Chancellery was still, in some respects, the supreme court of appeal in all matters of government. It did not simply submit the reports of the *consilium locumtenentiale* or the *Curia* on current affairs, or on the settlement of complaints, to the royal decision without comment ; it discussed the reports fully and freely, then it forwarded them—together with its own opinion on the matter—to the sovereign for his final decision.

In all cases in which the opinion of the council of war, or the Chamber, or any other of the chief authorities of Vienna seemed necessary, the Chancellery not merely corresponded with the body in question but held a deliberation with it in common council. The minutes of such conferences were then submitted to the sovereign, who decided the points at issue, by royal resolution.

The third department of the Chancellery was responsible for issuing royal decrees and resolutions regulating the administration of justice. This department also kept the national archives, and, being responsible for the issue of patents of nobility, letters of appointment, deeds of grant, etc., had a tax-office attached to it. Its sphere of authority was thus an extensive one, and embraced the whole life of the country. None the less, here as elsewhere, all this procedure displays, not the power of the Chancellery, but the extent of the personal authority of the King. In all matters, even of the most insignificant character, it was the sovereign alone who decided, and the Chancellery, after offering its humble advice, relapsed again into the character of a "despatch office." The influence of the Chancellery on the destinies of the nation depended not so much on its own procedure as on the decision of the sovereign to rule according to the accepted system, or to go his own way. The French King had at length acquired complete control, and the power of forcing his Parlement to pass all his decrees into law; in the same way the power and glory enjoyed by the Hungarian Chancellery became merely a reflection of the light of the royal sun. The social importance of the Chancellery officials formed a glaring contrast to the minimum of actual power which they enjoyed, though every Court councillor was practically a participant in the supreme power. The explanation of this apparent contradiction is that, during the reign of Maria Teresa, personal questions often received the precedence over political ones, as is general under aristocratic rule. The Chancellery had not power to compel the sovereign to summon Parliament, to annex the *partium* to Hungary or to reside in the country[1]. Its efforts in this direction were kept a secret. But no bishop, no *föispán*, no member of the *consilium locumtenentiale*, no *septemvir*[2], was appointed, except on the nomination of the Chancellery. The sovereign could have no personal knowledge of the respective candidates, and hence a very wide field lay open for the exercise of favouritism, whether avowed or un-

---

[1] When the Turks conquered Buda in 1541, the eastern counties came under the rule of the princes of Transylvania (*Partes Regni Hungariae*). After the expulsion of the Turks (1718) many resolutions of Parliament decreed the annexation of these counties; but the Court always hindered it. The annexation was not carried into effect in 1848. The counties of Zaránd, Kraszna and Middle Szolnok and the District of Kövár were the last remainders of the *partium* (v. map).

[2] *Septemvir*. The supreme court of appeal had at first seven judges. The name remained till 1869, though the number of the judges was then much greater.

conscious; and as a result the Chancellor and the "referendaries" of the respective departments were the most powerful patrons in the country.

The fact that the constitutional and patriotic activity of the Chancellery was shrouded in obscurity, and that any success attending its efforts was attributed to the sovereign, whereas the personal activity of its members and their intercourse with the other principal authorities of Vienna was familiar to everybody—all this is in itself sufficient to account for its unpopularity. In it we see a relic of the age in which an unlimited royal power was the sole factor directing the fortunes of the country, relegating its councillors to the position of servants. None the less, the whole course of Joseph II's rule will show that those men, to whom the defence of Hungarian interests in Vienna was entrusted, were eminently fitted for the task. Even in times of extreme gravity they were able to reconcile their love of their country with the service of the sovereign. They were worthy representatives of Hungarian society, permeated as it was with aristocratic and Catholic ideas. A very strict judge— Joseph II himself—emphasised the fact that the staff of this government office consisted of select men. We have already mentioned the names of the Chancellors. Among the councillors in office at the accession of Joseph II we find Joseph Ürményi, the organiser of education in Hungary, Joseph Izdenczy, a severe critic of the Hungarian constitution, Brunsvick, the chief collaborator in the work of drawing up the regulations relating to socage, and Count Francis Györy, whose name we have often had occasion to mention. Many important Hungarian families owe their prosperity and prominence to the work done by these Court councillors and to the royal recognition accorded to them. A glance at the list of these names, and an investigation of their zealous and successful activity, will convince us that despite all the disagreeable recollections it awakes, this system of government by corporations, though it restricted the chances of attaining eminence, none the less gave an opportunity for the labours and aspirations of some eminent Hungarians of undying merit.

After the Chancellery, the second chief national authority

was the *consilium regium locumtenentiale.* Its very name shows
that its origin and whole organisation was due to the absence of
the sovereign from the country. It could scarcely be called the
King's Council, for any Hungarian affairs that came directly
before the monarch were submitted to him by the Chancellery.
This *consilium* hardly represented the King's person and authority; it rather replaced the former power and jurisdiction of
the Count Palatine. Since 1549, discussion in council had been
substituted for the personal influence of the latter. Acts CI and
CII of 1723 reformed this *consilium* and very precisely prescribed
the limits of its authority. It was not dependent on any Court
authorities, but only on the sovereign. It submitted its reports
direct to the King, who informed it of his will by rescript or
decree, according to the nature of the subject[1]. When he
thought it necessary the sovereign could receive the reports
of its members in person[2]. Its independence of all other
authorities was vindicated by the law which declared that it
was in no direct connection with the Government boards of
the Hereditary Provinces, with which its sole intercourse was
through the sovereign. On the other hand, "contra positivas
Patriae Leges nihil determinet," and it was its duty to provide
for the execution of the resolutions of the Parliaments. In its
debates a majority decided, and a resolution once arrived
at could not be altered by any one. The wisdom and statesmanship shown by the Estates (of which this council was
really a committee) is seen by the fact that they selected as
the most important of their special tasks the repopulation of the
deserted parts of the country, in so far as it did not interfere
with the interests of cattle-breeding. According to the instructions issued by King Charles, its task—as a subordinate
instrument of royal power—was to supervise all political,
economic and military questions of importance in Hungary,
and to support all measures for the furtherance of the King's

---

[1] According to Chanc. Arch. No. 14,667 (1785) the difference between *rescript*
and *decree* was that the former was an ordinance issued on the basis of the existing
laws in explanation of the same, whereas the latter was merely a writ for the carrying
into effect of certain measures. The English counterpart is the difference between a
royal proclamation and an order in council.

[2] This very rarely happened—except when the King was in Pozsony.

service, the administration, the welfare and prosperity of the whole country, and the maintenance and subsistence of the inhabitants and tax-payers[1].

According to Baron Joseph Eötvös, the great political philosopher of new Hungary, the distinguishing feature of the modern State is that it provides for the welfare of the citizens as individuals, and does not confine its activity exclusively to the common tasks of government[2]. So far as we know, the above instructions are the first trace in Hungarian history of the State having become conscious of its duties in this direction.

Notwithstanding the fact that the *consilium* was entrusted with one of the tasks of a modern State, its composition, defined according to law, rendered it quite as faithful an expression of the privileged society of Hungary as was the Chancellery. At its head stood the Count Palatine, in whose absence the Lord Chief Justice presided, while the twenty-two councillors were appointed by the King from among the prelates, magnates and gentry. When a vacancy occurred in the council, the body itself recommended one person for appointment, though it also submitted the petitions of other candidates. In addition to the ordinary councillors, the permission of the sovereign might be obtained for young magnates and nobles to be present at the deliberations, that they might thus acquire experience in public affairs. The members were paid out of the royal revenues. In a speech at the inauguration of the *consilium locumtenentiale*, Philip Louis Sinzendorf, Chancellor-in-chief of the Imperial Court, thus described the significance of the council in its relation to the Estates of Hungary: "It shall provide for the maintenance of the authority of the Church, for the privileges of the magnates, for the rights of the gentry, for the commercial prosperity of the *bourgeoisie*, and for the undisturbed cultivation of his land by the peasant[3]." The country as a whole was still regarded as the aggregate of all the orders.

---

[1] The instructions were modelled on those of the *Statthalterei* in Bohemia.
[2] *A XIX század uralkodó eszméinek befolyása az államra* (*Influence of the prevailing ideas of the XIX century on the State*), vol. II. German edn. Leipzig, 1854.
[3] Bél, *Notit. Hung. nov.* vol. I. p. 432.

The *consilium locumtenentiale* did not belie its intimate connection with the ruling classes of society. In the questions that chiefly interested the age of Maria Teresa—religion and socage—the council has been reproached for allowing the interests of the hierarchy and the aristocracy to take precedence of national ones. We may give as an instance of this the fact that the *consilium* scarcely issued a single passport to non-Catholic youths who wished to continue their studies abroad, so long as the Primate Francis Barkóczi was at the head of the religious department[1].

As the activity of this council extended to so many fields, it was divided into several departments or commissions. The first was concerned with ecclesiastical affairs; its "referendaries" were always priests. The second was the commission on education; the third that on taxes and the maintenance of the army; the fourth dealt with economic and commercial questions[2]; the fifth with questions of a mixed character, and with all other questions not comprised under the foregoing heads.

In order to serve the public interests in every direction, this board of government exercised the chief control over the magistracies of the counties and of the royal free boroughs. "But, should any county or town delay or refuse to execute any measures, or fail to send in the necessary information required of them, the council shall bring such facts to Our notice, together with its resolution and its opinion for a suitable remedy in the matter."

This one point shows the weak side of the whole system of the *consilium locumtenentiale*. Though it was partly an organ of the Parliament, the several municipal authorities could oppose their constitutional rights to it, since it was also the instrument of the arbitrary power of the King. On its own initiative the council could take no steps against the said authorities, for the personal rule of the monarch was really the final guarantee of the maintenance of this system. The *consilium* itself merely wrote reports and made proposals: the execution of measures

---

[1] *Intoleranz, loc. cit.* pp. 150, 151.
[2] In these the toleration of Jews was also included.

was not its business, and it was in a dependent position both with regard to its superior and to its subordinates. The bishops and the county assemblies would not carry into effect the King's orders as communicated by the *consilium*, unless they agreed with the interests or the desires of their respective classes. The King did not entertain its proposals, unless he considered that they enhanced his personal authority and rule; and hence its recommendations had least influence just in those questions which aimed at the advancement of the whole country, and most in the furtherance of the interests of individuals or classes.

As the King's power was much more in evidence than that of Parliament, the *consilium locumtenentiale* became above all the instrument of the former. It was paid by the King, not by the country; it received orders from the monarch, and merely reports and requests from the national authorities. Consequently, Parliament very soon became conscious of the fact that the new institution regarded as its principal task the consolidation not of the constitution, but of royal prerogatives. The Parliament of 1741 very seriously thought of dissolving the council, and only refrained from doing so because it was unable to replace it by anything better[1]. Ever since the office of Count Palatine had become vacant and Albrecht, Prince of Saxe-Teschen— Maria Teresa's son-in-law—had been the head of the council, it had come more and more to resemble the German boards of government, which were directed solely by the sovereign, not by the Parliament. However, the system of government of Charles III and Maria Teresa was particularly favourable to the interests of the aristocracy and of the hierarchy. As a consequence, the whole spirit of the *consilium locumtenentiale* was imbued with a loyal and yet, at the same time, with a con-servative feeling. Though it could boast of eminent members, and though many councillors of the Chancellery were recruited from among its numbers, it sat at Pozsony, and thus its members had no chance of being influenced either by sound Hungarian national feeling or by the cosmopolitan culture of Vienna. The oft-repeated desire of Parliament, that the

---

[1] *Mus. Jank. Coll.* vol. XII. p. 9.

consilium locumtenentiale should be transferred to the centre of the country, struck at the root of one of the chief defects in the whole system of government[1].

It was to its closer connection with the country that the greater popularity of the third principal corporate body, the *royal Curia*, was chiefly due.

In the spirit of the Hungarian constitution, the King exercised his supreme executive power in the field of jurisdiction also through the Estates of the realm. With the conduct of the supreme control the Chancellery and the *consilium locumtenentiale* were entrusted; but the *Curia Regis*, the supreme court of justice, carried out the actual executive work[2].

Like the other organs of central government, this one too was an outgrowth of the personal prerogative of the King, and was as old as the kingship itself. In the earliest period, the Count Palatine, the Lord Chief Justice, and even the Primate, acted as the supreme judges of the kingdom. During the reigns of Matthias and Vladislav (Ulászló), the *octavalis*[3] court of justice was established, with masters of the court in ordinary, and recruited from among the magnates and gentry. The Ban, the treasurer, and the waywode of Transylvania also exercised jurisdictional powers of their own.

Out of this body the Parliament of 1723 evolved that form of the supreme national court of justice which it kept practically unchanged until 1848. The bench of *septemviri*, sitting under the presidency of the Count Palatine, received an addition of eight new members—two prelates, two magnates, and four from

---

[1] Cf. Acts XCVII of 1723 and III of 1764-65. The tone of both of these is very characteristic of the helplessness of the Hungarian legislature. The general drift of the first is, as soon as possible, the *consilium locumtenentiale* shall be transferred to the centre of the country, but for the time being it is to remain at Pozsony. The second runs as follows, *verbatim*: "the full legal activity of the royal *consilium locumtenentiale* being maintained, the Estates of the realm very humbly beg to hope that her Majesty, by carrying into effect the provisions of Act XCVII of 1723 concerning the transfer of the said council to the centre of the country, will graciously deign to offer them due consolation."

[2] Ürményi, *Jus Publ.* III. 7 cap.: "De jure summae potestatis executivo ac speciatim de Curia Regia."

[3] This court was so called because its terms were fixed for a sennight (octava) after a given feast-day.

the ranks of the gentry—chosen from all parts of the country. The presence of not less than eleven members of this bench was required in order that a decision might be valid. It sat at certain specified times. Act XXIV of 1741 added four to the number of members—one prelate, one magnate, and two members of the gentry[1]. This was the supreme appellate tribunal in the kingdom of St Stephen. The "King's Bench" (*Tabula Regia*) likewise sat permanently, except on the ordinary legal holidays. This was the supreme court of the nobility; to it were referred all cases dealing with grants of land and all criminal cases concerning nobles; it was constituted, like the bench of *septemviri*, according to orders. Its president was the King's *personalis*: it had seventeen members—two prelates, two barons of the Court, the *magistri* of the Count Palatine and the Lord Chief Justice, two prothonotaries of the same and two of the *personalis*, four assessors appointed by the King and two appointed by the Archbishops of the kingdom. The *director causarum regalium* also took part in its sittings, but he had no vote, and left whenever any affairs of the *fiscus* came under discussion. The King's Bench, as such, took part in the Parliaments; its *personalis* (who by Act V of 1764 had always to be a member of the order of gentry) presided over the Lower House (or Table); its prothonotaries drafted the bills; its young students were the most numerous among the youths who served Parliament in subordinate positions[2]. This custom of the King's Bench sitting in Parliament was a relic of the days of the Grand Assizes held by the King.

Nothing can give us a clearer conception of the peculiar character of these important courts of justice (which consists in their intimate connection with the class-system of the country)

[1] Consequently, besides the Count Palatine, the members of the bench of the *septemviri* consisted of six prelates, seven magnates and six members of the gentry.

[2] The representatives of the counties at the Parliament were accompanied by young men who acted as their clerks, and attended the sittings of Parliament as possible future members. Some of the young men—who thus attended Parliament— were young lawyers practising in the King's Bench. These young men gave the *personalis* much trouble, on account of their indomitable patriotic zeal. They were admitted to the sessions of Parliament and were practically the only source from which knowledge of its proceedings could transpire.

than the way in which their terms and vacations were arranged. From St Thomas' Day to the Sunday after Epiphany there was a Christmas vacation ; again, the courts were closed between the end of the Carnival until the first Sunday in Lent. During Passion Week and until the Second Sunday after Easter there was vacation ("that, namely, the prelates may be able to take part in the functions of Passion Week, and that the other judges too may be able to attend divine service"). From Whit Sunday until Trinity Sunday there was again vacation. These vacations point to the participation of the ecclesiastical order in this exercise of judicial authority. Hence the administration of justice, though already in the hands of the State, did not completely monopolise the attention of those members of the ruling classes who passed sentence in the King's name. A proof that the nobles engaged in this judicial work were of the landed class, is furnished by the fixing of "harvesting" and "vintage" vacations[1]. It was also a natural result of the judicial duties of the nobility that the courts should be shut for thirty days before the opening of Parliament, and should remain closed until the deputies dispersed.

The administration of justice did not therefore entirely monopolise the time of those engaged in it, and the arrangement was really a sort of transition-stage between the older patriarchal method of justice and the modern system where the judges are experts. It was because of this fact that the fixed salaries of the justices were also patriarchal (i.e. very trifling) in amount, and that there was a rapid growth in all the abuses characteristic of judicial corporations of this type. Thus, it was not considered by any means improper, in any particular case, to supply information to the judges and to accompany it with *douceurs*[2].

[1] The "harvesting" vacation lasted from June 27 (St Ladislas' Day) to August 20 (St Stephen's Day); the "vintage" vacation lasted more than a month and a half, from Michaelmas to Martinmas. The four terms, when the courts sat, were in consequence St Martin's, Epiphany, Easter, and St Stephen's.

[2] Townson, *Travels* (of the district court of Debreczen), p. 240: "Its members have the vile practice of receiving incidents. Are these bribes?—the reader will ask. God forbid ! They are only *douceurs* to engage the judges to examine more strictly into the nature of a cause." Cf. *Manch-Hermaeon*, p. 122: "Informationen, das heisst Belehrung der Richter vor dem gefällten Urtheil, mit Dukaten-Rollen in der Hand."

Such corruption was not unprecedented in more western countries, as is proved by the case of Beaumarchais in the French Parlement and of the great Francis Bacon in the English Chancery. In describing the organisation of the lawcourts of Hungary, Fessler quotes the words of Aeneas:

"Infandum, regina, iubes renovare dolorem[1]."

However, bribery never became absolutely universal; and the integrity of the judicial bench as such was beyond impeachment. Even Joseph II never went so far as to accuse the whole bench. The chief danger involved by the judicial system was that cases were protracted for so long, and that the employment of the methods of *oppositio* and *repulsio* (which every noble could claim on the payment of a trifling forfeit) might protract a suit *ad infinitum*[2].

The Parliament of 1723, which centralised the administration of justice, also established district courts (benches) in the four districts of the country. In Croatia also there was a district court of this kind, where the "Ban's Bench" was established. Such institutions were meant to replace the older circuit courts, for assizes were now to be held in settled centres.

During the eighteenth century the Hungarian laws remained the same as before. They satisfied the claims of a medieval society, and were adopted as their own by the nobility and clergy, who looked upon Verböczi as the main pillar of Magyardom: Verböczi was the authority to be used by judges in passing sentence in the county courts and the King's Bench, and his explanations and commentaries on the law were quoted in the inns of court. In other countries in this age theology

---

[1] Fessler, *loc. cit.* vol. x. p. 251.

[2] It was a natural result of an aristocratic constitution that the alienation of property—in particular of landed property—should be rendered as difficult as possible, if necessary by force (i.e. *repulsio*). This result is perhaps pardonable on political grounds. As for the *oppositio*, the *Manch-Hermaeon* (pp. 123, 124) relates the following case, which has since found its way into most of our historical works: "After a suit lasting 30 years, *A* wins a property valued at 100,000 florins, which is in the hands of *B*. The latter however resists the execution of the sentence and begins a so-called *oppositio*. If he has a good advocate and money, he can protract the case for years. If he loses it, he has only to pay a fine of 200 florins; while during the whole time *A* is deprived of the revenues of the property, which *B* enjoys without having any right to them."

was the most essential part of the culture that was common to all : in Hungary it was replaced by legal studies. No German or foreigner, uninitiated in this peculiar knowledge could be appointed to judge in Hungarian courts[1]. The laws themselves remained for a long time untouched by any external influence : there were indeed a large number of complaints, but all that Maria Teresa could do was to arrange for a collection of the judgments and decisions of the *Curia* (1769). Yet, owing to the very nature of the administration of justice, this organ of the central government was farthest removed from the sovereign's influence. Of all state institutions, that of jurisdiction is the one in which the body originally invested with power can maintain its ground best without provoking general attack, and its power of resistance is all the greater because it is almost imperceptible. In the *Curia* the authority of the most eminent of the magnates— spiritual and temporal—remained the deciding factor, and they not only sat in judgment themselves, but were responsible for the appointment of other justices. In the sphere of the judiciary, therefore, the nobles were the predominating element, and the sovereign scarcely seemed to exercise any effective control. Pest was the seat of the supreme court of justice ; and, though its inhabitants were largely German, its municipal importance was too small to influence the members of the High Court who resided there. The numerous *personnel* of the *Curia*, the young nobles studying and practising law within its precincts, the parties in the different cases, who flocked up to Pest from every part of Hungary—all these people did much to maintain the cause of Magyardom in this thoroughly German town. Many exceptions were taken to the proceedings of the *Curia*, but all its cases concerned the interests of the nobility, and those of other classes do not seem to have been injured.

In the lesser judicial courts, whether courts of the manor or of the county, the sovereign had absolutely no influence at all. These petty courts had the *jus gladii*, i.e. decided on questions of life and death, without the knowledge of the higher judicial authorities. It was not until the year 1758

---

[1] Maria Teresa, in her instructions to her youngest son, Maximilian, called Hungarian law "a not very interesting topic for study."

that the Chancellery issued an order that no trials for witch-craft should in future be begun without due notice being given[1]; nor was it until March 30, 1778, that the Chancellery decreed that there should be an appeal to the sovereign against certain kinds of capital sentences. Such appeals were some-what limited, being confined to those cases where the original courts had scruples or doubts as to the wisdom of the sentences passed[2].

It is not possible to deal in this place with the whole complex structure of judicial administration in Hungary: we must confine ourselves to establishing our contention that the Hungarian nobles still possessed almost the full measure of their old authority and influence in the law courts. The judicial system was the one institution in the State possessed of a peculiar character of its own, for it had the appearance of a caste-system. Against such a system many well-founded objections could be brought, but its national character—as revealed even in its very abuses—was enough to make it popular in the eyes of Hungarian society.

The organ of central government then which had the most national character was the *Curia*, the one of the most alien character was the Chamber (*Kamara*). By its name alone (a slender enough link of intimacy) was it connected with Hungarian society. At its head, indeed, were magnates (such men as Count Antal Grassalkovics, Count Paul Festetics and Count Francis Balassa); its councillors included seven magnates and eighteen of the gentry, but its whole spirit was German. This was not due to the fact that Hungarians showed any particular abhorrence of figures and of the economic system. The men whose names have already been mentioned, like Joseph Majláth and Ignatius Almási, together with others, were fitted to be at the head of the "Chamber" of any country. But the *Kamara* was the one institution that required a large number of subordinate officials. Such posts were detested by the Hungarian nobles, and not accepted by them if they could make a living elsewhere, which was not a difficult matter. Non-nobles found it no easy task even to acquire the education required of candidates. Of the

[1] Fessler, *loc. cit.* p. 271.
[2] Reviczky, *Status Regni Hungariae.*

noble councillors in office in 1756, only six were Hungarians[1]. Of the subordinate officials employed in the custom-houses (*harminczad*) and salt-depôts at the same time, barely one-tenth were Hungarians. The procedure of the *Kamara* scarcely permitted any question of independence or independent traditions, for everything was modelled on similar institutions in the Hereditary Provinces. The *Kamara* was therefore a direct instrument in the hands of the monarch; it had no spirit of its own, and possessed a staff consisting of paid officials, not of patriots.

This class of paid officials was the one most despised in Hungary: and this result was not due solely to the nature of their occupation, which naturally brought them most into conflict with the interests of the inhabitants of the country. Our oft-quoted Swiss traveller writes of them as follows: " Though eminent men are at the head of the several authorities (in Vienna) the general character of the imperial officials is proportionately the more contemptible. As a rule, there is not a spark of patriotism in them; they know nothing, are disagreeable and not even hard-working. For them the main point is the salary and the title: the work is a minor matter. Do not think I am exaggerating. Upon my word—taking them all in all—what I say is literally true. The native Hungarians, engaged in the administration of their country, possess a much sounder common sense, more friendliness and more zeal for their work, than the Austrians. Yet the latter are given the preference, as well as an opportunity of displaying their arrogance[2]." This was written in 1782—not later.

This institution of the *Kamara* therefore—a ready-made instrument of absolutism—not only did not fulfil its duties, but actually made the whole governmental system an object of hatred. The bad treatment which people experienced at its hands, robbed the system of the sympathy even of those who would otherwise have welcomed a transformation of the Hungarian administration. In the case of all the other authorities (*Curia*,

[1] Baron Paul Jászy, Adam Rajcsányi, Francis Török, Antal Grabovszky, Stephen Kruspér and Ignatius Végh.

[2] *Reisen eines Franzosen*, vol. I. pp. 451, 452.

consilium, Chancellery) the "caste" spirit and interests predominated. No attempts to counterbalance the latter could expect to
meet with success unless they supported the cause of the injured
classes. But the only possible field for such attempts lay in the
county assemblies, whose whole organisation precluded the influence of any superior power. Though the sovereign appointed
all the officials of the various boards of government from the
Chancellor to the *registrator* (registrar) and the salt *régie* officers,
he had no legal influence on the *alispán* and county magistrates
(*szolgabiró*), who were the "oracles" of whole large districts. It is
true that it had been a long-established principle of the Court to
use social influences to gain over these heads of the autonomous
administration, and that grants (*donationes*), the title of King's
Counsel, and the distribution of orders, had all served to
create a Court party. Yet this method was not only dubious in
value and, in many cases, unsuccessful, but it implied a tacit
recognition of the social independence and importance of the
men thus distinguished. If then a radical change were desired, it
could be brought about only by influencing the judicial and
administrative system in the counties. The King indeed had his
own officials even in the counties ; he nominated the high sheriffs
(*föispán*), the heads of the counties; and had not the older *comes*
been merely a royal official ? The high sheriff was the only
official who could be used to compel the counties not to throw
obstacles in the way of the uniform system of government.

This was the object of the instructions to high sheriffs
which were elaborated by the Chancellery in 1768[1]. Their first
business was to be the preservation of the Catholic faith and the
advancement of the educational system. They were to compel
the counties to prepare annual returns of the numbers and
religion of the inhabitants, of the teachers and so forth. They
were not to permit any county official to be under obligations
to any landed proprietor or royal free borough. They were
to preserve the county archives, to supervise the condition
of prisoners in the county gaol, to undertake the care of the
orphans of the county, and to keep the roads in repair. Their

---

[1] Chanc. Arch. for 1783. These instructions were based on those of April 8, 1752.

principal endeavour should be to provide for the carrying into effect of all royal decrees, by virtue of a resolution either of the *consilium locumtenentiale* or of the county assembly. Further, they were to accelerate the proceedings of the courts of law.

To attain all these objects, it was imperative that they should reside permanently in their counties, or at any rate that they should not absent themselves from the county assemblies, even if they had other occupations.

Here we have in outline the first principles of good administration. Not more perfect were the instructions given by Colbert to his intendants, who worked in all parts of the country as the instruments of the central power, and were responsible for building up the whole system of French administration. In France the intendants were either of *bourgeois* extraction or were impoverished nobles, and their very existence depended on the favour of the Minister or the King. On the other hand, in Hungary the *föispán* was as a rule the largest landowner in the county, and the office was hereditary in the most important families. In other counties, again, the office was an appendage of the bishoprics. In Vienna the *föispán* lived at Court, in the country in his own castle. Even when he had any enthusiasm for public affairs, or condescended to take an interest in county matters, his activity made no perceptible impression except where his instructions conformed to his own personal convictions or to the tendencies of his class. We have already had occasion to point out that, when instructed to do so, these officials did make energetic and effectual use of their influence against the Protestants. But, in executing the commands of the *consilium locumtenentiale*, or rather of the personal rule of the sovereign, the first men in the counties were degrading themselves to the status of officials. They would probably have put forth all their energies in defence of the constitution ; and, if the King had sanctioned or urged any attempt to overthrow it, the most that could have been expected of them was that they should throw no obstacles in the way of such endeavours.

Yet according to the constitution, the high sheriff was the only medium of intercourse between the county and the supreme power of the sovereign.

Of the boards of government and authorities in Hungary suitable to serve as instruments of absolutism, those which had any influence at all were established upon national traditions and on the basis of " caste." The whole spirit of the Chancellery and the *consilium locumtenentiale* was against their voluntary abettance of any attacks on the Hungarian Parliament and nation. The power of the high sheriffs, in so far as it existed at all, was on the side of Parliament, not of the King. The spirit of the principal courts of justice in the land was also that of a " class " ; the *Kamara* was the only one of all these institutions which did not possess a will and objects of its own.

Consequently the Parliament was not the chief opponent to be reckoned with by a sovereign bent on overthrowing the independence of Hungarian political life. Moreover, the boards of government—the instruments of his own power—would stand in his way, by passive resistance if not by other means. Yet, even if the sovereign carried the Chancellery and the *locumtenentiale* council with him, they had no influence on the people. Any King desirous of affecting the whole structure, of attacking the very foundations of this separate national and constitutional life, had above all to overthrow two deeply-rooted and far-reaching institutions—the organisation of the judiciary and of the county.

V.

In the continuous struggle of conflicting interests the centre of gravity was the *diploma inaugurale*, that fundamental law of the country by virtue of which, according to the constitution, the King began his reign.

In the case of State contracts of extreme importance, which turn the scale in favour of either of two elements in a constitution, it is only natural to think of material power as the cause. Similarly in the case of treaties of peace, which regulate the relative strength of various States, there can be no doubt that neither party to them will be ready to renounce any of its former rights, unless threatened by imminent danger. It is indeed impossible to refute the oft-repeated argument, that the laws of

1687 and 1723 (which established the right of succession) are to be explained by the apprehension of the Parliaments. Only this apprehension was not due to the violence of the moment but to a wise foresight. It was hoped to avert a greater sacrifice at the price of a less important one, and it is just those who most fervently desire the preservation intact of contracts putting the monarch under obligation to his people, who have no right to attack the validity of concessions dictated by a foresight of this kind. When a nation yields its King a more extensive sphere of authority, it does so often enough by instinct, to avoid external dangers, and without any pressure being brought to bear on it. It will suffice to refer to the decision of the Parliament of 1526 (which gave the King a practical dictatorship), of which surely no one will assert that it was forcibly wrested from the legislature by the King. On the other hand, whichever of the foundation-stones of Hungarian constitutional liberty and of the freedom of Parliament we regard, from 1222 to 1848, we shall find that not one of them was laid without armed resistance, without a strenuous struggle, or at any rate without preparations being made for one. It is this constant change and play of forces and their endeavour to perpetuate their triumphs in permanent institutions, which constitutes the very essence of constitutional life. Anyone who admits that the change is admissible on one side, must concede that it is justified on the other. For, by virtue of the law of evolution, every institution is capable of fulfilling the task before it only until it is replaced by another endowed with a greater power. The mightiest armies have striven in vain to arrest the course of history: what obstacles to it could, then, be offered by a simple *diploma*—unless backed at least by power?

Great indeed is the power of a law that has been duly sanctioned and solemnly accepted. The conditions of modern States are perhaps such as to encourage doubts as to whether the personal obligations of a sovereign are a sufficient safeguard against the dangers of personal rule. But the mere stipulation of such conditions, however often the ruling power may override them, always serves to remind the oppressed party that his foe is not invincible. Though unsupported by any army or material force, these stipulations at all times afford a definite starting-point to which a return can be made. This was the point of view that guided the creators of the fundamental laws. They were sanctified by the holy Church, and according to the requirements of chivalrous society the King, as knight, pledged his word of honour that he would keep all existing laws and cause others also to observe them. He took this oath on the greatest day in his life, when the crown of St Stephen was placed on his head, amid the jubilations of his whole people[1]. By his succession to the throne, the monarch was indeed already entitled to exercise the royal prerogatives, but it was not until he had been crowned and had taken the oath that he was qualified to enjoy all those rights which were the joint possession of the King and the Estates of Parliament.

The coronation of Maria Teresa in 1741 was celebrated with all the legal and customary formalities. The person of the monarch was a guarantee alike of an energetic exercise of the royal rights and of the preservation of the constitution of the country which she had confirmed by oath. The parallel development of the two, in a manner calculated to make each complementary to the other, did not seem at all out of the question. For centuries there had not been so close a connection of interests between sovereign and nation as then existed. The living record of this memorable episode is the coronation *diploma* of 1741. The two interests between which a wide gulf had so long been fixed, were now to be welded into one, not for the time being, but, according to the general tendency of all human institutions, for all time. It is true that the text differs

---

[1] The coronation oath is a purely medieval institution. It was unknown to antiquity, though the coronation as an institution is really based on Holy Scripture. From this point of view it is an important fact that the coronation oath occurs first in Hungary in the case of Andreas II (1205), the sovereign who signed the Golden Bull (1222). He was the first knight-King. His predecessors had all been patriarchal Kings. It is probably superfluous to lay stress on the fact that the ceremony of coronation and the oath accompanying it were in vogue in all medieval States in Europe. In fact the terms of the oath were practically identical everywhere. In all countries the King swore to maintain the royal rights, the Church and the laws. The anointing of the King, however, was not a universal practice. Besides the Roman Emperor, the Kings of England, France, Hungary, Jerusalem, and Sicily were anointed; those of Spain were not.

comparatively little from that of the *diploma inaugurale* issued by Charles III, but this circumstance merely proves that those factors, which had served as guarantees of constitutional rule since 1711, were still in force.

The principal contents of the *diploma inaugurale* of Maria Teresa, which was incorporated into law together with the coronation oath, as a sacred document[1], are as follows:

"The Estates of Our loyal Hungary and her borderlands (*partes adnexae*) summoned to meet at Pozsony on Exaudi Sunday the 14th of May of the present year for the occasion of Our coronation, appeared in Pozsony in full numbers at the Parliament—in which Parliament We too took part in person— and showed the obligatory fealty and homage due to Us as to their legal and hereditary Queen and Lord, and prayed Our Majesty, in fulfilment of the older laws, before the celebration of Our most happy coronation, to approve, confirm and bestow Our favour on the articles detailed below, and, having graciously accepted the same and confirmed them by Our royal authority, to deign graciously to observe them Ourselves and to secure their observance by all others whom it may concern:

"Firstly: We will piously accept and firmly observe and make others observe intact all the general and special liberties, immunities, privileges, rights and laws of this Hungarian kingdom and its borderlands, accepted by former Kings, Our predecessors (except only the clause of Andreas II's laws relating to the *jus resistendi*), in all their points, articles, and clauses, in accordance with the agreement come to between the sovereign and the Estates in Parliament, with respect to the use and interpretation of the same;

"Secondly: We will preserve the Holy Crown in this kingdom, according to the ancient usage and the laws of the country, entrusting the same to the safekeeping of the delegates elected for that purpose from among their own numbers, by the unanimous vote of the Estates;

"Thirdly: In accordance with the oath taken by Us, we will annex to the kingdom and its borderlands all parts and posses-

---

[1] *Sacrum diploma*, Act II of 1741.

sions of the kingdom already recovered or to be recovered with the aid of God ;

"Fourthly: In case (which God forbid!) all the Austrian archdukes and archduchesses descended from Our father and from the Emperors Joseph and Leopold, should die, by virtue of Acts I and II of 1723 the ancestral right of the Estates of the realm to elect and crown their King, shall again come into force ;

"Fifthly: Whenever, at a subsequent period, such inauguration of a monarch shall be undertaken in this kingdom by a Parliament, Our successors and heirs—the hereditary Kings to be thus crowned—shall at all times promulgate this acceptance of the guarantees of the *diploma*, and the confirmation of the same by oath.

"We accept and approve of all the above points and, by Our royal word, promise and engage that We Ourselves will keep the same and will compel all Our loyal subjects, of whatever order or rank, to their observance. In witness and proof of the same We have signed this document with Our own hand and have confirmed the same with Our royal seal."

If we examine the various provisions of this document, we must distinguish between those provisions which were generally used all over Europe and belonged, as it were, to the very essence of a coronation oath, and those which were the outcome of the peculiar conditions of Hungary.

Among provisions of this general character is the first, relating to the observance of the laws[1]; another is that which refers to the recovery by the sovereign of the possessions and rights of the kingdom. Among special provisions we may reckon the fourth, which serves as a reminder that Hungary had once been an elective monarchy, and as such was a little obsolete ; its real object, however, was rather to establish by documentary proof the legal independence of Hungary as

---

[1] The first coronation oath known to History, that of Caribert King of the Franks, dates from 561 and consists merely of the following sentence: "Juramento promisit ut leges consuetudinesque novas populo non infligeret, sed in illo quo quondam sub patris dominatione statu vixerant, in ipso hoc eos deinceps retineret." Stubbs, *Constitutional History of England*, vol. I. p. 147.

opposed to the Austrian Hereditary Provinces. The second point is peculiar—the inclusion in the *diploma* of the great reverence to the Sacred Crown and the obligatory preservation of it. It is explained by two things: first, the fact that the sovereign resided in a foreign country, secondly, the fact that, as the kingship had ceased to be elective, the coronation with the crown was considered by the nation not merely as a historic relic, but as a sacred object, for it was the only means by which the rule of the monarch could be brought into connection with Hungarian laws. For, so long as the King was a foreigner, his coronatioň in Hungary alone could establish his political relations to that country[1].

In the same manner, the abolition of the system of election was responsible for the fifth provision, in which the sovereign made the observance of the constitution obligatory, not only upon himself but on all his successors. In former days the election of a King had secured this guarantee[2], and the continuity of the constitution was now assumed as a natural consequence of the unbroken order of succession.

Those laws which form the basis of the whole political structure of the State and which, as a consequence, required special guarantees on the part of the newly-crowned King, are to be found enumerated in full, particularly in the *diploma* issued by Leopold I, the last King of Hungary who succeeded to the throne by virtue of election. Even the most royalist of all writers admits that these laws could not be changed without consent of Parliament[3]. Between 1681 and 1741, the Parliament did indeed make changes in most essential points, but none the less the importance of the old laws still remaining was very considerable, and, in consequence, the influence of Parliament remained, whether these laws were to be maintained or to be altered. We shall now examine these laws in order to see how

---

[1] In elective monarchies, particularly in the Holy Roman Empire and in Poland, the settlement of the political relations was connected with the election itself, not with the crown. In the former the election *capitulatio*, in the latter country the *pacta conventa*, corresponded to the Hungarian *diploma inaugurale*.

[2] In the *diploma* of the last King elected by the Parliament (Leopold I) this point is not even mentioned.

[3] Niczky, *Staatskenntniss*, ch. 3.

far their contents point to cooperation between the Estates and the Parliament in the government of the country.

Ever since 1687, when the *jus resistendi* of Andreas II's Act of 1222 was abolished, the Count Palatine had been the chief guardian of the Hungarian constitution. It was a fundamental law that he could be elected by Parliament only. According to Act IX of 1741, the office could not remain vacant for more than one year. This latter provision had already been made by Act III of 1608, which at the same time charged the Lord Chief Justice or the Treasurer (*tárnok*) with summoning Parliament to assemble, should the King "not desire to do so or fail to take the necessary steps."

Yet, after 1765, Maria Teresa did not summon Parliament to assemble, and she charged a lieutenant-governor of her own appointment with replacing the Count Palatine in the conduct of the internal affairs of the country. It was in vain that publicists endeavoured to convert the lieutenant-governor into a separate dignitary, endowed by the will of the sovereign with the authority belonging to the Count Palatine[1]. The lieutenant-governor remained after all a dignitary appointed by the monarch, whereas the Count Palatine had been a mediator between Crown and nation. It was in this way then that an important fundamental law of the Hungarian constitution was invalidated fifteen years before the accession of Joseph II. Now the Lord Chief Justice and the Treasurer could not summon Parliament to assemble; the days for such proceedings were past and over even though the law sanctioning them was still in force. Maria Teresa was able to vindicate her action by referring to an undoubted royal prerogative—viz. that the summoning of Parliament depended upon the will of the sovereign. However, ever since there had been a separate *consilium locumtenentiale* and a separate military command in the country (1757), the Count Palatine had become rather a relic than an actual power, and consequently his absence was scarcely to be felt.

Let us now examine the condition of those institutions which were engaged in supplying positive needs.

In the matter of taxes, no changes could be effected without

[1] Ürményi, vol. II. ch. 6. §§ 8, 9. Niczky, *loc. cit.* ch. 7.

the consent of Parliament. The collection of taxes depended upon the cooperation of the counties; but the amount of the *contributio* (impost) could not be raised by the several counties on their own initiative. The Acts of Parliament did not determine the amount of the annual taxes nor their distribution among the various counties[1]. That was the work of the *commissions*. Even in the sixteenth and seventeenth centuries the Parliament had voted the *subsidium* from year to year: and, when there was no Parliament, there were no taxes. For instance, no taxes were paid[2] between 1559 and 1563. Now, however, the taxes once assessed were not confined to a certain fixed period. The starting-point of the great Revolution in England (1640) had been that the King, by virtue of his royal prerogatives, had exercised the right of continually collecting the Tunnage and Poundage once voted by Parliament. In England the struggle occasioned thereby ended with the execution of Charles I; in Hungary the collection of the *contributio*—once it had been voted without the consent of Parliament—was not even called in question or resisted.

It is true that a one-sided raising of the rate of the *contributio* was impossible. But, as we have seen, the ordinary taxes constituted a comparatively small part of the royal revenues. When Parliament did meet, as in 1751 and 1764, it was only with the greatest difficulty and after protracted debates and bitter reproaches that it could be prevailed upon to impose an extra burden of a few hundred thousand florins on the serfs. Thus the amount that could be extracted from Parliament was by no means comparable to the advantages gained by the sovereign if he could rule without it.

There was one way of considerably increasing the direct revenues, which would certainly have been effective in enhancing the authority and importance of Parliament—viz. by abolishing that exemption from taxation which the nobles enjoyed. But the Parliament itself robbed its own members of the power

---

[1] According to Count Christopher Niczky (*Staatskenntniss*, ch. 16), the rate of the *contributio* was not incorporated in law, lest it should be thought that it was permanent, like the army.

[2] *Országgyülési Emlékek* (Parl. Records), vol. IV. pp. 399—401.

always exercised by those who are entitled to decide in questions of decisive national importance. It had previously resigned any right it might claim to control religious questions. Act VIII of 1741 formally converted the exemption of the nobles and of their land from all burdens into an unalterable fundamental law, of equal force to that which declared that Hungary could not be governed in the same way as the Hereditary Provinces. Consequently the most vital of all reforms had to be omitted or could only be effected in an illegal manner. But if we consider the whole social and economic system of the Hungary of those days, this reform would have involved, not merely a material sacrifice on the part of the nobles, but also, so far as we can judge, a renunciation of the separate existence of the country as a sovereign State. Over the question of taxation, then, the Hungarian nobles, otherwise loyal and dutiful, proved inflexible. The sovereign, however, had it in his power to acquire a pecuniary compensation elsewhere; for, though Hungarian nobles paid nothing direct to the sovereign, the Austrian Hereditary Provinces were yet enriched at their expense. Indirect taxation was imposed on them, not by Parliament but, as we have seen before, by the customs system elaborated in Vienna.

In another sphere of authority the powers of Parliament were of direct importance. The nobility, whose obligations to do military service formed the basis of the whole constitution, could not take up arms throughout the country in the *generalis insurrectio*, except by virtue of a resolution of Parliament. This was the sole surviving trace of the ancient national assemblies of armed warriors. On the one hand the wars of the eighteenth century had displayed the great superiority of properly trained men, of regular artillery and infantry, over troops of cavalry which, though brave and clever, were undisciplined. On the other, the sovereign could ordain an *insurrectio* (*particularis* though not *generalis*) without the consent of Parliament, and, in his capacity as the overlord of the magnates and prelates, was able to strengthen his army by the addition of large numbers of fully-equipped hussars, recruited by their authority and loyal generosity and maintained at their own expense. Finally—just as in the case of taxes once voted—the

Emperor was able to enlist the number of regular recruits voted in 1715, all over the country. Now in Hungary, in the eighteenth century, the right of raising levies was the direct equivalent of an obligation to do military service.

Absolute monarchy endeavoured in the eighteenth century to reorganise almost every country in Europe, not merely with a view to increasing its own power but in order to realise great ideals of civilization. In Hungary the chief obstacles, which it found in its way, were not the constitutional assemblies of the Estates. If it was to attain its end, the central royal power had to make its influence felt irresistibly and directly upon every grade of society, without being weakened or checked on the way by the intermediate classes of the nobility and clergy, acting as its instruments. In Hungary, such instruments were supplied by the counties in temporal matters, in spiritual matters by the great interests of the Catholic and Protestant religions (which made their influence felt on every class of the people) but in no respects by the Parliament.

The facts stated above should already have convinced the reader that the Parliament of the eighteenth century was no longer to be feared as an antagonist by the sovereign. The Hungarian State scarcely felt the absence of its activity, but the force of tradition was so great that the longer the intervals that elapsed between its sessions, the more effectually was every hope of patriotic Hungarians concentrated in its work. A great historian says of representative assemblies that, even when apparently restricted in their independence, they often give evidence of great internal vitality, of which the effect is always beneficial[1]. None the less, in Hungary the slow but unbroken work of centuries had gradually stripped the Parliament of everything that had made it in the past, and was to make it in the future, the chief expression of the national spirit and the chief director of political life. By 1780 it possessed scarcely any of those rights by virtue of which its activity had been an indispensable factor in the organisation of the State. Of its inheritance one part had devolved to the King, the other to various bodies, the

---

[1] Ranke, *Fürsten und Völker von Süd. Europa*, vol. I. p. 229 (of the Cortes of Castile).

counties, and the ecclesiastical corporations. It had become an unessential formality, whose final decay seemed only a question of time.

However—and this fact is proved best of all by the history of the age of Maria Teresa—the substance of this formality had not perished. The feeling of national unity, of the idea of a State, in a wo l, of patriotism, was just as living in this as in any period of the history of Hungary. Its outward form of expression, however, was no longer the Parliament, but the sovereign, and if we penetrate beyond the forms, to the essence of the constitution—the maintenance and keeping alive of patriotic and State feeling—we may ask whether the best Parliament could have done so much for it as Maria Teresa. Hungarian patriotism did not consider whether a Parliament or a King, the county or an official was at the head of affairs; it might change its instruments or create new ones, but it always wished to be sure that its leaders had national aims in view. Hence it was even prepared for the eventuality of a sovereign, who might again separate the interests of the Crown from those of the nation. In the great work of reorganising the State the lion's share fell to the monarch, but the basis was still formed by national institutions, which served the interests not only of individuals and classes, but of the whole nation. The downfall of Poland (the similarity of whose political evolution is in itself enough to account for the sympathy between the two nations) was due to the fact that the nobles overthrew the royal power only to replace it by private interests, and were thus unable to create true political and national institutions. In Hungary, on the other hand, despite the large number of privileges which the Estates and the orders enjoyed and the equally large amount of abuses which they committed, the Church, the judiciary and the county assembly were genuinely national institutions and formed an impregnable barrier between the monarch and the nobility. It was therefore not only in the monarchy, but in these organisations too, that Hungary sought and found an opportunity of evolving those political ideas and forms which are peculiar to her.

APPENDIX I.

MONEY, WEIGHTS AND MEASURES.

1. (*a*) *Coins*. **Gold.** The Hungarian "ducat," first coined in Körmöczbánya in 1330, has never changed in weight since that time, or in standard of fineness, viz. $23\frac{3}{4}$ carats. It was called the *florenus*.

Silver. Ever since the accession to the Hungarian throne of the Habsburgs (1526) the silver coinage has been the same as in Germany. The florin was a silver coin: and 2 florins made a "thaler." Out of 1 mark (troy weight) of silver 20 florins were coined. The *huszas* (twenty), the third part of the florin, was the coin most in circulation. A florin contained 60 "kreuzers" or "denars." A silver florin = 2 shillings; $2\frac{1}{2}$ denars = 1 penny. The ducat = 4 florins 30 denars: the Dutch ducat = 4 florins 28 denars.

Copper. After 1761 the kreuzer was coined in copper; half- and quarter-kreuzers were also issued. In addition, *fillérs* (farthings) were coined, 100 of which = 1 florin. So there were two standards of exchange, in the one (the Rhenish) 1 florin = 60 kreuzers; in the other (the Hungarian), 1 florin = 100 *fillérs*.

(*b*) *Bank-notes*. The notes of the Bank of Vienna circulated also in Hungary, though not sanctioned by any Act of Parliament. There were various notes, from 5 to 1000 florins in value.

2. *Measures* (*Lineal*). 1 fathom (*öl*) contained 6 feet (*láb*), and each foot contained 12 inches (*hüvelyk*). For measuring cloth and linen, 1 yard (*röf*) = $2\frac{1}{2}$ feet. For measuring horses, 1 hand (*marok*) = 4 inches. 1 Hungarian mile (*mélyföld*) = $5\frac{1}{5}$ statute miles.

3. *Measures* (*Square*). 40 square fathoms = $1600°\square$ = 1 *hold* (Hungarian acre). 70 *hold* = 100 English acres.

4. *Weights.* 1 pound (*font*) = 1¼ English pounds avoirdupois. 100 pounds (cental = *mázsa*) = 1 cwt. 1 stone. 1 pound contained 32 *lat.* 1 *lat* = about ⅔ oz.

5. *Dry Measures.* Corn was measured by the *mérö.* The *mérö* of Pozsony contained 80 *itcze*, that of Pest 120 *itcze.* 2 *itczes* = 1 pint. 1 *meszely* = ½ *itcze.* 2 *mérös* = 1 *köböl.* 1 *mérö* = 1⅔ bushels.

6. *Liquid Measures.* Wine was measured by the *akó*, which also contained 80 *itczes.* 1 *akó* = 1¼ *anker* (10 gallons). [N.B. The *antal*, used in Tokay, was 10 *itczes* more than the *akó* in general use.] 3 *itczes* = 4 English pints.

APPENDIX II.

DICAS OF THE COUNTY OF PEST.

Anno millesimo septingentesimo septuagesimo quinto, diebus sexta et septima septembris, sub praesidio spectabilis domini ordinarii vice-comitis Emerici Laczkovics considente pleno magistratu ac praesentibus etiam spectabilibus dominis Tabulae assessoribus seniore Gedeon Ráday, Daniele Tihanyi sequens elaborata est in antecessum pro futura dicatione materialis constitutivi clavis.

Coloni	per	4	Agri 1-ae classis jug. ... per	24
Filii	,,	6	2-ae ,, ,, ... ,,	26
Filiae	,,	12	3-ae ., ,, ... ,,	28
Fratres	,,	6	4-ae ,, ,, ... ,,	30
Inquilini	,,	4	seu una integra sessio.	
Subinquilini	,,	6	Omnia prata ad unam	
Servi	,,	8	classem a falcatione... ,,	24
Ancillae	,,	16	Vineae 1. classis a fossore ,,	6
Boves jugales proprii ...	,,	4	2. classis — ,,	8
Boves jugales mutuati	,,	8	3. classis — ,,	10
Saginati	,,	20	Molae fluviales 1-ae classis ,,	1
Vaccae mulgibiles ...	,,	4	2-ae classis ,,	2
— steriles ...	,,	8	3-ae classis ,,	3
Juvenci trium annorum	,,	30	Siccae Molae 1. classis ,,	2
— duorum annorum	,,	40	2. classis ,,	4
Vituli	,,	50	3. classis ,,	6
Setigeri	,,	40	Educillum commune a fl. ,,	40
Oves	,,	60	Torcular lini a flor. ... ,,	40
Domus a qua solvuntur titulo census fl. 100 ad			Opilionum arenda a sing. flor. x. 3. consideratis	
primam classem	,,	1	facient dicam ... ,,	40
a qua fl. 50 ad			Arendat. ex Lucro flor. ,,	40
2am classem ...	,,	2	Ahaena ,, ,, ,,	20

Alvearia ex Lucro flor.	per	40	2-ae classis	...	per	80
Opificia 1-ae classis	...	,,	2	3-ae classis	...	,,	90
2-ae classis	...	,,	3	Manualis opera in qua			
3-ae classis	...	,,	4	inquilini sumendi 1.			
Quaestus 1-ae cl. non datur	,,	—	classis...	...	...	,,	50
2-ae classis	...	,,	6	2 classis...	...	,,	60
3-ae classis	...	,,	8	3. classis	...	,,	70
Mercatura 1-ae classis...	,,	4	Lignatio focalis a personis			
2-ae classis...	,,	6	1. classis	...	,,	80
3-ae classis...	,,	8	2. classis	...	,,	90
Pascuatio pecorum ad			3. classis	...	,,	100
jugalia et mulgibilia			Lignatio aedilis a domibus			
restricta 1. classis	...	,,	40	1. classis	...	,,	80
2. classis	...	,,	50	2. classis	...	,,	90
3. classis	...	,,	60	3. classis	...	,,	100
Pascuatio pecudum 1-ae			Arundinatio 1. classis...	,,	100
classis ad oves mulgi-			2. classis...	,,	110
biles intellecta	...	,,	70	3. classis...	,,	120

Dein eodem 1775. anno die 17a decembris a proportione numeri dicarum in cohaerentia huius Clavis ex objectis conscriptis erutarum, pro exigentia huius comitatus quanti pecuniarium Dicae constitutivum pro contributionali cassa defixum est in f. 1. den. 62.

pro domestica den. 52.

The relative value of the objects or persons was about the same in the various counties. For example, a house, or a mill paid a whole *dica* : four serfs, as many oxen, or cows were also a *dica*, and as much was a whole session.

But the tax in money corresponding to a *dica* was different in the counties. In Pest it was 2 fl. 14 kr. In Sopron, at the same time, 2.52 after each *dica* ; in Máramaros, the poorest county, only 58 kr., in Bihar 1 fl. 12 kr. (1790).

APPENDIX III.

NUMBER OF THE PORTAE OF THE COUNTIES AND ROYAL FREE BOROUGHS 1723–1847.

	1723	1724	1729	1733	1780	1792	1847
Sopron county . . .	$336\frac{1}{2}$	$336\frac{1}{2}$	337	337	$302\frac{1}{2}$	$302\frac{1}{2}$	194
Sopron town	36	36	$34\frac{1}{2}$	$34\frac{1}{2}$	$36\frac{1}{2}$	$36\frac{1}{2}$	24
Kis-Marton town . .	$7\frac{1}{4}$	$7\frac{1}{4}$	9	7	$5\frac{1}{2}$	$5\frac{1}{2}$	5
Ruszt town	8	8	8	8	5	5	2
Vas county	$351\frac{1}{4}$	$351\frac{1}{4}$	$351\frac{1}{4}$	$351\frac{1}{4}$	301	301	212
Köszeg town	$10\frac{3}{4}$	$10\frac{3}{4}$	$10\frac{3}{4}$	$10\frac{3}{4}$	10	10	$6\frac{4}{8}$
Komárom county . .	90	93	93	93	90	90	92
Komárom town . . .					10	10	8
Szala county	$183\frac{1}{2}$	$181\frac{1}{2}$	$182\frac{1}{2}$	$182\frac{1}{2}$	$189\frac{1}{2}$	$189\frac{1}{2}$	170
N.-Kanizsa town . .	$3\frac{3}{4}$	$3\frac{3}{4}$	$3\frac{3}{4}$	$3\frac{3}{4}$			
Veszprém county . .	$89\frac{1}{4}$	$80\frac{1}{4}$	81	81	89	89	98
Fejér county	47	52	61	61	72	82	92
Sz.-Fehérvár town . .	9	9	10	10	15	15	$19\frac{2}{8}$
Baranya county . . .	$80\frac{1}{4}$	$94\frac{1}{4}$	$96\frac{1}{4}$	$96\frac{1}{4}$	112	$108\frac{3}{4}$	160
Pécs town						$3\frac{1}{4}$	12
Györ county	75	74	$74\frac{1}{4}$	$74\frac{1}{4}$	$63\frac{1}{2}$	$63\frac{1}{2}$	52
Györ town.					18	18	18
Somogy county . . .	90	90	90	90	102	102	123
Tolna county. . . .	$27\frac{1}{4}$	$35\frac{1}{4}$	44	44	63	$68\frac{3}{4}$	128
Mosony county . . .	$153\frac{1}{4}$	$153\frac{1}{4}$	$153\frac{1}{4}$	$153\frac{1}{4}$	162	152	120
Pozsony county . . .	$343\frac{1}{4}$	$343\frac{1}{4}$	336	336	303	288	200
Pozsony town . . .	$44\frac{1}{2}$	$44\frac{1}{4}$	40	40	48	40	40
N.-Szombat town . .	19	19	16	17	19	15	14
Sz.-György	8	8	4	5	5	5	$3\frac{4}{8}$
Bazin town	$12\frac{3}{4}$	$12\frac{3}{4}$	$11\frac{3}{4}$	$11\frac{3}{4}$	$8\frac{1}{4}$	$8\frac{1}{8}$	6
Modor town	$14\frac{1}{2}$	$14\frac{1}{2}$	$10\frac{1}{2}$	$12\frac{1}{2}$	$9\frac{3}{4}$	$9\frac{1}{2}$	6
Nyitra county . . .	$343\frac{1}{4}$	$343\frac{1}{4}$	352	352	$308\frac{3}{4}$	302	224
Szakolcza town . . .	$7\frac{1}{4}$	$7\frac{1}{4}$	$7\frac{1}{4}$	$7\frac{1}{4}$	$7\frac{1}{4}$	5	5
Trencsén county . .	$220\frac{1}{2}$	$229\frac{1}{4}$	$225\frac{1}{4}$	$225\frac{1}{4}$	200	195	130
Trencsén town . . .	$3\frac{3}{4}$	$3\frac{3}{4}$	$3\frac{3}{4}$	$3\frac{3}{4}$	3	3	$2\frac{1}{2}$
Bars county	$150\frac{1}{4}$	$150\frac{1}{4}$	$146\frac{1}{4}$	$146\frac{1}{4}$	$135\frac{1}{4}$	$135\frac{1}{4}$	88
Körmöczbánya town .	$8\frac{1}{4}$	$7\frac{1}{2}$	$7\frac{1}{2}$	$7\frac{1}{2}$	12	12	8
Ujbánya town . . .	$1\frac{3}{4}$	2	2	2	2	2	2
Zólyom county . . .	$76\frac{3}{4}$	$77\frac{3}{4}$	$76\frac{3}{4}$	$76\frac{3}{4}$	$76\frac{3}{4}$	$76\frac{3}{4}$	52

	1723	1724	1729	1733	1780	1792	1847
Beszterczebánya town .	11¼	11¼	11¼	11¼	12	12	8
Breznóbánya town . .	8	8	4	4	5	5	5½
Libetbánya town . .	1½	1½	1½	1½	1½	1½	2
Zólyom town	3½	3½	3½	3½	3¼	3½	2½
Korpona town . . .	5¾	5¾	5¾	5¾	4¾	4¾	3
Nógrád county . . .	112½	114½	114½	114½	115	115	100
Árva county	71½	71½	68½	68½	63	63	54
Turócz county . . .	46½	48	48	48	46	46	24
Pest-Pilis-Solt county .	104¼	122¼	140	140	177	197	244⅝
Buda town	24¾	24¾	29	30	44	52	38
Pest town	8¼	10¼	11	13	28	28	80
Esztergom county . .	31½	33½	37	37	48	53	56
Esztergom town . . .	5¾	5¾	6	6	8	8	8
Hont county	160	162	162	162	157	157	92
Selmeczbánya town .	12¾	12¾	11½	11½	13	13	11
Bakabánya town . .	1½	1½	1½	1½	1½	1½	2
Bélabánya town . . .	1¼	1¼	1¼	1¼	1½	1¼	1¾
Liptó county	64¾	64¾	64¾	64¾	51	51½	34
Bács-Bodrog county .	66	57	61	61	120	112½	290
Szabadka town . . .	—	—	—	—	16	16	46
Zombor town	—	—	—	—	13	13	30
Ujvidék town . . .	—	—	—	—	10	10	20
Abauj county . . .	85	73	77	77	73	73	65
Kassa town	10½	11½	14½	14½	14	14	18
Zemplén county . . .	172¾	180	180	180	134	134	104
Sáros county	144½	146½	140	140	100½	100½	74
Eperjes town	11	11	9½	9½	9	9	8
Bártfa town	6¾	6¾	6	6	4	4	5
Kis-Szeben town . .	4	3	3	1½	2½	2½	2
Szepes county . . .	104¾	103½	101	101	94	94	68½
Löcse town	14	13	8½	8½	6	6	7
Kézsmárk town . . .	8	8	9	9	10	10	5
Ung county	50	47	41½	41½	28	28	35
Szatmár county . . .	93	93	87	87	70	70	79
Szatmár-Németi town .	12½	13	13	13	8	8	12½
Nagy-Bánya town . .	5¼	5¼	5¼	5¼	4	4	9
Felsö-Bánya town . .	24	12	6	6	9	9	—
Szabolcs county . . . / Kálló and Polgári town	92½	84½	81	79½	73¾	72¼	70
Hajdu towns	35¼	35¼	34¾	34¾	37¾	37¾	31½
Gömör county . . .	115½	116½	116½	116½	113	113	92
Borsod county . . .	70	72½	82½	82½	91	91	84
Heves and Külsö-Szolnok county . .	88	94	100	100	114	114	148
Eger town	7½	10	9	9	9½	9½	
Jász-Kúnság district .	69½	67½	67½	67½	83	83	125
Bereg county	50½	50½	47	47	37	37	32
Ugocsa county . . .	20	21	21	21	14	14	12
Torna county . . .	15½	15½	13	13	13½	13½	12
Bihar county	160	176	200	200	201¾	201¾	214

	1723	1724	1729	1733	1780	1792	1847
Debreczen town . . .	38	46	46	46	52¼	52¼	41
Mármaros county . .	105	100	83	83	64	64	60
Kövár district . . .	25	25	25				—
Kraszna county . . .	21½	16	16	98½	98½	98½	16
Közép-Szolnok county	62	50	50				42
Csongrád county . .	28	28	28	28	35	35	61
Szeged town	11	9	11	11	23¾	23¾	46
Zaránd county . . .	60	53	53	—	—	—	15½
Csanád county . . .	15	13	12	12	21	21	39
Arad county	40	27	17	19	79	79	100+Arad town 10
Békés county. . . .	20	20	22	22	39	39	84
Szerém county . . .	—	—	—	—	60	51	81
Veröcze county . . .	—	—	—	—	58	58	91
Posega county . . .	—	—	—	—	55¾	55¾	55
Posega town	—	—	—	—	1¾	1¾	2
CROATIA							
Zágráb county . . .	—	—	—	—	81⅛	60½	66
Varasd county . . .	—	—	—	—	34¼	34½	31¼
Körös county. . . .	—	—	—	—	26¼	24¾	22¼
Zágráb town	—	—	—	—	1⅜	1⅜	3
Varasd town	—	—	—	—	2⅜	2¾	2½
Körös town	—	—	—	—	⅞	⅞	⅞
Kaproncza town . . .	—	—	—	—	1	1	2
Károlyváros town . .	—	—	—	—	1⅛	1⅛	4
Buccari town	—	—	—	—	2	2⅛	2
SP.							
Fiume town	—	—	—	—	1⅜	1⅜	4
THE FORMER BANAT							
Temes county . . .	—	—	—	—		229½	254+24 for Temesvár
Krassó county . . .	—	—	—	—	540	97½	112
Torontál county. . .	—	—	—	—		254	254

APPENDIX IV.

SPECULUM MODERNI TEMPORIS.

Inspice modernum Hungariae statum
    Intrinseca cui est videre datum
Et videbis cuncta quam male subsistant,
    Ni talibus magni prudenter obsistant.
Antiqui Magnates honeste vivebant,
    Arces, villas, terras in pace tenebant,
Nobilitas tota rusticum non pressit
    Et tamen argentum in arcas congessit.
Antiquus ornatus erant fortes panni,
    Quos non attriverunt duo vel tres anni.
Ex argento fusi nodi portabantur,
    Qui per Testamentum posteris dabantur,
Amphoras et scyphos celatos habebant,
    Vitrum, porcellanam numquam ambiebant.
Fictos uniones non fuit videre
    Voluit res firmas quivis possidere.
Hordeum in silvis apris non dabatur
    Dum cui placebat feras venabatur,
Phasiani nunquam triticum edebant
    Nisi quod in agris furtim sufferebant.
A Gallicis sibi tunc cavebant cocis
    Optime contenti Hungaricis focis,
Legumine, feris, pullis et pulmento
    Vescebantur cuncti semper pro contento.
Nunc vide ornatum in Hungara gente,
    Appetunt et gestant quod perit repente,
Aurum et argentum sic curant crispari,
    Ut secunda veste nequeat portari.

Pannos aspernantur, peruviem querunt.
  Vestem pretiosam vix modice terunt.
Abjicere solent, imo debent.   Quare?
  Ne ut canis pellem dicantur portare.
Prandium tunc sapit, quum ex porcellana
  Sumitur, me hercle, res est satis vana.
Amphoras et scyphos argento celatos
  Si convivis praebes, hos non habes gratos
Quodsi his infundas generosa vina,
  Omnes abhorrebit uti medicina,
Vitra sunt in flore, quae cito franguntur
  Heu! quam in vanum opes profunduntur.
Feras quas natura glandibus ditavit
  Quasque ager semper huc adusque favit,
Gula dominorum studet saginare,
  Agricola debet et pro his arare,
Venator ornatus auro et argento,
  Putares, hic artem scit ex fundamento,
Is attamen forsan leporem non vidit
  Qui eburem domi paulo ante scidit,
Coci speculantur cibos adaptare,
  Atque dominorum gulam satiare
Coquunt, assant, frixant bona miscent malis
  Ut neque dignoscas qui cibus sit qualis.
Luditur post mensam, ducuntur choreae,
  Curribus ornatis replentur plateae,
Servitorum turba gratis otiatur,
  Abdomini servit, fimbriis ornatur,
Taliter tractati domini, queruntur,
  Suasu medicorum pharmacis utuntur,
Vi medicinarum student reparare
  Id quod debuissent antea vitare.
Ecce vides mores, luxum et ornatum
  Hungaricae gentis, forsan minus gratum,
Haec sunt quae pessum dant opes proavorum,
  Haec est pestis acris, sentina malorum.
Nunc debita crescunt, deficit crumena,
  Quae fuit utcunque vivo patre plena.
Plures namque fiunt per diem expensae
  Quam solvere possit pagus toto mense.

Hoc ergo videte qui estis Primores
    Et quibus est datum corrigere mores
Quibus obedire debent omnes gentes
    Sub sacra Corona in regno manentes.
Disponite primum ut antiquo more
    Vivat in hoc regno quivis cum decore.
Vestes ordinentur pro quolibet statu,
    Cura sit in vobis et in magistratu,
Cuncti crispatores auri et argenti
    Moneantur ne res vendant rustrae genti.
Auri fabri solum redeant ad florem,
    Cudant ex argento solidum laborem,
Vitra, porcellana cum caro emantur
    Et in usum sumpta, cito confringantur,
Abrogentur prorsus et sint extra usum,
    Haec suppleat stannum et argentum cusum.
Feras quisque sciat in silva vagari
    Possit ut quilibet easdem venari,
Hordeum pro zytho domi conservetur,
    Phasianis posthaec triticum non detur.
Famuli Magnatum panno vestiantur,
    Qui tales exornant stricte puniantur.
Dedecet ut servus incedat ornatus
    Et dominus gemet debitis gravatus.
Extraneis cocis Magnas non utatur,
    Domesticis cibis quilibet vescatur,
Lusum Pharaonis qui sciet vitare
    Aes mutuum numquam debebit rogare.

MS. in the National Museum ascribed in a contemporary note to Baron Ladislas Amadé.

The same evolution is treated at length by Petrus Apor (1676–1752), in the *Metamorphosis Transilvaniae*, ed. 1863. It contains notes by Michael Cserei (1668–1756).

Boroughs, The Royal Free, statistics as to 63, 164–5 n.; relative unimportance of 163–6

Bourgeoisie, The, in Europe, influence of, in promoting absolute monarchy 10, 100–1, 346
—— in France, England, and Italy compared with that in Hungary 158–9
—— in Hungary, influence of xxxi–xxxii, 10–11; general treatment 148–70 *passim*
—— Emperor Joseph's judgment on 90
—— dependence of, on the King 108, 161–3, 315–6, 327
—— frequently German or Rascian in character and origin xxxi, 11, 108, 148 n., 149, 160, 163, 208, 229; Magyars not allowed to become citizens 161
—— connection of, with Calvinism xliii, 159, 161, 258; with Lutheranism 159–60, 208, 291
—— decline of importance of, in XVIII century 96, 110, 163–6; otherwise mentioned 291
Buda, population Rascian and German in XVIII century 62, 205, 208
Bulla Aurea xxviii–xxix, lvi, 103 n. 3

Calvinism and Calvinists, general political aspects of, in Europe lxii, 251, 289–9
—— in Hungary (v. also Catholicism and Toleration), xliii and n.; Calvinism and the nobles 139; chiefly among the gentry l, 129–30, 222, 289; Calvinism and the towns 161, 258
—— Calvinist relations with the Turks xliv, 248–9; with Francis II Rákóczi, his revolt largely Calvinistic in character lix, 250 and n., 251; relations with foreign powers lx, 136 n. 2, 222–3, 256–9 (v. also under Toleration)
—— religious policy towards, under Charles III (VI) 253 and notes, 254–5, 256 and n. 2, Bishop Biró's book against 257–9
—— Calvinist colleges and educational system 291–6; government assault upon, under Maria Teresa 237, 292–7
—— and relations with Catholics 248–9, 297–9
—— Protestant Estate represented in Parliament till 1681 251
—— in Transylvania (q. v.) 261–3
Camerae, comes 319
Camerae, lucrum 314
Capitulatio in Holy Roman Empire 352 n. 1
Castile, Cortes of xxxix, 321, 356
Castles, change in character of, in Hun-

gary in XVIII century 5–6, 69, 119 and n. 1, 120
Catholicism and the Catholic Church, comparison of, in Spain and Hungary 252–4; in France 255
—— influence of foreign states on, in Hungary 222–3, 256–9
—— general treatment in Hungary xxiii–xxv, 246–300 *passim*
—— its recovery after Reformation under Peter Pázmány xlix–l, 129 and n., 130, 248–9
—— more truly representative of national spirit in Hungary than Calvinism l–li, 224–5, 248–9
—— reaps fruits of Rákóczi's defeat 251
—— and intolerant policy of *Regnum Marianum* (q. v.) 237, 251 sqq., 256–9, 274–5, 323–4
—— hostile to Turkey, and to the Serbs, policy of converting the latter 205, 224–5; this policy religious not national in character 225 and n.
Cattle-breeding in Hungary, 25–6, 46–61 *passim*
Censorship, Government, in Hungary, effect of, in suppressing Protestant books and Hungarian literature 237
Chamber, Imperial, at Vienna 318
Chamber, Royal (v. also *Kamara*), powers and influence of 343–5; difference between, and the other organs of kingly government in Hungary 347; otherwise mentioned 209, 328
Chancellery, The Imperial, in Vienna 79
—— The Royal Hungarian, located at Vienna 79–80; general treatment 329–31, 335
—— ecclesiastical influence in 281
Chancellor, The, in Hungary 126
—— becomes a secular official 113
Church, The Catholic, in Hungary (v. also Catholicism and Catholics), an Estate of the realm in Hungary 109 and n. 1, 110; King's position with regard to 311–2; general treatment 246–300 *passim*
Civitas, Hungarian 103
Clergy, The lower, of the Catholic Church in Hungary, social position and education of 280–3
Cloth Industry, The, in Hungary 24, 62–3, 65–7
Coinage and Coins in Hungary v. 89, 315–6, App. v. and also under Mint, Royal
Colonisation in Hungary (v. also Immigrants, Germans, Swabians, Saxons, Slovaks, Rascians) 196–246 *passim*; otherwise mentioned 61–2, 70–3

Colony, Hungary in position of, in relation to Austrian Provinces 68–99, *passim*, esp. 94–99
Comes camerae 319
Comitatus (v. Counties)
—— *posse* (v. *Posse comitatus*)
Commerce in Hungary, policy of Austria in regard to 37–46, 78–83
Commissio in oeconomicis 38
Communitas, The Hungarian 305 n. 1
Compossessores (members of a family possessing an estate in common) 35–6
Conductus, salvus, to Parliament 317
Congregatio xxxvii and n., lxii, 143–4 (v. Counties)
Congrua of the clergy 283
Conscriptio (census) 170 n. 2, 271 n. 1
Consilium regium locumtenentiale (council of lieutenancy), lxii, main treatment, powers etc. 333–8, 325, 345, 347; economic control exercised by 38, 90–1; ecclesiastical influence in 281; records and opinions of, quoted *passim*
Contributio (war-tax) 8, 19, 20–24, 28–9, 31, 72, 179, 354, App. 1.
Conventa, pacta, in Poland 12, 352 n. 1
Cooptatio 312
Corn, Hungarian trade in 55, 57, 78, 94
Coronation, King's (v. also Crown of Hungary, Sacred), importance of, in Hungary 349–50
Coronation-oath of Caribert King of the Franks 351 n. 1
—— of Maria Teresa in Hungary 350–2
Coršle, use of, in Hungary 83, 173
Counties, The, and County-system in Hungary, importance of, as a centre of administration and local self-government xxvi, xxxvi–xxxvii, lxiii, 6, 356–7
—— influence of great ecclesiastics on 281
—— stronghold of gentry against magnates and peasant nobles xxxvii, xli, 7
—— unit of older Hungary 142; and strength of 147–8, 162
—— fix the list (*limitatio*) of prices for victuals and industrial wares in their own districts 72
—— elective system in 144; Emperor Joseph's criticism of 145 n. 2
—— assembly (*congregatio*) 143–4 and n. 2
—— officials of, empowered to deal with serfs 176
—— maladministration of counties 145–6
—— their power of resisting the *föispán* and the central power xxxvii, lxiii, 147, 325, 345–6
—— resistance of, to Emperor's attempts

to improve communications 84–5, 146; Joseph's decision to overthrow 90
Credit, conditions of, in Hungary in XVIII century 74, 89, 117 and n. 2, 125–7
Croatia, and the Croats xx, xxii, privileges as regards taxation 22
—— Ban of xxv, 113; Ban's Bench (Court of Justice) 341
—— Royal Free boroughs of 166 n.
—— Bishop of Bosnia and 281
—— nobles of 34; their relation to Hungary 103; numbers 226
—— Magyar language spoken in 227–9, 230; costumes of, Magyar 229 and n.
—— peasants of, petition to Crown 189–90; insurrection of, in 287
—— socage in 192; Greek Catholics establish themselves in 286
—— settlements of, in Hungary 214–6, 218–9
—— statistics of, in 1787 and 1847 219 n.
Crown, The Sacred, of Hungary xlviii
—— in relation to King 303, 350, 352
—— guardians of 113 and n. 4, 310
—— corporation of xxxii, 34, 110 and n., 155, 227, 318, 329
Csikós (horseherd) 48, 145
Cumanians, The, in Hungary xxii n., 104, 168–9, 197, 246; otherwise mentioned 87
Curia Regia (v. also *Tabula Septemviralis*), main treatment 338–41; 103, 329, 342
Currency in Hungary (v. under Coinage and Mint, Royal)
Customs, The, in Hungary (v. also *Harminczad*), main treatment 37–46, 75, 77 n. 2, 319; customs duties etc. not under control of Parliament 318

Debreczen, justice in 340 n. 2; fairs at 74–6; plague at 222 and n.; one of few towns with Magyar inhabitants 11, 157, 209; schools in 281; and Serbs 204; population of 164, 198; Calvinism in xliii
Decree, Royal, and rescript, difference between, in Hungary 334 n. 1
Dica (unit for the assessment of taxes), explanation 21 (v. also App. 11.), 26, 34, 360–1
Dicasteria, The 328–9
Diploma inaugurale lxi, 347–9, 352 and notes
—— *Leopoldinum* in Transylvania lvii, xlviii n.
Director causarum regalium 339

Domestica (a tax for the expenses of the *municipia*)
Donatio 104, 345
Dynasties, importance of native and foreign, to a country 14, 108, 135

Education, control of, in Hungary, given by Parliament to the Sovereign 1723 310; struggle for control of, between Jesuits and Piarists 282–5; *fundus literarius* (q. v.), how used 80; education of clergy 282–3; educational system of Calvinism (q. v.) 291–6; of Lutheranism (q. v.) 291, 294, 297, 300
"Empire," The Habsburg idea of 322, 323 and n., 324
Empire, Roman, comparison with Hungary 232, 233 and n.
—— Holy Roman, The 112 n. 1, 206, 251, 321, 352 n. 1
England, Stuart dynasty of, compared with Habsburg 6, 12; nobles of, compared with Hungarian 102; colonial policy of, compared with Austrian 97–9; the nation popular in Hungary 136 n. 1; Chancery of, compared 341; otherwise mentioned 139, 231, 236
Estates of Hungarian Parliament (v. under Prelates, Magnates, *Bourgeoisie*)
—— Evangelical, in Parliament 248
Evangelical religion in Hungary, i.e. Lutheranism (q. v.)
Expeditio 329

Fairs in Hungary, economic importance 74; fairs of Debreczen, Pest, etc. 74–6; Temesvár 76
Fiume, sea-port, union of, to Hungary, 1776, and importance of 76–81, 82
Föispán (high sheriff of county nominated by the King), office of, usually held by magnates xxvi, xxvii and n., xxxvii, 114 and n. 2, 143
—— relation of, to Court 147; instructions of, from King 343–5
—— office hereditary in some counties 114 n. 2; in others held by Catholic bishops 281; Calvinists excluded from 287
France, diplomatic influence of, on Hungary 251, 259–60; growth of monarchy in, compared li, 8, 10–12, 119, 321; in methods of administration 8
—— bureaucracy of, compared with that in Hungary 346; *bourgeoisie* of, compared 10–11, 149, 341, 346; nobility of, compared 6–7, 102 and n., 103, 104 and n., 105, 231; and Hungarian. exiles 15, 250; Calvinism in, compared with Hungary 289–90; religious policy

of, compared 222, 259–60; peasants of, compared 174, 243–6
Franciscans, The Order, influence of, in missionary work 270, 271–2
Freemasonry, influence of, in checking Catholic intolerance 299
Frontiers, The Military, explanation 318, 287 n. 1 v. also map and lxii
Fundus literarius (endowment for public schools, founded by Maria Teresa out of the confiscated Jesuit property 1780) 80
Fürmender (v. *Tribunus plebis*)

Gentry, The (v. also Nobility, Magnates, *Táblabiró*, Counties)
—— how distinguished from magnates xxv–xxix, xlvii n., 3 n., 6–7, 106, 120–1, 127, 128
—— relative decline of, in XVI century as compared with magnates xli, 107
—— general treatment of 127–48 *passim*
—— their economic independence of Court as contrasted with that of the magnates 128–9, 137–8
—— Calvinism (q. v.) and the xliii, 129–30, 222, 289, 291–2
German influences in Hungary, German. dress, wearing of, in Hungary 115 n. 3, 229
—— element in Pécs 151; in Pest and Buda 62, 208, 342; in north-western towns 157, 215; and in towns generally 148 n. 1, 163 and n., 205, 208, 216–8; German influence on Czegléd 196 and n.; and on Lutheranism 289–91
—— language, attempt to introduce, into Hungary, and protests by county assemblies against 229–31, 237–8
—— officials in Hungary 209, 343–4
—— settlers in Hungary (v. also Saxon and Swabian) xxii n. 1, 4, 33, 37, 71, 200; in Alföld after 1687 204–11 *passim*
—— soldiers in Hungary 179, 210–11, 318
Glandinatio (v. also under Pannage) 186 n. 1
Greeks, The, merchants in Hungary 30, 64, 72, 73 n. 1, 200
—— Catholic (or Roman) Church, establishment of, in Hungary 225 and n., 286–7
—— Orthodox (or Oriental) Church (v. also under Rascians) 73, 218, 224–5 287–8
Guard, The Hungarian Noble, created by Maria Teresa, influence on literature of 19 n. 2, 237 and n., 308 n. 2, 309, 325

Guilds in Hungary in the towns 72, 208–9; connection with citizenship 151–3; the Protestant 263
Gulyás (cowherd) 48
Gymnasium 285

Hajdú (Haiduk) nobles and towns, The, explanation 169 and notes, 104, 167–70 *passim*, 198, 213; otherwise mentioned 144, 175, 183, 246
—— Captain, The 169 n. 4, 170
Hármas Könyv (v. *Tripartitum*)
Harminczad (thirtieth), explanation 40 and n. 2, 42, 75, 77 n. 2, 279, 344
Haza (Fatherland), use of term 142 and n. 1
High sheriff (v. *Föispán*)
High treason (v. *Lèse-majesté*)
Hirmondó, Magyar (*The Magyar Courier*, first newspaper in Hungarian) 229, 238; quoted 69 n. 2, 77 n. 2, 295 n. 3, 326 n. 3
Hussars, The Hungarian 15 and n. 2, 262, 355

Immigration and immigrants into Hungary, effects of xxii n. 1, 61–2, 70, 72–3, 196–246 *passim* (v. also under Colonisation, Germans, Saxons, Swabians, Slovaks, Rascians)
Indigenae (foreign families naturalised in Hungary) 103, 232
Industry and industries, Hungarian, decline of, and causes 61–8
Infamia 314
Inquilinus (Mag. *Zsellér*), explanation 60 n. 1, 151 n. 3, 151–2
Insurrectio (v. also *Posse comitatus*), *generalis* and *particularis*, distinction between 355–6; xxv, lxii, 125
Intendants, The, in France, contrast with *föispán* (q. v.) in Hungary 346

Jesuits, The order of, influence of, in promoting Catholicism xliii–xliv, 249, 271; condemned by Rákóczi's parliaments 272
—— their influence on historical learning and in developing national ideas 273
—— character of their missionary and educational work 271, 280–3, 284 and notes 1, 2
—— struggle with the Piarists and abolition 285
—— funds of, how used, after their abolition 80, 125
Jews, The, in Hungary 30, 64, 72, 200, 261; and the toleration tax 319
Jobbágy (Minister), the term is first applied

to great dignitaries, e.g. in *Bulla Aurea* we hear of *jobbagiones*; afterwards, as in our period, it denotes Serfs (q. v.); general treatment 170–95, 182
Judices nobilium 131, 153–4 (v. *Szolgabiró*)
Juramentum decretale, effect of 267
Jury, trial by, introduced by Matthias Corvinus into Hungary 131 n. 1
Jus gladii 146, 175
Jus montanum 188 n. 3, 189
Jus nobilitandi 312
Jus patronatus 310 and n. 1, 313
Jus resistendi xxix and n., li, lvi, 103 n. 3; how abolished 1687 4, 324, 350, 353
Justice, in Hungary, administration of, central organs (v. under *Curia* and *Septemvir*, King's Bench) 133, 338–43; further centralization of 338–41; district courts 339
—— local administration of (v. *Táblábiró*) 131–4, 145–6, 342–3
—— Lord Chief, in Hungary 113, 274 n. 3, 353

Kamara (v. also Chamber, Royal), main treatment 343–5, 319
King, The, in Hungary, Otto of Freising on his position 9–10 and n., 105 n. 2
—— general estimate of his powers in the period 301–57 *passim*
—— elective character of, how abolished lvi–lvii, 4, 352; hereditary character established 308, 324, 351
—— relations of, to his subjects defined by *diploma inaugurale* (q. v.) and coronation oath lxi, 347–52
—— his relations with the Catholic Church 311–2
—— his control over the executive and administration 321–47
—— and *lèse-majesté* 115, 313
—— his personal prerogatives 309–15
—— his supreme control over peace and war 316–7; and education 310
—— his relations to Parliament 317–20, 353–7
—— power of resistance to his authority by the counties 147, 325, 345–6; decision of Joseph to overthrow counties 90
—— Montesquieu's erroneous view of King's powers in Hungary 317
King's Bench, Court of, in Hungary (v. *Tabula Regia*) 113, 313, 339–40
Kurucz, explanation xxviii n. and 201 and n.; liii, lix, 121, 211

Latifundia, The, in Hungary 49
Law, Hungarian, The, and Maria Teresa's opinion of 341–2 n.

Lèse-majesté and the King 115, 313
Limitatio (official list of prices for victuals and industrial wares fixed by the counties) 72
Literature, Hungarian (Magyar), value of, as a guide to national feeling lix, 234–43 *passim*
—— effect of censorship on 237
Lucrum camerae 314
Lutheranism and Lutherans, in Europe 289–90
—— in Hungary (v. also Toleration), German character of 289, 291
—— spread of, among the Slovaks 212–3, 232, 289
—— in the towns 159–60, 208, 291; generally xliii and n., 257–8
—— their system of education 291, 294, 297, 300
—— political status of, under Leopold I and Charles III lvi, 253 notes, 254–5, 256 and n. 2; and the *articularis* (q. v.) 248, 252, 265
—— intolerant and persecuting policy of Maria Teresa towards 237, 295–6
—— tolerance of Joseph, and political effects of 297
—— in Transylvania (q. v.) xliii and n., xlvi–xlviii, lvii, 263

Magistratus (town council) 73, 150, 187, 257, 268
Magnates, The, in Hungary (v. also Nobility and Nobles, Gentry), distinction between, and gentry xxv–xxix, xlvii n., 3 and n., 4–7, 105, 128
—— development of power in XVI century 106–7
—— policy of Maria Teresa towards, attraction of Hungarian magnates to Vienna 115–27 *passim*
—— wealth of 112–3, 120 n. 2; financial needs of, their dependence on the sovereign for loans 125–6; Risbeck's account of 122–3, his exaggerations 124–5; contrast with the economic independence of gentry 137–8; numbers and statistics relating to 123 n. 1
Magyar, and Magyars, The, meaning of word in Hungary in XVIII century 232–3; racial origin of, xxi n. 1
—— settlements in the Alföld after Turkish wars 211–46 *passim*
—— language, The, meaning, importance and influence of, in XVIII century, contrasted with modern view of 224–6, 228–38
—— literature, an index to national feeling 234–43; effect of censorship on 237

Magyar, nationality, inseparable from the Magyar nobility in XVIII century 231
—— nobles, The 226–31
—— serfs, The, insurrection of 1514 due to 172; character and position of xxxii, 212, 226, 243–6
—— Magyars excluded from royal free boroughs in Middle Ages, admitted in XVII century 11, 161, 217
—— population in Hungary, how far Magyar in XVIII century 218–9 and n. 2
Magyar Hirmondó (v. under *Hirmondó*)
Magyarisation, process and character of, in XVIII century 204–5, 220–46 *passim*, especially 224–5, 227 and n. 1, 232–3
Magyars, The (v. also Magyar), in Hungary, Emperor Joseph's judgment on 243–4
Mangcorn 55
Manufactures, various, in Hungary 31, 45, 62, 65–7, 69, 70–1
Measures and Weights, Hungarian v. App. 1.
Meat, preserved, trade in Hungary 77, 78 and n. 3
Mercantilism and Hungary 38, 68, 98–9
Mines, Imperial Chamber of 155, 157, 319
Mining Towns, districts and industry of 24–5, 30, 67, 71, 150, 155, 157, 161, 319–20
Mint, Royal, King's control of 315–6, 319
Miracles, Catholic 269
Money, Hungarian v. App. 1.

Nation (*populus*), meaning of, in Hungary xxxii, lviii, 110
Nationality in Hungary, problem of, in XVIII century 34; general treatment 211–46
Nativus 103
Navigation, school of, in Trieste and Fiume 79–80
Ne onus inhaereat fundo, principle of, established in Parliament of 1728 18
Nemes (also *Serviens*) xxv n. 1, 104
Nobility and nobles, Hungarian compared to English 3 n. 2; to Polish and French 6–7, 102–3, 104 n., 105
Nobility and nobles in Hungary (v. also Magnates, Gentry, Prelates, *Hajdú*, Peasant-nobles)
—— different kinds of xlvii n., 3 n. 2, 103–4
—— mode of life 69–70; privileges of 103 n. 3; King's Bench, supreme court of 339; attitude of, towards trade 85–6; nobles in towns 154 n. 1, 156, 157

Nobility, The use of Magyar language characteristic of 225
—— numbers of 104 n.; statistics of, in various counties 226–7 and n.
—— importance of national patriotism of, to Hungary 102–11, 355–7
Nonage 184–5, 195
North-West districts in Hungary, largely Slovak 32–5, 94–6; German element in 157–215; and serfdom 195; wine trade in 96; decline of material prosperity in 71, 96–7, 99, 129, 164
Nota Infidelitatis xxix, 130

Oppositio 341 and n. 2

Palatine, The Count, in Hungary, position and influence of xxviii, xxx, xlvii, liv, 113, 353; how chosen 279, 310
—— office of, open to members of gentry 128 and n. 2
—— nobles owing allegiance to 167 and n.; *banderia* of 105–6 n.; judicial functions of 338–9 and n.; from 1687 onward, liv; suspension under Maria Teresa 324–5, 334, 337, 353; otherwise mentioned 4
Pannage (v. *Glandinatio*)
Parliament, in Hungary, composition of xlvii n., 127–8, 129; representation in the boroughs xxxi–xxxii, 162 and notes; privilege of members of 317; powers of, and relation to King generally xxviii–xxxiii, 8, 38–9, 303, 307, 309, 316–7, 319–20, 322, 324–5, 327, 335, 339 and n. 2, 348–54 *passim*, 356–7; relation to county assemblies 143; financial powers of 128, 353–4; small amount of taxes voted by 319–20; invests the King with dictatorship (1526) 305–6, 348; and the serfs 171–2, 175–6; and the *Urbarium* 193; decline in power of, under Maria Teresa 338 n. 1, 351–4; and the *diploma* 348–54; Acts of, quoted *passim*
Partes adnexae (partium) 322 n. 1, 350
Patricii, The, in towns 154–5
Patronatus (v. under *Jus patronatus*)
Peasants, The, in Hungary (v. Serfs)
Peasants-nobles in Hungary 3 n., 104
Perpetuus miles 8
Personalis, The King's 339
Pest, largely a German town 205, 208, 342; Rascian element in 205; fair at 74–6; school founded at 281; population of 164
Piarists, The, order of, explanation 283 and n. 4; influence compared with that of Jesuits 283–5 *passim*

Plague, Oriental, The, a symptom of Turkish rule 222 and n.
Plebs, misera, contribuens 167, 187, 225 and *passim*; *plebis tribunus* (v. *tribunus*)
Poland, nobles of, compared with those of Hungary 7, 326, 357
—— influence of, on Hungary liv, 30, 254
—— constitution of, compared with that of Hungary 305
—— monarchy in, and in Hungary 12, 316 n. 4, 352 n. 1
Populus, The, in Hungary (v. Nation)
Porta, palatinalis, explanation 20 n. 5, 20–21; an index to growth of wealth and population 23, 25–6, 29, 32, 36, 166, 173; statistics as to 33, 38
Portiuncula 276
Portorium 43
Posse comitatus xxv, 8, 18–9, 110, 130; regulations of 1715 on 130, 167, 176, 191, 195
Postal Service in Hungary controlled by King 320; income from 88–9 and n. 1
Potato-growing, attempts to introduce, in Hungary 55–6
Praejunctura 179
Pragmatic Sanction, The lxi–lxii, 4, 308, 351
Prelates, The, in Hungary (v. also Catholicism and Catholic Church)
—— the first Estate in the kingdom of Hungary 109, 278
—— general treatment 247–300 *passim*
—— attitude towards Protestants 247 sqq.
—— powers and privileges of 279–80; influence in local government 281
Primate, The, of Hungary (Archbishop of Esztergom) 113 n. 3; powers of 278–80; nobles owing allegiance to 167 n.; *banderia* of 105–6 n.; otherwise mentioned 112, 223, 273, 281
Prothonotary (a magistrate skilled in the law who attends on a Judge) 339
Provinces, Hereditary, The (i.e. Austrian dominions outside the Hungarian kingdom), relations of, to Hungary 20, 38, 46–99 *passim*, 351–2
Prussia, influence of, in supporting Protestantism in Hungary 136 n. 2, 222 and n., 223, 257, 259 n. 4, 260–1
Publicus 292–3
"Pukova," a cloth 24
Puszta, The (waste-land, also *praedium*) xxx, 48, 53 56, 245

Rákóczi revolt, The (1703–11), general effect of lix–lxi, 3–4, 11, 13–4, 121, 203 n. 3, 204

Rákóczi revolt, The, largely Calvinist in character lix, 250 and n.; but also national 251
—— its relation to the peasants lix, 183
Rascians (Serbs), The, explanation 197 n., 198–9; settlement in Alföld xx, xxii n., 73 n. 3, 201–4, 205, 214, 218; settlements in Hungary 62–73; political status of, in Hungary 202–3, 319–20
—— Rascian element in towns 62, 151, 205, 208, 209, 218
—— Catholic policy of converting 224–5 (v. also Catholicism); the Sokácz and Bunyevácz tribes Catholic 225 and n.
Rectificatio portarum 21
Régie (excise) (v. Salt *régie*)
Registrator 345
Regnum Marianum (v. also Catholicism), policy of, in Hungary liii, lvi, 251 sqq., 274–5
Regulamentum militare 28
Repulsio 341 and n. 2
Rescript, royal and decree, difference between 334 n. 1
Resolutio 169
Reversalis 261
Rivers, The, in Hungary, attempts made to clear 83–5
Roads, The, in Hungary, importance of 78, 83; bad condition of 78–9
Roumans (v. under Wallachians)
Russia, monarchy in, compared with Hungarian 10–12
—— influence of, on Hungary, esp. as regards Rascians (Serbs) 89, 186 and n. 2, 202, 203 and notes, 211
—— commercial treaty with 44
Ruthenes or Ruthenians 195, 216–7

Salt, mines, income derived from 319–20
—— *régie* (i.e. excise) 75, 209, 319, 344–5
Saltpetre, manufacture of 38
Salvus conductus, members of Parliament 317
Saxons, The (v. also Germans), settlements of, in Transylvania xx n. 1, 161 and n. 4, 263
—— of the Szepes (Zips) district lvi, 162
Schools, The, in Fiume and Trieste 80
Sedria, also *sedis judiciaria* (the *congregatio* or county assembly in its judicial capacity) 134
Septemvir (v. also *Tabula Septemviralis*) 332 n. 2, 338–9, 341
Serbs, The (v. also Rascians), as traders 30, 72, 104; relation to Rascians 197 n.

Serfs, The, in Hungary (v. also Socage, *Urbarium*), condition better than that of peasants in France 174, 190, 243, 244–6
—— general treatment 158, 170–95 *passim*
—— general position of, after revolt of 1514 171–2; legislation with regard to 172–6; petitions of, to Crown 189–90
—— taxation of 22–3; *corvée* of 83, 173; remission possible 245–6; their economic condition much improved by Maria Teresa's *Urbarium* (q. v.) 191–2, and by Emperor Joseph 193–4
—— insurrections of 171–2, 178, 182 and n., 259 n. 1, 287
—— influence of, on political history lviii–lix, 182–3; decline of that influence in XVIII century 183–4
—— sentimental view of their condition expressed by aristocratic poets 177–8
—— folk songs expressive of their condition 179–80
—— of the Crown 193–4
Sericulture in Hungary fostered by Government 59–61, 65
Serviens 104
Sessio (session) (hide of land belonging to a peasant=about 30 acres) App. 11. 54, 150 and n. 3
Sheriff, The (v. *Alispán*), and high sheriff (v. *Föispán*), under-sheriff (v. *Szolgabiró*)
Slavonia (the Slavonian counties in Hungary) 161, 166 n. 1; annexed to Hungary 1750-1 19, 55; boroughs of 78, 166; peasants in 78, 189–90, 192; figures relating to 219 and n.
Slovaks, The, as pedlars 24, 89
—— nobles 34
—— in the towns 161, 212–3, 217
—— in the North-West districts xxii, 32–5
—— settlements in the Alföld after 1687 212–4, 217
—— relations to Magyars 37, 161, 214, 232 n. 1
Socage of serfs, contracts relating to (v. also *Urbarium*) 173, 175 sqq., 179, 186, 191–3; redemption of 194–5
Society in Hungary v. chap. 11. *passim*
South Hungary, in relation to the Alföld (q. v.) 25, 28; industry in 69
Spectabilis 142 n. 2
State, The, modern conception of 100–2 opposed to medieval 136, 142–3, 307, 327
Stola 265
Superstitions of peasants in Hungary 182 n. 1

Swabians, The (v. Germans), settlements in Hungary xx n., 62, 207, 209

Szatmár, Peace of, effects following on lx–lxii, 1, 3–4, 14, 37

Szatmár-Németi, one of few towns inhabited by Magyars 11, 209

Szeklers, The xxii and n., xlviii n. 1

Szepes (Zips district), part of, recovered by Hungary 11, 19, 30, 66–7, 74, 162, 326

Szolgabiró (*judex nobilium*), explanation xxxvi, 131 and n., 133–4, 345

Táblabiró and Táblabirák, explanation 131 sqq.; political importance of 135–6; character and mode of life 137–41, 142 n. 2, 143–8, 150; otherwise mentioned 257, 265, 267

Tabula Regia or Septemviralis (supreme court of appeal) (v. also Justice) 332 n. 2, 338–41

Tariff policy, Austrian, towards Hungary, main treatment 37–46 *passim*

Tárnokmester (i.e. Treasurer) 113, 308 n. 2, 353

Tavernici v. 308 n. 2

Taxation, system of, in Hungary, general treatment 18–37 *passim*, 166, 173.

Thwaites 185–6

Tobacco, becomes an article of export from Hungary 28–9, 43, 56, 75 n., 78

Toleration in Hungary (v. also Calvinism, Catholicism, Lutheranism), influence of foreign States in promoting 136 n. 2, 348–9, 256, 259; interference of Prussia to promote 222–3 and n.; Frederick II and, 257, 259 n. 4; puts pressure on Charles III (VI) and obtains condemnation of Biró's book against 258–9; violation of, under Maria Teresa 254–61, 290, 295–9; Emperor Joseph's edict of toleration 73

Toleration in Transylvania, xliii and n., xlvi–xlviii, xlix, lvii; violation of, under Maria Teresa 257, 261–3

Toleration-tax of Jews 319

Towns, The, in Hungary (v. also Boroughs, *Bourgeoisie* and Mining towns), representation of in Parliament xxxi–xxxii, 216 and notes; relative importance of, in XVIII century as

compared with rural districts 163–6, general treatment 148–70 *passim*

Transylvania, *voivode*, *waywode* (Governor) of xxv, xxxiv; his judicial powers 328

—— a separate customs territory 41; trade of 74, 92, 93 n.

—— independence of xlii, xlvi, 198; Bocskay's revolt in xlvi–xlviii, 104, 169, 248; Gabriel Bethlen's rule in, and importance of, to Hungary xlix, l–li

—— literature in 237

—— Maria Teresa violates toleration in 257, 261–3

—— Lutheranism and Calvinism in xliii and n., xlvi–xlviii, lvii, 222, 261–3, 277, 291–7

Treasurer (v. *Tárnokmester*)

Treasury, Royal 47, 112 n. 1

Tribunus plebis (Mag. Fürmender, Germ. Vormund) 151–2

Tripartitum, The, Hármas Könyv, unofficial code of Verböczy (1514) xxxviii, 7, 103 n. 3, 106–7, 127, 171, 304–5 and n. 1; quoted 109 n. 2, 110 n. 1, 313 and notes

Turks, The, relations with Calvinism xliii–xlv, 248–9; influence of their conquest on Hungary, xxxviii–xlii; and results of their expulsion 1–3, 13, 112, 133, 198 sqq., 221, 318

Two-field and three-field system of land cultivation 54 and n. 2

Universities, The (v. also Education) 285, 291–7

Urbarium, The (Mag. úrbér, the lord's fee) 175 n. 2; general treatment 178–9, 191–2, 193, 246; otherwise mentioned 171 n. 1

Viticulture in Hungary (v. Wine)

Vormund (v. Tribunus plebis)

Wallachians (Roumans, Wallachs or Vlachs), The xx n., xxii n., 34, 73, 195, 198–9, 216–7

Weights and Measures, Hungarian v. App. I.

Wine, Hungarian, export of 24–5, 30, 39–40, 41–3, 45, 57–8 *passim*, 94, 96

Woman, influence of, in Hungary 140–1

Wool, Hungarian, difficulties in way of exporting 42–3, 75, 95

Cambridge:

PRINTED BY JOHN CLAY, M.A.

AT THE UNIVERSITY PRESS